THE
MUTE'S
SOLILOQUY

THE MUTE'S SOLILOQUY

A MEMOIR

Pramoedya Ananta Toer

Translated by Willem Samuels

HYPERION EAST

NEW YORK

This translation is based on the author's original notes. Although substantial reference was made to the two-volume Indonesian edition entitled *Nyanyi Suni Seorang Bisu: Catatancatatan dari P. Buru* (Lentera, Jakarta, Vol. 1, 1995; Vol. 2, 1997; Joesoef Isak, ed.), the present volume differs markedly in both form and order from that edition and includes new introductions to each section.

Printed in the United States of America.

For information address
Hyperion,
114 Fifth Avenue,
New York, New York 10011.

Library of Congress Cataloging-in-Publication Data
Toer, Pramoedya Ananta, 1925–
[Nyanyi sunyi seorang bisu. English]
The Mute's soliloquy / Pramoedya Ananta Toer : translated by Willem Samuels.
p.   cm.
ISBN 0-7868-6416-8
1. Toer, Pramoedya Ananta, 1925–   2. Toer, Pramoedya Ananta, 1925–
—Imprisonment.   3. Authors. Indonesian—20th century—Biography.
4. Political prisoners Indonesia—Biography.   I. Samuels, Willem.
PL5089.T8Z4713   1999
899'.22132—dc21   98-46316
[b]   CIP

FIRST EDITION

Designed by Joseph Rutt

3 5 7 9 10 8 6 4 2

This book is lovingly and tearfully dedicated
to both the living:

my children,
Pujarosmi, Indriarti, Anggraini,
Astuti, Arina, Setianing Rakyat, Tatiyana, and Yudistira,

and the dead:

those companions in misery whose untimely departure from
Buru Island preceded my release.

CONTENTS

FOREWORD

The notes, essays, and letters in this collection were hastily written under adverse conditions—in a penal camp on the Island of Buru, Indonesia—and, almost without exception, were not looked at again prior to the preparation of this volume. This is true even of the letters to my children, most of which were never sent, once again because conditions did not permit. Had these materials fallen into unwanted hands, they no doubt would have been the reason for yet another interrogation. Thus the opportunities I found to write very much depended on my intuition for safety.

These are personal notes, nothing more. There is no grand plan here; these notes are a stream of water flowing unchecked, with no thought given to their final shape or form. No doubt they are rife with redundancies which I would have found unacceptable under normal conditions.

This volume contains only a small portion of the notes I wrote during my time of imprisonment. Aside from the numerous pages that the military authorities destroyed on Buru Island, I myself was forced to destroy hundreds more when, following my release, an acquaintance of mine from Yogyakarta reported their existence to the authorities, causing me to be called in several times for interrogation. Included in that large stack were most of my notes about the time I spent in prisons in Jakarta, prior to my transfer first to Nusa Kambangan and later to Buru. Notes about my first few months in Buru are also missing. They were burnt by the authorities following a search for papers in my unit. Hidden among piles of rice sheaves, they were confiscated, never to be returned to me.

One government official who disagreed with the way we prisoners were being treated once advised me "to deal with life as you would fly a kite: when the wind is strong, give it more string; when there is no wind, pull the string in. If not," he said emphatically, "you're all going to die." This man's words influenced the shape of the notes and letters in this collection. Had I disregarded his advice, I am quite certain these notes would never have been published, regardless of their shape or form, and I, their author, would have been turned into a dried fish wrapped in a funeral shroud. To this unnamed man, I extend my thanks.

I also extend my thanks to each and every person who, out of international solidarity and humanitarianism, made it possible for me, beginning in 1973, to write in detention. Special thanks must be given to the Indonesian Section of Amnesty International, and at a more personal level to Dr. W. Wertheim and Ms. Carmel Budiarjo, who did so much to keep the plight of the Indonesian political prisoner alive in the international press.

I had originally intended these notes as a means for recalling the past and as a method for preserving the opinions of a certain day and age, thereby preventing them from fading with the passing of time. Understandably, therefore, this collection is very personal in tone and could not be otherwise.

The decision to publish this collection was based on the view that an individual's personal and sensory perceptions, particularly those that have been testified to in writing, form one part of that person's nation's history and of humankind in general. This is what made me shunt aside whatever reasons I had for not publishing these notes.

Preparation of this manuscript for publication made certain parties apprehensive. There are many people who would prefer to forget or even to expunge from their lives certain events and certain experiences, those knots in the larger net of experience that ultimately bind together all people who find themselves caught in the same web of time.

Evil permits no witnesses, they say. But what am I to do? Destroy these notes? Forget my experience? "Experience" is every person's right and it is up to the individual to decide what to do with his experience. No power can take that right away. People can try to discredit a person and his experiences—and for that there is an entire arsenal of reasons ready for use, especially for people with access to money and power.

On a final note, I would like to extend my thanks to several persons without whose assistance this publication would not have been possible. It was my friend and tireless companion, Joesoef Isak, who first gathered these pages together, edited them, and put them together in a readable form. Without his labors, the original two Indonesian-language volumes in which these notes appeared would not have appeared and the notes themselves would have remained nothing more than a pile of scrap paper. Willem Samuels, my English-language translator, spent a countless number of hours going through the original manuscript both alone and with me, discussing with me what sections we felt would work best in English. Long ago, even before the two Indonesian volumes appeared, we had already decided not to include all the materials that were to appear in the Indonesian edition. (Nonetheless, before the initial cuts were made, Mr. Samuels did translate *all* the original language materials; eventually they will be stored for public use with the Library of Congress.) It is only by virtue of Mr. Samuels's unstinting love and appreciation for Indonesian culture that it is now possible to read these notes in English.

Since before the appearance of the American edition of *The Fugitive*, published in 1989, William Schwalbe, now of Hyperion Press, has served as my literary representative. Not only has he helped me to keep meals on my family's dining table, he has also, as much or more than anyone

I know, worked tirelessly to keep the plight of the voiceless Indonesian writer—mine being just one—in the international limelight. To him I also extend my thanks.

Each of the three gentlemen just mentioned has left his mark on this happenstance of a work but all the shortcomings that are found therein are my own.

—P.A.T.

Jakarta, 1984; revised in 1988 and 1998

INTRODUCTION

In 1965, Pramoedya Ananta Toer was forty-one years of age. Having already published a wide range of novels, essays, and collections of short stories, he was highly regarded both in Indonesia and abroad, and was then entering what should have been the most productive period of his life. He had several manuscripts awaiting publication and had researched, created detailed outlines for, even partially finished a dozen more. But on the night of October 13, 1965, when he was kidnapped from his home and thrown into military prison, his life as he knew it—as a writer with the freedom to air his views—came to a sudden end. For more than fourteen years his voice was silenced. He was a mute, not to regain his voice until after his release from the Buru Island Penal Colony. How the river of life that carried this acclaimed author from his hometown of Blora on the banks of the Lusi in East Java to a forced labor camp on the edge of the Wai Apo in Buru Island, two thousand miles distant, is partially described in this volume. Through his notes, letters, and essays that survived his years of incarceration—most of them surreptitiously written, all of them smuggled out of the penal colony—the author provides a partial picture, a fragmentary memoir, of his life.

•

Born on February 6, 1925, Pramoedya Ananta Toer was the first of his parents' nine children. His father was a man of many talents—teacher, activist, composer, and writer, among others—but it was in his role as educator that he exercised the greatest influence on his son's life. His steely academic focus became the model for his son to imitate. In that respect, he might be credited with instilling in Pramoedya the discipline required to produce the more than two score titles he has thus far published, particularly those that were written under the adverse conditions of Buru Island.

However strong his father's influence, one may conclude from the author's notes that it was his mother who gave direction to the author's life. It was she whose nightly bedtime tales filled him with the desire to create a better world, even if it was only in his imagination; she who urged him to become an independent person and to carve a niche for himself in the world; she who found for him the necessary funds to continue his education. As Pramoedya affirms, throughout his life his mother has served as the standard by which he judges others. It was she who provided the "soul" so evident in his work.

At the age of seventeen, following the completion of courses in radio engineering at a vocational school in Surabaya and the death of his mother from complications of tuberculosis and childbirth, Pramoedya moved to Japanese-occupied Jakarta. There he enrolled as a junior high school student at Taman Siswa, a nationalist-oriented educational institution, and found work at the Japanese news service, Domei. During this period (1942–1945) he began to develop his writing skills, first at a technical level—becoming a speed typist, proficient stenographer, interviewer, and archivist—and then at a more creative level, by writing feature articles and stories and editing his school magazine.

The military defeat of the Japanese and the proclamation of Indonesian independence in August 1945 was soon followed by the arrival of Allied Forces in Indonesia and then the return of the Dutch occupation army. Pramoedya was one of the hundreds of thousands of young Indonesians who jumped at the opportunity to serve his long-claimed but newly-born nation and defend it against the reestablishment of Dutch colonial rule. To this end, he enlisted in Badan Keamanan Rakyat, a civil defense unit, and served as the unit's press officer. Following the reorganization of the army in late 1946, he joined Voice of Free Indonesia. In July of 1947, he was arrested by the Dutch military for possessing anti-Dutch documents.

His subsequent imprisonment at Bukitduri Prison in Jakarta marked the first of Pramoedya's three periods of incarceration as a political prisoner. Unlike his second time from 1960 to 1961 and, more significantly, his third time, in Jakarta and then on Buru Island from 1965 to 1979, where during the first few years of his stay even the possession of paper or other writing tools was a warrant for death, at Bukitduri he was given both the freedom to read and the means and impetus to write. It was in Bukitduri that the author wrote the first few books that established him as a rising light in Indonesia's literary world. His first published novel, *The Fugitive*, which was written at Bukitduri, was awarded a national literary prize.

While at Bukitduri, Pramoedya also came to know Arfah Iljas, one of a group of young women who paid regular visits to the political prisoners. The young couple married shortly after his release and had three children together before they were divorced in 1954. His second marriage, to Maimoenah Thamrin, with whom he was to have five children, followed in 1955 and has lasted to this day.

Indonesia in the 1950s was a fragile nation, which the centrifugal forces of ethnic, social, political, and religious rivalry as well as economic disorder threatened to tear apart. The country's shaky financial base—World War II and the four years of resistance to Dutch attempts to reestablish hegemony over the archipelago had severely depleted the country's resources—combined with the determination of the young nation's first president, Soekarno, to keep the country "nonaligned," not bound to the political doctrine of one particular foreign power, kept the nation in a state of heightened tension. The Cold War raging outside Indonesia, with the Western Imperialists marching toward a showdown with the tyrannical Red Menace of the East, further heightened pressures at home.

Pramoedya's populist views, at least those evident in his writings from this period, along with his sympathy for the downtrodden and his championship of "people's power," earned him frequent invitations to travel abroad to nonaligned and Communist countries—China, the USSR, East Germany, Romania, Poland, and Czechoslovakia, among others. At home he was often called to speak on behalf of socialist causes; in 1958 he was given an honorary seat on the governing board of Lekra, the Institute for People's Culture, the cultural wing of the Indonesian Communist Party (PKI) and thereafter served as one of the Institute's unofficial spokespersons. In 1962 he also began to edit "Lentera," the literary column of *Bintang Timur,* a newspaper backed by the Indonesian Nationalist Party. Even though many people assume he was a member of the PKI, he says he was not. He has written, "I've never been a party man, never an organizational sort of person." The only organization to which he claims ever to have belonged is Gelanggang, a short-lived association in the early 1950s of writers devoted to the cause of universal humanism.

Pramoedya considers himself an individualist and has been unswerving in his refusal to be dictated to by others, much less by a particular ideological or political doctrine. Another former political prisoner once remarked that the chairman of PKI, D. N. Aidit, had specifically requested that Pramoedya *not* apply for party membership. When asked about this, the author couldn't recall such a request but added, "Even if the PKI had wanted me to join, I wouldn't have. I won't be anyone's gofer."

Pramoedya's unwavering views and his sometimes strident criticism of people he felt were inconsistent in their support of the populist goals of the Indonesian revolution earned him many enemies, and might very well be cited as the main reason for his detention in 1965 and subsequent exile in Buru. However, five years before that time, in 1960, he was forcibly detained by the Indonesian military and imprisoned for the second time in his life for publishing what was then regarded as an overly sympathetic history of the Chinese in Indonesia (a subject, as evidenced by recent horror stories from Indonesia, that remains sensitive to this day).

From 1960 to 1965, Pramoedya's fortunes fluctuated. Though he was, by this time, one of the most well-known names in Indonesia's literary circles—his books were being translated into numerous foreign languages and earning him critical praise abroad—fame did not translate into fortune. Domestic publishers refused to publish his works and remuneration from translation rights was negligible. Many foreign publishers didn't even bother to ask his permission to translate and sell his books (a situation that in some countries has continued to this day). Living by the pen, the writer was having a difficult time making ends meet; but a far worse time for him and his family was yet to come.

The spirits of havoc that had plagued Indonesia from the time of its proclamation finally merged in 1965 to start a blood bath never before seen in the nation's history. While to this day no irreproachable chronology or analysis of this period of Indonesian history has ever been put forward, almost all historians agree that the trigger for this cataclysm was the kidnapping of six senior army officers in the late hours of September 30, 1965, and their murder in the early hours of the following day. Regardless of whether this incident represented a "coup" or a "counter-coup" and without regard to "who" tipped the first domino—right-wing military officers or PKI supporters—the results of Gestapu or the Thirtieth of September Movement (as it is somewhat erroneously called) were unquestionable: the eventual downfall of President Soekarno; the emergence of a military-controlled "new order" government; the massive roundup of members and supporters or suspected supporters of the PKI and its affiliated organizations; and the extermination of as many as one million innocent people.

During the first week of October 1965, tension was at an all-time high in Jakarta and the twenty-one gun salute that marked the burial of the six murdered military officers at the National Heroes' Cemetery was followed by a nationwide cry of revenge on the PKI and all godless leftists.

On the night of October 13, Pramoedya was at home editing a pseudonymous collection of short stories by President Soekarno. Several other projects, including a social history of Indonesia and a trilogy of novels, were also on his desk. The house was almost unnaturally still. None of the four daughters of his second marriage were there to ask him to tell a bedtime tale or help with homework. His three-month-old son was not crying to be fed. Having been warned by a friend that he was likely to be attacked, Pramoedya had taken the precaution to move his family to his mother-in-law's home. The front door of the house was locked as was the gate to the lane that led to the main road beyond. At the back of the house his brother Koesalah, recently returned from study abroad, was on his way to bed.

At 10:30 P.M., Pramoedya was jarred from his work by the sound of voices. Looking out the window he saw that a crowd had gathered outside his gate. Most of the people were wearing masks. They demanded to be allowed in. Having gathered stones from a nearby construction site, the mob began to pelt the house, breaking windows and shattering doors, threatening to burn the author's home to the ground, with him in it.

Pramoedya's brother attempted to flee out the back, intending to slip away through a neighbor's grounds, but the neighbor wouldn't let him pass for fear that his house, too, would come under attack.

Having no intention of bowing to mob violence, Pramoedya picked up a Japanese long sword he owned, along with a wooden mop handle, and went outside. At the gate he faced the troupe of devilish masks and called for their leader to step forward. "Take your masks off. Then I'll talk to you," he said. The crowd responded with jeers and threats and thrusts of the knives they carried. More stones were thrown at the author's home.

Suddenly, there was a round of automatic gunfire. The crowd fell back slightly from the gate. Four or five police officers and soldiers emerged from the lane. The crowd parted as they walked toward the gate.

"We're here to take you to safety," one of the soldiers said to Pramoedya. "Gather up the things you'll need."

Pramoedya opened the gate and told the soldiers to come inside. As they waited in the front room, Pramoedya collected the trilogy he had been working on, along with his typewriter, a bag of clothes, toiletries, and an envelope of money for his wife. His brother also made ready to leave.

When they had finished packing, Pramoedya and his brother were led out of the house and toward the front gate by two of the armed escort. At the end of the lane the author's hands were tied behind his back and a noose placed around his neck.

Pramoedya asked his guards to safeguard his library, to remove it from his house and turn it over to the State. Instead, as he was trundled toward the military truck that was waiting on the main road, the men who had remained inside his house began to ransack his library. They threw his thousands of books, documents, and years of accumulated research into a pile at the back of the house and started a bonfire.

At the truck, when he again begged the soldier who was guarding him to save his library, the man raised the butt of his gun to smash the author's face. Quickly turning away, Pramoedya took the brunt of the blow on the side of his head. (That blow, combined with others that were to follow, left him deaf in his right ear and very hard of hearing in his left.)

As the air in the neighborhood filled with the ash from Pramoedya's papers, the truck in which he sat sped away, first to the Army Strategic Reserve Command Post (Kostrad) and then to the Regional Military Command Post (Kodam), both located in central Jakarta, where he would find all his belongings as well as his freedom taken from him. There, he demanded of the officer in charge that his brother be released. Surprisingly, given the officer's sadistic reputation, his brother was allowed to leave (though he was once again arrested and imprisoned some time later).

In the months and years that followed, the New Order regime was to arrest an estimated one and a half million people. Indonesia's prisons, special detention centers, and military guard posts were overflowing with political prisoners. Many of them initially felt themselves lucky—at least they had been spared the fate that met the hundreds of thousands of people whose hacked bodies and corpses littered fields and clogged waterways and canals.

The huge number of people who were detained presented immense logistical problems for the newly established military regime. While the regime never pretended to make a show of caring for the prisoners under its control—it was the prisoners' families that provided them with food and clothing; many of those without families or whose families were ignorant of their whereabouts died of neglect—it soon became apparent that if cases were to be built against all of the political prisoners, it would take years if not decades to work through the roll. A solution had to be found. Buru Island was part of that solution.

The military authorities developed a classification system. The political internees were categorized as A, B, or C prisoners. An "A" prisoner was one who was accused of being directly involved in the attempted overthrow of the Indonesian government (through the Thirtieth of September Movement). This included military officers, members of the PKI Political Bureau, and other high-level political personages. In category "B" were those prisoners who were suspected of being involved in the movement but whose cases would take time to build, while "C" was reserved for people who were members of the PKI or its affiliated organizations.

To a certain extent a prisoner's classification also depended on "merit." If, for example, a prisoner had traveled in a Communist country he was awarded extra merit points. Writers by their very profession were also given extra merit. In many instances this resulted in a higher "grade" for the intellectuals who were imprisoned. This was part of the reason Pramoedya was "awarded" a "B" rating.

The prisoners in category "A" were either killed or thrown into the maximum security wings of Indonesia's prisons. Prisoners in category "C," poor people for the most part and considered to be of limited risk, were held in regular jails and military posts. It was the "B" category prisoners, a relatively large percentage of whom were educated, that gave the military room for pause. This is where Buru came in. Just as the Dutch had once exiled Indonesia's nationalist leaders to the far flung reaches of the archipelago, the military regime decided to send 12,000 of its "B" category prisoners to Buru, a virtually undeveloped island in the Moluccas. Pramoedya was on the first shipload of prisoners to be sent there.

In Buru, as in Java, the military regime demonstrated almost no concern for the prisoners' welfare and provided the barest essentials of food and provisions the prisoners needed to stay alive, and only for a minimal period of time. After that, the prisoners had to fill their own needs.

For the next ten years Pramoedya and his fellow prisoners developed Buru Island by hand, opening thousands of acres of land for fields, building hundreds of miles of roads and waterways, constructing from the trees they themselves felled the barracks they were to call their homes.

Drought, floods, and pestilence—the very hardship of life on Buru— drove some prisoners to suicide. More succumbed from torture, and a far larger number died from what can only be called intentional neglect. As soon becomes evident from even a cursory reading of the "List of the Dead and the Missing," which the author compiled and is included in the final section of this book, what generally might be viewed as minor ailments, easily treated in a developed world, were the cause of death for hundreds of political prisoners.

At the age of forty-one, when Pramoedya was imprisoned, the author should have been entering the most productive period of his life. Exiled for fourteen years, that period was stolen from him. Nonetheless, despite the hunger, adversity, and constant threat of death first in Jakarta and later in Buru, he somehow managed to write and, with the help of sympathetic missionaries and visitors, smuggle from the island five historical novels, a play, and an estimated thousand pages of scattered papers.

Before leaving Buru, all of the author's belongings and remaining papers were confiscated and destroyed. Fortunately, a partial testimony to this period of Indonesian history continues to survive in the form of the materials that were smuggled out of the island previously, including the papers on which this volume is based.

These days, most mornings find the author dressed in a threadbare white undershirt and a tattered checkered sarong, picking up the debris that accumulates every day in the empty lot catercorner from his house. As if serving as the local trash collector, he makes a pile and sets it afire, using a machete that he smuggled home from Buru to aerate the pile and keep the flames burning.

Before returning to his house to bathe, he pauses beside a row of makeshift wood and wire bird cages to chat with a clutch of entrepreneurial youngsters who are raising pigeons for competition and sale.

After his bath he climbs the narrow, vinyl-covered stairway to the second floor of his house, his shoulders brushing the family photographs that hang on the stairwell's wall. At the top landing he enters his study— no computer there, just an Olympia typewriter next to an ashtray as full to overflowing as the bookshelves that line the room's three interior walls. He then begins his daily routine of clipping and pasting news articles, answering correspondence, typing up responses to written interviews and, sometimes, attempting to write. But for this once exceedingly productive writer, this is an onerous task. "Who's going to read me, anyway?" he asks. "Who's going to publish what I write?" It is a sad fact indeed that as of this writing, his books remain on the attorney general's list of banned and subversive books. And who is it for whom he has always written but his fellow Indonesians?

Selected publications by Pramoedya are now available in more than three dozen languages but that honor means little to him as long as his own children can't pick up their father's books at the local bookstore. Possession and distribution of Pramoedya's books is still a punishable crime.

When Pramoedya is tired he retires for a nap in a small and Spartanly furnished room adjacent to his office. Almost completely deaf, Pramoedya can't hear the rumble emanating from the overhead expressway nearby, but, as if the backfire of a passing truck were the belch of a military truck, he clenches his fists as if preparing to defend his home once again. "But now," he has said, "having had so much of my life taken from me, I will never be taken forcibly from my home again."

—Willem Samuels

THE
MUTE'S
SOLILOQUY

I

THE

MYSTERY

OF

EXILE

On the night of October 13, 1965, when I was picked up by the military, I was at home editing a collection of short stories by President Soekarno, which he had written under a pen name.

It's a mystery to me why I was exiled. Prior to my arrest and imprisonment I had never been threatened and even to this day I still don't know, and have never been officially informed of, the reason for my arrest and imprisonment.

Also unknown to me is why the whole incident ever took place. For myself, as a student of both ancient and modern Indonesian history, I see behind almost all the monumental events in this nation's history something I'll call "Factor X," namely an external factor that has played a determinantal role in the shaping of Indonesia. During my years in prison I spent a great deal of time trying to discover who or what was Factor X in this case.

After I was led from my house that night, my military escorts and I were immediately surrounded by a mob of masked men who had gathered outside my house, all of whom were armed with knives or other kinds of blades. At that point, my hands were tied behind my back and the rope that bound my wrists was then looped around my neck. In the early days of the Indonesian revolution that kind of knot was a sure sign that the captive was to be killed.

From my home I was taken that night to the Army Strategic Reserve Command Post and, later, to the Regional Military Command. Following my captors' instructions, I had carried a bag of belongings with me—they told me they had come "to remove me from harm's way" and that I should take my work with me—but at the latter place, my typewriter and an unfinished manuscript I had brought along were taken from me.

A week later, I was transferred to Military Police Headquarters on Jl. Guntur and there all the rest of my belongings were taken from me, including six months of emergency wages from Res Publika University where I was giving lectures, and six months of emergency wages from a pencil factory on whose board I served as an advisor. These funds were all the money my family had to live on.

After two days, I was moved to Salemba Prison and, in November, moved again, this time to the Tangerang Correctional Institution for Juvenile Delinquents, which had been taken over by the military. I was told that I was being moved there "in preparation for release." That didn't prove to be the case.

My family didn't find out where I was being held until three months after my initial capture, and six months passed before they were allowed to visit me. This was natural, I suppose, since the detention centers in which I was held for that first half year were sites of mass torture; the authorities would never allow visitors to see the political prisoners there.

For the first few months, torture was the prisoners' constant diet. I saw prisoners whose hands and legs were bound tightly being thrown out of trucks. I witnessed how one young man, who was being interrogated beside me, had pencils placed between his fingers, at their base, between the middle and lower knuckles. Every time the interrogator asked the boy a question, he'd crush the young man's fingers together, causing him to scream and moan in pain. The interrogator also set the leg of the table on the young man's large toes and intermittently slammed his fist down on the table or sat on it.

In May of 1966, I was transferred back to Salemba where I stayed until July 1969, when I and a trainload of other prisoners were sent to Cilacap, a port town on the south coast of Java. There we were put on a ferry and taken to the penal island of Nusa Kambangan, where I was first held in Karang Tengah Prison but a week later moved to Limusbuntu, one of the island's other prisons. I was there until August 16, 1969, when I and a crowd of other prisoners were put on *Adri XV*, a military ship, to begin our journey to Buru Island.

We were the first group of prisoners to be sent to Buru and, after our arrival, were placed in what was then known as Unit 3, the unit farthest away from the coast. In 1971, I and fifteen or sixteen other prisoners were placed in quarters separate from the other men, which is where I lived in isolation until July of 1973.

It was that same year I began to write again. This was following the visit of General Sumitro to Buru, who gave me official permission to write.

Most of my notes about the period before 1973 were destroyed: some I myself was forced to destroy in the interest of my own safety; others were destroyed by the authorities. I have no idea how many pages of notes I wrote in the end, but what we have here is some of what I managed to salvage.

1998

NATANT
RUMINATIONS
(A Letter for Pujarosmi)

It's unlikely that you'll ever receive this letter. It's unlikely that I'll ever be able to send it. But I'm still going to write it—you see, I told you I would!—for you, who are now happy in newly wedded bliss.

I remember so clearly the time when you came to me with your fiancé and the religious official who would administer the wedding ceremony. You were in such a rush, so afraid you might miss the train of good fortune.

I'm sure you knew that I would have no objection to your taking a husband of your own choosing. And I'm sure you remember the words I said to your husband-to-be when he stood before me prior to your wedding: "This young woman is my first child. I love her. Her grandmother had hoped that she would become a doctor, but now she is to be your wife. I ask you, therefore, to do nothing to obstruct her from continuing her studies after she marries you. I also ask you—no, I forbid you—to ever strike her or hurt her in any way. And because you have asked for my daughter's hand in the proper manner, I also ask you that if something happens and you find that you no longer want to be with her, that you return her to me just as she is now, in good health, and that thereafter you never call on me again."

After that time you never came to see me again. When was that? I

6

can't remember the day or the month. Even your husband's name, his ethnic background, occupation, and education seem to have slipped my
mind. But whatever they are, everything is up to you now. You made your
choice and in so doing took on the responsibility for that choice.

The year? That I do remember. It was in 1969 that you took your leave
from me at the Salemba Prison, the "Special Detention Center" as it was
called, to embark on your new life as a married woman. Before reaching
the mammoth door that opened on to the main road, you turned several
times to look back at me. The man beside you, your husband, bowed, dip-
ping his shoulders slightly as a sign of respect for me. But after that, after
that huge door closed behind you, all such niceties ended. You left on
your honeymoon. Then I, too, went away—into exile.

If a person cannot free himself from three-dimensional time—from either
the past, the present, or the future—how must this be viewed? As God's
gift or His curse?

During the Revolution when I was being held by the Dutch in
Bukitduri Prison, I memorized a Negro spiritual, the first line of which
went "There's a happy land somewhere..."—a symbolic promise for
every person's future.

With hope as his guide, sweat as the symbol of his labor, the present
as his starting point, and the past as his provisions, a person goes forward,
toward a happy land somewhere. But because one can never be sure of
reaching that place, the second line of the song goes "And it's just a prayer
away...."

The song is a beautiful one, especially so when the time is right and
one is not plagued by matters that set one's nerves on edge.

"Somewhere," my child, but where? Where is this "happy land"?
People are raised to believe that happiness is the land to which they are
destined to travel. But that belief, which one so easily accepts as true,
might just as well be a mirage.

It's August 16, 1969, and you are off on your honeymoon to a happy
land. I, too, am off to a happy land somewhere, to Buru I've been told, an

island in the Moluccas about the size of Bali. We're supposed to leave tomorrow, on August 17, Independence Day—a birthday present for the nation!—if our departure is not postponed yet another time. I and eight hundred other prisoners will leave on *Adri XV*, a ship of some 300,000 tons in dead weight, but to board we must first go to Sodong, port for the island prison of Nusa Kambangan, located across the strait from the much larger harbor of Wijayapura in Cilacap, southern Java.

I will not close my eyes, neither those in my head nor those in my soul, as the ship carries me away, along with my future, my dreams, and my beliefs. Buru Island is no happy land somewhere; it's but a way station on my journey in life—though to believe even that much will require no small measure of hope.

The whistle blows and slowly the ship leaves sight of Sodong and Wijayapura. A green wall, the forests and mountains of Nusa Kambangan, moves alongside the craft as the white strip of shoreline gradually disappears from view. As one turns toward the south, only the open sea is visible, the Indian Ocean a limitless expanse of azure stretching beyond the horizon. To the north are the steep and jagged cliffs of Java's southern coast.

Don't listen, shut your ears to the labored breath of this rusted and asthmatic vessel. Like our distant ancestors in the age of migration we are on a voyage of discovery, a journey toward a new land and life. Only our education gives us the knowledge that we are passing through the waters of our own country, a maritime nation of more than thirteen thousand islands.

But the lesson that now seems more real, more easy to comprehend, is the one that was drilled into us by the chief warrant officer of Salemba Prison: "The only right you have is to breathe!"

For some of us, even that right has been rescinded, making the lesson we learned in school nothing more than an exercise in hypocrisy. And it's not just the sea I'm referring to, but all its contents as well—the land and everything else found in it. And the sky, too, for that matter—as far as the eye can see, the entire solar system. Between reality and promises there is no status quo.

Our ship rocks and shakes. Our cabin is one of three large barred areas in the cargo hold. Its huge door of steel bars is securely locked and bolted.

But we no longer have the right to look at the sky, or so it seems, much less dream of claiming it, even a small part of it, as our own. We are coolies on Captain Bontekoe's ship, the kidnapped Chinese on Michener's ship bound for Hawaii; we are the four million Africans loaded onto British and American ships for transport across the Atlantic. Nonetheless, even among the eight hundred hostages on this boat, I still feel myself to be an individual, a person with the power, the strength, and good health—for the time being at least—to act for myself. For far too many of the prisoners on board, this journey is not only their first time at sea but also the first time they have ever set foot outside their home village. Can you imagine? These men are supposed to be citizens of a maritime nation. In primary school, Indonesian children are told that they are the descendants of a maritime people who roamed the seas. Yet here on this ship, most of the prisoners are sprawled helplessly on the mats that line the deck. As the ship cuts through the open sea they heave their guts, then retch and heave some more.

Remember the time we sailed to Europe in 1953? You were just a little girl, only three at the time, but on that sixteen-day voyage you never once were seasick.

One must refrain from staring or smiling ruefully at the men whose stomachs are bloated from malnutrition. Many have come here directly from prisons where, for a year or more, they received no more than three shoe-wax tins of food per day. One of the men is five foot three inches in height but weighs only sixty-four pounds. What a high price one must pay for the right to call oneself an Indonesian citizen! Generally speaking, prisoners from Jakarta, whose jails opened far more easily to foreign scrutiny, are far more fortunate.

You've probably never witnessed the abnormal physical movements or the odd mental manifestations of a person whose body weight is less than fifty percent of what it should be. The man's eyes bulge from their sockets; yet his vision is blurred. His skin is cracked and dry, and when he moves his joints are stiff, like those of King Kong in the silent film. When he walks he looks around himself, his head bobbing slowly and uncertainly, but his stare is blank and without direction.

Such a sight was a common one during the Japanese occupation and now today is a common one again among Indonesia's political prisoners. Yet even as they wallow in their own regurgitation, their spirit for life continues to burn. Not, I'd say, because our first meal on board this ship was a full plate of rice with a piece of meat and an egg. No, not because of that at all. Simply because it's their wish to see an end to all of this! And also because they know that life can indeed be beautiful, especially for people with ideals, and know how to make best use of it. This is true even for those prisoners who can no longer rise from their beds or lie down again without the assistance of others who are more healthy.

I have no doubt that this year, just as in previous years, at the beginning of the fasting month my mates and I will be treated to a lecture by a religious official specially brought in from the free world, on the importance of fasting and controlling one's hunger and desires. Imagine the humor of that!

You yourself have never known real hunger, but then you are the child of a free nation and logically should never have had to feel hunger pangs resulting from the incompetence of others. But I, being the child of a colonized people, have had to experience sustained periods of hunger in my life. Thus the hunger I'm feeling now is in no way extraordinary. While I don't eat all that much, the hunger is still real, though I have come to accept it as a hapless and miserable friend.

During the close to four years that I spent in Jakarta's Salemba and Tangerang Prisons, I wasn't nearly as hungry as many of my fellow prisoners. The family did its best to provide for me, sending packets of food as often as two or three times a week. And though I didn't receive all the food that was sent to me—a good third vanished even before it reached my hands and most, if not all of the rest, went into the cooperative meal plan that we prisoners started—at least I (and those other more fortu-nate prisoners with families able to help) did not die of hunger.

In speaking of hunger, I'd like to ask what's the difference between hunger and murder when the former is the systematic consequence of the prison officers' greed? There is absolutely no doubt that if we had been forced to depend for sustenance on the food rations that the prison authorities provided, we would have starved to death. What a weapon food can be when its distribution is controlled by the hands of murderers! And this is Jakarta, the center of power I'm talking about, not Klaten, Sukoharjo, Pacitan, Kebumen, or any other isolated town where the local jail was far from the vision of international eyes.

At Sodong Harbor in Nusa Kambangan, even before the ship left port, hunger had begun to perform its drama. For the better part of a day we were forced to sit there beneath the hot sun, trying to still our hunger pangs even as we watched the guards beat other prisoners just for exchang-ing items of clothing—uniforms had been passed out to the prisoners with no regard to body size. Those of us who ended up sitting beside the hedge that bordered the holding area tore off the leaves and chewed them in desperation. Though coated with dust and with nothing to wash them down—even if there had been water available, we couldn't have left our place without risk of being beaten—we ate the leaves raw. And we con-sidered ourselves fortunate.

Imagine a diet of gutter rats, the moldy outgrowth on papaya trees and banana plants, and leeches, skewered on palm-leaf ribs prior to eating. Even J.P., one of our most well-educated prisoners, found himself reduced to eating *cicak*, though he always broke off the lizards' toepads first. He'd become quite an expert at catching them. After amputating the lizard's toes, he would squeeze the nape of the unfortunate creature between his thumb and forefinger, shove it to the back of his throat, and swallow it whole. That man's will to defend himself against hunger was a victory in itself.

Our ship is nothing like the *Oldenbarneveldt,* with its speed of sixteen nauti-cal miles per hour, on which we sailed to Europe, nor like the *Oranye* on which you returned to Jakarta. The difference between the *Adri XV* and those two ships is that between earth and sky. The Dutch-owned ships on which you sailed were finished with brightly polished wood. Their decks were spotless from daily scrubbings. Not a single cockroach was in evidence—unlike on this ship where they are on constant patrol, interpreting the world and the prisoners through their bobbing antennae.

The prisoners come from jails and detention centers throughout Java, not just from Jakarta, though most of the men in my cell, the one farthest forward in the bow, are from the capital.

Because of the position of our cell in the front of the ship, it is relatively higher than the other two. In front of our cell, in the jut of the bow, is a combination bathroom-latrine. You can't imagine our disgust at having to use that place, at least for those of us with any knowledge of hygiene. At the entrance to the room you must slap your hand over your nose and force your legs to go forward to stop yourself from fleeing from the veritable mountain of feces found in there. Yet that is our ship, the *Adri XV*—and it's still operational! Are we really the offspring of a maritime people?

Even without being told to do so, the men in my cell set out to clean that god-awful room. We got out the brooms and barrels for water, then turned the water faucets on, but in no time at all the huge mound of fecal matter had turned into a muck-filled swamp. The drainage pipes were blocked! Satan himself would have had a hard time finding where the drains were supposed to be. We couldn't believe it. We poured barrel after barrel of water into the room but still the fetid tidal pool refused to ebb. And as the bow of the ship rose with the waves outside, the liquid excrement of this manmade swamp rolled across the deck to lap at, then to leap over, the low steel divider to flood our cell.

Now ask me if we would-be conquerors of this fecal mountain were surprised. Ask me if we were astonished. No, not in the least, because when we entered the barracks that had been assigned to us at Karang Tengah Prison on Nusa Kambangan, we had found there, too, a hill of human shit. In each barracks it had been the same: a petrified mound of shit starting from just inside the door and continuing all the way to the latrine. The only difference between Karang Tengah and the *Adri XV* is that the floors of the barracks were hardened earth while the floors of this ship are rusted steel.

With its three hundred thousand tons of dead weight our ship wheezes and puffs as it makes its way forward. Oh, we are making speed—about as much speed as a leisurely ride on a bicycle! Time and again the engine stalls and the ship, chug-chug-chugging to a stop, becomes a bobber on the mid-sea waves. Yes, this is our ship, possession of the largest archipelagic nation in the world!

Suppose the ship sinks, we prisoners would go down with it, all eight hundred of us. The doors to our cells are locked. But so what? What would be wrong with our dying? At least then we would give the world something to to read about: a headline for a day, a sensational story. How many creatures have been wiped from the face of this earth without eliciting a bit of fuss? How many kinds of insects are now extinct because of insecticide? Has anyone ever got upset about them? Why then should anyone make a fuss about us?

Following the events of 1965, I lost everything or, to be more accurate, all the illusions I had ever owned. I was a newborn child, outfitted with the only instrument a newly born babe finds necessary for life: a voice. Thus like a child my only means of communication was my voice: my screams, cries, whimpers, and yelps.

What would happen to me if my voice, my sole means of communication, were to be taken from me? Is it possible to take from a man his right to speak to himself?

I truly am sorry that I was unable to attend your marriage celebration and that the only wedding gift I have for you are these notes, which are unlikely to ever find their way to you, but for the past four years all I've been able to do is to follow the pointed index fingers of those who rule these concrete and wooden cells. That doesn't mean I haven't been thinking about you. No, that's not true at all.

Where are you living now? How is your new life with your husband? I'd like to know. But supposing that I did, what good would it do for you? Four years in a person's life is not a short period of time. A *kadal* lizard doesn't even live that long.

In my cell in Tangerang I once caught a fly in a plastic bag. In just three and a half days, the animal had died of old age. All in all, four years of not knowing what charges have been brought against me is a bit excessive.

I can't count the number of times that other ships have passed us by. From a distance we must be a heartrending sight: a leper in the midst of natural splendor. Every waking moment I am aware of the ship's wheezing and the creaking of its rickety joints. And how many times have I heard the wheezing completely stop, then felt the shudder of the ship's steel skin as its engine gasped and died.

A thousand years ago, our forefathers passed through these waters— our teachers wouldn't feed us rubbish, would they?—in boats they had fashioned with their own hands, ones that were no doubt much cleaner than the *Adri XV*. No, our teachers wouldn't have fed us rubbish. The Bugis, Macassarese, and Madurese are famous for their sailing ships. Even today their ships are much better tended than this one that was bought and paid for by the state.

I am sure there are those who pray that a gale-force easterly will sink this ship and transform its human cargo to shark bait. I'm sure those same people also feel that the dead have no voice. Theirs is a stone-age sensibility with a criminal blush. They rob us of our civil rights, they steal our very lives. They give us inadequate sustenance, yet time and again we prove ourselves capable of slipping through the eye of the needle of death.

We are refugees who carry on our shoulders a bag of provisions that we shall not discard till death, one chock-full of the symbols of spiritual and sensory experience, a crystallization of undying energy, something more lasting than flesh and bones and even unscissored ivory. These symbols speak forever, each in its own language, whether that language be German, Russian, Dutch, English, Spanish, or Indonesian.

In his novel *Darkness at Noon*, Koestler described a scene in a Spanish jail: As night falls, the tinkling of bells can be heard as an anti-Fascist soldier, a priest at his side, walks toward death at the hands of the executioner.

But what of those anti-Fascists who managed to escape death? How long did they have to remain confined in their cells, waiting for Franco to fall? How did they fare? As they waited, the years passed; between 1933 and 1965, they were murdered one after another. For thirty-two years their loved ones—first their wives, then their children, and, later still, their grandchildren—queued outside the door of Burgos prison to bring them food. And still the Franco regime did not fall. Even after thirty-two years, their torture and oppression had yet to become past history.

In 1965 Marcos Ans, an anti-Fascist Spaniard who had spent twenty-three years in one of Franco's jails yet somehow managed to escape death, paid a visit to Buchenwald. There, when he began to weep, a woman expressed surprise that he, who had spent twenty-three years of his life in prison, still had tears to shed. He said to her: "I cry for all those who fell: whether they were on your side or my side, it doesn't matter; they are part of us all."

Yes, the dead do speak, but in their own way and at their own time. Buchenwald, Ravensbruck, Dachau, Auschwitz, and all the other human slaughterhouses, even those in Indonesia, cannot silence the dead.

And that bag we carry on our shoulders—how long will we go on filling it? Will it be for us as it was for the prisoners in Spain? I suspect that the answer depends on the West and its use of arms and capital.

How ironic it is that in 1948 when I was in Bukitduri prison I wished that I would be exiled to the Moluccas, along with the nationalist leaders who had been sent there, instead of being confined in jail. And now, years later, my dream is about to come true—that is, if the ship does not sink before we arrive.

There's nothing ironic about the food distribution system on our ship. It seems to be following the same model that was applied at Nusa Kambangan. There, for the first few days, things weren't so bad, but after that our ration of rice began to shrink, and soon the other kinds of food began to be whisked away to the home of the gods. The very same thing is happening here. Most likely, for the rest of the voyage, all we'll get is rice, served twice daily, with a little chili water on top. But who's going to protest? Our jailkeepers have used our own fear to intimidate us ever since we were imprisoned, and they have been fairly successful in their job.

The ship sailed due east until it reached West Nusa Tenggara where it turned northeast and headed in a beeline toward Buru. This was a faint surprise—I expected that other plans might have been made for us. When crossing the Banda Sea, the ship stalled twice. Three or four centuries ago, Western sailors had surveyed this sea, and now I, a prisoner of uncertain fate, was doing the same thing.

If you were here with me, you'd be startled by the blueness of the afternoon sky. At night I stare at the millions of phosphorescent dots that rise and fall with the waves that strike the ship's keel. This is all that I can see from the porthole but in my ears I can still hear the words of the information officer who spoke to us prior to our departure. He said, "Remember, that island is part of your country, too, and you have a duty to defend it from outside attack." Can you imagine!

One good thing about this surprising craft—"surprising" because it is still afloat—is that it means I'm far from the prisons of Nusa Kambangan where bathing had been difficult at best. The bowels of this ship are full of water; bath water is so abundant I almost feel like I'm a child again, bathing at my grandmother's large house. It's interesting how one can rediscover the pleasure of carrying out the simplest of tasks, especially when knowing that all around, wherever one looks, are symbols of death: the wide open sea, this shit-house of a ship with its ceaseless creaks and moans, the bullets, bayonets, orders, roll calls, rank insignia, hand guns, rifles, and camp knives.

The other men seem to take no notice of the radio even though, throughout the journey, it has never stopped spewing a constant barrage of sentimental *kroncong* songs and a preacher's prayers for a safe voyage, wishing us "Good luck in your new life."

No matter what you do in life, no matter where you go, the grave is your ultimate destination. Every person is delivered his death sentence at birth. Napoleon's journey from Corsica to his victories on the battlefield may have given birth to new legal institutions and codes, but the distance from the École de Guerre to Les Invalides, from the School of War to the emperor's grave, is but a few hundred yards.

What can I say? Here, in this cage of a ship, it is difficult not to think about death.

Just as on the *Oldenbarneveldt* sixteen years ago, the passengers on this ship, too, feel compelled to introduce themselves to me. Why? Because of my "fame"? Because in the free world they had once heard of my name? I find it somewhat disturbing that people seem to think a famous person must also be a fountain of knowledge or arbiter of truth.

What is fame if not a social manifestation—or should I say social effluence? Look at the famed prostitutes of today's world, those men and women who through the successful use of their skills have found the upward path to glamour and luxury. Have they ever had their civil rights stolen from them or had to suffer officially sanctioned humiliation and oppression? No, because of their fame, diplomats and heads of states open their arms wide to bid them a proud welcome. Fame trumps all political and moral qualms.

When I was your age one of my teachers was the writer Mara Soetan, a fairly well-known man in his day and age. All the students stood in awe of him. Though he was never a large man, his body seemed to have grown smaller with age. His face was shrunken but his eyes, peering from behind his gold-framed spectacles, sparkled and shined. It was he who taught me that everything a person comes to know is the product of what that person does with his life.

But the other prisoners don't seem to want to recognize that I am no different from them, and that I, too, am ignorant of the charges against me. What am I supposed to say when asked how long we'll have to stay in exile? Until death, or maybe only until we've sunk into a semiconscious state?

People seem to think that "freedom" is in the interest of the downtrodden and the oppressed and forget that freedom is also in the interest of those who purloin and oppress. The difference lies only in how "interest" is defined. We political prisoners, *tapol* as we are called, have one interest only: our release. Nothing more, nothing less. Freedom. But what are the interests of those people "across the sea" who control the world's capital. Go ahead. Ask that question to them. I for one believe that if and when our freedom comes it will be because of the West.

Meanwhile the loudspeaker continues to belch saccharine *kroncong* songs, official announcements, sermons, and advice from nameless authorities who wish for us good luck in the new life that we are headed for.

If one were to attempt to follow the logic of the information officer, it wouldn't matter whether this boat were to stop dead in mid-ocean, arrive at its destination, or sink to the bottom of the Banda Sea. The result would be the same: We'd still be in our own country where both land and water are in abundance. The depth of the Banda Sea offers sufficient guarantee of water.

There is at least one advantage to being an Indonesian citizen: With this country's expanse of land and even greater expanse of sea, it's not difficult finding space for one's grave.

Once again, I hope you'll forgive me for offering you this as a wedding gift. My gift to your mama when we married was a short story entitled "The Wedding Gift." Now, years later, my gift to you is made up of these natant ruminations which I'm not even sure you'll ever receive.

In monetary terms, these notes are worthless. Their value resides in their testimony, the witness they bear to the poverty of this nation's first generation of citizens. I would not imagine that to be an American or a Brazilian, for example, would be as difficult. You, of course, got your citizenship for free. Maybe you don't give the question of citizenship much thought, but I have been in prison for four years, now going on five, and am now on my way toward exile without even knowing what charges lie against me.

Exile—a birthday gift for people who would prefer to see me dead! There must have been some mistake. For a thousand years or more, the stories of the shadow theater have taught us that even the gods can be wrong, that even the gods can make mistakes and are not free from ignorance and error. What, therefore, can one expect from the human castes? We, the pariah, occupy the final position of a very long line of numbers.

The journey across the Banda Sea on this tuna warehouse they call a ship has been a slow one. Did you know that for a tuna to stay alive, it must swim at a continuous speed of at least twenty miles per hour? If not, its circulatory system, which is directly beneath its skin, will begin to clot and cause strangulation. The fish will choose to stop rather than to die. When caught in a net it chooses death.

Below this ship, in the sea's coral mountains, your favorite fish lays its eggs. These eggs are washed on to the shore where people scoop them up with seashell shovels and raise them in ponds. After they've hatched and grown, they're taken to the market where your mama buys them, then takes them home to cook and place on the dining table. Below this ship are millions of tuna, but there's not a bit of meat on my plate.

After ten days at sea the southern coast of Buru Island finally appears. The ship skirts the island's eastern shore. The hills and mountains cluster so tightly together, they form a rugged natural barrier. They are to be our guard and our keeper. Festooned atop the island's baked and cracked soil is a headdress of elephant grass. One of the men assures us that the fish on this island are slow-witted, that using even a stone for bait will guarantee a healthy catch. Our bodies so desperately need protein, we are cheered by the man's assurances. When catching sight of deer running across the savanna all we see is protein in flight.

The iron doors are opened. The men who are suffering from malnutrition and lack the will to ever rise again are carried on to the deck by their friends. The ship swings round to enter lovely Kayeli Bay, which curves inward toward the coast, a natural bay resembling a forgotten naval base from ten centuries before.

Kayeli is, in fact, the world's largest and oldest recorded producer of maleleuca oil. First came the Portuguese to this bay, and then the Dutch ships, one following the other, in search of this island's mace, nutmeg, and cloves. But that was centuries ago. And now we *tapol*, known as the "yellow drill army" because of our uniforms, come to these shores, but not to collect the fruits of the labor of the Buru people.

The wind from off the shore at once robs us of our breath and announces the island's intense humidity. It also carries a warning for us to take especially good care of our lungs and stomachs.

There stands the port town of Namlea with its miniature cardboard cut-out houses. The ship's whistle screams, but not for search of a quay; the ship is far too large and must anchor at sea. Two landing craft come out to meet us. A mosque with minarets that rise silently upward peers out at us from the shore. Namlea looks completely uninhabited.

Several officers emerge from the landing craft and board the ship. A few dozen of the prisoners, those in the best physical shape, are ordered to disembark first in order to set up a kitchen. The highest-ranking officer then comes forward to greet us.

The chosen group of pioneers lands on the island of New Life with a cartful of kitchen needs. They come on shore at Namlea, lifeless except for the squad of soldiers from the Pattimura division who welcome them with rifle butts and fists.

So, my child, young bride that you are, in return for this wedding gift to you, I hope that you will say to me, "Good luck, Papa." I am a prisoner about to enter a period of exile. To you, my child, I bid good luck as well. To you, and to your husband whose name I cannot even remember.

Now it is my turn to leave this ship. Your father must board the landing craft that will take him to a place I'm not so sure is somewhere.

CHANGING
COMMANDS

In the last week of February 1976, a fellow prisoner, Saud Surjono, came to my room in the barracks where I was living at Camp Headquarters to deliver a travel pass. I was to go to Unit 3–Wanayasa, the camp in which I had first lived in Buru, and meet Captain I. M. Sudiraka, the unit commander.

Saud and I left the unit together, following the road from Command Headquarters that led to Unit 2–Wanareja where we turned and headed toward the village of Wailonangan where we would cross the Wai Apo. Wailonangan had grown considerably since the first time I had been there over five years ago. Once consisting of only seven or eight houses, the village now contained at least twice as many.

The Wai Apo was so high that day, the swamp on Wailonangan's outskirts had virtually become one with the river. The current was very strong but on such a sunlit morning, the sight was very satisfying. It was there, in one of the hooks of the river, that I had once set up a survey camp: a simple bamboo hut. Since that time, both the river's banks and my bamboo hut had been felled by the river's current.

I always found crossing the Wai Apo by raft a pleasurable experience. The craft, made from two long dugouts strung together and a deck attached on top, plies the breadth of the river, making use of the current's own force to propel it forward. The raft was large and strong enough to carry horsecarts and motorcycles. It was tethered to a rope that straddled the river. As long as the rudder was properly set on the one riverbank, it could cross the river without a navigator.

No more than a few dozen steps from the opposite shore, we came to the main road of Unit 3–Wanayasa in Airmandidih. This road was the second one in the Buru interior that I had worked on more than five years ago. Just putting my feet on the road meant recalling the daunting time during which the road had been opened.

About one and a half miles down the road there rose from a patch of savanna a new unit whose buildings were of hewn wood with tin roofs. Except for the guard post the unit was empty.

When coming to the swamp-filled area of Wanayasa I could see that sites where huts had once stood were now under cultivation. A silence took hold of me as I thought about how much Buru's political prisoners had built over the past few years. On virgin land, almost absent of fruit trees and covered with grassland and forests, we had built a self-sustaining village that was now surrounded by dense banana groves. I noticed that the one original mango tree in the area was still standing, and that a few of the twenty-six mango trees I had planted now shaded the home of the commander and the guard post.

The quaint grass-roof houses I had left behind two years ago were now in a state of disrepair, nothing more than run-down hutches. The same was true of the so-called "arts building" and the unit's ad-hoc clinic.

The day was quiet. Only a few men were about. Most were out working or fishing. With the exception of newcomers to the unit, I knew all of the men there, though not everyone by name—we had built Wanayasa together. At roll call they greeted me with handshakes and laughter. The years had taken their toll and the men, both the young and the old, looked even older. Only a few seemed to look the same.

When Captain Sudiraka received me that evening, he told me that because my name was not on the official prisoners' census for Command

Headquarters (where I was living at the time) I was to return to Unit 3 of which I had originally been a member. He then asked me to write about my experiences in Wanayasa.

The date was September 4, 1969. The two landing craft, filled with political prisoners, left Kayeli Bay and entered the Wai Apo estuary, leaving in their wake the Bugis fishing village of Kakiair to head upstream, north to Buru's interior. The equatorial sun was shining, the morning sky bright.

The Wai Apo is not particularly wide but its current is strong and its banks are covered with forest. *Manau* vines, a thick-stemmed rattan, encircle the trees to climb skyward, reaching heights higher than even the trees around which they are entwined and giving the impression, to newcomers at least, that this is a virgin jungle not yet conquered by man. But none of the trees visible from the river, even those along the river's edge, are very large in size and behind them, what appears to be a green jungle wall, is in fact young forest.

The Wai Apo twists crazily, its sharp turns forming an endless meandering thread. This fact alone tells one that the Wai Apo Valley is a low plain with a slight gradient; the river's strong current tells one that its course was not formed by the shape of the mountains' folds but by the movement of the water itself which, when coming to a flat area, will seek its own path. Buru's physical geography, nature's panorama, becomes for me a lesson book, but one with no known table of contents. This upstream journey becomes a memorable event.

Large rivers served as seedbeds for many ancient societies and cultures, but along the Wai Apo the only sign of civilization is a cluster of Bugis houses on one side of the river and a string of native homes on the other. All the roofs are made of sago palm leaves.

Our boat docks at the "Transmigrants' Post," a structure erected by the transmigrants who had been sent to the island before us to make initial preparations for our arrival. Built on forked stilts with a tarpaulin roof, the structure stood within a small grove of trees. Immediately apparent was the fact that the forest was far younger than it had originally appeared; the trees were fewer and farther between and there were no fruit trees except for a few *melinjo* growing here and there. A glance at the ground was enough to tell that these trees were growing not on top of an earlier stand but on virgin soil. The land was that young.

The path leading away from the dock ran straight into brush. The number of trees grew fewer. The footpath proved to be a difficult passage. We were forced to crawl beneath numerous large trunks lying across it. Rattan thorns, the devil's own—long, thin, and razor sharp—were everywhere, some still on the vine, others fallen from their stems onto the path below, ready to pierce a prisoner's bare foot.

Many of the prisoners were suffering from edema, a side effect of the starvation diet in the prisons and detention camps in Java from where they had come. For these men it was difficult to lift their own bodies, much less the supplies they were forced to carry.

When finally emerging from the brush our eyes were blinded by the light of the open sky above the savanna, which from a distance looked like a field fenced in by interlinked stands of trees. The air, which is at least six Celsius degrees hotter than in Jakarta, heated the lungs. The whole savanna steamed as if it were a huge frying pan.

The high-grass plain reminded me of stories I had read about the American Great Plains, but there were no Indians here, and no horses either. There didn't seem to be any sign of habitation. And the footpath, only two and a quarter miles in length, seemed to go on forever.

Along the route, we passed thin and scraggly trees as well as miniature marshes where *mujair* eels slithered peacefully, oblivious to the attention of their prospective customers. This spattering of marshes was clearly part of a former riverbed. In fact, I later learned that the map of Wai Apo has to be redrawn every year because the twisting river's course keeps shifting, with a bend in the river becoming a swamp the one year and the next year part of the river's course.

We were in that first wave of five hundred men sent to this most isolated of places. The last group being transferred to Unit 3 arrived at around seven o'clock in the evening. It had taken six hours to traverse the two-and-a-quarter-mile footpath.

Seeing our barracks surrounded by barbed-wire fence, I was reminded of the detention camp described by Asmara Hadi in his book about imprisonment under the Dutch. Such a world of difference there was between his experience and mine—like heaven and earth.

I had been detained a number of times before, and had once visited the Nazi concentration camps of Ravensbruck and Buchenwald. I had seen with my own eyes Japanese detainees; I had read Anna Seghers's writings on Auschwitz and Dostoyevsky's *The House of the Dead*; I had toured Siberia; and now I, too, was going into exile, entering yet another barbed-wire dominion.

Of the ten barracks planned for the unit only five had been built but we were forced to sleep in them anyway, crowded together, one man on top of another, on floors of pounded earth damp with creeping moisture. The barracks' beams and pillars were the trunks of young trees. Their roofs were made of sago palm leaves, and their main walls and door frames from staves of pounded bamboo. Because the end walls were also made from sago palm leaves, from a distance the barracks looked for all the world like a herd of giant hairy beasts.

Shortly after we had laid down in an attempt to regain some of the strength we had lost during our long and difficult journey, the signal gong, a large drum made from a hollowed trunk, sounded, calling us to our feet. Shit! We could do nothing but. Over the course of the past four years the signal gong had come to exercise such power over us that we were little more than Pavlovian dogs.

It was still dark outside but the first thing we had to do after rising was exercise. A sergeant led us in exercise. "One, two, three, four!" he called out. "Watch how I do it!" But the only thing I could see was darkness; the sergeant, with skin as dark as early morn, was invisible.

Supervising our exercise was the first commander of Unit 3, Lieutenant Eddy Tuswara, who was a former Cakrabirawa officer, one of President Soekarno's special troops. One man, still weak from the previous day's journey, was unable to do the exercises and was the first one to be sentenced to crawl around the exercise field, yelling, "This is exercise and I'm having fun." I was put in charge of watching over him, a truly revolting and humiliating job.

By this time most of us had already been in detention for four years, and for myself, at least, this period was one of constant tension, of witnessing and experiencing punishment for unclear crimes—sentences that had never been meted out through a system of justice where a moral person might know what is right and what is wrong. I sensed that this tension would continue to be a constant companion in this journey of ours to a new life. Doesn't tension burden human nerves? And the burden itself: was there an economic, cultural, or educational reason for it? Or was it a punishment for animals? I found myself unable to bid farewell to my worries. It seemed at that moment my tale of woe would be a long one indeed.

Our breakfast that first morning was a joyful event. Going from a starvation-level ration of food to twenty-one ounces per day, we had made a quantitative leap. We had rice, not bulgur, and were told that we were guaranteed a supply of staples, including sugar, salt, dried fish, and tobacco, for a period of eight months. We imagined that the four years of hunger we had already experienced were finally going to end.

I was in relatively fair physical condition, as were most of the men coming from Jakarta's Salemba Prison. There we had been able to receive food packages from our families three times a week. I was thankful for the possible improvement in conditions. What an illusion I was under. Within the New Order's power structure, built as it was on a foundation of mass murder, the only thing the authorities had room for was assuaging their consciences. Forget about making sure the prisoners' food was taken care of.

Our first order that morning was to clear land for a new road, but we had no tools! The road was to cut straight through the grass plain. The high grass, a kind of elephant grass, had triangular-shaped blades with razor-sharp edges. We had to pull it out with our bare hands. And not everyone had a hat. The only respite from the savanna's intense heat and humidity was a scraggly bush here or there. It proved impossible to clear the grass completely, especially the roots. The job went on for six days, leaving our hands bloody and swollen.

About a week after our arrival it was announced that our food ration was to be reduced from twenty-one to seventeen and a half ounces per day. Three and a half ounces per prisoner was now to be "put on deposit"! Not only were we never able to "redeem" that deposit; later, and with no ado whatsoever, the seventeen and a half ounces were further reduced. There was no tobacco. Sugar was not to be had. The stock of dried and salted fish, which lasted slightly longer, had a bitter medicinal taste.

Ten days after our arrival, we finally received some tools: crowbars, axes, saws, and some fairly decent hoe scoops, but the machetes given to us seemed to contain not a trace of steel in them. When using them to clear the grass, the grass wasn't felled but simply fell in a faint. They were no better for cutting branches or twigs which would end up hanging from their trunks or getting stuck in the crotch of the tree. They might as well have been stage props.

On our first day out with the new scoops, we were ordered to turn over at least sixty-four square feet of land per man. Because of our improved physical condition, resulting from our intake of *mujair,* snakes, lizards, and other kind of meat that we had captured and eaten, our performance improved. Also helping us was the fact that we had begun to uncover the secret of how to use a hoe.

I, for one, had no experience at all in using such an instrument, and being faced with the reality of having to survive by farming was most unsettling. None of my education had prepared me to be a farmer or a farm worker, much less a skilled one. Now, going on forty-five years of age, I was being forced to learn a new livelihood, a new way of life. The awareness crept in that the future I had built for myself would, slowly and over time, find its perdition here.

Even though I had always been physically active, I was incapable of swinging a hoe scoop all day long beneath the burning sun. Baked by the sun, untouched by rain, the soil was rock hard and the first time one of the men turned over forty-three square yards of land in one day, I could express only awe. Most surprising for me was that the man had achieved this despite the fact that he was suffering from malnutrition and had a bloated stomach from lack of food.

The dark clouds that gathered in the sky quickly fled behind the surrounding hills. Steam rose from the Wai Apo lower plain and the air was heavy with humidity but the rain did not want to fall. The Wai Apo Valley is like a large cauldron with a lip of locked hills. The heat was more intense than in Java, and the island's cold much colder. Then, too, besides the heat that blistered our skin, the mosquitoes and flies were almost unbearable. When taking our midday break, we were forced to sit inside a mosquito net.

Arable soil averaged, in flat spots, about six inches, and, in sunken areas, slightly more. The soil wasn't crumbly to the touch, like the mineral-laden volcanic soil of Java. And the fact that stones were to be found only along the rivers and in the hills provided evidence that the Wai Apo Valley was the result not of the river's sedimentation but upward pressure from below the earth's surface. When we made drillings for wells near the barracks, the drill always ran into a layer of sand with coral or shell deposits.

Our extremely limited knowledge of Buru's natural conditions was a cause for depression, especially among those prisoners who were farmers or had in them farmerly instincts. Yes, this was indeed a new beginning; we could only guess what the coming years would bring. As no one provided us with information on the weather or climatic conditions, we were forced to collect our own. Our initial agricultural efforts at Unit 3 were akin to operating a boat without a rudder.

The land's aridity was especially daunting but we also had to deal with a lack of tools and poor transportation conditions between the unit and the harbor as well.

When Lieutenant Eddy Tuswara, the commander of Unit 3, was transferred to Unit 1, command for our unit was given to Captain Daeng Masiga, an educated man and a former adjutant to President Soekarno, who had spent a good deal of time abroad. I sensed that he could see that four years of detention had caused the prisoners to lose their sense of self-confidence, and knowing that this would ultimately prove to be obstructive to the government's goal of development, he set out to rebuild the men's spirits.

The cassava we planted didn't take root and with the rain in such short supply the sugarcane plants we planted showed no sign of growth even after a month, though they were fertilized regularly with urine and watched over by a man who was an expert in sugarcane cultivation. The food situation went downhill rapidly, both in terms of quality and quantity. When we first arrived in Wanayasa our supplies had been brought to the unit by boat, but with the drop in water level, the boat was able to make it only as far as the Transmigrants' Post, a little more than two miles away, a difficult trek at best but even worse when one was loaded down with supplies. The distance from the landing site at the unit to the warehouse was only about 150 yards, yet for eight men carrying a hundredweight of rice it was a hike that sapped them of their sweat, breath, and strength. And now we had to contend with a distance of over two miles! Few of the men were from rural areas. Most were city people unaccustomed to using brawn in their work.

We had no choice but to try to improve the condition of that two-miles-plus path. It was our economic lifeline. So it was that "roads improvement" became my first job. Not only did the footpath have to be widened to three yards, but because of all the twists in the river resulting from the low plain's topographical structure, we had to build bridges over every twist in the course, whether there was water or not. Natural barriers, which caused the path to turn, were also to be "corrected." We had to fill in sinkholes, fell trees in some places, clear trees in others. The most formidable natural barriers that we had to "correct" were swamps, riverbeds, and bamboo or rattan groves. Because there were only seven of us working and all of us were inexperienced, the job took a fairly long time even with the assistance of a chain saw that was given us. Nonetheless, I, for one, preferred to work in a small group. Out amid the quiet of the forest or the plain, I was able to let my mind wander without too much fear of reprimand.

While I was at my job, other men were engaged in farm work. As planned, the first stage of our agricultural endeavor was to focus on field crops, including dry rice cultivation. But opening up fields in a savanna, which grew ever harder without rain, was very slow. An additional problem was that we were in desperate need of seed stock; the search went on everywhere, especially in the abandoned fields of the native inhabitants, but about all that the men managed to find was cassava stock, and very little of that.

For all practical purposes, the native people did very little farming. Their primary food was sago, which they harvested from sago palm swamps; for meat they hunted deer and boar. Being seminomadic, they would leave their village after living for a time in one location, and establish a new one elsewhere. Because fields per se were not all that important for them, it was difficult for us to obtain seed stock; even finding cassava required trekking great distances through the savanna and forest.

As the felling of trees at the unit had only just begun, it was impossible to begin dry rice cultivation. Housing for the unit was also lacking. And because of the falling water level, poor administration, and inefficiency in transport, the unit's food ration rapidly grew smaller.

As a solution to the problem, Captain Daeng Masiga decided that supplies must henceforth be shipped to the unit directly instead of first going through Units 1 and 2. But the only way for this plan to be made feasible was to open a new road between Unit 3 and Airmandidih, the Bugis village located downstream on the Wai Apo.

In the work on the road to the Transmigrants' Post only a third of a mile remained, but now boats couldn't make it even that far and had to stop at Airmandidih. The captain ordered us to forget about finishing that road and move on to the new project. The job of planning this new road was assigned to me.

I knew the job would be a difficult one. There was no existing path and the road had to pass through very rough terrain. We lacked the proper tools. We didn't have a compass. Writing implements were hard to come by, and we weren't allowed to look at, much less own, a map.

Fortunately, as a result of a meeting between the captain and a lieutenant from the Ambon Special Forces, we were able to obtain a promise of the tools we needed. With these, I said, we might be able to build the road to Airmandidih.

I chose three men to serve on my survey team. Together we explored the Wai Apo Valley with only the sun as our guide. Fortunately, one of the men had a strong sense of direction. It would have been very easy to get lost in the vast plain of grass without guideposts to lead us back home.

Because of the endless number of twists in the Wai Apo—there was virtually no straight stretch at all—the distance downriver was very misleading. There was no footpath made by native inhabitants that we could use as a guide. More often than not, they used the river as their road and entered the savanna only to hunt or to fish in the marshes there, activities that left virtually no trace on the terrain.

After two days of survey work, we came across the site of a former home near the bank of the Wai Apo. In the immediate vicinity we found a fair number of coconut trees, two jackfruit trees, a mango tree, some lime trees, coffee bushes, and some grave markers as well. The air around the site was gloomy, darkened by the thick foliage of banana trees, brush, and stands of bamboo.

From the bank of the Wai Apo we could see, across the river on the opposite bank, a village where women were washing clothes and hauling water in covered bamboo containers. Spotting a dugout canoe tethered to the bank, I ordered two of the men to cross the river to ask the villagers whether there was an overland route to Airmandidih. The two hadn't ever been in such an unstable craft before, and though they managed to make it to the other side, it was not before they had upset the boat and fallen in the water. The commotion created by the men and their arrival on shore caused the women to scream and run away. The men followed in pursuit and disappeared from sight into the village.

We spent the next two hours worrying while waiting for the two men to reappear. What had happened to them? Why were they taking so long? We called their names until our voices were hoarse and it wasn't until they reappeared on the opposite shore that our tension eased. As it turned out one of the men had taken a fancy to one of the women there.

The advice the villagers conveyed was simple: Walk straight until you come to Airmandidih. A sweet piece of nothing that was.

We set up camp near this site, constructing a bamboo hut with a sago palm leaf roof, with the intention of carrying out our survey from there. From that time onward, the villagers came frequently, using various reasons and ruses to ask for food. Generally speaking, they were able to understand basic Indonesian. They refused to eat *melinjo*, the boiled gnetum nut that we prepared, and wouldn't have anything to do with breadfruit or jackfruit either, except for the seeds. As for greens, their diet was limited to amaranth and *kangkung*, otherwise known as swamp cabbage.

From our small base camp, we gradually made our way through the lowland and jungle to finally establish a line to Airmandidih. Somehow, without shoes to protect our feet, we had managed to make our way through fields of elephant grass and rattan groves and not get lost in the labyrinth of maleleuca trees whose branches formed a mesh in the water. When we finally spotted Airmandidih—the tops of its coconut trees, the green of its banana groves, and haphazard-looking fields in the forest— we screamed with joy; we had succeeded in doing what our ancestors had done thousands of years before.

The Bugis settlers of Airmandidih, traders or the children of traders who had moved to Buru from Sulawesi, were pleased to hear of our plans to open an overland road to the interior. Their livelihood came from trade in the agricultural and forest products that the native people produced, and from the milling of *gembol* wood which they sold in Namlea. For them, the road to the interior meant the arrival of greater prosperity.

Three days later construction on the road began. With what tools we had, we were able to clear a path six feet wide and five miles long in a period of three and a half days. We celebrated our venture's success with an "arts night" in Airmandidih.

Our hope of getting supplies directly from the landing had become fact, but the job of hauling food that distance proved not to be as easy as we had anticipated. There were bridges still to be made. Rivers and swamps we had to cross on foot, often over foot bridges made from tree trunks. Whatever the case, our supplies began to arrive at Unit 3 in far greater volume and in better condition than had previously been the case.

In December of 1969, just after we had begun the job of improving the road and its bridges, Major Kusno, chief commander of the penal colony, ordered that all nonagricultural-related activities cease. In a sense, I could understand his decision. The men of Unit 3 had been the first to arrive on Buru, but of all the penal colony's units, Unit 3 was farthest behind in terms of self-sufficiency in food needs.

With the issuance of Major Kusno's order, we were forced to leave our road-building work and go into the forest to start opening fields. For my work there I used an old American-made Legitimus machete. Manufactured in 1945, the machete's blade was both flexible and sharp, thereby making my work a great deal easier. That said, there is no easy way to clear bamboo and rattan groves and I was frequently bashed around by the same poles I was felling when they sprang back into the air after hitting the ground. A fellow worker had his nose crushed by one of the poles. Another prisoner had a tree branch fall on him and was incapacitated for a month.

I hated working in rattan groves, and not just because of their thorns. For every three clumps that I cleared, at least one of them had a nest of black snakes at its base. Constant assurance that only snakes with triangular heads are poisonous made me no less afraid. There were lots of different kinds of snakes, most of them the long and skinny sort, but the kind I most often came across was a slow-moving yellow snake, skinny with an oversized head. Once its head had been cut off and its body skinned for eating, all that remained was a skeleton with a thin layer of meat.

We also came across numerous cuscus, a nocturnal animal about the size of an adult cat with brown, gray, or white fur and long, sharp nails. Their huge round red eyes become mirrors when struck by light. The animal's pace is so leisurely that it's a very easy prey. When trapped in a tree, it won't even move when the tree is felled. We tried skinning and eating them but didn't learn how to rid the carcass of its rotten smell for quite some time. Our hunger forced us to eat whatever we could.

Two or three days after felling trees, we began the burning. Leaves and branches of the small trees that lay beneath the larger ones had begun to dry and served as kindling, making the fire easy to take hold, to spread and rise upward until it licked the sky, creating a reverie of crackling thunder. Smoke blackened the sky. This was the first time I had seen so many bats, thousands of them, wave after wave filling the air with their screams. I had a hard time understanding how so many animals managed to find food. For me the jungles of Buru seemed to be almost absent of animal sounds.

When finally our fields were finished we planted dry rice. The plants grew well—almost as well as the weeds that encircled them.

That month, without prior warning of thunder or lightning, the rains began and one particularly heavy rainfall turned the unfinished road to Airmandidih into a river of mud, sewage, and swamp water. In some places the road was nothing more than a mud hole. Because we couldn't stop using the road, the damage to it grew worse. Even though I felt sad about it—after all, I did play a major role in its construction and every inch on that five-mile stretch had been marked by drops of my sweat—I was also aware that my sentimentality was a useless and petty luxury.

At the request of Captain Masiga, I chose a name for Unit 3. I called it "Wanayasa." I took the name from the historical tale of the long march of the army of Sultan Agung from Mataram who attempted to wrest the Dutch Royal Trading Company from its position in Batavia. Wanayasa is the hamlet south of Purwakarta where in the early seventeenth century the Mataram army first established its supply base before proceeding to Purwakarta and clearing the land between Cikampek, Krawang, and Bekasi for preparation as rice fields, which is what made possible the land battle for the fortress city of Batavia in, if I'm not mistaken, the year 1629.

That same month two other prisoners and I were ordered to go to Unit 1 for an "interview" with Attorney General Sugiharto and a group of officials who were visiting from Jakarta. The only reason I mention it here is because, following the visit, Major Kusno came to Wanayasa and called together those prisoners who had met the attorney general for the purpose of engaging in a "dialogue" about his visit. At the meeting's close he presented me with a gold Pilot fountain pen, a bottle of ink, and a thick legal-size writing tablet. That the major had presented these gifts to me in public implied that I had permission to write. And, indeed, an accompanying letter signed by the major granted me restoration of my right to write.

Since 1950 writing had been, in all practical terms, my family's sole source of income. It was the only work I felt capable of doing. But in the four years since my imprisonment in 1965, the only thing I had been allowed to write was my signature on official documents. In that period the thinking process, which serves as a prelude to writing, had in me been paralyzed. There was brain activity, to be sure, but all I could do now was "react" and I wanted to do much more than that.

Look at me, I thought. Here I am, with paper, a pen, ink, and official permission to write, and I find myself unable to do so. Suddenly, focusing my attention was not nearly so easy as I had thought it would be. Then it dawned on me that I, like most of the other prisoners, had also lost my self-confidence. Four years of detention and the uncertainty of my future had inflicted severe mental damage indeed. I was forced to ask myself, "Do I have the strength to restore my former capabilities? Or is this the end of my life as a writer? Do I no longer have a role to play in this nation?"

Further reduction of our food supplies made my "recuperation" much more difficult. I couldn't gather my thoughts. Just to remember the name of one of my children might require a week's time. As a person who had made his living from writing, I now found myself lacking in the additional skills necessary to supplement my income, a necessity for increasing my food supplies. Further, unlike other prisoners, I simply couldn't make myself eat just any kind of meat. And then rice, our staple food, was replaced by bulgur. With the intense labor that went into clearing fields for cultivation during a time of incessant rainfall, my body weight and the general state of my health had plummeted. And then our ration of bulgur

was cut. Even the quality was worse: All we got were the sweepings—
moldy clumps of the stuff not infrequently mixed with chunks of rubber
from the transport ship.

My stomach, my body's weak point, came under attack. Every time I
ate I found myself suddenly having to run to the outhouse. And there, after
squatting to relieve myself, I'd find my legs to be so weak that I almost
couldn't lift myself back into an upright position. I'd be forced to lever
myself into an upright position with my arms. With the loss of more than
twenty pounds, I was thinner than I had ever been, even during the Japanese
occupation when I thought I had reached the lowest weight possible.

I have always been proud to be an Indonesian and a citizen of
Indonesia and have carried myself with the awareness that I, too, contributed to the making of this nation. I had the right to be proud of what
we had achieved. But the situation I was now in caused me to ask myself,
"Am I no longer worthy of being an Indonesian or an Indonesian citizen?
Was my contribution to national freedom insignificant, a complete waste
of time? Were the people of Indonesia not willing to recognize me as a
fellow citizen, one with full civil rights?"

Hoping to still my disquiet and as medicine for the treatment of my
mental and physical decline, I began to write, a quarter of an hour each
day. Initially this form of treatment proved unsatisfactory; its effectiveness
was gradual and it was some time before I was able to make my brain work
again. But eventually, through this exercise, I rediscovered myself as an
Indonesian, a person of respect, living and operating with a sense of values; I rediscovered myself as a man in all his nakedness, free from pretensions and ambitions, a creature not powerless but, in fact, equipped with
the will to define his own course in history. I found, in the end, that the
man is far more important than his pretensions and ambitions. The man
himself determines who he becomes.

At night, before falling asleep, I'd try to recall books and stories that I
had once read, but often an image that I had tried to forget would just as
frequently emerge: a rail of a man, bare-chested and hunched over as he
squatted on his heels, studying the earth outside the Outer Block of

Jakarta's Cipinang Prison. The year was 1961 and the man had already been in prison for eleven years since 1950, without trial, without a chance of freedom, because no agency or individual was sufficiently interested in handling his case. "When they first arrested me," the man said, "I was young, still in my early twenties. But now look at me and what I've become."

The other suspects in this man's case—they were accused of robbery and murder—had been freed five years previously, yet he was still being held as a material witness. He hadn't been called because of an administrative error; his name wasn't listed in the attorney general's files, only in the administrative files of Cipinang Prison.

"If I get out first," I promised him, "I'll see to it that you are freed." But after my release, I found myself under house arrest and unable to fulfill my promise. I learned later, however, that he was released that same year. He hadn't experienced the honor of being freed, however; he had simply been kicked out of prison. What then was the meaning of the eleven years that he had passed in detention? Was the same thing to happen to me? And what would be the meaning of anything I had to write when compared to that?

Even though my writing tablet was more than half full of notes, I wanted to destroy it. It was meaningless, nothing but a prophylactic for personal anxiety. Yet each time my hand moved to burn it, my conscience told me to stop. "These notes, regardless of their worth, are a part of me," I told myself. And so, even though I felt what I had written to be unsatisfactory, I still couldn't destroy it.

When Lieutenant Eddy Tuswara was made deputy commander of Unit 3 he was given direct control over the unit. He forbade the cultivation of any crops except rice. Not even vegetables! And ridiculous as this might seem, those were his orders. So supposing that the rice we planted grew well, that was all we would have to eat: rice, only rice!

Work on the opening of wet-rice fields began. A feasibility study on the construction of building terraced fields proved the idea rash. Nonetheless, I was given the honor of opening the first wet-rice field, which we later named

"Terrace 1," though, at that time, no dikes had been built. The virgin land was covered by pools of river water with sandbars all around them and stands of towering elephant grass on their sides. Deer droppings were everywhere. When cutting the grass, we sometimes came across nests of *maleo* eggs or the eggs of other birds, which we immediately ate raw.

Our first job was to open up a channel to permit the pools of water to drain. This task we finished in a short time. After that came cutting, mapping, and leveling. Gradually the first wet-rice field came into being.

To keep from dying from malnutrition, I began to eat rats and lizard eggs as well. Though the unit received some outside assistance in the form of milk powder, I knew that we could not expect this assistance to be permanent. And, indeed, after the third shipment we received no more.

In 1949, I wrote a story about a refugee who tried to keep her children alive by feeding them stray animals, cats included. Now I found myself doing the same thing. Eating snakes was common. Some of the men ate wood worms, too, disposing of the head first and then eating the fatty lower part of the body, sometimes raw. Dogs, too, found their way into our stomachs. For a half year we had almost no vitamin C; we had no vegetables or fruit. My vision declined and when out in the field I couldn't see well enough to put in rice or to weed. The sight of anything moving made me dizzy, especially in the wet-rice fields where the water would be constantly moving around me. And vitamin A? Forget it.

The humiliation, the beatings, the forced labor; these things made the situation more worrisome. Once, when we were out trying to harrow the soil—using water and our bare feet to turn the clumps of earth to mud—the guards beat us up. They had never seen farmers prepare a plot of land for wet rice and thought that we were playing. Another time, when I was trying to clear an area and gather some kindling for a fire, a young guard nearly strangled me to death. And then there was the time when the guard commander called me into his office for an "interrogation." When I returned to the barracks, the men in my work detail bowed when seeing my blue and swollen face.

•

A good first harvest in 1970 put rice back on the menu. This and the cassava we had finally gotten used to eating meant an increase in sustenance, at least as far as our carbohydrate intake was concerned. Thank God we were no longer forced to eat *cabin*, roasted pieces of sugar palm stalk which, when you ate it, you had to keep spitting out the fiber. And though our forced work schedule was strict, some of the men managed to slip away to catch fish.

Our unit produced eighty tons of dry rice but eating, especially eating nothing but rice, is not the sole requirement of life. Being able to fulfill one's most basic biological need does not yet make a man; that makes him a biological creature, an animal. There are a large number of other requirements that must first be fulfilled to change human animals into civilized creatures with the dignity and respect that is due them. Human history is but a series of struggles toward this goal. And the cessation of food supplies from the government made it clear to me that I would have to live by my intuition. That was a fact I learned to accept.

When I was a boy, there was a woman living in exile in my hometown. People said that the Dutch government paid her a stipend of forty guilders per year. I don't know whether this was true but I did know that her son, who was living in exile with her, was also able to survive from that stipend and that he owned a new Raleigh bicycle, one of the few to be seen in my town.

Nationalist exiles sent by the Dutch East Indies government to Digul, in then Dutch New Guinea, and other parts of the country in the 1930s were also provided financial support. But here, in the middle of this fruitless savanna, we political prisoners were forced to survive by intuition. This manifestation of an unjust and uncivilized society, one lacking in any sense of humanitarianism, must be engraved in national memory.

The announcement by the authorities that we prisoners had to "stand on our own two feet" was something we had no choice but to accept. Nonetheless, when the authorities then suggested that we bring our families here, I was dumbfounded. Our per capita income for food wasn't sufficient to even fill an individual's needs, much less that of a family.

It was around this very time that I temporarily lost my hearing. I was deaf, suffering complete degeneration. I was frightened and panicked. Would I never again hear my children's voices? A week later my hearing had improved yet was not completely back to normal; I couldn't hear or understand low voices. I was forced to silently accept the fact that I was now a semi-invalid. I imagined before me a gloomy stretch of time whose end I could not foresee.

A memory from that time: a soldier screaming at us at morning roll. We are filthy, he says, and don't know the meaning of cleanliness. Our punishment is fifty push-ups. That shouldn't have been a problem for me. At Salemba Prison, I always did a minimum of sixty-five push-ups in the morning. But here some of the prisoners could barely lift their stomachs off the ground. The sight almost made me want to laugh. By the time the soldier had counted to fifteen almost all of them were stuck to the muddy soil. That's when my silent chuckle turned to anger. By the time he'd reached twenty-five I, too, was pasted to the ground.

Our crime that day? There wasn't one. He had found drops of shit, a track of them, running from the guards' hut to the river. But the shit was light yellow in color, the fecal tracks from someone who had eaten too many sweet potatoes. None of us had eaten sweet potatoes. Even going out at night without permission was forbidden. It was obvious, to us at least, that our garden had been raided before the proper time for harvest.

Another memory from the last quarter of 1970: Eddy Tuswara, the deputy commander, comes to my hut to tell me that he is going back to Java. He brings with him a letter from Unit Commander Captain Daeng Masiga, informing me that he is unable to say good-bye personally because he has hurt his leg but that he's leaving a used towel and a pair of underwear for me.

The captain wasn't trying to insult me with his going-away gift; when out in the wet-rice fields, some of the men were forced to work completely naked in order to save their clothes for sleeping. He left the other men underwear too. Given my situation, I had no choice but to accept his gifts.

When leaving Salemba Prison, we had been allowed to take no more than two sets of clothing and after two or three months of working in the rice fields, my clothes were in tatters from sweat, field water, and rain. It wasn't until later I learned that the underwear had been provided by humanitarian organizations.

Before leaving that day the first lieutenant apologized to me for the treatment I had received but then added, "I was just doing my duty."

I followed him out of the hut, descending the ladder and tracing with him the course of the large drainage ditch under construction. "Just doing my duty," that's what he had said. How many prisoners had suffered at the hands of soldiers just doing their duty?

Masiga's replacement was Captain Samingun. During his tenure a film crew from the State Film Corporation visited the unit. The crew was led by a German-born cameraman who, before leaving, presented me with two shirts and a pair of corduroy trousers. His gift meant that I could put away the shirt I usually wore, which was made from a bulgur sack and had been a gift from my younger brother who was sent into exile after me.

I'll never forget that stranger, a person who did not know me but in whose country I had once traveled, and his willingness to help me out here in the middle of this savanna. He gave me his gifts completely freely, without thought. Sure, the clothes were used, but that was all he had. Regardless of his own motives, his gifts made me aware of my growing dependency and brought back to me childhood memories of elderly people with no means of income, whose own families were poor, coming to my parents' house to ask for used clothes. And my mother always gave them, whatever it was they asked for, with a smile on her face. I was becoming like those old people and felt ashamed of myself.

Working in the fields, we wore out our hats quickly too. I was forced to trade the fountain pen that Major Kusno had given to me for a *caping*, the large cone-shaped hats made from woven bamboo that farmers wear to protect themselves from the sun and the rain. With the loss of my pen I no longer could write.

Then something extraordinary happened: A German priest, Father Roovink, from the Namlea parish, visited Unit 3 and brought with him a packet of clothing from my wife. Thus, for the time being, my clothing needs were taken care of. For free people this might seem to be a minor thing, but for me at the time, it was a matter of incredible importance.

In July of 1971, Captain Samingun called together a "special" group of prisoners. We were ordered to move out of our respective barracks and into the Maranatha church. As it turned out, the church was in such a state of disrepair that we were ordered to build our lodgings beside it. Starting then, we were called the "Model Group" and were isolated from the rest of the men. We cleared and tilled our own separate fields. We raised our own ducks and chickens as well. Only at roll call did we gather together with the other men. This period of isolation went on for two full years.

This was not my first time in isolation. I had been put in isolation twice at the Salemba Prison, both times for more than a month and for reasons unknown to me. Here we weren't told the reason either.

In 1960–61, I was incarcerated for a year at the Salemba Military and Cipinang prisons and never had my crime pointed out to me. It was during these periods of isolation-without-explanation that I gained greater respect for the age-old values of humanity and humanitarianism. I meditated on the principles of liberty and freedom that had been instilled in me by my teachers prior to the Indonesian Revolution of 1945. Though present reality differed so greatly, in both sound and tune, my respect for such values deepened and Multatuli's voice became ever more pleasant to hear: *"De plicht van een mens is mens te zijn"* ("Human duty is to be human").

Because I had no writing implements I didn't write anymore, but as a form of compensation I studied German for five minutes every day. Who knows, I thought, I might someday be able to read German this way. I tried to forget about reality and the difficulties of being an Indonesian citizen. I came to sense the wisdom in the words of J. A. Cronin who, in *The Keys of the Kingdom*, warned people not to eat too much because "the door to heaven is a narrow one" and that while there are many religions and beliefs "there is only one kind of reasoning." But with my powers of reasoning as they were, it became ever more difficult to understand the situation I was in.

The next commander of Unit 3 was First Lieutenant (later "Captain") Sudjoso Hadisiswojo who replaced Captain Samingun. He was a short, thin man with dark skin and a thick head of hair so black that it looked unnatural. He was forever frowning, possibly just to cover his buck teeth, but maybe to make himself look more intimidating.

The period of his tenure was a most anxious one for me and I was constantly being punished for reasons I was unaware of. Once I was forced to push a cart to Airmandidih and back twice in one day, a total distance of twenty miles. The new commander put a stop to our cooperative, the initial capital for which had come from the wages that were paid to the prisoners when we built new units farther upriver. Because the individual wages were so small, we had pooled them as a means of improving the general welfare of the unit. That's how we had been able to establish the cooperative.

With the cooperative's closure, there was no more accounting of prisoners' funds. In the past the cooperative's financial standing had always been publicly announced. Now, the results of our work disappeared without a trace. The entire inventory of the cooperative became the personal belongings of the new commander.

Somehow, no matter how the commander dressed—and I don't know whether it was because of his constant frown, his diminutive size, his dark skin, stooped posture, or buck teeth—he always looked slimy. Sliminess, it seems, was an integral part of his personality. Shortly after he was appointed commander, he issued an order to deliver to him each day three grown chickens and fifteen eggs. At that rate, I calculated, we'd have no chickens left in less than a year. As a solution to this problem, we established a number of hatcheries, using chickens that were individually owned as layers to produce future stock.

A few days after making our first "installment" of chickens we learned that our tribute was being sent to Namlea where it was sold to fatten the man's own wallet. Our eggs were used to finance his affair with the wife of a Bugis peddler from Kakiair. Later, when he began an affair with another woman, he ordered that we provide him with enough planks to build a large house for his mistress to live in.

The man was like some kind of warrior from a former uncivilized time, whose power and authority were based on fear. Whenever he went out to the fields, he went alone, and in areas where the grass grew thick and high, he'd always fire his revolver at least twice. For the work crews who were far away, the sound of gunshot became for them a signal to stop and rest.

In the early hours of the morning he'd spy on the barracks. Once, when he found some prisoners still sleeping, he had them punished by making them lie on their sleeping platforms for three days straight. The only time they were allowed to move was when they had to urinate or defecate.

Under his leadership, five men in the unit died, the most under any commander. Under him, food conditions grew most worrisome. Even with our surplus harvest of rice, we were receiving, per capita, no more than five ounces a day. At this same time, eighty-four tons of rice and seven hundred and thirty cubic feet of wood planks were loaded and sent off to the harbor with no clear accounting whatsoever. Even our supply of chaff, which we used to feed the animals, was reduced by tens of tons. And all this was on top of the prisoners' forced daily tribute of chickens and eggs to the commander.

Our work day was lengthened until working as late as nine at night was nothing extraordinary. One man, after already putting in a full day of work, was ordered to continue hoeing up elephant grass from six in the evening until six the next morning. It wasn't a rare sight to see men out in the woods in the middle of the night sawing planks. And the only recompense for this work was continued beatings.

Once during his tenure, the commander escorted me and another

prisoner across the Wai Apo to Unit 2 where a team of reporters was waiting to interview us. I mention this meeting only because one of the
reporters, a Dutch man, gave me a notebook and ballpoint pen before he
left. After our return to the unit, the commander asked me to tell him
what I had written down.

After roll call that night I burnt whatever writings I had, and suffered
no regret from doing so. This wasn't the first time my papers had been
destroyed.

I find it very difficult to write about this period for, in putting my memories on paper, I recall incidents certain to disturb my sleep. For instance,
the final act of Captain Sudjoso Hadisiswojo in his role as commander of
our unit: It's morning roll and the commander is set to return to Java. His
replacement and that man's deputy are standing, stiffly in place, beside
him. From my place in line I catch sight of smoke rising from several loca-
tions. The outgoing commander had ordered the huts in the fields to be
burnt. Their destruction also means the destruction of our seed stock.

Early that same evening, I am working in the field and I see him,
through the clumps of bamboo, walking away. He is alone and leaving
Wanayasa forever. He doesn't look back, doesn't turn his head to the right
or the left. He walks away, straight toward his own grave.

We heard later that he contracted ascites. The serous fluids that collected in his abdomen caused his stomach to bloat and eventually brought
about his death. He never returned to Java alive.

There are so many bad things that I could note down. Fortunately,
good things, too, are eternal; like steam they rise and evaporate before
transforming into lasting values that return to earth once again as a guide
for living.

After Captain Sudjoso came Lieutenant Kusnadi. Soon after his arrival he
announced, "If I should take even a kernel of rice from you, I'll be damned
to be a monkey." Captain Sudjoso had said the same thing. And it's true,
he didn't take a kernel of rice from us—he stole eighty-four tons. But the

new commander proved to be true to his word and, in time, the anxiety and tension that ruled over our unit gradually declined.

In July of 1973, the "Model Group" was disbanded. Finally, after two years of unexplained isolation, we were allowed back into the general prison camp population. Two years! I could only think of how incredibly cheap freedom is for Indonesians like myself.

Members of the "Model Group" were put to work in the unit's rice-processing division, unloading unhulled paddy from carts and winnowing the chaff. This was a job that left me with time on my hands. After winnowing a cartload of paddy and waiting for the next cart to come, I had time to write. Gradually I began to see take shape my former dream of writing a novel about the period of national awakening. I knew that what I wrote would be, at best, notes for a first draft but soon nine writing tablets had been filled.

One morning, my notebooks were confiscated by the guards and turned over to the unit commander. They were never returned to me. Like personal rights, Indonesia appeared to offer no guarantee of copyrights either.

In October 1973, I and a number of other prisoners were ordered to go to Unit 4–Savanajaya where we talked to members of a psychological and psychiatric team that had been sent to Buru. Thereafter, we proceeded to Unit 2 where we met General Sumitro. Among the remarks that the general made that day was, "Go back to practicing your skills while waiting for your release."

One month later, the same group of prisoners was called to Unit 3 where Brigadier General Wing Wirjawan presented us with a letter from President Soeharto. On November 14, 1973, I left Wanayasa and moved to the command headquarters of Unit 1–Wanapura, leaving behind me its fields and the road to Airmandidih on which my sweat had fallen during its construction four years previously. Exactly four years.

On March 5, 1976, after a week in Wanayasa, Captain I. M. Sudiraka, the commander of Unit 3, returned my travel documents to me. I was to return to command headquarters the following day.

The next day I left Wanayasa, traversing the road to Airmandidih. I looked off to my right to where the churches we had built once stood, but both structures had bowed to the earth. Parts of them had been turned into chicken coops; other parts had been dismantled for use as firewood or for the construction of other buildings. The Buddhist temple and the mosque that we had built were still standing but were no longer in use because of disrepair.

The only thing that seemed to be the same was the green of the plants cultivated by the prisoners, who were now in their eleventh year of life without freedom. The same silence that took hold of me five days earlier embraced me again as I asked myself how much Buru's political prisoners had built and how much of our lives had been destroyed.

WHEN THE GODS CAME DOWN TO EARTH

When I was young, I was taught that man's position is higher than that of angels—man is made of earth while angels are beings of fire—and that the devil himself is an angel who betrayed God. In my study of Old Javanese, I learned that man's position is higher than even that of the gods, that the gods are only messengers. Nonetheless, in tales of the shadow theater the gods frequently go beyond the limits of the duties proscribed for them. Not only do they sometimes choose sides in order to enable a person to vanquish his foes, at times they even dirty their own hands by interfering in worldly affairs.

In their role as messengers, the gods often come down to earth from *kahyangan*, their heavenly home, to make contact with mortals. But that's only in shadow plays. Only there do the gods peregrinate between heaven and earth. In my entire life I, a man of the twentieth century, had never heard of a mortal being called on by the gods.

One day, I went into one of the large swamps near the camp to look for fish. Around the swamp's perimeter was a stand of wild sugarcane several yards deep. For lack of rain the swamp water had receded and its gray mud bottom was visible; in shallower sections, this muddy ribbon was fairly wide and in one of the pools of standing water I spotted scores of *muria*, the large variety of eel that inhabit the waters of the Wai Apo plain.

As I prepared to fish, I suddenly caught sight of something large, something very large in one of the stagnant pools—a huge *muria* with teeth the color of gold. Being on kitchen duty with the responsibility of cooking for my mates, I immediately imagined the ample meal an eel this size would provide. Not about to concern myself with where such an eel might have come from, I opened its mouth, attached a line, and dragged it back to camp. But when arriving at the cook house, do you know what happened? I woke up. It had all been a dream. For some time that night I sat alone on my sleeping platform, mulling over my dream of the gold-toothed monster.

The next day one of my mates told me that in dreams the color gold is a symbol of death. The man's information made the dream seem even more strange to me, but as strange as the dream might have seemed, I was soon to learn that reality can be even stranger and that even now, in the twentieth century, there are instances when the gods do come down to earth.

On the morning of October 6, 1973, I was in the field turning sod in preparation for planting corn. It was just at that time of the day, when the sun is burning so hot you can feel the strength being siphoned from your body, that an order came for me to report to the command post. "Get moving, double-time!" I was told, so I handed my mattock to a mate and sped off toward the command post where I found six other prisoners already waiting.

We were told that we were to go to Unit 4–Savanajaya and that we were to take with us enough clothing, sleeping gear, and supplies to last for three days. After going to our barracks to gather together our bundles, and then fetching the necessary supplies from the storeroom, we returned to the command post to tell the officer in charge that we were ready to leave. By this time it must have been one o'clock in the afternoon.

Still unaware of the reason behind the more than twelve and a half mile trip on which we were to embark, we boarded a large dugout canoe and began to make our way upstream, using the banks of the Wai Apo as our guide.

After leaving the Wanayasa area behind, we crossed the river and landed on the opposite shore in Wanakarta. Traveling on foot now, we walked away from the river several hundred yards before turning right and heading toward Wanareja two and a half miles away.

At Wanareja we made another turn, this time to the left, and made our way toward the Wai Babi forest that bordered on Unit 16—Indrakarya. At Indrakarya we made another right turn, then climbed and descended a hill until we came to Indrapura, where we took our meal and tried to gather together what little reserves of strength we had remaining before continuing the journey once more. Having worked in the field that morning, our packs seem to grow heavier and the sun hotter with each step we took. For those of us who were barefoot, the journey was lighter than for those who were wearing boots, but none of us had any water left to quench our thirst.

Outside of Indrapura the road led through a large stand of trees and by the time we made our way through the woods it was already night. None of the men had ever traveled this route before, and it wasn't until we reached Bantalareja, Unit 14, that we were able to find more specific directions on where to go.

The remainder of the journey to Savanajaya was made through the black of night. We got lost once and were forced to retrace our steps, but finally we made it to the rickety footbridge on the outskirts of Savanajaya. After trudging over an embankment we reached our destination, or at least the unit's command post, where we rested and ate before being told where we were to sleep for the night.

By the time we made it to our lodgings it was already 11:00 P.M., but even before we had the chance to wash our feet, we were called to the unit commander's home. There we were separated into two groups. My group was led to the upper floor of the house where we found seated, as if waiting for us, four men in civilian dress.

One of the men had a tawny complexion and with his narrow nose and lean features appeared to have some Arab blood in him. This was Fuad Hasan, a doctor of psychology and member of the Faculty of Psychology at the University of Indonesia. He was in Buru as head of what was called the "Inter-University Psychology Team." It was he who opened the meeting, informing us that the purpose of the team's visit to Buru was to learn the prisoners' true feelings and thoughts. He told us to speak freely, to not hold back. "After all," he said, "the team is not an interrogation squad." Its members were made up of representatives from the University of Indonesia of Jakarta and Gadjah Mada University of Yogyakarta.

Immediately following this brief introduction, the question and answer period began. Following is a transcript of the questions that were addressed to me, in so far as I can remember them (FH = Fuad Hasan; PAT = Pramoedya Ananta Toer; TM = Team Member):

FH: How have you been since you've been here?

PAT: Fine.

FH: Are you able to write?

PAT: Yes, when I have the time and I'm not too tired, but in general I only have a quarter of an hour a day for writing and between three and five minutes a day for reading.

FH: What is it that you read and write?

PAT: Lately I've been working on a novel about the first part of this century, the period of national awakening—but as an era, not as an event. I was given permission to write and had written about one hundred and seventy pages but my manuscript was confiscated. My reading materials consist only of what is available at my unit and the books I myself have managed to obtain.

FH: What would you think about having your family brought out here to join you?

PAT: Before responding to that question, I'd like to say that in answering it I am speaking for myself only, not for anyone else. That said, I must also say that it would be impossible for me to consider such a thing. First of all, my wife is not well. And second, regardless of whether my own contribution to the cultural development of this country is insignificant, I do feel that my children must have the right to actively participate in the national culture. That would be impossible for them here.

FH: What do you think would be the best way to develop this island?

PAT: That's a difficult question to answer, but let me give you an example. Dilar Darmawan, one of the prisoners here, was once a professor of English literature at Surakarta University. He's been here for eight years, a period of time during which he might have helped to produce several Indonesian scholars of English literature. But what is he doing here? He's tilling fields. What's the value of his work here when compared with the education of, let's say, even two scholars of English literature that he might have helped to produce? I, for one, feel strongly that this situation provides no advantage for the country.

Thus, as far as the development of Buru goes, I look at the problem from the point of view of the prisoners here who are developing it. The government should stop fretting about how the prisoners are going to develop this island and how much money must be spent for that purpose. The answer is simple: free the political prisoners. That would not only be the easiest thing to do; it would make for the development of a much better Indonesia as well.

TM: But you must view the situation from an objective point of view.

PAT: Having been in detention for eight years, all I can speak of is my experience as a prisoner. For me, that is objective. I know nothing of what has gone on outside of here.

TM: But you do know that you're here, don't you, because of G-30-S [the Thirtieth of September Movement], and the violent murder of the generals.

PAT: My answer to that is the same as the one I gave to the team that first interrogated me. I know nothing about that incident whatsoever.

TM: What's your opinion about G-30-S?

PAT: Frankly, I feel there's little need to dwell on that particular event. The fact is, ever since the time of Ken Arok in the eleventh century, the history of Indonesia has been one of coups d'état.

TM: When Ken Arok rose up against Tunggul Ametung that was not a coup.

PAT: You're right, the term "coup" was not used at the time.

TM: The publications of yours that I've read would indicate that you are a Marxist.

PAT: Which publications would that be?

The Team Member didn't answer my question but instead turned to address the other prisoners. Later, Fuad Hasan asked me another question:

FH: Can you see any *rechtsvaardiging*, any legal justification, for your presence here?

PAT: I feel that I have not been treated in accordance with law. I've never been brought to trial, never been officially sentenced. I'm a writer who writes under his own name. If I make mistakes or there are errors in what I write then anyone may, and has the right to, criticize them, especially the government which has its own Ministry of Information.

Why don't you tell me why I'm here. If I am guilty of something, I would willingly accept the sentence imposed on me. But look at how I was removed from my home and look at the kind of people who arrested me. I asked them to save my books and documents. They were, for me at least, of invaluable worth. At Kostrad, the Army Strategic Command Post where I was taken, I told the lieutenant colonel on duty there the same thing. It had taken me close to twenty years to build that library. I told him that if the government wanted my library, then fine, take it, but don't destroy it. Regardless of any personal interest, my library would be of great value for the nation.

But what happened? It was completely destroyed. Was this good for Indonesia? I'm not talking about the current government; I'm talking about Indonesia.

At any rate, if I'm wrong, then dole out the appropriate sentence. But if I'm not, then let me go. The treatment that has been shown me has not been educative and will not contribute to the development of a better society.

What is the use of studying the principles of freedom if one has no personal guarantee of freedom? For the prisoners here, what can education in this subject mean but greater suffering from their knowledge of freedom's loss?

I have a story to tell you: one day a mother asked her son, a primary school student, to go and find his father who had disappeared. And so the boy left home and went from one detention center to another until he finally found his father. Yes, his father was a political prisoner, and because the boy loved his father and didn't want to leave him, he stayed with him in prison. Some time later the boy's father was released but not the boy. He'd been registered as a political prisoner. Worse still, the boy was then sent to Buru. He's here now, in Unit 3–Wanayasa. His name is Asmuni.

Having told you this story I'd now like for you to define the meaning of "legal justification." The point I'm trying to make is that this place provides no foundation for the growth or development of a better Indonesian society. Just think of that boy, the number of years that he has been here, and the harm that has been done to him.

TM: What is your idea of a "better society"?

PAT: A democratic one.

TM: And, in your opinion, what kind of democracy is the best? The kind of democracy that was practiced in Indonesia between 1950 and 1957, the years of "Guided Democracy"?

PAT: In speaking of democracy I'm speaking of democracy as an idea. Thus the kind of democracy that would have been most appropriate for Indonesia during the 1950s would be difficult to determine without first assessing the collective nature and morality of the people at that time as well as the origins of those who held power.

    The kind of question you ask demands scientific research, something I have never undertaken. Let me ask you how far the *cultuurstelsel,* the cultivation system that was forcibly imposed by the Dutch colonial authorities, went toward destroying the character and values of the Indonesian people. What was the impact of destruction of the indigenous trade network by foreign-owned shipping fleets? You're going to have to answer these and other questions before you can come up with a formula for democracy most appropriate for Indonesia's needs. And it is whatever form that is most appropriate that would be the best.

The other prisoners were also asked about the issue of "legal justification." Fuad Hasan then asked if any of us had experienced any "religieuze beleving" or "spiritual awakening" during our time on Buru. I refrained from answering this question but at the end of the interview had this to say:

PAT: I apologize if there's anything that I have said that might seem odd or rude. If there is, blame it on my having been here too long without any freedom of movement. I'd just like to say that I am willing to assist you at any time in answering your questions.

During the next two days, October 7 and 8, the other prisoners and I spent most of our time clearing an area of tall grass that was to be used as a soccer field. We also underwent a battery of written psychological examinations.

At around ten o'clock on the morning of the third day, October 9, a helicopter from Namlea arrived in Savanajaya and landed on the playing field we had just cleared. The helicopter's principal passenger was General Sumitro, Chief of Kopkamtib, the Operational Command for the Restoration of Safety and Order, which had been established by the government following the events of 1965 and 1966.

At around one o'clock in the afternoon, I and several other men were called together, reportedly for the purpose of meeting the general. We were taken to an office but there were told that the general and his entourage had already returned to Namlea. There were a number of journalists who attempted to interview us but who were prevented from doing so by the unit officers. We prisoners were ordered to return to our barracks.

At seven o'clock that evening, we were ordered to pack up our belongings and go to Unit 1–Wanapura. That very same night, we set off on the twelve-mile journey through darkened forest and shrub. We arrived at our destination at one o'clock in the morning.

Very early the next morning, on October 10, we were given the honor of riding a horse cart to Wanareja, about a mile and a half away. Shortly before our arrival, a helicopter landed. As soon as its passengers had disembarked, the craft rose and was off again. The helicopter's passengers were escorted to Command Headquarters; we were ushered into an adjacent building.

The first person to call on us that day was the commander of the Pattimura Battalion, Brigadier General Wing Wirjawan. He informed us that General Sumitro would be meeting with us later and that if the general were to ask us a question we were to answer him properly.

"What do you mean by 'properly'?" I asked.

"By telling the truth," he advised.

After he left, the next person to enter the room was Brigadier General Wadly, head of the planning division for the penal colony, an agency known as Bapreru, the so-called Buru Island Resettlement Implementation Board. After giving me the once over, he said, "Well, Pram, you're looking better than ever."

"Naturally," I replied.

At about that same time we heard the sound of the helicopter returning. This time it was carrying General Sumitro and his entourage. Not too long after, we prisoners were called before the general in a room that was crowded with visitors, including a number of Indonesian journalists, two of whom I knew personally, Mochtar Lubis and Rosihan Anwar. In the room with General Sumitro were the two brigadier generals who had spoken with us earlier and several other high- and mid-echelon officers. Also present was the Inter-University Psychology Team.

The meeting that day began with an interminable speech by General Sumitro, which is described in detail in my original notes. In brief, after first telling us how happy he was to be in Buru and to have the chance to engage with us in a "direct dialogue," he announced that since we had been in "isolation" since 1965, he himself would present for us a historical and chronological rundown of national and international developments. Needless to say, the picture he painted was a rosy one.

Though he did admit that in the past "some mistakes had been made" and that some people had been "falsely arrested or detained" it was the Indonesian Communist Party's own policies that had led to the "excesses," i.e., the mass killings, that had occurred following the events of 1965.

After the meeting was adjourned the prisoners were divided into two groups, and the group I was in was moved to another room where we were interviewed by members of the press, the Inter-University Psychology Team, and a number of high level officers. Asking me questions that day were the journalists Mochtar Lubis (ML), Rosihan Anwar (RA), and Gayus Siagian (GS), and a military officer, Major General Kharis Suhud (KS).

ML: Well, Pram, have you found God here?

PAT: What was that you said?

ML: Oh, I see you're hard of hearing. Which ear's been affected?

PAT: Both of them.

ML: I'll buy you a hearing aid.

PAT: Thank you but that's not necessary.

ML: You look fit.

PAT: That's because I work hard. Starting at Salemba Prison, I began to exercise.

TM: Isn't that the same as physical labor?

PAT: It's very different.

RA: Do you still write, Pram? [*He addressed me as "jij," the Dutch familiar "you."*]

PAT: I started again recently and have finished about half of a novel on the period of national awakening.

ML: So, you're writing about history, are you? Why not write about the present?

PAT: Because I'm sick of all the unpleasant things that are going on right now. And besides, if I were to write about the present it might be misinterpreted.

GS: But why not write about those unpleasant things? Why not write about them?

PAT: What I write about is my choice. I am the one who decides what will give me personal satisfaction and in this instance I don't care whether anyone else likes it or not.

RA: I think you're right, Pram. I just wrote a historical book, one about the pirates my grandmother used to tell me about. But, maybe because your name isn't on it, the book didn't sell!

TM: Where do you get your materials from?

PAT: From my research before I was detained. But now, because it's based on memory, there are bound to be lots of shortcomings.

TM: Where do you get your paper from?

PAT: I own eight chickens.

TM: And how do you make money?

PAT: Sometimes an officer buys my eggs.

ML: Make a list of the books you need and give it to me; I'll send them to you.

PAT: Thank you.

ML: What have you been doing all this time?

PAT: All sorts of things: farming, smithing, road building . . .

KS: I wonder, Pram, do you still remember me? [*The major general spoke in a highly presumptuous tone of voice.*]

PAT: I'm not so sure anymore.

KS: Weren't you once in Cikampek?

PAT: Yes . . .

KS: Then how could you forget me? I was in the First Battalion, and you were on the regiment's staff.

PAT: That's right! I'm sorry to be so absentminded.

KS: Why don't your write about our experiences?

PAT: I have. [*Obviously, the man had not read many of my early works.*] In fact, some of the stuff I've written has been translated into other languages.

But let me say something here. I'd like to say to you here that I am a survivor, one of a select number of souls. I remember when I was in Karang Tengah Prison on Nusa Kambangan Island, reading on a blackboard there, "Started out with four hundred; now two hundred or more are dead!"

Yesterday, in Savanajaya, I came across a young man, another one of the survivors, if that is what you can call him, who has been bedridden for two years as a result of hepatitis. His name is Isnarto. Now, after he has survived this long, I don't want to see him die. I ask your help in saving this man's life.

TM: That makes me ask how have you managed to survive all this time? Has this period been one of any spiritual value for you?

PAT: I have a story about that, too: In 1948, after having spent two years in detention under the Dutch, I felt bereft of hope, ready to kill myself. But *ik ben meer mystisch dan religieus aangelegd,* I guess I am much more mystic-oriented than religious-oriented, and I called out, "Kill me if life has no use for me!"

RA: What are you saying? That you had an *openbaring,* some kind of revelation?

PAT: Yes, I did, but I won't say just what.

ML: You've studied history. What do you think about Gestapu, the Thirtieth of September Movement?

PAT: What I think is that at the time of the incident I was compiling material for an encyclopedia on the history of the independence movement for the period 1900 to 1945. I was working at home and knew little or nothing about what was going on outside. When I was arrested on October 13, 1965, I had already compiled about seven hundred and fifty pages.

RA: That must have been a tragedy for you, Pram.

PAT: I wouldn't call it a tragedy.

RA: Why not? It is a tragedy!

ML: But from a historical point of view, what about Gestapu?

PAT: Maybe someone else can answer that question but not I.

Questions were then addressed to the other prisoners before coming back to me.

ML: What have you been reading during your time here?

PAT: One thing I enjoy reading is *America,* a magazine the Jesuit Society puts out.

RA: Do you read any books on Islam?

PAT: I read whatever is interesting.

TM: What do you think about the development of Buru?

PAT: I think that Buru should be turned back to the jungle and allowed to remain untouched for another hundred years.

TM: Why?

PAT: Because the soil here is too young; it doesn't have enough minerals. This isn't a volcanic island; there's savanna here, large stretches of grass dotted with small forests. When compared with the size of the savanna, the amount of area that's been opened up is minuscule, but even that small amount of agricultural area is already plagued by infestation.

TM: Aren't there any insecticides?

At this point the interview ended; our intermission was over, and we were called back to the room where we had earlier met so that General Sumitro could continue his "dialogue" with us.

About the only significant thing that General Sumitro mentioned in the "dialogue" that followed was that "now that we have achieved political stability, the situation is calm enough for us to permit a resolution of the problem of political detainees. But how are we to resolve the problem of you here on Buru?" he then asked rhetorically, before presenting us the choice of being shipped back to our place of origin or remaining on Buru. He advised those who chose to return to Java to consider carefully a number of factors: political stability in Java, one's personal safety, and social and economic issues. He warned us, "Don't expect your old job to be waiting for you. Unemployment is a big problem in Java. Transmigration out of Java is now the on-going thing."

We were told that while waiting for the "problem" that we prisoners represented to be "resolved," we were to be "regrouped" based on our abilities and expertise. The general said, "This will give you the chance to retrain your mind to think and keep it from becoming rusty."

He then begged us not to give up hope. "Hope is, after all, a beautiful part of human life, and a life without hope is a meaningless life. I know that you live in hardship, but while waiting here in this calm and peaceful natural environment, find enjoyment in your suffering. And later, when you are happy, exercise caution as well." He then looked directly at me and said, "I have learned that your research materials were destroyed. I know that for you, as a writer, your documents represent a source of pride. Therefore, I ask you to make a *verlanglijst*, a list of the books and other reading materials that you need. I promise that I will have them delivered to you. I will also send you newspapers so that you can keep up with outside developments and with President Soeharto's important political speeches.

"To you personally, Pram, I'd also like to convey greetings from your friends. It seems that you still have lots of friends in the outside world. Anyway," he added, "think about the problems you're experiencing here and, on another occasion, we'll discuss them."

In closing he said to us all, "Please convey what I told you today to all of your other friends and mates here."

After returning to Wanayasa I thought that my life as a prisoner would return to normal. It didn't. On November 13, Brigadier General Wing Wirjawan, commander of the Pattimura Division, paid a visit to the unit, and I and a number of other prisoners were summoned to command headquarters to meet him.

In our meeting the brigadier general repeated much of what General Sumitro had told us a few days previously, adding only, at the end of his lengthy speech, "I won't go on at great length because General Sumitro has already clarified most of these matters for you. But knowing as you do that our nation is rich, fertile, and prosperous, I want to remind you that you are being both educated and invited to participate in this country's development." He then mentioned that he had recently been summoned by the president to Jakarta and that when the president had asked him, "How are our brothers on Buru Island?" he had assured him that his "brothers" on Buru were doing well.

He also announced that he had brought gifts with him, farming tools that we needed. "But because they're expensive, take care to use them properly." He told me that he had brought some of the books that I had requested as well as a letter from President Soeharto. "And though the letter is addressed to you personally," he said, "it is intended for everyone here on Buru.

"Let this letter be an incentive for all of you. I'd say it's rare anywhere in the world that a president would take the time to write a

letter to detainees like yourselves. The president is constantly busy with
the job of governing the nation, yet he still takes the time to write a letter to you!

"It is a great honor that President Soeharto has shown you, a true sign
of his kindheartedness."

The letter from the president read as follows:

The President of the Republic of Indonesia
Jakarta, November 19, 1973

To: Pramoedya Ananta Toer
    Buru Island
    I received a report from the Commander for the Restoration of
Safety and Security and General of the Indonesian Armed Forces
about the condition of you detainees.

    For every person a mistake in judgment is common, but that
must of course be followed by its logical consequence, that being:
"Honesty, courage, and the ability to rediscover the true and accepted
road."

    I pray that God the Most Powerful and Most Loving provides
protection and guidance to you in finding that route. Amen.

    Strive for and pray to Him for His guidance.

                        President, the Republic of Indonesia
                        Soeharto
                        General, Indonesian Armed Forces

On the evening of November 17 the same group of prisoners was
summoned by Colonel Sjamsi, commander of the Penal Colony, and
ordered to draft a reply to the president's letter. The colonel warned us,
however, "I will read the drafts of your letters to see if you have been
straightened out or not."

This is the letter I wrote:

To the President of the Republic of Indonesia,
General Soeharto

Respectfully,

I was both surprised and moved to receive your letter for I had never imagined that a political detainee would ever be shown such a great honor. I express my sincerest thanks and my greatest respect for the valuable time and attention that you have bestowed on me.

There is obvious truth in your letter of November 10, 1973, i.e., in that "for every person a mistake in judgment is common," and that "that must of course be followed by its logical consequence."

To you, the honorable President of the Republic of Indonesia, I would like to say that my parents, as with most other parents, I assume, educated me always to cherish truth, justice, and beauty, as well as a knowledge of our nation and our people.

It was with this education as my provisions that I made my way into the world. And the mark that I leave behind, the traces of my footsteps, are there to be judged by anyone. For that reason, in your letter, when you asked me to seek "Honesty, courage, and the ability to rediscover the true and accepted road," I read that as a call from my own parents who held in high esteem the message that the magnanimous soul will forgive mistakes just as the strong will extend their hand to the weak.

I extend to you my deepest thanks for your prayers to God the Most Powerful for there is no true protection or guidance outside of His own.

I shall forever strive and pray. With the deepest regards and greetings, I am . . .

> Political Detainee No. 641
> Pramoedya Ananta Toer

And so it was that even in the twentieth century gods still come down to earth . . . Incidentally, I never did receive the books.

THE BACK SIDE OF
THE MIRROR

During these past twelve years I have indeed seen far too much death. At the Tangerang Detention Center there was a period when between two and four prisoners died every day. The same was true at Salemba Prison. The prisoners' reserves of strength were sapped by forced and constant hunger; the end result was beriberi and all the complications that ensued. Even well-fed soldiers like the members of Cakrabirawa, the army's elite unit, who were arrested and detained in Salemba Prison for their alleged involvement in the events of September 30, 1965, were felled by beriberi after only three months of incarceration!

Here I must state that, for all practical purposes, the tens of thousands of political prisoners, the *tapol* who were first detained in prisons around Indonesia and later exiled here on Buru Island, paid for the cost of their stay in prison. For us to have depended for our well-being on the authorities who detained us would have meant beriberi, malnutrition, distended bellies, and wearing rags on our backs.

Most of the first men to die were farmers who, because of the physical labor they were forced to do, required larger rations of food—rations that were not given to them. After suffering a month of near starvation, when their families were allowed to visit and brought with them baskets of boiled cassava, they would eat until their intestines ruptured. Heavy smokers were also among the first to go. They'd trade their food rations for a bit of tobacco and then try to satiate their hunger by eating scraps from the garbage. Dysentery usually got them.

The hunger that the political detainees endured behind Indonesia's prison walls between 1965 and 1968 resulted in a mortality rate even higher than was found in the rural areas of the country between 1942 and 1945, when the country was ruled by Japanese bayonets.

In 1966, during the first year of my initial detention, the first man I knew to die in prison was a man by the name of Sugeng who had been a member of the anti-Fascist underground in the Netherlands during World War II. Consummately polite and forever easygoing, this middle-aged man carried on his shoulders a wealth of experiences invaluable for humankind. Yet he was tortured to death. Strange, isn't it, in this day and age, to think of torture as a form of persuasion? The "nobility of mankind," spoken so highly of in school, at the mosque, in the church, and even on mother's lap, is but an empty phrase it seems, quite meaningless in the situation that Indonesian political prisoners have found themselves.

As I write this I think about an incident that happened just yesterday. Around midday, when I was on my way down to the river a friend asked if I were going to Unit 14 to pay my respects. Pay my respects? Yes, to Mulyoso, another prisoner, who had died the previous morning. A graduate of the Banyuwangi Sports Academy, he had been murdered while eating breakfast by B., a young man from the Palmerah area of West Jakarta.

Mulyoso was forty-three years of age and B., twenty-seven. B. had struck him from behind with a roughly-hewn spade handle. Initial word had it that B. killed Mulyoso for not being allowed to participate in the unit's Ping-Pong competition. B. wanted to serve as his team's pivot but Mulyoso, the team's coach, had refused.

I knew Mulyoso, but only distantly. He was a robust man. Physically, he was a bit on the short side and rather stout besides, and had salt-and-pepper hair. We usually just nodded at each other when we met. In fact, the first time I actually spoke with him was only five days ago, on the evening of July 10, 1977, when I visited at Unit 4 where he lived. I was on my way back from Unit 14 to my own unit at the time and had stopped to see my brother, Hartoyo, and another friend, Ruslan. Ours was thus a chance meeting. I met him in the mess hall. I can't now recollect what we said to each other but I can see him eating peanut brittle as he talked, while the rest of the men sorted and shucked peanuts.

I might have spoken with B. at one time or another but I didn't really know him either. He had been imprisoned as a teenager, at the age of fifteen. During his twelve years of internment he had come of age. He was quite a good-looking young man—a quiet fellow, perhaps, but nonetheless active in the unit's sports and arts activities. He played Ping-Pong and soccer and in the *ketoprak* plays that his unit put on, he often played female roles.

I found it very hard to believe that B. had murdered Mulyoso for not being allowed to participate in a Ping-Pong competition, a suspicion that was later strengthened by the news that since mid-1975 B. had begun to engage in homosexual relations. B., it seems, served as a surrogate female for his sexual partners. The fact that he played female roles in *ketoprak* plays was not just a coincidence. Mulyoso, I learned, had once tried to dissuade B. from such behavior. I also learned that B. had once tried to stab Mulyoso with a dagger and, on another occasion, had gone to Mulyoso's sleeping pallet at night, intending to smother him, but had found nothing there but an empty mosquito net.

But that was then, and now, on July 15, Mulyoso was dead. It was not he who occupied my thoughts, however, but B., the young man who had spent twelve of his formative years in prison. Perhaps for having come of age in detention this young man was capable of premeditated murder, of killing in cold blood. When shown his victim's corpse he had shown no sign of remorse. I found myself wondering what would become of this child-man in the free world after his release—if he were ever to be released. What becomes of a person who is raised in a world of legal uncertainty and constant abuse of authority? If B. could be cited as an example, then such a man becomes a cold-blooded killer, a man capable of premeditated murder.

The incident caused quite a stir. All of the prisoners faulted B. for killing a fellow prisoner, a person who shared the same fate. But B. had killed only one person. How many of the other prisoners had killed their mates, if only indirectly, by snitching on them for some regulatory offense? For that matter, how many of the prisoners had been murdered by camp guards for no justifiable reason whatsoever?

The basic fact is that for the person without civil rights, death is always present in the background, forever dancing, each second of the day, before his eyes. Look on death if you will, but only silently. There is no need to beckon; the darkness that is death will soon come to you uninvited.

I remember one time in 1971 stopping in at Unit 3 when returning to my barracks from work in the field. I wanted to see Suproyo, one of the older, better-educated prisoners. I hadn't intended to stay for very long but he persuaded me to tarry by offering me a glass of sweetened water. Because I myself hadn't had anything sweet to drink in at least six months, I was somewhat surprised but also grateful. The glass of sugared water he gave me was enough to make my eyes shine once more.

One week later, Suproyo had to be carried from his barracks to a dinghy for transport downstream to Unit 1, site of the closest infirmary. He died even before the boat reached its destination, yet another victim, one of the almost countless number of prisoners to die of para-typhoid. And yet the one or two spoons of sugar that he needed to preserve his health, he had willingly proffered to his guest.

His mates said that three days before his death he had received a letter from his family containing a recent photograph of his wife and that no matter how hard he'd looked at the picture he couldn't find in it the wife that he had once known. Before being photographed, it seems, his wife had treated herself to a visit to the beauty salon—a simple act for most people but one completely incomprehensible to a person with no civil rights.

In Unit 3, the first unit I lived in, everyone knew Kayun. Not yet twenty-five, this young graduate from Malang Teachers' College was one of the most friendly, helpful, and easygoing men in the unit. I was among the first group of detainees to be sent to the far interior of Buru, site of Unit 3. Altogether, there were fifty of us, most of us older men who were unable to perform the hard physical labor the establishment of a new camp demands. Kayun, one of the younger men in the group, couldn't bear seeing old men having to work the entire day just to survive. And to lighten our burden he used up his own reserves of youthful strength. He toiled for the men as if they were his own parents. As a result, his caloric expenditure was not commensurate with his caloric intake and he fell ill.

In March of 1970 a bout of malaria left him feeble, unable to perform the chores he had once done, and he found himself being cared for by the very same men whom he had wanted to help. He moaned in his sleep and became dispirited and ashamed that the older men were now having to do his work. Their words of encouragement seemed only to make him feel more helpless and more guilty for being a burden on these men.

One day, the commander of Unit 3 marched into the infirmary and ordered the sick and helpless men who were there to run around the roll-call field. Later, when he found Kayun sunning himself on the field he beat him with his billy club. (He also beat another prisoner, a man by the name of Samtiar, who died the following day.) That evening Kayun's stiffened body was found in a hut in the field. His skin was bluish in color, his mouth agape and foaming. The hut was a shambles: The place had been torn apart; bamboo containers of seeds, pot ash, and ground glass from bottles used for sanding hoe handles were everywhere. An empty container of insecticide was also found lying on the ground.

Anyone who has ever seen a chicken after it has swallowed endrin-tainted food can easily picture the miserable bird squawking and flying about madly before it falls twitching to the ground to die. That is how Kayun must have died.

Ashamed of having to be cared for by his elders, unable to endure the captain's insults, Kayun had chosen to take his own life. The day was March 11, 1971. In the outside world, in free Indonesia, people were commemorating the transfer of power from Soekarno to Soeharto. Poor Kayun. He probably never got the chance even to pen a few last words to his mother.

All the prisoners in Buru, but especially those who came from the jails of Surabaya, knew Tjiptono or, if not the man himself, at least his name and his legendary kindness. The first time I met him was at the communal kitchen at command headquarters, where I was living, shortly after his arrival. With his athletic build, handsome features, and creamy brown skin, he looked both healthy and masculine. His eyes shone with self-confidence. When I met him, I told him straightaway what a good-looking man he was. His grasp was firm when he shook my hand.

A week later, when he and some of the other prisoners residing in Unit S were on the way to command headquarters, an accident occurred. They came by way of the pontoon that spanned the Wai Apo behind the headquarters complex. The pontoon, which was constructed of light-weight *pelaka* wood, would have been next to impossible to sink, but it seems that too many of the men from Unit S had tried crossing the bridge at one time and had upset its balance, causing it to tilt dangerously. When this happened some of the men had panicked and jumped into the water. Others had fallen in and, being unable to swim, started to drown. Tjiptono, who was an able swimmer, jumped into the water to rescue one of the men but then found himself unable to break the stranglehold of the man he was trying to save. Both of them as well as a number of other men were swept away by the river's strong current.

The fortunate reached the safety of the riverbank, though not until far downstream. The unfortunate, seven altogether, drowned though it was not until the following day that all of their bodies were found. Tjiptono's corpse was found caught in one of the rapids, still in the embrace of the man he hoped to rescue.

During his time in detention in Surabaya, Tjiptono had lost so much, even his wife who had promised to be faithful, yet he had somehow managed to survive East Java's deadly gauntlet of prisons. And then, after giving all he had to ease the burden of his mates who, like himself, had everything taken from them, after traveling so far, across the Java and Banda Seas, he had found death in Buru.

One of my fellow prisoners once said that death is God's affair, a natural comment, I suppose, in times when the wiles of fate seem impossible to comprehend. But no one here speaks of natural death or death by natural causes. That's not one of the choices here. Here, the list includes medical, biological, economic, and, last but not least, political causes.

In my life I have seen a great deal of death. Some deaths have made me ponder and caused me to think but, in the end, I have made my peace with them. For me death is not something extraordinary. It's not a specter that has haunted me since childhood, the outcome of wrongdoing so frequently cited in children's stories and oral tales. No, death is nothing extraordinary.

There are many euphemisms for death, one of the most popular being that the deceased "has returned to God's side." It's never been clear, at least to me, why people talk of His "side," but, regardless of the answer to that, you can be sure that in the prayers of those who try to maintain the pretense of fearing and loving God, they include the request for a delay or, if at all possible, a rescindment of the call to return to His side.

It is not death *per se* that brings these thoughts to mind, but the drama and tragedy of it all. Maybe such thoughts are a waste of time; maybe everyone thinks such thoughts, but then just swallows them along with their phlegm. Am I wrong in holding the opinion—if a prisoner has the right to hold an opinion—that there are noble thinkers or philosophers of death? Though a possible exception might be Gautama Buddha, I can see that even Mahayana Buddhism might well have sprung from his latter-day thoughts about death. For that matter, might not the *Tantrayana* contain the essence of such thoughts? But what am I doing? What kind of luxury is this I'm engaging in, mixing up thoughts of Gautama, the *Mahayana,* and *Tantrayana* with life here in the middle of this savanna?

One thing certain is that the dead have no more problems—at least in the view of those parties who don't wish to concern themselves with the dead.

Animals are not supposed to have the power to reason and therefore don't care whether there is life after death. But imagine animals trying to cheer themselves up in the same way that our own ancestors did when faced with death, by believing that there is life after death. How would they resolve the problem that in the afterlife they might once more be eaten by man?

Reason is the creator of happiness and suffering, of truth and falsehood, of everything except nature and oneself. To give an animal reason, they say, would be to make that animal human. That being the case, the animal without the power to reason can be neither right nor wrong. An animal is an animal. Nonetheless, observation tells one that an animal does gather information and based on that store of information "decides" how to act.

And so it was that in 1970, a bull "decided" to use its horns to split open the chest, lungs, and back of one of the prisoners.

Suyadi, the man I speak of, came to Buru from Kalisosok Prison in Surabaya. He was a man of slight build and a person who stuck to himself, preferring to live alone in a hut out in the field to the communal barracks. In the mornings he worked the rice field; at night he worked, too, chasing away the deer and wild boar.

Unlike most of the prisoners, Suyadi had once been a member of PNI, the Indonesian Nationalist Party, and maybe because of his political background felt himself estranged from the rest of the prisoners. Whatever the reason, he seemed to be a man in need of a friend and often, when I was on my way back to the barracks after work in the field, he would wave to me and signal with his hands for me to come to his hut. He always had something to give me, a morsel that he had somehow managed to put aside even in the midst of the forced labor: a sweet potato that he had harvested in his secret garden, a piece or two of the *muria* eel that he had caught and made into soup, or a slice of *durian* fruit that he had found deep in the jungle. Though kind to me, Suyadi showed true friendship toward the unit's bull that had been entrusted to his care. Every evening, after work in the field, he would lead the bull down the steep bank and into the water of the Fisroit River where he washed the animal clean, even its legs, with a swatch of grass.

It was on one of those evenings, no different from any other, that the bull thrust his horn into and through the man's chest. Critically wounded though he was, Suyadi managed to crawl up the river bank, and with one hand covering the hole in his chest stumbled to the hut that served as the unit's infirmary. There he breathed his last, without the chance to say another word.

If the bull recognized Suyadi as a friend, it must have also realized that he—the bull—was nothing more than a slave, forced to work long hours, made to transport materials even at night from the camp to the work site, five miles each time. And even if he was given enough food to eat, he wasn't allowed to rest, even in the mating season. Unfortunately, my fellow prisoner could not understand the bull's mind.

One of the prisoners spent an extended period of time on the penal island of Nusa Kambangan before being shipped off to Buru and there, while fishing one day, he pulled from the waters a miraculous catch, the novel *Ilona* by Hans Habe. When the man was put on the ship bound for Buru he brought the book with him, intending to translate it. By the time I met him, he had translated more than a third of the book, an amazing feat considering that he had no access to a dictionary or other reference books.

He came to me one day asking for my advice. He wanted to know whether or not to attempt to continue his translation. Pages from the novel were missing, having been ripped out by his fishing hook and lost in the Cilacap Strait. But it was not only the missing pages that caused him to doubt the worthiness of his venture. My friend had spent his formative years in Hungary and in *Ilona*, Habe paints that country as a whore among the nations of Europe. He also portrays old people as a collection of souls merely awaiting their execution. My advice was that he not continue the translation. My friend agreed and gave the copy of the tattered book to me.

In opposition to Habe's view, I contend that whoever is born spends his life waiting for the implementation of his death sentence. Whatever one's opinion, in the final denouement the question of death is determined by how and from what angle it is viewed. The answer thus depends both on the kind of lens one uses, as well as the material it is made from.

Buru's political prisoners come from almost every prison in Java and are the survivors of many previous screenings by death. No, one cannot say that the dead are silent. Their energy survives in different shapes and forms and is made manifest by various routes and means, but especially through the memory and, more particularly, the words of those who have escaped death's draft in Buru.

Prisoners who failed the screening process have all been noted down, transformed into interlinear notes written in ink made from soap and found in sentences uttered by tourists about Indonesia's high level of culture, its remarkable civilization, and the extreme friendliness and politeness of the Indonesian people. At some future time there might be someone capable of writing about them without his hand shaking uncontrollably or his note paper becoming wet with tears. But that person will not be me. In the world of the dead there are so many souls whose presence I know nothing of. All I can do here is try to make note of the souls whose names I do know.

Death, I know, is everywhere. And whenever I look in the shard of mirror I found in the rubbish heap at Limusbuntu Prison on Nusa Kambangan, I am always struck by my hair—how white it is, how it has changed in color and texture, and how tufts seem to have migrated to other areas in a desperate attempt to find more fertile ground. My eyebrows are almost gone.

Then I think of my limited reserves of energy and how they, too, have been diminished, sapped from me like the sweat that has fallen from my brow and dampened acres of Buru soil during my time of forced labor here.

My mirror is a pitiful thing, nothing more than a foggy and scratched shard, yet it can still hold an image—even if on its back side is death. And though all of us will one day make our way to the back side of the mirror, for now, there is still incentive to go on living, something that continues to goad me, perhaps that I might do something of significance before I die. Chairil Anwar once wrote, "after meaning, comes death." Is that true? Of what significance did this pioneer Indonesian poet have for the people of his own time? How far can we go before we stop thinking of life?

In such times as these when I am completely exhausted, both physically and spiritually, I hear voices whispering to me from an unknown source: Wouldn't you like to rest? Wouldn't it be lovely to stay like this forever? Yes, you, old man! No one needs you anymore, except maybe the thieves and extortionists. Your children, your grandchildren don't even know you. They have grown up by themselves like the seeds of wild grass, without concern for who it is that sired them.

But the incentive for life is not so easily dimmed. A voice rebels inside me: Just look at you! Not only have you not finished your work, what you have done is shoddy and poor. You lack imagination. You must stay alive! You need another thirty years at the very least. So put up with it and be its witness.

Several months ago I found myself loading rice onto the ship, skittering up a wooden plank set at a forty-five degree angle, loading tons of rice into the hold, one hundred pounds at a time. I'm sure that even now, in the state I'm in, I could still do the job but the weariness I feel at this moment stirs an incredible sorrow in my bones. What kind of prize do I earn for such work? A hernia, perhaps, to further reduce my mobility!

I try to listen to my own advice. You're working too hard. Reduce your workload. Stop exercising so much. Those dumbbells you're lifting are too heavy! But then comes the other voice: Exercise can give a person self-confidence. Physical fitness makes even a hopeless tomorrow seem brighter than it is.

This reminds me of the story a friend once told me about a Japanese war criminal he had seen at Glodog Prison jogging but a few minutes before he was taken away to meet the hangman.

And whether or not there really is any hope, the only real capital a person has in life is his body and of that you only have one. You have no choice but to make use of what you have. Others may steal your strength and extort your body's capabilities, but it's only you, its owner, who is going to feel the loss. Those thieves fail to understand that your loss is also their own.

Such an interminable weariness I feel, one that clings to me and shows no sign of loosening its hold.

The tone of these notes might be so depressing because of my decline in physical strength during the past two weeks. As has happened numerous times before, I've begun to doubt my own resiliency and strength. I can't even manage to make a workable rat trap from bamboo staves. The sly devils refuse to go into the tube where I affixed the trip wire.

Also weighing down on me is the knowledge that my novel *Mata Pusaran*, which I had thought was in the final-draft stage, must be rewritten from the very start. Why? Simply because I obtained a batch of data more reliable than what I previously had access to. And I had actually begun to believe that I was going to finish the book. "Belief" I guess is not the final word. There is no final word.

I feel the twilight of my life floating before me, amoeba-like with no clear limits to its form. But the incentive for life keeps returning, coming back time and again, like a recording of His Master's Voice: Thirty more years, Pram, you need thirty more years.

One by one, mates have gone, not to return. Each passing means another speech. A few of them managed to die on their own, without assistance from the authorities. No need to strangle them, or to strike them down with the rod of Moses or a blast of fiery breath. Free victims. Regardless, we have lost so many others as sacrifices to the greed of thieves and extortionists who have turned them into clumps and clods of earth.

Meanwhile, we grow weaker, older, and more ignorant and blind to the happenings of the world outside. Indeed, it wasn't for nothing this place was selected for us. Around you all you can see is a circle of mountains. The only fissure in the giant bowl is the Wai Apo and that is bounded by sentry houses festooned with machine guns.

Even so, it's nice to know I don't have to listen to the sermons and "mental guidance" lectures that were given to us each morning at Salemba Prison immediately after roll call and right after I had taken care of the remains of another fellow prisoner who had died alone, without his family, or had dealt with the family of a prisoner who refused to accept his corpse. But that is what happens to ye of little faith and to ye of little conviction. Even in death political prisoners must pay their way. Yes, a neat three thousand rupiah for the prison's administrative costs, though of course it is the deceased's family who must pay for their loved ones' funerals.

Death. Life. Thirty more years.

Beyond twilight comes a beautiful night, the kind of night the weary dream of. And to all my good friends, to those who have already gone to the back side of the mirror, I bow my head. I remember the kindness they gave freely to the world and to their friends.

These men took part in transforming this arid stretch of savanna into an agricultural bowl whose produce the people of the Moluccas now enjoy. Their skills and artistry have enriched their neighbor's homes. And their drops of sweat, though invariably foul in smell, have produced multiple benefits for the families of thieves and extortionists.

I remember their kind and unpretentious greetings. And even if there were any pretense, that would still not have made them wrong. For they are buried now, under a plot of land they had never before imagined and never been told of even by their teachers in primary schools.

IN THE MIDST OF
IT ALL

At eleven o'clock on the morning of August 19, 1969, what seemed to be an unending line of political prisoners came to occupy the interior of Buru Island, "empty land" or "frontier territory" as it was deemed, where the island's lowland plain begins to meld into hills and mountains. Five hundred prisoners marched slowly forward to settle on the savanna, an area of about 2,200 acres, bordered on both the east and the west by rivers, the Wai Leman and the Wai Apo, and on the north and south by broad stretches of elephant grass and jungle.

But the Buru interior was not empty; there were native people living off that piece of earth long before the arrival of the political prisoners forced them to leave their land and huts behind. Then, as the prisoners converted the savanna into fields, the native people watched their hunting grounds shrink in size. Even the area's original place names were stolen from them and they, too, were calling the area "Unit 10." With ten large barracks planted in their soil and five hundred prisoners settled on their land, what other choice did they have? But the strangest thing of all was when the prisoners began to build fences, erecting borders where no boundaries had ever been. The native people had no word for "fence"—

the concept was completely foreign to their culture. They didn't recognize such manmade limitations on land-use rights.

The political prisoners, the native people: two separate communities separated by language, race, religion, and culture. Yet somehow, beneath the island's blue sky and in the midst of the upheaval that the prisoners' arrival caused for the native people of Buru, there came to be interaction between the two communities. Only six months after the prisoners' arrival, relations between the two communities could even be described as cordial.

During their first half year at Unit 10, the prisoners had suffered extreme hunger for the simple reason that the food rations provided by the government were far from adequate in fulfilling dietary needs. And though the military officials strictly forbade free association between the two communities, the prisoners' hunger pangs exercised far more influence over their actions.

The chief of the village closest to Unit 10 was a man by the name of Moni, and it was his house that became the locus of trade activity. Shirts, trousers, hoes, eyeglasses, and watches that prisoners carried into his house left in the form of cassava, soybeans, coconuts, and tobacco.

Eventually the authorities yielded to necessity and granted the "locals" permission to enter the unit. Local men, even their wives and children, began to visit the prisoners in their barracks and sometimes eat the food that the prisoners prepared. Not surprisingly, after a period of time, this level of interaction led to more interpersonal mingling between the two camps.

All of the political prisoners were men and for most of them, having been cut off from the opposite sex for so many years, their meeting with the local community represented the possibility of or an opportunity for sex. In conflicts that later arose between the prisoners and the native community, "sex" was generally, though not always, the grounds for dispute. Buru women were chattel, owned by the adult men whose prerogative it was to do with them what they pleased. That a native man's wife might choose to engage in sexual relations with a prisoner was not in itself a problem; the problem only arose when the prisoner didn't provide his sexual partner's husband or "owner" the proper recompense.

The Wai Tina was the sole source of water for irrigating the fields of Unit 10. As there was no dam across the river, the prisoners had to construct a two-mile canal with which to divert water from the river to their fields. It was when this canal was under construction or, more precisely, on the evening of February 16, 1971, that one of the prisoners failed to return to the barracks. The prisoner's name was Wahyudin. Originally from Jakarta, he had once worked at the head office of Bank Indonesia, the country's central bank, on Thamrin Avenue.

The other prisoners searched for Wahyudin until 11:00 P.M. without success and, in the end, were forced to report his absence to the unit commander; concealing a prisoner's absence would have been highly risky if not impossible.

After roll call the following morning, the prisoners were mobilized to look for him again. At around 8:00 A.M. he was found, his body floating in the middle of a swamp, his head almost severed from his torso.

An investigation into Wahyudin's death produced the following scenario: After finishing work the previous evening, Wahyudin had set off to go fishing. Judging from the number of cigarette butts found at the fishing hole by the edge of the swamp, at least one other man had joined him, a native it was assumed. Though Wahyudin himself was a shy, somewhat reticent man, not particularly given to mixing with other people, the other man's presence probably did not arouse suspicion in him. After all, the site where he was fishing was at the crossroads between the village of Waitina and the other villages near Unit 10. It was very common for prisoners to meet or to run into local inhabitants at that place. But at some point during the meeting—maybe a fish bit on Wahyudin's baited hook and his attention was drawn away from the man to the moving bobber—the man brought his machete down on Wahyudin's bare neck.

Though all the local inhabitants were questioned, Wahyudin's murderer wasn't found. One man did say, however, that a week before he had seen a stranger tramping about in the jungle nearby. He was described as wearing a loincloth and letting his hair hang free, not fastening it beneath a head cloth as was customarily done. It was concluded that Wahyudin must have been the victim of this wild unknown stranger.

Whether the cause of Wahyudin's death was "sex" is unknown but, for a time, his murder brought out previously suppressed tension between the two communities. The prisoners could not look at a local man without wondering "Is he the one?" Suspicion smoldered in their eyes. It was now unthinkable for a prisoner to go off into the jungle alone. Going fishing far from the unit was strictly forbidden.

The natives made their feelings known in other ways. In Wailo they destroyed the large trough that the prisoners had made for pounding sago. (This was something some of the prisoners seemed to understand: After first having their hunting grounds taken from them, the local people couldn't have been pleased to see the prisoners taking over the production of their primary food source.) Crossed wooden stakes were also placed on the footpaths leading into the jungle: nonverbal signs that the area was now off bounds.

Easter Day, May 12, 1972, was a day of commemoration if not celebration and the prisoners were permitted a day off from their work. After Easter services that morning, two of the men, Suharman and Sarna, decided to spend the day fishing. Both prisoners came from Ciamis and were true farmers to the core, with hardened bodies and defined musculature that clearly revealed that they knew how to turn an untamed piece of land into a cornucopia of sustenance. Not surprisingly, because of their expertise, these two men had been chosen by the other prisoners to plot the unit's wet-rice fields.

The place they usually fished was a swamp not far from the rice fields, close to the site where Wahyudin had met his death. With none of the prisoners working that day, the rice fields lay silent and anyone crossing the dikes would have had the swamp and not the field as his destination.

At 10:00 A.M., with the sun climbing quickly upward, the sky was rent by the cry of a man calling for help from the direction of the jungle. A prisoner by the name of Kabul, who was resting in a hut a few hundred feet from the forest's border, leapt from his place and ran in the direction of the sound. What he found was Sarna, sprawled on the ground with a spearhead lodged in his stomach and his body covered with blood. Kabul immediately went pale but quickly called together the other prisoners who were in the area and, together, the men carried Sarna back to the unit, directly to the medical ward.

"Where's Suharman?" Sarna moaned, which is when the men knew that Sarna had not been alone.

Several dozen of the men grabbed their *parang* knives and set off in search of Suharman. The unit commander ordered the guards to accompany them. Drops of blood determined the posse's course and they soon found Suharman, or at least his headless corpse. Several of the men hoisted Suharman's corpse from the ground and carried it back to the unit. The rest continued the search, following the blood drops for almost one and a half miles until that sign was gone. Even so, they continued their search, scouring the hillside, the jungle, and the swamps, but by 8:00 P.M. they were forced to give up their search and return to the unit.

Suharman's corpse was buried that same day. Sarna, meanwhile, lay whimpering in the medical ward with the four-pronged spearhead still deep in his abdomen. Unable to risk pulling the spear out, one of the prisoners, working as carefully as possible, forced the spearhead inward until the points emerged from Sarna's back. Only then, after the points were broken off, could the spearhead be dislodged from Sarna's stomach. Sarna screamed in agony as blood gushed out of his wounds. Without any medical tools to assist him, the unit's nurse, another prisoner, was powerless, and at 9:00 A.M., on the morning of May 13, Sarna took his final breath. His body was buried next to that of Suharman.

On December 6, 1977, the commander of Unit 10 was idly fishing in a pond that the prisoners had constructed next to the rice fields when a man's scream suddenly woke him from his reverie. Turning his head he saw a prisoner called Karnudin running toward him with tears streaming from his eyes. While trying hard to catch his breath he managed to blurt out that a prisoner was dead.

The prisoner was Harjo, a popular man in the unit, who had chestnut-colored skin and a mop of curly hair. He was the son of a farmer who had been raised to follow in his father's footsteps but, somewhere along the line, he had become a petty trader and small moneylender instead.

Harjo's one wish in life was for a child, and although he married several times none of his wives succeeded in producing for him an heir. First in prison, then in exile, he felt himself to be a man alone in the world. As a means of filling the vacuum inside himself, he told the other prisoners stories, and he had an endless series of tales. But because he didn't always have a ready pair of ears to listen to him, his loneliness wasn't easily assuaged. It was probably to keep his mind busy that he began to create other worlds: sculptures, and carvings of thatch and wood.

Harjo became quite a proficient carver, and the pride of his collection was a wooden statue of a tiger roaring from within a snake's tightening coils. His carvings earned him personal satisfaction and plentiful praise. Unfortunately, they could not prevent his untimely death.

The commander immediately called together the rest of the prisoners who were in the vicinity. He ordered them to form a line and then to find Harjo's body. Footprints and drops of blood led the procession about 150 yards upriver to where Harjo had been working with a sickle to clean the stream of the refuse that was impeding the water's flow. And this is where they found him shortly after noon, sprawled on the riverbank with a spear in his chest and his sickle on the ground at his side. This man, whose hands had never stopped working, was now lifeless. The blood that once coursed through his body had now begun to clot in dried masses on his gaping wounds.

In the investigation that followed it was learned that three "locals," a man by the name of Mansen and two of his friends, had been waiting near the spot where Harjo was killed since early morning. The three men concealed themselves in the bushes until their hapless victim arrived, when they greeted him with the thrust of their spears. Harjo had fought back and managed to wrest one of the spears from the three, but the blood that drained from his wounds carried with it the strength he needed to drag himself to safety. Alone in the heartless savanna, he died where he was found. He was buried that same evening with all the prisoners of Unit 10 paying their final respects.

Mansen and his two compatriots managed to escape into the hills of Mount Batabual. Their attack, it was learned, had been planned months previously. They were among the local inhabitants who did not like newcomers, no matter who they were or where they came from. It was their hunting grounds that were shrinking, their sago production that was ruined.

Harjo's death, like that of Wahyudin, Suharman, Sarna, and so many others, was soon forgotten. Death in Buru is commonplace and, anyway, what's the difference between being killed by the natives or by the military officials? The fact is, for those in power, wouldn't the eradication of all the prisoners residing on this insular piece of land come as welcome news? Isn't that what they really want?

A CONFLUENCE OF COINCIDENCES

A person and his experiences are inextricably and inexorably linked, and a person without experiences is a person without a past, one who has been left behind by the unstoppable current of life. One must always try to avoid the repetition of painful experiences; one must also hold on to the experiences that have proven beneficial and use them as a compass for further movement.

From the time the Buru Island Penal Colony was established until its authority was officially dissolved, there existed an unbridgeable chasm between the political prisoners and the authorities, and the only place the two parties could meet was at the demarcation line between duties and rights.

The authorities—including both the headquarters commander and unit commanders as well as their staffs and the regular soldiers and guards—held positions that demanded absolute subservience and respect. With victory on their side, the mandate of truth was theirs and each word they spoke was a rule or command. The prisoners were the defeated, the ones in the wrong, and it was their duty to attend to the wishes of the authorities and to show them the honor that was their due. Words spoken by prisoners were tools of resistance.

Throughout the history of the Buru Island Penal Colony the authorities held all rights, the prisoners all obligations. The prisoners were responsible for serving the needs of each and every authority figure in camp and every government official who visited the island. The prisoners provided their food and accommodations and filled, it seemed, their every need. Unit commanders, to whom the government provided a salary and special food rations, placed the burden of their cost of living, including bathroom supplies, cigarettes, and entertainment, squarely on the prisoners' shoulders. When returning to Java for home leave or at the end of their tour of duty, they demanded additional tribute in order to purchase gifts for their families. Not included in the above expenses is the value of the labor of the three prisoners who worked in the camp guest house as servants or cook. Setting that value at 1,500 rupiah per day begins to give one an idea of how high was the annual "service cost" for each unit commander.

Every unit had a security post manned by a platoon of guards. The prisoners took care of their needs, too, from the provision of food supplies to the preparation of their meals. The only food the prisoners didn't provide the guards was their rice.

A special honor for Unit 2—Wanareja was the placement there of the Battalion Command, including the Headquarters and Reserve Companies as well. Cadets in training were also stationed there. Responsibility for filling their needs was also given to the prisoners of Unit 2, from cooking and ironing to the maintenance of the soldiers' practice field and the road on which they marched.

No monetary figure can be assigned to the value of the funds and services that the authorities extorted from the prisoners. The greed of the military authorities on Buru infested the entire rank and service, from the uppermost level down to the lowliest soldier. The most frequent source of conflict arose when the prisoners were ocassionally unwilling to meet the soldiers' demands. Examples include times when the prisoners, not having enough food to feed themselves, refused to provide the soldiers with vegetables; when they protested the soldiers' poaching of fish from their ponds; when they didn't want to honor a soldier's "request" to sell to him one of the fighting cocks they had raised; and when they shirked at selling the handicrafts they produced at far lower than normal prices.

The soldiers' greed, and the constant forced labor that was demanded of the prisoners, together acted as the catalyst for two incidents—one a murder, the other an escape attempt. The two events were unconnected but their coincidental confluence led to tragic consequences.

Usually by mid-November there is some sign of the approaching rainy season, but as late as the second week of November 1974 there were still no clouds to obscure the night sky. Even in darkness, the paths and roadways of Unit 2 gleamed almost white beneath the light of the moon.

Since the visit to the island by General Sumitro twelve months earlier, supervision over the prisoners and their activities had been somewhat relaxed, and it was now much easier for prisoners to travel between units. At night, Savanajaya Village, the family unit, almost resembled a small town, with numerous prisoners from the surrounding units visiting there or staying overnight.

Wanareja, too, was livelier than it had once been. Evenings found the prisoners honing their dramatic and artistic skills: in Barracks 4 there was *gambyong* dancing, while over in the arts building there were *ketoprak* plays and rehearsals for fledgling puppeteers and *wayang orang* performers.

The authorities seemed more relaxed than ever before, but then they might have been too busy counting the profits from their lumber trade and other forced-labor activities to concern themselves too much with the docile prisoners.

On most nights at Unit 2, the prisoner from Barracks 9 who was in charge of tending the unit's livestock would go outside sometime after midnight to replenish the animals' food. But on the night of November 12, or rather the morning of November 13, he decided against doing so. He could see in the darkness the blurred shapes of moving figures—and not just a couple, there was movement all around the barracks outside. He also noted that the animals were not in their pen; someone had let them out.

At around this time, the barracks chief was awoken by the sound of gunfire coming from the direction of the unit's kiln, about 250 yards away. The kiln was the center of the unit's lumber trade and also the site where soldiers gathered at night to gamble. He got up to inspect the situation but put off going outside because he, too, could see suspicious movements in the dark.

When the man in charge of livestock reported to the chief about the suspicious figures he had seen and told him that the cattle were not in their pen, the two men concurred that the mysterious figures must be soldiers stealing their chickens. That being the case, they decided, there was nothing they could do to stop them. Nonetheless, the barracks' chief remained puzzled by the sound of gunfire he had heard.

Earlier that night, at around 10:00, prisoners who were sleeping in the hut in the Karsotani rice fields also noticed suspicious movements in the dark. The barracks' chief immediately responded to this report by heightening the watch. He had heard rumors of a possible uprising and wanted nothing to do with it. Suspicious of some of the men under his charge, he forbade any of the prisoners from leaving the barracks; everyone was assigned to bed.

Sometime after midnight on November 13, no one knows exactly what time, the prisoners of Unit 2 were roused from their sleep by the guards and ordered onto the field for roll call. Many of the men, having just fallen asleep, were sluggish and were having difficulty opening their eyes. All they knew was that it was late—the night air vibrated with the sound of insects and frogs—and that they had to stand ready for roll call. The suddenness of the order and the uncertainty of its meaning made their hearts beat faster. The pounding of feet on hardened earth as the men scrambled toward the field accelerated their fear.

The path leading to the field was thick with prisoners. Near St. John's, the Catholic chapel adjacent to the field, a camp lantern glowed. The closer the men came to the field, the faster their hearts beat. They could hear from up ahead the unmistakable sound of soldiers screaming orders, shouting at them to pick up their pace.

The next sound they heard was the thud of hard objects—batons, slabs of wood, and pipes—as they fell on human flesh and the howls and screams of people in pain. In the cool night air the men's torpor vanished instantly. All eyes were now wide open, bright and burning with questions.

The prisoners who approached the field from its western side—men from Barracks 1 through 7—had to be particularly fleet-footed to escape the soldiers' blows. There, an entire squad of soldiers was standing, but there was no other route to take. When one prisoner went down, all the soldiers would start in on him, beating him until he couldn't move from his crumpled position. Rifle barrels and bamboo truncheons the thickness of soldiers' forearms were used to move the flow of prisoners forward. Those prisoners who managed to escape this gauntlet unharmed scrambled the last 50 yards to join the other prisoners already standing in place on the field.

Outside St. John's the scene was repeated time and again as one after another, groups of men came onto the field. The air reverberated with the pounding of metal and wood on flesh, the thump of bodies falling to the ground, and the rapid footsteps of prisoners trying to escape death. Because there were so many soldiers—the prisoners were completely surrounded—it was almost impossible to escape being the target of a rifle butt or a bamboo pole. Victims of the beating fell in droves.

After all the barracks were represented on the field, roll call and a steady round of punishment began, with the military guards roaming the area to divvy out shouts and blows. Rifle butts, bamboo poles, and slabs of wood turned out to be extremely effective pounding tools. The soldiers didn't seem to have a particular target; they swung their weapons indiscriminately, not stopping until their weapon of choice had broken or been shattered.

At 1:00 A.M. the prisoners were ordered to place their hands on the backs of their necks and to stand on one foot. The beating continued while they were in that position. The prisoners were nothing more than rats trapped in a gutter.

At around 1:30 another group of prisoners arrived; they had been staying at the lumber mill and were late because the sentry had been tardy in calling them. Not a single man escaped beating and many who fell to the ground were to lie there unconscious until the sun came up. No one could help them. Everyone thought they were dead. Many of the prisoners on the outside of the roll formation began to fall, unable to stay on their feet beneath the constant beating. Then, when the soldiers were either tired or bored of beating the prisoners, they discarded their weapons—their bamboo poles and slabs of wood—by throwing them at the prisoners. Human flesh was no barrier against the onslaught of these flying objects and many more prisoners fell to the ground. The night air was filled with moans of pain.

At 2:00 the prisoners were ordered to take off their outer clothes. Those who, because of their meager financial resources, owned no underwear were forced to stand naked in the cold night air. What might have looked funny in another situation had no humor now; death was present, ready to wipe the smile from a man's lips. The field was scattered with broken bodies. It was impossible to know how many were dead. The prisoners were then ordered to lie facedown on the ground. At around 3:00 they were then ordered to turn over so that they faced skyward and to go to sleep. Though the soldiers' beatings had stopped, at least for the time being, their screaming and shouting had not.

The soldiers brought out four machines guns and set them up around the field, their muzzles pointed at the prostrate prisoners. The naked and near-naked prisoners stared upward but the stars in the sky had no answers for their questions.

The barracks' chiefs were called together and taken off to battalion headquarters where they were given both a dressing down and a beating as well as being subjected to a shower of questions and threats. The most frequent question asked of them was, "How many of the men in your barracks took part in the uprising?"

The drubbing given the chief of Barracks 1 was especially brutal. Many of his men had failed to show up at roll call and his beating was so severe, he fell unconscious to the ground and his head swelled to twice its normal size. It was not until six months later that he was able to do light work again.

Punishment of the barracks chiefs continued until around 5:00 A.M. At that time, when a soldier raised the national flag on the flagpole to half-mast, one of the command post's staff members asked, "Do you know why the flag is at half-mast?"

"Because there's been a death, sir," came the hushed answer.

"That's right, and it was your men who staged the uprising, wasn't it, and who got one of our men killed?"

With that comment, the picture of what had happened and the reason behind the soldiers' extraordinary brutality began to emerge, but it was not until sometime later that all the pieces were complete.

With the return of the barracks chiefs to the field, the prisoners lying on the ground were ordered to stand. The bodies of those men who could stand were wet with dew, but many were unable to get up; they were either dead, unconscious, or had no strength left to stand. A sour smell of blood and human waste clung to the air.

The guards continued circling the rows of prisoners, venting their fury with fists, guns, and bamboo, completely ignoring their superior officer's orders to stay off the field. Dawn brought with it another shower of blows. More bodies fell to the ground, silent companions for the prostrate bodies on the pathway.

Then another soldier came running toward the field. With a semiautomatic, which he held by the barrel in his hands, he rushed up and down the rows of men, looking for targets for his anger. His blows toppled more prisoners. For a moment he appeared satisfied but then began to run away. At a distance he stopped, turned around, raised his gun, and took aim at the prisoners, but before the man could fire, other soldiers had wrested his weapon from him.

Around sunrise two prisoners whose names were Supriyadi and Eko Tunggono came running to the field. When asked where they had been, they answered that they had been out in the rice field stealing rice. Not believing their answer, the soldiers turned the two men into punching bags. Even after the two had fallen to the ground the beating didn't stop. The soldiers whacked them with bamboo poles until the poles were broken and the men motionless. They appeared to be dead. In fact they were unconscious and were to remain so for several more days. Neither could move of his own accord for several months thereafter.

At approximately 6:00 A.M. a reprieve finally came when Colonel Samsi, who had recently been promoted to the position of commander of the penal colony, came into the camp on a motorcycle. Even before doing anything else he began to scream at the soldiers for acting without orders. Those soldiers who were still torturing the prisoners suddenly stopped and removed themselves to a distance.

"How long have you been in the army?" the colonel yelled at the battalion commander. "Don't you know the meaning of discipline?"

"I ordered them to stop, sir," the man answered, "but they didn't hear me."

"You idiot!" Colonel Samsi continued. "If you want to kill the prisoners you can do that in less than a minute. Get your men off the field now."

With that the torture ceased and, after the soldiers had left the field, Colonel Samsi ordered all of the officers present, from platoon commander upward, to gather for a briefing. We don't know what was said.

At sunrise the sky turned bright, just as it had the day before. But the previous day the men had been able to smile, even to make jokes about the uncertainty of their lives as prisoners. Yes, but that was yesterday. On this day, under the new day's sun, there were no smiles on the men's lips and no cheer in their hearts. One false step could mean pain or death. Everyone was in pain, except for those prisoners who hadn't shown up for roll call.

What were those other men doing now, the bedraggled prisoners wondered. Dancing in freedom? Planning a follow-up to their success? Or maybe they were just as cold and still as their friends who were lying on the ground. Maybe their skulls had been shattered by soldiers' bullets.

Who could know what was going on? The prisoners who were able to stand remained in place. Their calves trembled. Even the soil on which they stood seemed to be their enemy. Their legs were pins and needles, their muscles ready to give out. Their eyes remained fixed on some point in the distance—maybe at a time nine years earlier when so many other friends had been butchered.

At around 7:00 A.M., Colonel Samsi's briefing ended and the company commanders were dismissed. The prisoners were then herded to the arts building. Some of the prisoners who were seriously injured still managed to make their way but wobbled crazily as they walked. The unconscious prisoners were carried in by the few men who had any strength left.

After all the prisoners were inside the arts building, Colonel Samsi finally resolved some of the questions buzzing around in the prisoners' heads. "A number of the prisoners have fled. And that was a mistake. The government knows Buru Island in minute detail and there's no place to hide. They're not going to find any food in the jungle, and the hills are bare. If they stay in the jungle they'll die of starvation or be eaten by snakes. If they try to seek shelter among the local people they'll soon be discovered because they look different from the people here. Even the sea around Buru is different from the Java Sea. Saying they do manage to reach the sea, they're going to get caught because they won't know how to use the boats from around here.

"There is no connection between the murder of one of the soldiers and the men who fled. For that reason I ask you now to go back to your barracks. Those of you who are injured will be given medical attention. For your own safety, follow all orders given you. If you go out at night you must carry a light. Follow my orders well."

While leaving the arts building no one said a word. All thoughts had returned to former times, to other days of darkness and blood, and cries and moans. By the time the men returned to their barracks it was 10:00 A.M. Forty-eight prisoners were still unaccounted for.

•

The following night Unit 2 was absolutely still. No prisoner left his barracks, not even with a lantern. Outside were soldiers, concealed in darkness and foliage. Prisoners who wanted to defecate forced themselves to wait until morning; those who needed to urinate relieved themselves inside the barracks. Only when the sun finally rose the next morning did the prisoners begin to feel the beat of life inside them again. Faint smiles appeared on faces; glimmerings of hope flashed in prisoners' eyes. But when evening fell, thoughts of death came again to threaten them all.

Around midnight they were ordered outside for roll call. The prisoners steeled themselves for a new round of torture. But nothing happened—it was just a numbers check.

In the morning life pulsated through their bodies once more but, unlike before, none of the men felt they had control over their bodies any longer. Now, whatever the authorities asked of them was freely given. If a soldier was hungry for chicken, all he had to do was to order one of the men to catch him one, dress it, and cook it for him. The same was true of vegetables, and eggs, and fish, and handicrafts.

Having only partially succeeded in their attempt at murder, the soldiers were now trying their hands at theft. And not just of the petty kind. Barracks 9 was ordered to turn over to the Reserve Company one ton of its mung bean harvest. The prisoners never got a chance to harvest their corn; the soldiers had already picked the stalks clean.

Listlessness took hold of the prisoners; they now knew that at any time anything they owned, including their lives, could be taken from them. And what lives did they have anyway? With the plunge in their food supplies, they now faced starvation.

On the third day after the incident the prisoners were allowed to return to the fields to harvest rice. On the fourth day they were allowed to work in the forest, as long as they carried a permit. On the fifth day life—if that is what our condition can be called—was pretty much back to normal.

An Afterword:

It will never be known whether the soldier who died the night of November 12, 1974 was killed for being caught cheating in a card game, or because of problems in the lumber trade, or because another soldier wanted his money, but what is certain is that he was not killed by a political prisoner.

Following the sound of gunshot that the chief of Barracks 9 heard, two soldiers were sighted hurrying toward the command post. Their clothes were ripped, they were covered in mud, and they were wearing no shoes. They were carrying with them a dead soldier. The two soldiers are said to have reported to Colonel Samsi that the prisoners of Unit 2 had rebelled and killed their fellow soldier. After looking over the two shoeless soldiers with their rolled-up trousers and their guns with bayonets, he then inspected the body of the dead soldier. The man hadn't been stabbed to death but had been shot several times. He then ordered the two soldiers to be put in the stockade. The corpse of the dead soldier was taken to Namlea. What later became of the two soldiers is unknown.

That the prisoners who planned to escape from the penal colony staged their flight the same night as the soldier's death was a stroke of bad luck. But more unlucky were the other prisoners who didn't know anything about the escape plan and had to suffer as a result.

According to the information gathered after the incident, on the night of their escape the participating prisoners were to have gathered at midnight at a reconnaissance point in the jungle and from there gone on to make their way out of the penal colony by way of the Wai Omo River. They carried weapons—sharpened bamboo poles—with which they intended to attack Reserve Company headquarters. Once they had disarmed and killed the soldiers there, they would then attack and overpower battalion headquarters with their newly acquired weapons.

Unfortunately for them, their escape route took them close to the kiln where the soldier was murdered. When they heard the sound of gunfire and, soon after that, the order for a roll call, all their planning and coordination began to unravel. This became apparent when, over the next few days, the escapees began to return to camp, not together but in small groups or individually, and turn themselves in. Some of them had actually hidden near their own barracks but were afraid to come in for fear of being beaten by their fellow prisoners.

The entire Hassanuddin battalion was mobilized to search for the other escapees. Helicopters were used to search for the men from the air and those who were caught were flown directly to Namlea. Most of the prisoners who were caught were very thin from not having eaten for a week.

Two prisoners, Basri and Agus Suroto, were making their way across a barren hill when they heard a helicopter roaring overhead. They tried to run but the soldiers shot at them. Basri was hit in the leg and he fell. The soldiers continued to fire at him. Before falling unconscious he saw his companion trying to fend off the bullets with his bare hands. When he opened his eyes next he was in a village north of Buru. Agus was dead.

Two other prisoners, Amat and Jembrang Suwardi, were caught stealing cassava in a field in Unit 6. They were taken by the guards of that unit and tortured until they died the next day. They were buried by the men of that unit.

Sukarjo Sukir, Dalari, and Nyamad tried hiding in the mountains and even built themselves a hut. One day a soldier who got lost came to their hut, looking for something to drink. When the three men ran away the soldier immediately became suspicious and fired his rifle at them. Sukarjo Sukir was hit in the chest. The other two, Dalari and Nyamad, got away but were later captured at Unit 10. When Sukarjo Sukir was taken to the command headquarters he was still alive, but died later.

Of the forty-eight prisoners who fled, twenty-seven are known to have been captured and died. Eventually the remaining twenty-one prisoners were either captured or turned themselves in. Initially they were imprisoned in Namlea but were later transferred to Unit 12–Bhirawa Wanajaya.

II

FRAGMENTS

OF

MY

LIFE

The penal colony was originally planned to be comprised of fifteen units. When I arrived, there were only three, each with ten barracks, some of them holding five hundred or more prisoners apiece. After we had finished building the additional twelve units, three more—the "R," "S," and "T" units as they were called—were established. Their barracks were built for "only" two hundred and fifty prisoners. Still later, another unit, this one named Savanajaya, was opened. This unit was reserved for prisoners whose families had joined them. A final unit, Jiku Kecil, was established for what the authorities called "incorrigible" prisoners. That unit, even more than the others, was a death camp where the guards could treat the prisoners any way they pleased.

The barracks were little more than frames made of tree trunks, which served as both supports and cross beams. The roofs and walls were made of rising layers of sago palm leaves. The floors were packed earth. There were no walls or dividers; it was just one large open space with a long pallet, stretching the length of the building, on which the prisoners slept. Our latrine, at least at the beginning of our stay, was the river. At first the area in which the barracks were located was surrounded by a barbed-wire fence but after about a year that was removed.

Every unit had its own platoon of soldiers whose guard house was always situated in the most strategic location, all the better for keeping an eye on us.

Other buildings in a unit included the commander's house and office, a clinic, mosque, church, and, in units where there were enough Hindus, a temple as well. The only other substantial structure was what we called the "arts building," a sort of community center.

My family home, the house where I grew up, was in fact two homes that my parents had joined with a common steeped roof. Its supports and beams were teak; the floors and walls were stone. In the central part of the house was a long room, stretching the length of the house, which was divided into a front room that functioned as a parlor and a back room where the dining table sat.

Off the central area were five bedrooms. Our kitchen, which also served as a go-down or storage space, was at the side, structurally separate from the rest of the house. Our property measured approximately 2,990 square yards.

For Blora, my hometown, our home was fairly substantial, but then we needed it. My parents had nine children—me, followed by Waluyadi, Koenmaryatoen, Oemi Syafa'atoen, Koesaisah, Koesalah, Soesilo, Soesetyo, and Soesanti—as well as a constant stream of foster children, students, and assorted relatives. At any one time there were up to twenty people living there.

Three of my brothers were also imprisoned. Waluyadi, the second oldest, was working as a translator for the USSR embassy when he was arrested in October 1965. He now lives at the family home but suffers from an acute nervous disorder as a result of the torture he underwent while in detention.

Koesalah, the sixth child, was taken in the same night as I. He had recently graduated from Lumumba University with a degree in Russian language and literature and was home in Jakarta to finish work on his dissertation. He now works as a freelance translator. In addition to being fluent in Russian, he has also mastered English, German, and Dutch, and can read French, Spanish, Javanese, and Old Javanese.

Soesilo, the seventh child, who had obtained a degree in Economics and International Trade from the University of Lomonosov in Russia, had gone to work in West Germany, which is where he was in the early 1970s when Adam Malik, Indonesia's foreign minister, made a visit to the country. He called on all Indonesian scholars, whose skills were needed for national development, to return to their homeland. But as soon as Soesilo got off the plane at Kemayoran Airport in Jakarta he was arrested and thrown into prison. He now supports himself by operating a small *warung* no larger than six by six feet where he sells daily household goods.

Like me, none of my three brothers were ever informed of the reason for their detention nor were they ever put on trial.

Sometimes I feel I was fated for hardship. I can't say that I have ever in my life experienced complete satisfaction. As a boy I had to work to help my parents and then, after my mother died, I had to support my younger siblings. I became a soldier to fight for this country's freedom but since independence I've experienced a good deal more repression than freedom.

It's only through writing that I've ever been able to suppress life's personal disappointments. When I can't write I feel anxious and out of sorts and am easily riled, though I'm usually able to control my emotions.

Of course there are times when my temper flares and I'll stand up to anyone whom I see as not supporting the principles of right and justice. This attitude I owe to my parents, to the political education they gave me as a child, and also to my own effort to create a modern and democratic nation. It's a pity that the country I imagined became, in reality, a primitive and fascistic society ruled by militarism.

Thank God for my wife. In my second marriage I've had a helpmate with whom I've always gotten along. We've always been able to work out our problems in a sensible and peaceful manner. Her strength has supplemented my own. It's possibly my knowledge that she could survive without me that gave me that extra little bit of stamina I needed to survive those years on Buru.

Indeed, knowledge of my family's well-being helped me to maintain my mental balance—that, in addition to my own determination not to break. I had my own ways of resisting the government's heinous use of power and used them every chance I got, especially when meeting with journalists, but even more so when called to meet high-ranking officers or government officials who would always do their best to belittle me.

In 1950 when my father was critically ill, I made a promise to him that after he was gone I would renovate the family home; over the years it had fallen into disrepair. And after he died, I kept my promise, doing up the house in a new, more modern style. But the years passed, I was imprisoned, and wear and tear took its toll. Today my family home, that fragment of my life, is in the same poor condition that it was in before my father died. It's amazing, isn't it, how much energy it takes to keep one's home in good repair and how easily it can be torn down?

1998

ONE LINK IN A CHAIN

There's a Dutch proverb, *"De appel valt nier ver van den boom,"* the English translation of which would be "The apple falls not far from the tree." In Javanese, however, one would say *"Kacang ora ninggalake lanjarane,"* or "A string bean doesn't break free from its vine." What this means is that a child will not differ greatly from his parents. Long before Mendel was born and the secret of chromosomes was discovered, agrarian communities had developed their own genetic theories, ones based on the mystery of blood.

Since ancient times blood has frequently held, for primitive peoples, mystical properties, but ones that could be explained in simple terms—apples or beans, for instance, which were also used to explain generational bonds, that endless chain corresponding with the law of genetics. Of course other more "human" terms are also used, such as "culture," "civilization," and "tradition."

The point of this is that each and every person is a link in the chain connecting one person with the most-recently-born representative of the human species. The connection between these links is entirely biological, unlike other human links, which hold mysteries that can never be fully explained, not through rational thought, feelings, or intellect.

In the biological chain I am the link between my parents and my children. This is one that is irrevocable and cannot be broken, differing, let us say, from a social link, which can be severed by a break in tradition—between myself and my children, for example, because I have not had the opportunity to communicate with them in their adolescent and young-adult years. Thus, while I am a father, because of my current situation, I am prevented from fulfilling that role for my children. Since I can't be with them myself, other people may tell them about me and provide them with stories, interpretations, and assessments. In that way a picture of their father will emerge, however blurred; still more blurred will be the link between them and my parents, the generation above me.

Filling these gaps of information—drawing in the links—is every parent's responsibility. Every bean must know its vine, and every apple must know its branch; that knowledge gives one the ability to evaluate oneself, to determine where one stands in relation to one's parent, and to determine the progression or decline in the genetic line. Is the child wiser or more foolish than the parent?

Toer is the name of my father, founder of the Toer family. It is an odd name—not at all "Javanese"—and in the 1950s, when the name first began to become known nationally through my published works, it stirred numerous questions about its origins, especially among those who knew that its bearer was ethnic Javanese. But in the 1920s and 1930s it was a familiar name in the social and political life of the small town of Blora.

In a conversation with a Polish painter in the city of Canton in 1956 I learned that in Polish the word "toer" means "cow." In German, the word, when pronounced the same way, means either "crazy" or "gateway." In Javanese it means something else altogether. But whatever the meaning in whatever language, I will be proud to carry the name until my dying day, for it is not just the name of a particular family's founder; it is the name of a founder of tradition. That name appeared for the first time in 1923, a year of escalation for Indonesia's nationalist movement. Only one year before, the land of my birth had found its own official, political name: Indonesia.

It was at this time that a certain young man, twenty-six years of age, a graduate of the Kweekschool in Yogyakarta and a teacher at Hollandsch Inlandsche School (HIS), the Dutch medium primary school in Rembang, declared his intention to leave the colonial civil service and to practice "noncooperation," the nationalists' term for the tactic of not cooperating with the Dutch colonial authorities, either directly or through their administrative arms.

The young man, a farm boy with an athletic build, had been raised to despise feudalism. This fiery nationalist who could play simple tunes on the violin but loved Javanese culture was my father. Born in 1897, he was the son of a man who earned his living by working first at the mosque in Ploso Klanten and later at the mosque in Ngadiluwih near Kediri.

In 1923 the young man married my mother, a graduate of HIS in Rembang who was a former student of his. Born in 1908, she was the daughter of Haji Ibrahim, a prominent religious leader, being the adviser in religious matters to the regent of Rembang. Her name was Saidah, and at the time of her marriage, she was fifteen years of age.

Though the couple shared a similar religious background, their marriage was one of dissimilarities. My father's hardened body matched his opinions and attitudes, but the trait I myself came to most respect in him was his patience in coming to a decision and his ability to live with the consequences. He was a liberal thinker who gave short shrift to religious duties. He was a man who detested feudalism yet held Javanese culture in high esteem and never raised his voice against Javanese feudal culture. His knowledge of Javanese literature was extensive. He was an activist, a writer, and a composer. He translated the text for "Indonesia Raya," the national anthem, into Dutch and is credited with writing the lyrics for "Petruk, Gareng en Semar," a once-popular song. Even today I find the range and breadth of my father's interests and talents to be impressive.

My mother, who was from one of the "better" families of Rembang, grew up in a religious environment. Her family lived in a former East Indies Army building located on the southwestern corner of the city square. (There, when I was a child, I often discovered little treasures: kohl and shards of porcelain with Arabic letters that my grandfather had brought back with him from his trips to Arabia.) On the left front side of the building was a prayer house, even though the city's Grand Mosque was located directly across the square. Her home was an imposing edifice and with its stone walls, one acre of grounds, and a six foot high wall that completely surrounded the property; it's not entirely surprising that her family was considered well off.

My mother was given a Western-style education, and her parents even hired private tutors to come to the house. She knew little about Javanese culture and was unable to read Javanese script. Not brought up for manual labor, she was raised like a feudal princess and was never allowed to sweep the floors or cook. She was a fragile child and her father purchased a cow after her birth, to provide her with milk for the nourishment she needed. Even so, she remained slight and thin as an adult.

In 1923 my parents moved from Rembang to Blora where my father immediately set out to reorganize the local branch of Budi Utomo, the Java-based nationalist organization. When the branch opened a primary school he took on the position of director.

That same year, in Yogyakarta, an attempt was made on the Dutch governor general's life. The grenades that had been thrown at him failed to explode, but did set off an expulsion of political dissidents to Digul Prison in West New Guinea. Life in Java took on a new edge with the growing nationalist movement.

In the spirit of these times, my father hoped to "revolutionize" Budi Utomo and turn the Institute into a nationalist school, but he failed to convince the mother organization to agree with his goal. As a result he could only nod his head in acquiescence when yet another member left to join a more radical organization.

I am not sure how the rift between my father and his administrative superiors at Budi Utomo's headquarters occurred, but because of the static condition of the organization's local branch in Blora, the Budi Utomo Institute where my father worked became a near autonomous educational institution.

I was born on February 6, 1925, and my father, a Javanese who had a near-mystical feeling about words, named me Pramoedya. Reflecting the revolutionary spirit of the time, the name was constructed from the phrase "*Yang Pertama di Medan*" or "First on the Battlefield."

As a child I absorbed the influence of many older relatives—aunts, uncles, and grandparents—all of whom were representatives of their own particular background and social group in that period of time. I didn't know my paternal grandfather, but I do remember my father's mother, a large woman with an unshapely set of teeth. With her rounded features she looked typically Javanese. Although she lived with us for some time, she left no lasting impression on my life.

My maternal grandfather, whom I mentioned already, I knew somewhat better. He was a tall lean man with a straight nose and sallow complexion, probably because of some Arab or Indian blood. As an older man he contracted an illness that left him both deaf and paralyzed. I don't know how old he was when he died, but he had made the pilgrimage to Mecca three times. I'm not sure what my grandfather contracted, but my mother told me that her father raised leeches in jars and would sometimes use the leeches to suck blood from certain parts of his body.

As was the custom at the time, my mother's father, Haji Ibrahim, went through several "trial marriages" before he finally married a woman who was his social equal. Wives from the trial marriages were summarily divorced and sent away; their children remained behind. One of the wives he sent away was my grandmother, my mother's mother. I don't know my maternal grandmother's own name but she was a petite woman who appeared to be at least partially Chinese with her small nose, rather narrow eyes, and slightly yellow complexion. She had been a "village flower" when my grandfather met her. Like my paternal grandmother, she had no formal education. Nonetheless, she was a person of extraordinary energy and occupies a very important place in my life. She was lighthearted but also patient, optimistic, and industrious—the eternal worker. When, after bearing a child for my grandfather, she was "discharged" from further duty at her husband's palace, she immediately embarked on a life of labor, selling used goods for a living, piling her odd collection of items in the large basket that she carried on her back. She never asked my parents for help. For that matter, I don't think she ever had a conversation with my father, her son-in-law. The only thing I ever heard her say to him was *Ndoro*, the very polite Javanese term of address. When she came to the house, it was her grandchildren she sought first, ready with a handful of treats from the market.

Her second marriage was to a feckless man who seemed to have no skills at all. He once tried to earn a living as a traveling soup vendor. Another time he tried his hand at selling chicken satay. Yet another time he tried to eke a living from a rice field that had been given in usufruct to the village officials. The only thing he appeared to be good at was *not* turning a profit. Their home on the northern outskirts of Blora was little more than a hut whose walls were plastered with cow dung.

My grandmother had no other children except my mother. And even though whenever she spoke of my father's mother and my mother's step-mother, her former husband's official wife, she referred to them as "Ndoro"—"sir" or "madam"—she was the woman I loved most in the world apart from my mother.

Even when her husband died she would not live with us. Only one time, when she was sick with a stomach ailment and her grandchildren forced her, did she consent to spend a few days with us. Then, after returning to her own home, she died on the road outside of her house. She had not wanted to cause us any trouble.

In 1926, the Indonesian Communist Party (which had changed its name in 1923 from the East Indies Communist Party, thereby becoming the first organization in the East Indies to use the word "Indonesia" in its name) staged a rebellion against the colonial authorities. The rebellion was an utter failure but sparked the mass arrest by Dutch authorities of revolutionaries, regardless of their political stripe or religious beliefs. Numerous other nationalists were placed under surveillance, including my father, who was unable to go anywhere without being followed.

In Bandung, in 1927, leaders of Indonesische Studieclub, the

Indonesian Study Club, one of whom was the country's future president, Soekarno, changed the name of the organization to Partai Nasionalis Indonesia (PNI), the Indonesian Nationalist Party. Very soon thereafter, my father registered as a member and was chosen to head the Party's local branch.

People have told me—and I don't mean my aunts or uncles—that my father was a powerful speaker, a lion at the rostrum. He canvassed the entire area, speaking to crowds not only because of the spirit of independence at the time, but also to live up to the spirit of Soekarno's doctrine about mass action: A leader must talk not only *to* and *before* his people, but *to* and *against* those who did not agree with him, even other leaders when necessary.

At his workplace my father found his position increasingly untenable. He was a nationalist and a revolutionary yet he was having to work in a conservative, "nonrevolutionary" institution. It was like trying to paddle two boats at one time. Finally, in or around 1930, he resolved to cast off one of his boats and put all his energies into charting the course of the other, more revolutionary ship. Setting out to revolutionize the Budi Utomo Institute, he dropped the government-established school curriculum and replaced it with one that had a nationalistic orientation, one that he himself developed. No longer were history lessons straight out of *The History of the Netherlands* or *The History of the Netherlands East Indies*. Now they focused on the history of the people of Indonesia. He had his brother, my uncle Imam Barsah, paint life-size portraits of historical figures whom he considered to be heroes in the struggle against the Dutch. He also wrote songs about these people and taught them to his students.

Among the school's authorities, my father's attempts to excite revolutionary fervor proved to be as effective as trying to make a wet thread stand upright.

At the national level, repression by the colonial authorities was bringing the early "leftist phase" of the nationalist period to an end, and even the religious-based nationalist groups, whose politics could hardly be described as leftist, were now seeing their authority emasculated by the colonial rulers.

The only bastions left for leftist nationalists were their educational institutions, which the government set out to destroy as well. Using a bludgeon known as the Unlicensed Schools Ordinance, all private schools that were not using a government-established curriculum, even ones that received no subsidy from the government such as my father's, were to be closed.

Government officials confiscated from the institute the lesson books my father had compiled and had printed in Semarang. They also cut the electrical power to the building, leaving the school without essential lighting for the Eradication of Illiteracy Program and the Teachers Education Program that were conducted at night. The situation destroyed the working relationships my father had established between the institute, local shops, and savings banks, forcing him to provide a personal guarantee against debts. To make matters worse, the country's self-sufficiency movement, which had been modeled on the *swadeshi* movement in India and, at least for a time, had helped to stimulate local textile and handicraft production, also came to a halt. Large suppliers of imported items were able to undercut local producers' prices. Consequently, my parents, prominent supporters of this movement in Blora, found themselves faced with the prospect of gloomier, more difficult times.

In a traditional Javanese family, the husband stands stage-front, in good times and in bad, in fortune and during failure. The wife who remains in the wings may witness but not join in her husband's performance. Her duty is to bear his children and all the other burdens that raising a family entails. It is, as the feudal Javanese saying goes, "*Suarga nunut, neraka katut,*" meaning that a wife has no choice but to follow her husband's fortunes: In good times she may go with him to heaven, but in bad times she must follow him to hell.

But my mother, an obedient Javanese wife, was not alone in having to bear the consequences of my father's dwindling fortunes: Following my arrival, she gave birth to a child practically every two years. The household expanded further with the addition of several of my father's siblings and a number of nephews and nieces as well. Then, too, there were always in the house a few foster children whose parents had turned them over to my parents to educate and feed either because they themselves were incapable of doing so or the children were unmanageable and out of their control. At one point my mother was responsible for providing food for nineteen mouths—and this doesn't include the assistance she provided to the numerous in-laws who had fallen on hard times. This feudal princess, who had never been trained to work, who enjoyed reading and writing, and who had once dreamed of continuing her education at the Van Deventer School for young women in Semarang, was now responsible for running a huge household.

With all those obligations, from nurturing the children under her care to tending the garden and hoeing the fields, she still managed to find time to devote to the nationalist women's movement, to read the newspapers and books, and to perform her religious prayers. My mother had a gift of foresight and any extra money she came by was used to purchase porcelain ware, eventually enough to fill a large cupboard buffet. She rented out the dishes to people holding parties. She bought pressure lanterns for the same purpose and took in sewing as well. She never stopped working, oblivious, it seems, to her own physical limitations.

A literary critic once chastised me for paying too little attention to my mother in my semiautobiographical works. The fact is I didn't focus enough on either of my parents. That would have required a greater degree of objectivity than I possessed. I say here, however, that in my early years my parents played an especially influential role and their attitudes, manners, thoughts, and ideals became a part of me.

Though, even as a boy, I knew from my parents' disparate attitudes that they must have been in perpetual conflict, I never saw them fight, either physically or verbally. Three years after my father died I came across a notebook that my parents kept jointly. In one section my mother accuses my father of ignoring his family. My father's reply to her criticism was a poem, written in Roman script but with Javanese words and meter, wherein he related that he had done as much as a man could possibly do but that the result of his efforts was outside of his power to determine.

•

The Unlicensed Schools Ordinance, which resulted in the closing of the Budi Utomo Institute, presented a serious challenge for my father. The school's closing left his teachers hungry and uncertain of their future. Various members of the Volksraad, the People's Council, the nationalists especially, strongly protested the ordinance, and eventually Governor General de Jonge retreated somewhat and softened the decree's harsh terms. Private schools were allowed to reopen but could be staffed only by certified teachers with diplomas. But the nationalist schools, the seedbed for the independence movement, were not places where upper-class teachers wanted to work. Teachers at the nationalist schools saw themselves as freedom fighters: teaching was not just a job, it was a cause; not an assured source of income but a voluntary offering.

Further protests caused General de Jonge to relax his stance one more: Under the amended ordinance, noncertified teachers were allowed to teach but were obliged to pay taxes. Yet another wave of protest ensued. How could private-school teachers who were earning, on average, no more than ten rupiah a month possibly pay taxes? Being teachers they had to dress appropriately. They also had to buy more toiletry items, let's say, than a railway coolie who paid no taxes yet was earning more than a private-school teacher. De Jonge gave in a final time and revoked the ordinance.

My father reopened his school as an independent institution, not as a hero but as a common teacher. When he left the house for school each morning he was dressed in a homemade head cloth, a white long-sleeved shirt with a narrow collar, and batik sarong. His feet were bare. Using his left hand to lift the bottom edge of his batik cloth, he kept his right hand free at his side. He carried himself with noble bearing, his body erect, his eyes not looking right or left but focused straight ahead.

The tone of my father's voice, the brilliance of his eyes, and the surety of his movements all signaled authority, but such traits as these could not affect the power of the East Indies authorities. When the school reopened, the number of students dropped by two-thirds, and most of the students who did return were ones who either couldn't pay, who refused to pay, or who paid reduced fees. Admittedly, however, some were upper-class children, even though the government had done its best to spread the word that graduates of unlicensed schools would not find employment in the government civil service.

Corn replaced rice as the family's staple food, but neither my mother nor my father were willing to accede to pressure. My father remained true to the oath that he and other nationalist colleagues had made several months earlier when they, with the Red-and-White in their right hands, pledged their loyalty to the nationalist flag.

No, my father would not give up. He went to school every day to teach his seventh-grade students though many benches in the other classes were empty, like so many holes in an old man's dentures.

The decline in my family's fortunes was reflected in the decreased level of activity at and the circulation of materials through our home. Our house had once been the production center for all sorts of forms, leaflets, and teaching materials. We had at first used an old-fashioned manual press, but, because printing in this manner was too slow, we acquired a newer, more modern press and a stencil machine. The two machines ran constantly, all evening long. Large crates full of paper were also there along with seven standard typewriters—secondhand perhaps, but still in good condition. A European woman taught people how to use the printing machines and my father hired a professional typist from Semarang to teach people how to type.

Inside the house were rows of small desks and chairs for the kindergarten. In one storeroom we had a full *gamelan* orchestra that we lent out for events whenever it was needed, free of charge. Outside, in the front grounds, were stacks of metal, raw material for the smithing and woodworking trade school that was being planned. In another storeroom were piles of hoes, possibly there in preparation for the opening of an agricultural trade school. My family had all these things but we didn't own a gramophone, a common household item in the "better" homes of Blora. My frequent complaints to my mother about this fell on deaf ears.

My father paid for or subsidized all of the activities at home. Thus, when his fortunes took a turn for the worse, the equipment in our house began to disappear. First it was the printing machines, then the typewriters until not a one was left. The only evidence that we once had a printing shop in our house was two rollers that were now of no use at all. The crates for paper stood empty. The grounds weren't cluttered with students' bicycles and the small desks and chairs for the kindergarten gradually fell into disrepair. Household items vanished. Even the pile of hoes began to disappear. Whenever a farmer came to the house my mother always gave him one to take away.

Governor General de Jonge issued his Vergader Verbond, a decree that forbade public gatherings. The East Indies was being turned into one giant prison. Even so, the independence movement would not die; it went underground instead. People took to holding parties or celebrations as a ruse to meet and discuss pressing issues. People gathered to dredge the river together or to go fishing as a way to meet and talk.

With all the diminished activity, our house was quiet and still, and the only time my father seemed to be at home was in the morning, before leaving for school, and at noontime, when he returned home for lunch. He spent all his free time at friends' homes, gambling I was quite sure. What this had to do with Governor General de Jonge's decree I couldn't ascertain, but it did make me dislike him.

To cap the family's financial worries, a friend of my father's ran off leaving my father, who had acted as guarantor for a loan to this man, with a large debt to the bank.

My father grew more and more distant from the family. When he was at home all that he would do was sit in his chair, saying nothing as he chain-smoked clove-scented *kretek* cigarettes. If he did speak, it was only to order someone to fetch him an ember from the kitchen because his lighter was out of fuel or its flint was gone. At some point in his silent reverie he would suddenly rise, change his clothes, and disappear. It was a rare occasion when he spent the whole night at home.

•

In 1936 Governor General de Jonge returned to the Netherlands and was replaced by Tjarda van Starkenborgh-Stachouwer. Because the former had effectively pulled out the rug from under the nationalist left, the latter could afford to be more lax but, by this point, the nationalist political parties had been so weakened by fear of imminent dissolution, they were unable to take advantage of the change. As a result, the independence movement entered a period of extreme malaise.

During this middle chapter of Indonesian nationalist history, nationalists began to consolidate what little power remained. Their efforts stimulated a fusion of political parties and nationalist organizations, the Greater Indonesia Party, which was known by its acronym Parindra.

Under Parindra's banner the country's nationalist movement reverted to a form that had been more popular in the first part of the century, becoming a "social" as opposed to "political" movement (though one, admittedly, on a national scale) within which people focused their energies on helping one another, establishing self-help groups and savings-and-loan banks, and collecting funds for various good causes—the construction of a building, the opening of a printing company, and so on. No one seemed to have the courage to open their eyes and stare straight in the face of power that was Dutch colonial rule in Indonesia.

My father, still mourning the dissolution of the nationalist left, was able to muster scant enthusiasm for this turn of events and, for the time being, chose to confine his nationalistic activities to the classroom.

At his school my father refused to use government-authorized textbooks and instead of teaching his students the Dutch songs that were taught in the government-licensed schools, he taught ones that he or other Indonesian song writers had composed. He removed from his classroom walls the poster-board pictures that were sent to schools by the government for the teaching of history and destroyed them. These larger-than-life pictures always showed Europeans in a favorable light and depicted indigenous people as primitive. When the bamboo walls of his school were replaced with teakboard he had maps painted on them showing Java and its administrative regions, Indonesia, and all the continents. He refused to allow the school to celebrate Dutch royal holidays and would not permit the Dutch Tricolor to be flown.

It was for the above reasons, perhaps, that more problems for my father followed: One night something extraordinary happened—my father didn't leave the house. He sat in his chair, positioned at a safe distance from the constantly sputtering pressure lantern, as if waiting for something to happen. And then three visitors appeared, members of Budi Utomo's board of directors, who soon had my father engaged in a spirited and laughter-filled conversation. After a time, however, the tone of their conversation suddenly turned serious when one of the visitors announced, "We're here, *Meneer* Toer, to talk about the school."

My father responded in Javanese: "After all these years, with no one around to help me with the school and its problems, out of the blue you suddenly take the time to come here. What is going on?" As the seriousness of the conversation increased, less Javanese was used, being replaced by Dutch and Indonesian. One of the men explained that a commission had been set up to handle the management of the Budi Utomo Institute and also that "we have received a number of complaints from your teachers suggesting that you pay insufficient attention to their needs and that you're using the students' school fees for gambling purposes."

There was a long pause before my father answered: "Go on, tell me the rest," he then commanded.

"Both the commission and the teachers hope that, in the better interests of the school, you will voluntarily resign from your position."

It appeared that Budi Utomo wanted to oblige the colonial government by returning my father's school to its former status and using the government-approved curriculum that had been in use prior to the school's politicization. One of the board members intimated that if this were done the government might then be willing to provide the school with a subsidy.

"Upon whose authority was this commission formed?" my father asked his guests. He spoke forcefully, as if at a public forum, then paused, as if waiting for a reply. "And who gave this commission the authority to interfere with the Institute's internal affairs? The assistant district officer? Or has Budi Utomo reestablished itself in Blora?" He paused again but still found no reaction. "Who asked me to direct this school? Who signed the agreement with me? Wasn't it you yourselves? Do you remember the organization promising me, without my asking for it, a salary higher than I would have received in government service plus a further increment every two years? Do you know what my monthly salary is now? Never since I have been the director of this school has the organization kept its promise to me. You can check the books of the school's treasurer yourself. As an organization Budi Utomo doesn't exist here, so where is the money for the school coming from? Not a single cent has been lost to the gambling table.

"If you will look at my contract you'll see that the salary I should have received for the past ten years surpasses the monetary value of both the school building and its grounds. If I were to take this matter to court you can rest assured that the court would side with me. Even with everything in it there still wouldn't be enough money to pay me off. If I were a greedy man it would be easy for me; I'd have this matter settled in an instant.

"And what are the teachers complaining about? At our weekly meeting on Fridays everyone has a chance to speak his mind. Their accusations are false and those who made them are traitors. They're content to ride on the school's prosperity and fame but unwilling to share in its defeat . . ."

The end result of that conversation was that the following day a number of teachers did not show up for work. Because there were only four teachers remaining, my father was forced to close the school while waiting for the arrival of new teachers. But even when they were found, the quality of education that the school offered could not compete with that of the government-run Hollandsche Inlandsche School. The situation was such that my father could not hoist himself from the well of his depression and disappointment.

•

During this chapter of the nationalist movement, my mother also curtailed her outside activities. With her health suffering, she began to spend more time reading and tending to her children's needs. She rarely sat down at the sewing machine, and the Singer, her pride and joy, waited for her silently.

Around this time my father's sister, her husband, who had been living underground since the Communist uprising in 1926, and their children came to my parents' to live. Physically weakened by chronic tuberculosis, the man was unable to work and the doctor predicted that he would die within a year. The number of mouths my mother had to feed continued to grow.

All of the difficulties that our household encountered caused me gradually to move, step by step, closer to my mother and farther away from my father, whose only interest in family life seemed to be occasional garden work.

The year 1937 brought with it tension and heightened security. Princess Juliana of the Netherlands was to marry Prince Bernhard, a paint salesman from Switzerland and descendant of the German royal house. The princess was twenty-eight years old; the prince, twenty-six. The Javanese, who have a bent for numerology, predicted that the couple would produce no male heirs, that they would have female children only. Large celebrations in honor of the marriage were planned and my father found himself with another trial to face.

The government declared it mandatory that all schools participate in the grand celebration but my father refused to sing the Dutch anthem, "Wilhelmus," to fly the Tricolor, and to participate in the parade. There ensued a period of nonstop negotiation between my father and the local authorities. My father refused to budge on the issues of the "Wilhelmus" and the Tricolor and, finally, it was the assistant district officer who gave in. The school didn't have to sing the "Wilhelmus" or to fly the Tricolor as long as the students participated in the parade and displayed the symbols of the royal wedding.

Teachers with painting and woodworking skills were mobilized and on the day of the parade, the students of my father's school showed up with a float made up of a massive portrait of the princess and the prince on top of a homemade howitzer cannon whose muzzle was the trunk of a papaya tree, symbolizing a marriage made in the midst of preparations for war.

Our school's contingent was flanked by rows of flag-waving students, but we ourselves had none; our hands were empty. While the other contingents sang their respective school songs, ours didn't sing at all. When our float appeared not a word of praise was heard. Even so, we were awarded third prize.

I was proud of my father. He had won an honorable victory. He was my hero and, at least momentarily, I forgot the poor manner in which he treated his family and especially my mother. He probably wasn't aware of the pride I felt toward him, so occupied was he with his own feelings of disappointment.

Change in the situation at home was brought about by events in Europe. The Germans, after a successful demonstration of their weapons in Spain, where General Franco had snuffed out democratic forces, were busily arming themselves. And Fascism, with Mussolini as its crown prince, now ruled in Italy, Germany, and Spain.

The common people of Blora were awed by German power. They sympathized with things they knew, respected, and loved. The pictures of Nazi and National-Socialist parades that filled the front pages of newspapers were cut out and pasted on the bamboo walls of their homes. The orderly ranks of German soldiers, all sporting high boots and swastikas, were an impressive sight, and their steel helmets as fear-inspiring as anything produced by Dutch factories. People had the names of new weapons to memorize—torpedo, tank, armored vehicle, sea mine, land mine, missile, and other items of war—that had never appeared in any shadow performance they had ever seen. The ocean swallowed ships of all nations, the prey of torpedoes fired from submarines. "What's a blitzkrieg?" people asked. And what is "anschluss"? They ignored the Russian invasion of Finland and forgot about the Netherlands altogether. Germany's neighbors fell beneath the feet of the swastika-bearing soldiers in a matter of a few days. With the fall of Czechoslovakia, Austria, Hungary, and Poland, the meaning of "blitzkrieg" became well known. My father did his best to explain these developments to his seventh-grade students.

France's Maginot Line was hailed in the propaganda-filled press as unassailable, a bastion that the German troops could never breach. But the Germans didn't mount a frontal assault; they went around the line, and France fell. Dutch defenses against the German blitzkrieg lasted for only three days. The water-sodden fort they boasted of was powerless. Belgium fell in a week.

The East Indies authorities arrested Germans and other Europeans who sympathized with the Germans, especially members of the National Socialist Movement. Images of Hitler, Himmler, and Von Ribbentrop appeared in the papers daily. Then Italy attacked Abbysinia and that country fell. In Asia, Japan arose, and the Berlin-Rome-Tokyo Axis was like an eagle's talon with the world in its tight grasp. In the East Indies, Parindra leaders sympathized with the Japanese and the Party's youth members, in imitation of the Japanese, took on the rising sun as one of their symbols. They adopted the Hitlerian salute as their own. People's heads began to turn from the direction of Germany to Japan. The authorities grew more nervous.

Abroad the call went out for everyone, regardless of one's political beliefs or the state that one's country was now in, to join together in an anti-Fascist front. The satanic Berlin-Rome-Tokyo Axis was a threat to all of mankind and must be opposed. Outside of Asia the Communist and liberal-democrat countries agreed. In Asia, the United States began to establish an anti-Fascist front in the Philippines. In Malaya and Burma, the British began to do the same thing, arming *their* "colonial children" with weapons and giving them lessons in modern warfare practices. The French followed suit in Indochina. All in the name of fighting Japan. It was only in the East Indies that the colonial overlords hesitated, unsure as to whether an armed Indonesian populace might not turn its guns on them.

With the establishment of anti-Fascist fronts in other countries, Parindra and its affiliated organizations demanded that the government provide them with arms. A militia was of paramount importance, they argued, but the government ignored them. Parindra then tried another tactic for obtaining arms by requesting that Indonesia be given its own parliament, but this demand was also ignored. The sympathy shown by Parindra's leaders for Germany and Japan heightened the government's suspicions of this organization.

As a tentative step toward the formation of an anti-Fascist front at home, the colonial authorities began sending feelers to the nationalist, leftist, and Communist underground movements but made no promise of supplying weapons. So untrusting were the authorities of their own subjects and so lacking were they in confidence that they preferred to place their hope of survival on the colonial bastions of Indochina, the Philippines, and Singapore.

At around this same time, something remarkable happened: The government asked my father to teach at the government-run Hollandsch Inlandsche School. My father discussed this request with both my mother and his colleagues. For me, ignorant of the meaning of "anti-Fascist front," this was an earthshaking event. My father and his family had always belittled civil servants. They had scorned anyone who served in the Dutch Indies Army and shown disgust toward anyone who joined the colonial police force. Now my father was being asked to become a civil servant! This man, whom I respected and viewed as the epitome of masculinity, a person utterly devoted to the cause of national independence, held in esteem by friends and feared by enemies, whom local government officials avoided like the plague, had now been offered a position as a civil servant in the very same government that he, as a noncooperator, had left sixteen years before.

Because I was so sure that he would refuse the offer, my trust in my father's convictions was sorely shaken when he accepted. This was not the man I was proud of. He was no different, no better than anyone else. My disappointment in him could not be eased and my opinion of him as an unswerving idealist was not to be restored for quite some time, not until after I myself had begun to study the history of the independence movement.

As a teacher at HIS my father's monthly salary was six times larger than the one he received at the Budi Utomo Institute where he continued to teach the upper-level students in the evening. But, due to my ignorance of history, my father was for me my father no longer. I felt unimaginable shame around my friends, neighbors, and anyone else whom I knew or knew me. I hated him. I didn't respect him. If this was his real character, then why hadn't he stopped being noncooperator a long time before? At least then my mother wouldn't have had such a hard life.

My father disgusted me and nothing he could say at the time could make me change my mind. I was only fourteen, a seventh-grader, and struggling with inner turmoil and a sense of enmity that I could not reveal to anyone. I vowed to break free of my father's influence. Starting from that point on, I vowed to become my own person.

The snake that was the Japanese military proved unable to swallow whole the entire Chinese frog and so it turned, winding its way southward. Two British warships, *Repulse* and *Prince of Wales,* were early victims. The Japanese then attacked Pearl Harbor, but this action was answered only a few hours later by a declaration of war by the Allied countries, including the Dutch East Indies.

One by one, the colonial bastions fell to the Japanese. The ABCD Front, made up of the American, British, Chinese, and Dutch forces, was broken. The British immediately withdrew from the alliance. Why not? They had no reason to defend their colonies: Malaya and Singapore had already fallen.

When Singapore fell, everyone knew it was only a matter of time before the East Indies fell, too. The oil-rich areas of Sumatra and Kalimantan were to be the first targets for the Japanese. The naval battle in the Java Sea turned out to be the final show of strength by the East Indies government.

At the beginning of the Occupation, management of the Budi Utomo Institute was taken over by the Japanese military authorities and soon people at the school were studying Japanese. I know little of my father's activities during the Occupation but I do remember that when the Japanese ordered all *keris*, daggers, and other ceremonial swords to be surrendered, my father ordered me to deliver his personal heirloom *keris* to the office of the assistant subdistrict officer. When I arrived there, I saw an entire room filled with *keris*.

"This is from the Toers," I said, handing the man my father's *keris*.

The man wouldn't touch the dagger. He looked at me and mumbled hurriedly, "Take that back to where it came from."

After the death of my mother and my move to Jakarta, almost everything of value in my parents' home was gradually sold: my mother's china collection, the family library, even my father's notes and papers, which were sold as wrapping paper. From an article in a Semarang newspaper I learned that among all of the students studying Japanese in the Residency of Pati, my father had finished number two. He was forty-six years old at the time.

In a letter from my father around that time he mentioned that he did not intend to remarry; his marriage with my mother had been bound by a promise both parties had voluntarily given, that regardless of which partner died first, the surviving party would not marry again without the permission of the deceased party. Such an odd man, my father . . . He would never show disrespect toward anyone nor consciously violate another person's rights. If he had any weakness it was his fondness for gambling, but to others he was generous to a fault, always willing to lend a hand to those in need. He raised, taught, and put through school a large number of other people's children. He once gave a house to a person who was in need of one at no cost. He gave a rice barn to another person, again at no cost. For another person, he put up his own funds for the establishment of a workshop and provided the shop with tools, again with no thought of recompense. He gave numerous people money to start their own businesses. He also educated a large number of potential nationalists. More than anything else, however, the thing that makes me most proud of him was that he was a nationalist who gave his full support to the independence movement.

He died in June 1950, a time of peace, not long after independence and freedom had come to the land of his birth. Never having left Java himself, in life he never was able to fully savor the taste of national independence for which he had so long struggled. I described the last part of his life in my novella *Life Is No All Night Fair*. Once when I was abroad, and paying a visit to a university where Indonesian was taught, a teacher's assistant in the foreign languages department asked me to read into a tape recorder several pages from that book. When reading the section I had been asked to record, I started to cry. That was in 1960, ten years after my father's death.

In another letter he wrote to me, all my attention fell on the words, "You are the first child, the one to carry on our family's strength."

I see above me two links that I do not know. Below me are two more that I do not know or, more accurately, have not yet come to know, though they themselves might know something about me.

Am I a link that ties the links above me with those links below? That I do not know. But can an apple fall far from its tree? Can a bean free itself from its vine? You tell me. I have done all that I can do.

FLOWERS FOR MOTHER

A woman may have many children or she may have few or none at all, but
a child can have only one mother. Even if a child never knows his mother,
this will not alter that undeniable fact—though it does not necessarily
mean that he will ever have the opportunity to come to know the qualities
of the woman who once carried him in her womb. The native people of
Hawaii, I once read, view a mother not as the woman who gives birth to a
child but the one who takes care of the child and raises it. In strictly soci-
ological terms, this view seems to be a valid one, yet it fails to take into
account the biological, psychological, and possibly even mystical links that
exist between a mother and her child.

I also read somewhere that a man can never be sure if his child is in
fact his own offspring. At one time this was something only the woman
could know for sure.

If in former times people saw there to be some kind of mystical bond
between a mother and her child, that view, we must accept, is a product
of the age before logic came to reign. The Indonesian tales of Malim
Kundang and Dampo Awang are legacies of that age. Other ancient tales,
such as the Greek *Oedipus Rex*, the Javanese *Prabu Watu Gunung*, and the

Sundanese *Sangkuriang* also reveal a bond between mother and child that far surpasses customary links.

Over the ages the relationship between mothers and sons and between sons and mothers has produced many tales, each of which represents both a product of and a building block for societal life. In this I am no exception and the link between my mother and myself is far stronger than either that between me and my father or me and my siblings.

When I was growing up, I didn't know my mother's name. It was only when she died and I read the painted wood-post marking her grave that I learned her name was Saidah. Such was the fate of a woman of that time: In marriage a woman lost not just herself, she also lost her name. But each time I think of her, especially when I'm trying to write, my mother is always vaguely present, hovering in my father's shadow. I suspect that the two-faced Oedipus complex, with a son loving his mother and hating his father, might very well be operating in my subconscious. Even if my mother stands in the shadow cast by my father, she represents for me my childhood. This is why I want to write about her. I shall gather flowers for her. And though I might well err in my choice of blooms and show scant flair for flower arrangement, these notes of mine shall be the bouquet I place at her feet.

My mother was a woman of slight physical stature, even by Indonesian standards, though for the generation of males that preceded me, she represented the physical and sexual ideal. She resembled her mother, my grandmother, a woman whose name I never came to know. Both women were physically energetic, always working, rarely taking time to relax, but there were differences between them, too. My grandmother was the hearty type, while my mother was much more frail.

Their facial type was similar, yet there were differences here as well. My grandmother had a clear complexion that was highlighted by a constant smile on her lips and a bright glint in her eyes. My mother, on the other hand, had sad eyes and looked on the world timidly. There was a dark cast to her features and her skin was marred by tiny specks like hard whiteheads that would not burst. Of the two women, my grand-mother looked the younger.

Once, when my mother was telling me about the past, she said, "When I was pregnant with you, I dreamt that an old man came to me and gave me a small knife." The tone of her voice can only be described as that of a Javanese with the misfortune not to possess material wealth and who views dreams as an integral part of life. For this kind of Javanese, dreams are harbingers of the future, omens of a person's unalterable destiny. Typically, a knife symbolizes sharpness, but regardless of what the image meant for my mother, it no doubt influenced her opinion about my future role in life and place in the world.

Her stories stirred in me, this young and impressionable Javanese boy, a sense of uselessness and futility. But given the nature of Javanese thought, with its inability to adopt an objective worldview, I cannot entirely blame my mother for this. She represented her generation, one that was only just beginning to discover modern civilization and thought. Her worldview, the Javanese worldview, was one shaped by poverty, thereby making it difficult to promote the adoption of one of greater objectivity, especially in regards to material wealth.

So it was that in my childhood, superstition occupied an important and determinant role. Superstition determined one's attitude toward life. And though a person's mind might be razor-sharp, superstition will control him as long as he lacks the ability or willingness to adopt an objective approach toward the material world.

I don't blame my mother for trusting the words of an old woman—a trader in woven sarongs who, as an added service of her trade, read palms as well—when she took my hand, peered at my palm, and predicted, "You are a flower, my boy, a strange bloom that will be loved by half of the people and despised by the other." In my mother's world and frame of mind, this prediction would also have been a marker for the course of her son's future.

On another occasion, during a visit with an elderly acquaintance, my mother's friend asked to see the sole of one of my feet. Because this man had no reputation as a *dukun* or fortune teller, his request was quite surprising. Nonetheless, I showed him my sole, which he studied carefully. "My, my, what a sole we have here," he then pronounced. "It's clear that you're never going to be a man of high rank!"

I don't know if my mother was upset by the man's prediction, but because of my way of thinking at the time, I had already accepted as fact that I would never attain a high government position. That didn't bother me. Mother herself had said that she didn't want any of her children becoming civil servants or government workers. As the wife of a fervent nationalist she rejected anything "colonial."

Once, when I was in sixth grade, we were harvesting corn in a field across the Lusi River. During a break, when I and the other kids gathered around her, my mother asked me what I wanted to be when I grew up.

"A farmer," I told her straightaway.

"You're not made out to be a farmer," she immediately replied. "You're too lazy for that. You're a person who's meant to be free, an 'all around' person," she added in English before explaining to me the meaning of that foreign phrase.

My mother liked to read and could understand Javanese in Roman script, as well as Malay and Dutch. She kept up with the Surabaya and Semarang daily papers and all the books and magazines that we received. (My father, as the principal of a school, was given numerous publications free of charge.) At night, when encircled by her children, or sometimes when lying down and nursing the youngest child, she'd weave for us stories based on the materials she had read. She was a brilliant storyteller, able to entwine us in her spell. Over a series of nights she might relate the story of *Angling Darmo* and her favorite hero, Amir Hamzah. Or one of the many stories published by Balai Pustaka. Or a Western story or fairy tale.

From when I was in the fifth grade, she began to tell me stories about contemporary nationalist figures, for example, the life stories of progressive women she admired such as S. K. Trimurti and Rasuna Said. She spoke spiritedly of Gandhi and the Indian nationalist movement and was forever throwing into her stories excerpts from Svin Hedin, Marco Polo, and Pinkerton mysteries. Though my father included among his prized possessions copies of the Javanese classics, *Pustaka Raja Jarwa* and *Pustaka Raja Purwa*, she never drew stories from them to tell to us.

Her stories, with their beautiful fantasies, stimulated the imagination and nurtured in our young souls the dream of building a better, more perfect world.

In the middle of a story my mother might interrupt her tale with a song. Though she liked to sing, her repertoire was limited. Most of the songs she knew were Malay, not Javanese. One of her favorites was "Sang Bangau." She also sang Dutch songs she had learned in school, but preferred to sing nationalist tunes or melodies my father had written.

For reasons unknown to us she revealed little about her own childhood, almost never going into detail when speaking of her father, mother, and stepmother. It seemed as if there were a steel door separating her from them. Though her family was one of obvious comfortable standing she never talked about material wealth. She told us about people she knew who had gone to school in Europe and one time, as if adding a postscript to her story about Indonesian students in Europe, she said to me with a tone of decisiveness in her voice, "One day you must study in Europe, too, until you obtain a doctoral degree."

There lived in our town a well-off man whose name I no longer remember, but I accompanied my mother to his house several times and twice went on my own to take him food that my mother had prepared. The most memorable thing about the man was the German shepherd he owned. Gangs of us kids would gather outside his gate just to stare at what was absolutely the largest dog we had ever seen in our lives. But the other memory I have of him is the misfortune that struck his family: Shortly after his son had graduated from Technical High School in Bandung, the boy was waiting at the train station in Bandung when he was struck by a locomotive and killed. When my mother returned home after calling on the grieving parents, she remarked, "Even a boy that smart can have an accident if his mind isn't on what he's doing." Those words have always stayed clearly with me.

My mother spoke of the doctors, lawyers, and engineers who were active in the national movement but, for some reason, never talked about activists among graduates of the humanities. Was she trying to say something to me? It was years later when I found myself with my own fast-growing children that I understood why my mother felt it so necessary to tell me those stories—not just to demonstrate the pride a parent might feel when having a child whose name history will record, but to indicate a road to that end.

Perhaps it was because my mother had been raised *not* to work that in her married life she underwent a spiritual revolution, which ended with her placing great honor on work. My mother did anything and everything: She cooked, baked, wove cloth, and made batik; she manufactured sweet soy sauce and coconut oil; she tilled and hoed the garden and developed skills in dressmaking and tailoring—all this in addition to raising her own children and a large number of foster children as well, with no thought of recompense. She was active in the women's movement; she read books, newspapers, and magazines; took care of the house, and raised chickens, goats, pigeons, geese, and ducks. It was only when her stepmother came to Blora to visit that she consciously refrained from manual labor.

Amid all her activities, and whenever finances permitted, Mother was always ready to take us children for an outing, either for a jaunt outside of town or a trip to the city—Rembang, Kunduran, or Semarang—where she introduced us to urban life.

On one of our trips to Semarang she took us to the city's main emporium, a Japanese-owned department store by the name of Saerah, where she purchased a large number of Japanese-made household items. After that she led her gaggle of kids to the children's department where she told us, "Choose something for yourself."

What a lovely time that was for us; even at my present age, I still remember the feeling. The foster children had come along and she told them to choose something, too, just as if they were her own children. Our first choice naturally fell on toys that we had never seen in our hometown, as well as clothes, sandals, and Japanese-made bamboo fountain pens with glass nibs. When leaving the store that day, we had to rent two horse carts just to carry us and our purchases to the guest house where we were staying.

Whenever there was a night fair in town, the entire household went out to watch, except for Father who almost never went along. Mother even brought the servants along. At the fair she would treat us to a meal in a restaurant. This, too, was wonderful. But most days, normal days that is, my mother spent working herself to the bone. I recall overhearing a neighbor once say in surprise, "Can you believe it—a woman from a wealthy family and the wife of a wealthy man, working like a farm wife?"

If my mother heard such comments she certainly didn't listen to them. In fact, she put my brother Prawito and I in charge of raising goats and she herself took me to the animal market to choose a whip, one that "felt good in my hand," and a small sickle for gathering fodder. Thereafter, with sickle in hand, I'd go off looking for *petai cina* leaves, which the goats liked to eat but which were not readily available near the house. The older I got, the more embarrassed I became when meeting my friends on the road, especially those who studied at the government school. When I told Mother of my embarrassment, she smiled sympathetically, took hold of my arm, and pulled me down beside her on the long wooden bench where she was seated. "But what are you ashamed of?" she asked. "Didn't you once say that you wanted to be a farmer? You're not going to be a man of rank or a civil servant. You're going to be a free man, self-employed. Isn't that right? Any job that causes no injury to others is honorable work. You're a brave boy. I'm sure your friends have neither your strength nor the fortitude it takes to raise and feed goats. Just ask them. They'd probably be too embarrassed to do the job. I'm sure you can get over your embarrassment, can't you?"

And so my brother and I continued to raise goats, herding them to the soccer field or the graveyard in search of food. There we would play games with farm kids, children who would never have the opportunity to go to school or to study Dutch, or I would relate to them stories that I heard from my mother or in school or that I had read in books.

My mother's words of advice remained constantly within me—perhaps because she spoke them so softly and with such surety, or possibly because she herself served as their model.

As I once wrote in *Stories from Blora*, my mother was a soft and gentle person, but she was also very strict, and of all her children I believe that I was the one she pinched and spanked most often, so much so that I decided once to run away. Nothing came of that decision, however, as I didn't have the courage to leave.

One day a young beggar appeared at the house, a thin boy about my age with scabious legs. Mother led him to the kitchen and told him to eat his fill. When he had finished eating, she called him to her, and though she had children of her own and numerous foster children as well, invited him to live with us: "You said you don't have any parents and that you've never gone to school. If you wish, you may stay here and study and work with my children. Would you like that?"

The boy nodded his head in assent. Mother ordered me to give him some clothes. For the next three days the boy lived with us, ate in the kitchen with us, and worked with us in the field behind the house. The following day he disappeared never to return again.

"Look at that boy," my mother said of him. "He can spark people's sympathy, but is afraid of work. I just pray his future won't turn out to be as bad as that of other people like him."

Every year at Lebaran Mother could be found making loads of holiday cakes and other sweets. All the children clung to her side hoping to grab the discards, the ones that had broken or got burned. She also sewed, making formal *kebaya* blouses for customers. For one made of fine cloth she would receive twenty cents. She made all the children's clothes, too, and it was she who first taught me how to cut and sew. She also taught me to knit so that I could make my own woolen vests. After that I was able to make my own clothes. Not that I liked to. "They look so homemade," I told her.

"But you made them with your own hand," she said in avid praise. "It's not just anyone who could do that."

Her words made me proud and kept me from being disturbed by my friends' snide comments. I stuck out my chest when I told them that I had made my clothes myself. My mother was right, and their sarcasm changed to admiration.

Mother kept two she-goats that she milked. One night, when one of the goats began to bleat in pain—it had probably eaten too many *kara* leaves—Mother lit a lantern and went out to its pen. Some of the foster kids followed. Seeing the state the goat was in, she ordered the kids to fetch some coconut juice and the sheath of a papaya leaf. She poured the coconut juice into the animal's mouth and inserted the sheath in the animal's anus as an ad-hoc pipe for the release of gas. Her measures failed to save the goat and in the morning it was dead. It wasn't the failure of my mother's exercise that stuck in my memory; it was her quickness of mind in dealing with the situation.

My father had a great deal of initiative and was forever coming up with new projects and schemes but in terms of stick-to-it-ness, my mother was the family's role model. My father once purchased a grove of coconut trees but when he wearied of looking after the grove, it was mother who took over the job. The same thing happened with a couple of fields my father had purchased from farmers who had received government land grants. And with the rice barn he had built as well. Who was it that did the chores and maintained the building? Mother and us kids.

Yes, indeed, in terms of diligence there was a world of difference between my mother and father, at least at home. My father's diligence was evident at school. There he exercised iron discipline.

Despite my father's role as an educator, neither he nor my mother ever demanded that their children get high marks in class. When I failed to advance in class, I prepared myself for a tongue-lashing, which I thought would be unavoidable, but neither of them said a thing.

Though Mother never volunteered to tutor us, she was always ready to help if we asked her to. She never inquired, "How are you doing in school?" though she did demand that we study. On that point there was no bargaining. But as to whether we were smart or not, or whether we succeeded or not, she didn't put pressure on us at all. That said, I still suspect that of all my parents' children I was the greatest disappointment to them. I remember Mother once saying to me, "Your father has educated so many children, many of whom have gone on to become successful adults. What would people think if his own children weren't able to keep up? I can imagine how they would laugh . . ." The implication of her words was readily apparent to me.

I entered the Budi Utomo Institute's primary school in 1929 at the age of four. I was enrolled early in order to get me out of the hair of the people at home, or at least that's what I was told. At school we had to learn Dutch, a foreign language for me, one that we did not use at home. The same was true for my classmates but at the end of the year, when grades were announced, I was the only pupil not to receive a passing grade. As a result, it took me two years to finish the first grade. The same thing happened in grade two, and then in grade three as well, meaning that after six years in school I was only in the fourth grade.

I don't know what my parents had to say to each other about my lagging learning skills but after only a few days in the fourth grade, my father suddenly forbade me to go to school. Thereafter I stayed home and helped Mother with her work. I was content to spend the mornings washing the floors, splitting kindling, and pounding corn for cooking. It didn't bother me not having to go to school; I was indifferent to my parents' concern and didn't realize until much later how worried about my future they actually were.

The family's fortunes during this period of time were in a precarious state. The stacks of rice sheaves that after harvest had once filled the grounds, the rice barn, and even the guest room were gone. Piles of squash, harvested in the dry season before the wet monsoon, were not evident. Worse for me was that my father, who used to spend most of his evenings outside the home, was now there every day, at five o'clock, to educate me. What torture this was for me. He had me sit on the chair in front of him as he gave me lessons in arithmetic, Javanese, Dutch, geography, grammar, and other subjects, almost all of which seemed to end in tears. Not that my father ever struck me; he never raised his hand to me but his sharp voice, somber demeanor, and flashing eyes were far more frightening for me than the ogres I witnessed in shadow plays.

To these lessons my father later added instruction in Arabic language and script and, on Saturday evenings, Javanese dance as well. For the latter he hired a special teacher, but he later dropped these two lessons. Mother never asked me directly how I felt about receiving instruction from my father. Whenever I left my seat in front of Father with tears streaming from my eyes to go to the bathroom to wash my face or to the kitchen to look for something to eat, she bowed her head and would not raise her eyes to look at me. I knew that she preferred not to know what I was going through. As hellish as these lessons were, it was only when I was studying with my father that I could truly focus my thoughts. I was never able to do that in the classroom. Five minutes into a lesson at school and my thoughts would have already wandered to a realm of fantasy that was far more exciting and beautiful than real life. I was a dreamer, a trait that has lasted until the present.

On occasion, after my lessons with father had begun and he could see that I was going to cry, he'd rise from his chair and tell me softly, "That's enough for now. Go take a bath and put on your good clothes." These words always meant that he was going to take me for a stroll. We'd walk to beyond the city limits or loll in the town square, watching passersby as the sun silently slipped behind the mosque's dome and minaret. He used these times to relate tales of heroism and parables from the Javanese and stories from the shadow theater. In those times all friction between us disappeared, and he was no longer the scariest person in the world for me.

The end of my direct education from my father took place one dark night. Just the two of us were sitting on the long wooden bench in front of the house. Father spoke to me in a slow and sonorous voice: "Everything is a struggle. Whether you're watching a shadow play, or listening to a story, or reading that same story yourself, it's all about struggle. . . . Never be averse to joining the struggle. Don't think about shortcomings or mistakes.

In a struggle the victor is always the one who is right." (But he never explained why the Dutch were always victorious in their battles against us.)

After that evening he never called me for lessons again. Almost a year had passed since his lessons with me had begun, and now the hours of torture were over.

In the new school year, I returned to school as a fourth-grade student. Dutch was still difficult for me. I couldn't seem to remember the gender of words, so that I was forever making mistakes. When my father was reading or teaching Dutch, he almost never had to make use of the large dictionary resting on the table. Why then was I so stupid? And in mathematics, which I hated so much, I could never seem to keep up with the other students; yet my father was such a whiz that he could, off the top of his head, add, multiply, and subtract tables of up to six or seven digits. My father was the brains of our small town. Why was his son such an idiot?

I wanted to change, but there didn't seem to be anything that I could do to help. But that same year my parents held a circumcision ceremony for me, my brothers, my foster brothers, and a number of friends and after that, for no explicable reason, I found it much easier to study and was never held back in class again.

One afternoon, when I was in sixth grade and returning home from school, my father overtook me on the road. He turned to me as he passed and said in Dutch, "Study your Dutch lessons well. Master that language and the world will be yours. That is the key. With that language you can find all the knowledge there is to find."

Unfortunately, I paid too little attention to his advice. It was not until later that I discovered it was true. Dutch, the language that had always been such an unwieldy instrument for me, eventually became my true helper, leading me to far-distant worlds I had once thought unreachable. I might never forget the misery I felt when studying that language in primary school, but now I give thanks to the fair-skinned Dutch, whose language became for me an irreplaceable tool for my advancement in life.

Another memorable quip from my father, this one told to me about six months later, was, "I'll respect you more for the one cent you earn honestly, from your own sweat, than for any grade of '7' your teachers might give you." The thing was, as my father knew quite well, I never got any "sevens" on my report card. But unlike his advice about studying Dutch, this particular kernel of wisdom fell on rich and fertile soil, and I began to work hard, as did my siblings.

My parents never gave us an allowance; at most, around Lebaran, we'd be given five or ten cents. We weren't like other kids who were used to receiving treats. "The best food, the cleanest food, and the most honorable food is the food you eat at home," my mother always told us. "If you're given treats all the time, you'll end up not respecting either your home or family."

One way we had of earning spending money was picking the canaga flowers that grew near our well and selling them at the market. We also sold leeks and celery that we grew in earthen pots. Mother helped us with our venture but never asked about the income we made from it.

Eventually we used our savings as investment capital to buy and sell cigarettes, tobacco, and flavored syrups. But after only three months we had to stop selling cigarettes because our older male relatives kept relieving us of our wares and never paying their debts. Instead, with the money we had collected, we purchased a goat for breeding. Later, when we told our mother that we wanted to raise cattle, too, she took us to the livestock market and chose a choice young calf for us—a large, strong, white-haired, female calf.

We turned the calf over to a farmer to raise, in payment for which he was to receive its milk. We, on the other hand, would receive the calves that it bore. Our eyes remained fixed on that beautiful young calf as the farmer led it away toward his village. That was the last time that we saw the calf. When the harvest failed, the farmer sold what was now our cow and its calf without ever telling us about it.

Because my mother never raised the subject of our lost cow, I was forced to pluck up the courage to talk to her about it myself. To this all she had to say was, "Leave it be. You and the rest can still work. The man was in harder straits than any of you."

With those words we accepted our loss and didn't think about it again.

With the passing of the days we grew accustomed to earning our own money. Around this time my parents were having financial problems and now when there was a night fair my brother and I went, but not to watch. Instead we unrolled our mats outside the gates of the fairgrounds and sold candies and cigarettes. Each night fair made us a little richer. I saved all the money I earned because I had a plan, which even Mother didn't know about.

An uncle of mine who had returned home from New Caledonia brought with him a thick book on electricity. Finding the subject interesting, I went through the book, time and again.

I took my savings and bought several liters of sulfuric acid, copper, and glass bulbs, then proceeded to make a cell battery. When it was finished and the light bulb lit up, I felt that my heart would burst from glee. As our home wasn't wired for electricity, this meant that I was the very first person to introduce electric light to our home. Even though the bulb glowed for only a few seconds, I roared inside; I had done it by myself.

I then set out to learn how to do electrolytic plating, but in no time at all my savings were completely gone, and I had to disband my exercise. By this point Mother knew what I was doing, but I didn't have the nerve to ask her for money. My parents, especially my mother, encouraged self-initiative. Neither of them interfered in my activities and though they offered me little assistance, they never forbade me to do anything either. At a much older age, when I came to understand that they used "self-initiative" as the standard for judging their children's capabilities and determination, my respect for them grew by bounds.

When I was thirteen years old, my mother began to share her feelings with me. Perhaps it was because I was her first child, the oldest in the family, that she came to me to express emotions she had suppressed for many years. I learned, for example, that she didn't care for my father's family. "None of my family has ever been a burden for me," she began, but then went on to say that my father's relatives were good only for making children and shrugging off responsibility for raising them on the better-off members of the family, the effect of which was to drag the entire family down. "They somehow seem to feel they have the right to put the burden on me. Just look at how I've wasted away; I'm nothing more than skin and bones." Just looking at her was enough to verify her statement. She was at that time quite sickly indeed.

"What with all the children I have to take care of, they now want to give me more—seven altogether. But I refused. They begged me to take pity on them, but I still refused. I have lots of children of my own and I don't know how I'm going to get you all an education."

Another time she said to me, "And look at the children I've already raised and put through school. Now that they've gone away, they can't even write a letter of thanks. They must not even think about you or your siblings." Because of the family's depleted finances, her words took on greater truth and became an even heavier burden for me. "I don't regret having helped someone if he turns out to be of use for the people. Your uncle Moedigdo is one example. After graduating, he began to support himself straightaway. But the others? What's become of them? It's almost as if I didn't have a hand in raising them.

"That's why I've always told you to be a free person, independent and in control of your own life. You have to be a person with 'all around' talents," she stressed, "not someone's slave, but not a slave driver, either."

I had no real image of what my mother's desires were for me at that time. Certainly I sympathized with her and, in listening to her, came to sense that her home life, which on the outside appeared to be so smooth, was in fact turbulent and that she, a person roundly praised for her kindness and beneficence, was suppressing a storm within herself. I gradually came to see this, but it wasn't until later that I realized the reason she shared her troubles with me was because she didn't want me to have to experience the same difficulties. She wanted me to be able to stand on my own two feet. This is why she drove me to work so hard.

In my budding state of emotional development, I was so moved by her predicament that one day I penned a note to her: "My beloved Mother, please permit me to quit school and to do service for you." It was late at night when I wrote the note and, before going to bed, I folded it and placed it beneath the light of the only lamp still burning in the house, the one on the tall stand in the center of the hallway.

At one o'clock in the morning my father knocked on the outside door. I jumped out of bed and went to open it. Then, remembering the note beside the lamp and, not wanting my father to read it, I hurried to the stand and grabbed it just as he was passing by. The letter appeared to be still in its original fold but, regardless of whether my mother had read it or not, what I came to realize at that time is that I loved my mother with all my heart. Any irritation I might ever have felt toward her—because of her strict ways and her demand for discipline and hard work—dissolved in an instant, leaving absolutely no trace. I knew then that if there were no other person in the world who would pay attention to her needs, there would still be one. That would be me, this boy of thirteen.

By the time I was in the seventh grade, school lessons didn't seem as difficult as they had been in my younger grade-school years. In fact I now liked to study and to think about subjects other than the required ones in school.

My mother took pleasure in seeing me with an open book in my hands, even if it wasn't a text book. She'd watch me from a distance and not ask me anything directly. She seemed especially pleased when I began to pay more attention to my appearance: making sure my clothes were freshly ironed and combing my hair neatly into place after first slicking it back with coconut oil that was fragrant from the flowers that had been steeped in it.

Mother no longer spun yarns for us. She didn't even join in listening when father took on that task. Her health was so poor that she had to spend much of her time in bed. One day, when lying prone on the bed, she told me that more and more dead people were appearing in her dreams. From a book I had read in Javanese about prophesying the future, I learned that dreams about death are a sign that the dreamer is himself close to death, and that the more frequently one dreams of death, the closer to death he is. I also learned that when a person begins to smell the scent of a corpse, he has only a few months more to live. This knowledge, if that's what it can be called, began to plague me. Had Mother read that same accursed book? I certainly hoped not.

My seventh-grade graduation diploma contained several "sevens." That precious piece of paper was beautifully printed with dark brown script on a background of cream-colored flowers. At the top was a *garuda* bird on whose arrow-pierced breast were the initials for Budi Utomo Institute. At the bottom of the diploma were my teachers' signatures. For me, at the age of fourteen, this lovely piece of paper represented the pinnacle of happiness. When I showed Mother my diploma I felt as if I were flying in the clouds.

"What do you intend to do with it?" she asked me.

I answered without a thought: "I want to be an electrical engineer!"

"That would be nice," she answered, but with a listlessness that said she was taking extra care to guard her strength. Possibly flashing through her mind were numerals of the sum of money necessary to turn my dream into reality.

Toward the end of each school year, my father always received promotional materials from private schools: teachers' colleges, vocational schools, and other secondary schools. One brochure that he received that year was from a private secondary school in Madiun that showed a picture of the school and a dormitory. I felt the brochure had been sent especially to me and, even before my father had a chance to look at it, I showed it to my mother.

"How about if I go to school here?" I asked, pointing at the picture of the school.

My mother merely turned her head aside and I, without the tenacity to press her on this, immediately left her room.

I spent an enjoyable vacation visiting friends, almost all of whom had already made their plans for leaving Blora. I knew there would be no telling how insignificant and unsuccessful I would feel if I were to remain in Blora. The only former classmates who intended to stay were those with almost no hope of advancement. Those who planned to go away were high-spirited. Inversely, those who were going to stay seemed fainthearted, as if their diplomas were meaningless.

I got up the courage to talk to my mother again about my problem, but the only answer she gave to my query was, "Ask your father." That took an extraordinary amount of willpower for me to do, but I finally did it one evening, at around five o'clock, just as my father emerged from his bedroom after a nap. I stopped him with my entreaty: "I want to go on to school, Father, to the private Mulo in Madiun."

I willed myself to look at him and saw his face redden and his eyes begin to shine. His voice was like a bolt of lightning for me: "Idiot! Maybe if you were smarter, you could. Maybe you should go back and repeat seventh grade."

I left without saying another word. It wasn't anger I felt but the need for vengeance. How could he insult me like that, as if I weren't even his own son? I felt hurt. I ground my teeth and felt myself breathing hard and hot. I swore to myself that I would be a better father to my children, that I would never insult one of my own. I would do everything in my power to make them proud of themselves! For the next few days I lacked the nerve to face my mother. I knew she had heard what my father said and knew that his words had hurt her even more than me. The value of my diploma had faded to nothing.

Taking my father at his word, at the start of the new school year I returned to the classroom I had left not too long before. When the bell sounded I entered the classroom first, my legs trembling as I found a seat for myself at the back of the room. The other students looked around at me with astonishment. I didn't care; I was ready to accept my father's torture.

My old teacher, *Meneer* Amir, came in and addressed the students in Dutch. He began to call the roll. Those whose names were called had to stand. It turned out he had an extra student. When he saw me, the cigarette he'd been smoking fell from his fingers to the floor. He picked the cigarette up, placed it on the desk's edge, and walked over to where I was seated. He struck me on the shoulder and spoke to me in Dutch in a nearly inaudible tone: "Young man, what are you doing here? You've finished, haven't you? This is not your place anymore."

Ready to burst with emotion, I rose from my place and ran from the classroom, not stopping until I had reached the cemetery, where I threw my arms around a tree and began to sob. In that graveyard I had tended my goats. Now I was there on my own, and, perhaps for the first time in my life, I felt that I was completely alone in the world.

I didn't go back to school after that, and my father never questioned my behavior or admonished me again. As a silent protest, whenever he came home from school I would be at the gate waiting for him. I'd take his bicycle from him and then clean it. Maybe he didn't say anything because, as an educator, he saw the wrong in what he had done. As for me, the hurt I felt came back to haunt me frequently, and even in my old age continues to pain me whenever I relive the memory in my mind. But however much pain I felt, I suspect it was my mother who suffered most from seeing me doing a gardener's work.

The midyear harvest of 1940 was a successful one. All the farmers in the Blora area were talking enthusiastically about their yields. It was very early one July morning that a knock on my bedroom door pulled me from my sleep. It was my mother, urging me to my feet: "Get up and take your bath, then come along with me." I glanced at the clock. It was only four o'clock.

After I had bathed I followed my mother as she led me down the road to the Kaiwangan bridge, which connects the outlying agricultural areas of Blora with the town itself. Even at that hour farmers were already crossing the bridge and heading toward the market laden down with sheaves of rice.

My mother began to stop them and to buy their rice. Whenever she and a farmer had reached an agreement on the sale's price, the farmer would take his rice and fall back away from the road to wait beneath the awning of a closed store. When she determined that she had made enough purchases, she had the farmers carry the rice to our house where she had me stack the sheaves in her bedroom. She wouldn't permit me to store it in the rice barn. This rice was her own, she insisted. We repeated this venture the next day and each day that followed until the end of the harvest season. Then we waited.

Weeks passed and as the rainy season approached, farmers found themselves to be in need of seeds for planting; they had sold off the major share of their harvest and eaten most of the rest. Now they came to my mother for seed.

One day my mother called me and handed me a silver *ringgit* worth two-and-a-half rupiah and told me to buy myself some shoes and socks. I bought a pair of Bata brown leather shoes with rubber soles for two-and-a-quarter rupiah. I was fifteen years old and they were my first pair of shoes. With the other quarter, I purchased two pairs of socks. When I returned home with my purchases she asked, "What is it you want to study in school? And where is it you want to go?"

I didn't know what to say. I knew that my going to school would mean additional work for her but more than anything else at that moment I wanted to be away from there. I didn't want to be a burden anymore. In my imagination I flew to Borneo and Sumatra.

"Go get information from your friends," she advised.

In the end, based on the data I collected from friends on their return home from the city, I chose to go to the Radio Vocational School in Surabaya. The course was only three terms, each lasting six months, after which you could immediately start to work. With my destination now known, Mother began to call on friends who had children living in Surabaya.

Before my departure for Surabaya, my mother bought me a wristwatch and gave me two gold rings, one with a chain motif, the other with a split rattan design. And then one dawn, I left alone on the train bound for Cepu, where I would change to another train for Surabaya. My going was, I knew, my mother's silent rebuke to my father. Thus when I left, I asked for neither his blessing nor his permission.

At Pasar Turi Station in Surabaya a young man with a bicycle was waiting to greet me. He placed my belongings in the bicycle's baskets and pushed the bicycle ahead as we walked on foot to the home where I was to board. I was almost unable to endure the pain that my new shoes and blistered feet were causing me.

I roomed at the home of one of my father's former students. In addition to myself there were several other boarders, all government or office workers, but they lived in an adjoining pavilion. I was given a bedroom at the back of the house in which there was a large armoire containing a small library of books. I gradually began to work my way through these but from the public library I borrowed other books as well. I pretty much read anything, even some privately published pornographic material and some detective books as well.

At school I consistently received high marks in electronics and radio theory, yet I didn't find the coursework very interesting. "Practicals," sessions in the laboratory where I was working with actual equipment, were special torture for me, though I must say I felt pretty full of myself when donning the school's white laboratory smocks. The source of my fear in the lab was the thought that I might accidentally break one of the radio sets. I had a vivid image of how much my mother would suffer if I had to buy a replacement.

Only a few months after I had started school my mother sent me a bicycle. When I commented that my bicycle was not nearly as good as the ones my friends owned, she sent me the money to buy a better one. After that I always had a good bicycle. My high marks at school made my mother happy, and when I went home during school breaks she seemed to welcome me with extra special cheer. She'd take me out on walks, just the two of us, to homes of friends, thereby giving her a chance to show off her son.

One night, at my boarding house in Surabaya, I dreamed that I was standing on a beach. I couldn't tell whether it was morning or night but the sky was dark with rolling clouds. The northern horizon was pitch black and the waves on the sea were enormous. And then, directly to the north, ribbons of fire leapt into the sky from the horizon. It was a volcano erupting but, strangely, the spot where I was standing was unaffected. And then I caught sight of my mother coming in my direction with my baby sister in her arms. Though my youngest sister wasn't really that small, I knew that the baby was my sister. I called out, but the harsh wind made it impossible for Mother to hear me, and she proceeded calmly along the shore, as if unaware of my presence. I called again but still she didn't answer. Then, at the water's edge, I noticed a boat, which she boarded along with my sister. The boat pulled away from the shore and began to sail northward, toward the volcano and its streams of fire pulsing into the sky. I ran after her, screaming, "Come back, Mother, come back!" But all I could hear was the thunderous wind and the roar of the waves breaking on the shore. She continued sailing northward. In vain, I kept on screaming her name.

At that moment I awoke, my face wet from tears. I sobbed where I lay and continued crying until morning, but it didn't ease the intensity of my pain.

Among the long-term boarders was a bespectacled man of about thirty-two by the name of Saat. He owned a book on the interpretation of dreams, and when I asked him about the meaning of mine, he told me, "Your mother is going to be very ill and will die along with your youngest sibling."

I immediately sent an express letter to my mother but it was my father who replied: "Your mother is just fine." So I sent another express letter, and this time Mother replied: "Why are you asking about my health? I'm fine. Don't worry about me." Despite my mother's assurance, my Javanese superstition caused me to link together my mother's dream about meeting deceased loved ones with my own dream and Saat's prediction. I grew apprehensive each time I thought about it.

A magazine the boarders subscribed to was *Panyebar Semangat*, a nationalist-oriented journal founded for the purpose of supporting the social and economic betterment of the Indonesian people. From an article that appeared in the journal I learned that my mother was a "middleman," a person who found no favor in the editors' eyes. While I agreed with the article that brokers "took advantage" of farmers, fishermen, craftsmen, and the like, I didn't quite know what I was supposed to do. I reasoned that my mother was far more knowledgeable about the situation than I. I also decided that she had been forced into the position of middleman because there was no other way she could earn enough money to put me through school. It was a puzzle I could not easily solve.

Another magazine that sometimes showed up at the house was *Terang Bulan*, an entertainment magazine. Generally speaking, the magazine contained few articles of interest for me, but one that did catch my attention was a piece about Herawati Latif, the first Indonesian woman to go to university in the United States. The article and the pictures that accompanied it described a life and what I assumed was a level of happiness and prosperity that would be impossible for me to obtain. Both her parents had a college education. My mother, on the other hand, was forced into being a middleman. I sensed that my own education was an unlikely foundation for a bridge to the goals this young Indonesian woman had achieved. I saw an unbridgeable span before me. Nonetheless, that article as well as the ones I read in *Panyebar Semangat* gave me an inkling of what my mother had in mind for my future and humbled me as well, making me feel that I might not be able to live up to her expectations.

Hoping to please my mother, I joined Blora Bond, an association of students hailing from Blora. When I returned home during school break, I received an invitation from the association to attend a gathering at the Piroekoenan pool hall, a favorite place for young people. This was the first time I had ever received a personal invitation to attend a party.

Before leaving the house, I went to say good-bye to my mother who first looked me over—at my clothes, the way I had dressed, the part of my hair—then smiled, nodded, and told me to go. I was now taller than her. My once-skinny body had filled out from boxing and bicycling around the Surabaya area. I could tell from the way she looked at me that she was proud of me and, when she said good-bye that evening, that she had begun to see me as a nearly independent person.

At Piroekoenan Hall I hesitated to go up the steps after catching sight of two former classmates who were standing on the street watching the people enter. Neither of the two was wearing shoes and one had even pulled a sarong over his head to keep from being recognized. These were examples of classmates who hadn't had the good luck to be able to leave Blora. Only two years had passed yet how incredibly fast differences between former equals had emerged.

Inside the hall I felt like those two former classmates who were standing outside and peering in. Many of the other young people present at the gathering were graduates of Blora schools far more respected than mine. I felt uncomfortable, embarrassed, and insignificant. While others entertained themselves with musical instruments that I had no idea how to play, and sang, and joked freely, I sat alone, silently in my chair.

A young woman who had been a classmate of mine got up and sang "Bengawan Solo." As she sang, her body moved freely in time with the rhythm, but I sat stiff-shouldered and tense, uncertain what to do. I felt inferior to the others, those from the more respected schools who had gathered together in a separate clique separating themselves from us. I remained alone throughout the party. The event did nothing to cheer me or raise my hopes about my future. I found it to be absolute torture and soon thereafter quit the organization.

Of all the students in my school I was the one with the least amount of pocket money: a total of one ringgit or two-and-a-half rupiah per month with which I was expected to fill all my needs, including the purchase of notebooks and textbooks. To augment my income, my landlord tried finding me part-time jobs, but his efforts proved unsuccessful.

As meager as my pocket money was, I still managed to see films twice a week at the cheapest theaters in town. I viewed the films as a way of expanding my knowledge about Europe, the United States, and other countries. Usually, I entered the theater after the lights had been turned out and the film had begun. Because it was so dark the ticket taker often failed to notice that my tickets were used stubs that I had pieced back together. Around the time of final exams I went to the movie theater almost every night as a palliative for my growing apprehension. What I feared most were the practicals and drawing. For the latter section I prepared the diagram of a television, an instrument not widely known at that time. I was nervous about whether I would receive a passing mark.

One of my weekly pastimes was a visit to the home of Soedarmadi, an older friend of mine, one of my parents' foster children, with whom I'd share a meal of grilled skewers of milkfish. He always told me not to worry about my examinations. "If you fail, nothing is going to happen. What's the meaning of school anyway?" he asked rhetorically. "In the end, what's important is that a person be able to contribute to the betterment of his people."

I didn't find my friend's advice completely convincing, especially since he himself, who was in his late twenties, was living in a bamboo hut with a dirt floor. He shared the hut with an older Madurese woman he had neglected to marry. The hut was divided into two rooms, the larger of which was used for everything except cooking and bodily functions. The smaller room, which measured about three by six feet, was used as the kitchen. The only furniture the couple possessed were a sleeping platform made from the slats of a used packing crate and a soap box in which they stored their valuables.

One evening Soedarmadi pulled from the crate a small English-Dutch dictionary. "Here," he said, "this is for you." He advised me to study English language and literature. "It's an absolute must. With Dutch you might make it as far as the Netherlands, Surinam, and South Africa, but no farther. With English you can travel the entire world and, for that matter, to space and to the bowels of the earth as well."

Though usually full of hot air, my foster brother's words contained some truth this time.

•

At the time of school examinations, the country was preparing for war.
Night fairs were being held throughout Java, Surabaya included, to collect
money for the purchase of Spitfire planes. Radio broadcasts from Japan
were playing the nationalist anthem "Indonesia Raya." Members of the
National Socialist Party were under continual scrutiny, and German citizens were being placed in detention camps.

The first part of my examination, the theoretical section, I passed with
fairly high marks, and my diagram for a television was given a "six." Now,
it was only the practicals I had to get through, but on the day of the examination, right at the time we were to be tested, the test was postponed. We
were seated in the laboratory and just as the radio was turned on, a news
flash from Batavia announced that following a surprise attack by Japanese
planes on Pearl Harbor in Hawaii, the United States and Great Britain had
declared war on Japan. This news brief was followed by the statement that
the government of the Dutch East Indies had also declared war on Japan.
Immediately, the students jumped from their seats and rushed out of the
classroom en masse to grab their bicycles and speed home.

At my boarding house when I announced the news of war to my land-
lady, the color drained from her face. Her lips tightened; then she
screamed and began to cry. The woman's next-door neighbor looked over
from her verandah and asked me what had happened. When I told her she
immediately turned on her radio, which was still repeating the declaration
of war. When the radio finally fell silent, I could hear the neighbor crying
too.

On the following day, the students gathered again for the practicals.
Most of the test material left me completely confused and, in the end, I
received only a "five-plus," meaning that I would not be able to work as a
technician. So be it, I said to myself. I would study for an additional six
months until I obtained a diploma in Marconism, a section that had
recently opened at the school. With a qualification in that subject I could
easily find work: on a ship, in a terminal, or at a news agency. Because of
the declaration of war, I knew that it was unlikely I would ever be able to
go abroad for further study.

The war-time atmosphere intensified. The news in the papers and on the radio was about war and the war only. Suddenly, it seemed, the gods of war and upheaval were everywhere: in Europe, Asia, the Pacific, and in my own life. We students waited in Surabaya for our diplomas to arrive— one week, two weeks—but the school's director said they hadn't arrived from Bandung. "Leave your address and a photograph," he finally told us, "and they'll be forwarded to you."

Even though I had not done better than a "five-plus" on my practicals, I had still graduated and could now go home to Blora.

My mother was pleased to have me at home and one evening asked me to go with her for a walk. I didn't know where we were going and didn't much care: My small hometown had been transformed in my mind and was now of little interest to me. It was insignificant, dead. Whenever I caught sight of another young townsman—one who had remained in Blora—I saw a person without hope for the future. Though I had only just graduated from technical school, I felt that I had somehow been blessed with far greater opportunities.

By and by our feet led us to the office of the Green Cross, which offered consultation services for lung diseases. There, my mother informed me that she had tuberculosis. She then went inside and was led away by an attendant to an examination room. When the door closed behind them, I was left sitting alone on the wooden bench. There were no other patients that evening.

Seated alone in the empty waiting room beneath pictures of ravaged lungs, morbid thoughts and images came to my mind: the dream my mother had related, my own dream, and my friend Saat's predictions.

On the way home from the clinic, I became all too aware of my mother's difficulty in breathing; how slowly she walked; the stoop of her shoulders; how small she seemed when compared to only a few years previously.

The only treatment for tuberculosis at the time was rest, relaxation, and nutritious food. But who could stop working? People I knew who suffered from tuberculosis continued to work even as they vomited blood. One man I knew suffered from a combination of tuberculosis and asthma. Every night, before going to bed, he took two jimson seeds to help him sleep. Jimson seeds are a narcotic but also poisonous in excess dosages. One morning, when sitting on the roadside bench beside the runoff ditch, the man fell into a faint. It turned out he had taken an extra two jimson seeds the night before. Neighbors carried him back to his house. The next day he was back at work. The cycle continued until he died.

Immediately upon our return home, Mother went into the bathroom where she washed her feet and then retired to the bedroom not to come out again that night. For the following two months she wasn't able to work. I knew that the rapid failing of her health had been caused by her desire to put her son through school. And that son was none other than myself.

I knew that I was going to lose my mother, and when I was around her I tried to control my emotions as best I could, both to bolster her hopes and to prevent her from becoming annoyed with me. But with her health fading so quickly, she grew older by the day.

She was my mother, the only woman in the world for whom I have felt unfettered love. It was she who became for me the standard against which I judged every woman I later came to meet. She was a woman who wanted for her child an independent life, a simple but noble goal for which she willingly and uncomplainingly gave her life. And now all I can do is to give her flowers, to compose a bouquet of eternal values and place it humbly at her feet.

DEATH IN A TIME
OF CHANGE

It is February 6, 1942 and I am living in Blora. I just received a postcard
from Soedarmadi, one of my parents' foster children whose acquaintance
I renewed when I was a student at Radio Vocational School in Surabaya.
The last line of his brief note reads, "Show devotion to your parents, espe-
cially your mother..." A few days later a Japanese bomb fell on
Soedarmadi's house, destroying it completely.

It's my seventeenth birthday today—I'm almost an adult!—but in my
family birthdays are not celebrated and the person whose birthday it is
observes the day without fanfare. And what is there to celebrate? Inside the
house, in the rear bedroom, Mother lies on her wooden sleeping pallet,
severely ill with tuberculosis. Occasionally I hear her low and very weak
cough. On the front verandah is my grandmother, my father's mother,
cradling a newborn child, my newest sibling. From time to time she, too,
moans, releasing a soft almost symbiotic complaint for the newborn child
who hasn't the strength to make a sound.

What can I do to change this situation? I'm seventeen years old, the
oldest child in the family, but without an income of my own. So here I am,
caught in a vise of sad sounds: my mother's cough, my grandmother's
moan. As I ponder and compare the difference between these sounds, my

head is pulled upward by the heavy roar of a plane passing overhead. Grandmother speaks with certainty: "That plane must be carrying an awfully heavy load to be making such a sound."

For the people of Blora, my family included, this sound marked the beginning of the war. It was a midair confrontation between an Allied plane and a Japanese bomber. The crackle of automatic gunfire that rent the air caused the entire town to fall silent. It was the first time anyone in Blora had heard this particular sound of death and my grandmother, no small woman, dived beneath the wooden platform on which she had been seated, along with the baby in her arms.

That one retort of gunfire was the only one we heard that day. It was not the Japanese plane that fired, but the Allied plane. For the Japanese, bullets were a precious commodity. The roar of the airplane vanished in the clear midday sky. That evening we heard that a bullet had been found in Nglobo, a small village a few kilometers to the southeast. "It was as big as a thumb," people said, "and had buried itself some twelve inches in the ground. There was smoke that came out, too. Imagine if it had hit someone!"

My father, who was almost never at home, returned that evening to find me digging a hole in the ground. I was making a dugout.

"Forget it," he quipped. "Nothing's going to happen. We'll all be safe here." No one spoke of Mother or the newborn that evening. The only thing on people's minds was the coming of the Japanese and war.

A Dutch Colonial Army unit set up camp to the west of town. In the evening the men of the unit scoured the village and searched the fields. They didn't bother anyone, and didn't steal anything either but then, after a few days, they picked up and left. The camp was suddenly empty and bare and no one knew where they had gone.

The town's signal for danger from the air—a long unbroken drum-beat, bamboo against bamboo—became a common sound. Teachers soon lost the power to control their students. The authority of local government officials and the police had severely diminished, too. Now the town's most powerful authority was the Air Patrol Service. It seemed that planes buzzed over our small town constantly.

The local policemen, who had previously strutted around like little kings, rarely showed themselves, and their sabers and truncheons, previously symbols of pride and power, were now nothing but useless weights to carry around.

By the time the newspapers reported the news, it was already old; even the batik seller's radio, which was attached to a loudspeaker and hung from the guava tree outside his house, was not much better. For current news, one relied on rumor and gossip.

In Cepu, when three open parachutes descended to the ground from a Japanese plane, the soldiers who had been guarding the oil refinery there immediately fled. The three parachutes were found. Attached to two of them were man-size straw mannequins, but the third parachute was empty. Whomever or whatever had been attached to that parachute was gone.

The people most frightened by the arrival of the Japanese forces were the Chinese shopkeepers who, a couple of years earlier, had begun to boycott the purchase of Japanese goods. They had refused to patronize Matahari Grossier, the area's only wholesaler, a Japanese-owned enterprise. As a result, they had seen their share of the market shrink significantly. They cut prices and sold some goods at hefty discount prices. Their customers increased in number, but so did their shoplifters.

I don't know what the Chinese shopkeepers did to combat that particular problem but it was common knowledge that at Matahari shoplifters who were caught red-handed were tortured by the store's Japanese staff. Though everyone talked about it, the police did nothing to stop this sadistic practice. Even the town's highest-ranking official, the Dutch Assistant Resident, had lost all authority. He went to Matahari one time to investigate the reports but the store's manager refused to allow him inside. When he raised his hand, apparently to strike, the Japanese immediately retreated inside, only to return moments later dressed in a Japanese army captain's uniform. The Assistant Resident immediately saluted and walked away. After that no government official set foot in Matahari again. But then, around the time the Japanese military began its attack in the south, Matahari closed its doors, and all the Japanese in Blora left town.

Except for the Air Patrol Service the wheels of government stopped spinning. Everyone, myself included, was preoccupied with the predictions found in *Jangka Jayabaya,* a book of prophecy that the Javanese hold in near-sacred esteem. Therein was written, "A race of yellow people will control Java for the time it takes corn to grow..." Three and a half months, we thought. Maybe for that reason it wasn't so much fear that we felt toward the Japanese at first; a much more mystical feeling controlled our emotions. We anxiously awaited their coming. We tried to keep abreast of the most recent report.

And then the evening came that I once described in my short story "Blora," when the twilight sky was bathed in a red so brilliantly red it startled me. But as all the lights had been covered with sacking, a precaution taken several months previously, the night that followed was one of gloom.

At three o'clock in the morning of March 2, 1942, I heard the sound of thunder, a whole series of recurrent thunderclaps. At six o'clock in the morning the thunder rolled once more and the clapping resounded again and again. At around nine o'clock a man on a bicycle came pedaling down the deserted road outside my parents' home. He shouted as he passed, "The Japanese are coming!" and his cry brought everyone out of their homes; the entire city perched on the side of the road, waiting. My mother and younger siblings might have been the only people still inside. Even my grandmother, with the newborn in her arms, had come out to watch from the verandah. The sudden roar of approaching vehicles caused people to scurry back to their homes. Seconds later two large trucks passed by. Inside were colonial army soldiers dressed in camouflage fatigues. The trucks moved slowly, almost hesitantly, and, when turning the corner, left only a trail of dust behind.

A number of families came out from their homes with loads of belongings on their heads and shoulders, all set to evacuate town, but then another roar of transport vehicles swept the road free of people once more.

Two more trucks appeared, both pulling trailers with howitzers. Atop the trailers were Australians. Even from a distance we knew their nationality because of their light green uniform of shorts and shirts and the small steel hats on their heads. They were young, very young, probably not much older than me, and as they passed I noticed that the gunners' legs were bound to the cannons with iron chains. When the trucks turned the corner, I rushed outside and saw from behind that the men in the trucks were also in chains.

I suspect every witness that day felt at least some measure of sympathy for those young Australians. They had done nothing wrong toward us; their country had committed no crimes toward us. It was the Dutch, people assumed, who had, without cause or consideration, chained those men to their cannons.

Then a cry was heard—"The Japanese are in the town!"—which caused everyone to run out to the main road leading into town. We all wanted to witness for ourselves the arrival of the Japanese army. The excitement of the moment had made everyone forget his fear about the possibility of battle.

At the closest junction, about three hundred and twenty yards down the road, we saw a Japanese soldier crawling on the ground, his head turning to the right and left as he moved forward. We couldn't guess what he was doing. A few hundred yards behind him several trucks tagged along, slowly making their way down the road to the south. Finally the soldier stood and then waved his hand. With that signal the trucks picked up speed and he hopped on the advance vehicle as it passed. We ran behind the trucks, scurrying to keep up. The Japanese soldiers on the trucks began to throw out fliers, which the crowd fought to retrieve. On one side was a red circle and red rectangle, symbols of the Japanese and Indonesian national flags. On the other side, printed in black ink, were the words "*Dai Nippon-Indonesia sama-sama!* Japan and Indonesia together!"

The soldiers began to loudly hum "Indonesia Raya," the aspiring national anthem, which was broken by intermittent cries of "*Banzai!*" and "*Nippon saudara tua!* Japan is your older brother!" From behind the trucks we could see that the men were sitting or standing on a pile of corpses, their fellow soldiers. After crossing the Kaliwangan bridge, the trucks picked up more speed, leaving us behind. People made their way home with fliers in their hands while shouting, "*Nippon saudara tua!* Japan is our older brother!"

With the arrival of the Japanese just about everyone in town was full of hope, except for those who had worked in the service of the Dutch. Nonetheless, there was a bad smell about the whole thing, a stench that rose from the bodies of the Japanese soldiers.

The dirty earth-colored uniforms of the soldiers were tattered and worn; their fatigues didn't even cover their ankles; they wore caps, not helmets, which were also faded and worn, and patched with pieces of cloth. In the townspeople's eyes they looked uncivilized. The only thing people could do that day was talk about the arrival of the Japanese. Once called people from "Jepun," they were now from "Nippon" or "Dai Nippon." Japan! Japan! A race of yellow men would rule Java for the life of a corn plant! After that we would be liberated and free.

Even though she was in obvious pain my mother managed to inquire about what was happening outside. My grandmother, with the baby fixed to her arms, could only say, "Dear God! First it was *Jepun*; now it's *Nippon*. Whatever happened to the Dutch?"

The Dutch, it seems, were on the run. We heard a volley of gunfire coming from the southern side of town. After that we heard nothing more, at least not until *magrib,* the time for evening prayer, when we learned that farmers living to the south of town, across the Lusi River, had killed a squad of police. The act of taking vengeance on the servants of the East Indies government had begun.

At home that night we heard a low and distant rumble. The sound made me jump up and run, along with my brother Prawito, the second oldest, toward the center of the town. As we made our way we had to avoid a rush of people who were trundling goods out of town. The closer we came to the business district the larger was the crowd. Chinese-owned stores were being broken into and looters were taking everything they could.

At Toko Tik, a store with a large glass front, the owner was standing outside, directly in front of the main door, which had been locked from the inside. Though not armed, he became a breaker for the human wave and no one tried to force entry into his store, though Toko Gladak, the popular store right next door, was looted within a few minutes' time. More and more people arrived and even heavy pieces of household furniture were carried away. The crowd advanced from one store to the next, then spread to ware-houses, and on to office buildings. When the looting spree did suddenly come to an end it was not because several people who had broken into the rice-supply warehouse were crushed to death beneath falling sacks of rice, but because the Japanese soldiers began shooting looters on the spot.

Less than a week later, there were no goods in circulation. Those stores that had managed to survive were locked and bolted. Posters on walls announced that the Japanese Army would, in the interest of restor-ing order and safety, take stern measures against anyone who defied army commands.

With the market empty and the store shelves bare, the specter of hunger began to reveal itself. There was no rice, no vegetables, no fish, no meat. Nothing. Even salt appeared to be unavailable—though everyone knew the city warehouse was full.

One day I walked down to the salt warehouse where a crowd of peo-ple had gathered. Perhaps it was because of the announcement that loot-ers would be shot on sight that people were not attempting to break in at that point. But they were restless as they waited outside, as if expecting the building supervisor to willingly open the building from inside.

I watched as a tall, muscular man climbed on top of a bench or table to raise himself above the heads of the people. The man was a local celebrity due to his skills as both a soccer player and actor and was wear-ing an open jacket with a white kerchief sticking out of the top pocket. On the kerchief was a red circle, symbol of the Japanese rising sun. He shouted and screamed, ordering people to step aside and make room for him, as if they were a group of unruly fans. But he wasn't kicking a ball or acting a part. Like everyone else, he was there because of salt, a fact the crowd soon recognized; in no time at all the man's fans had grabbed him and thrown him from his place.

Leaving the warehouse, I then walked to the town square. There, the central post office building, now lacking in windows and doors, looked like a toothless old man. The town's premier billiard parlor, where the local notables passed their time, was in a similar state, its floors littered with debris and trash, looters' residue.

When the two colonial army trucks and the Australian trucks with their trailers and howitzers left town, they left for good. Their departure symbolized the end of Dutch authority over my people and my land. The sound of gunfire in the sky and to the south of town was their death rattle. With the arrival of the Japanese, the Dutch fell as if from a mountain peak to a muddy wallow. Not much older than a schoolboy myself and ignorant of the world's intrigues, I, too, rejoiced in the demise of the Dutch East Indies. I was finally free from the sense of inferiority caused by not being able to speak Dutch well. There was no need for me to study that language any longer. I would no longer be tortured by friends using words that I couldn't understand.

At the same time I wondered whether as a result of this change I would be able to find a place for myself with the new Indonesian society. With the eradication of the Dutch language, wouldn't students from village schools have the freedom to enter and fill more influential positions within society? Would I be able to compete with them? With what was I to equip myself? Only later did I begin to think that the defeat of the Dutch also meant for me the loss of access to a written world of civilized values. The vacuum of authority effectively erased social differences. There were no longer "the upper class" and "the masses," there were no police; no guardians of law and order, and no diplomas as well. There were only people in need of food.

"Look at him now!" people silently cheered when seeing a former student of Algemene Middelbare School, the residency's highest institute of learning, going from door to door, trying to sell soy sauce, *krupuk*, and shrimp paste. Prior to the arrival of the Japanese, that same young man would not have been caught dead lifting an empty bottle.

People also cheered, if only to themselves, when seeing the confusion of former civil servants who had lost their authority and their salaries. What was I to do? I didn't know. The fall of the Dutch East Indies government had been followed by a collapse of social mainstays. In just one day life as we knew it, as if by conjurer's magic, had been completely changed. All stores, offices, and schools were closed. Children were free, left on their own. But the problem everyone faced was the same: finding the next meal.

The sense of instability that people felt soon changed into one of fear after Japanese soldiers began to roam the town in small groups of three or four, taking from people whatever they wanted to take: rings, wristwatches, pocket watches, bracelets, and necklaces. No one would have anything to do with them anymore; their very sight gave people a shudder. Their clothes were dirty, even filthier and more tattered than farmers', and more foul-smelling too. But they were the victors and no one was about to oppose them.

In time theft was followed by rape and the soldiers didn't care whether the woman was underage, married, or old. As if by command, the women in town began to darken their clear skin with soot and stopped using all forms of beauty aides.

An image: A Dutch family climbing up the riverbank to the road beside our house. The father's skin is burnt red and he's dressed not in European clothing but in Javanese traditional dress. His wife and children are similarly attired. They're all barefoot. All eyes turn toward them and walk beside the family with sympathy—imagine the desperation and fear holding them in a viselike grip!—but no one dares to offer them a place to hide. They walk slowly northward, toward the main road, until they finally disappear from view. And then down that same road comes the Japanese army, a power now as frightening as it is invincible.

A memory: The thick silence that blankets the town after the Japanese begin to detain people found in public meeting places. They order people to sit cross-legged in the lotus position on the bare ground, and any man who cannot carry out the order is, regardless of the reason, arrested and charged with being AWOL from the Dutch East Indies Army.

A Japanese soldier who was caught raping a woman was publicly executed in the town square. This helped to decrease the incidence of rape and to diminish public fear. To bolster the people's courage, the Japanese arrested a Moluccan-born forest ranger and tied him to a support on the Kaliwangan bridge, which connected the town proper with its outlying areas and hence was a major thoroughfare for farmers, vendors, and tradesmen—many of whom detested the man. He always seemed to be catching them when they were out trying to cut down a few trees. All they wanted was to make some charcoal or sell some lumber in the city. The Japanese exploited this desire for vengeance and whenever a tradesman crossed the bridge they would force him to torture this defenseless man. At first it was just spitting on him but then it was belt-whipping and, finally, after that, they were forced to shred the flesh, slice by slice, from the poor man's bones.

This incident more than any other served to open people's eyes to what the future held in store. What we saw was the family's welfare in dire straits. My father had no income and my mother showed little sign of recovering. Because something had to be done my brother Prawito and I tried our hand at trade. The market was near lifeless with only a few people selling there, most of whom were, like ourselves, completely new to the business, with little or no experience. With the value of money tumbling and the price of goods rising, the more experienced traders stood back, waiting to see what would happen.

We sold items that we had purchased from people who didn't know what they were used for. As it turned out, many people bought our wares and we soon began to see ourselves as professional used-goods salesmen. Because of our little business scheme my brother and I were able to support our family; for a time we even made enough money to buy medicine and clothing. Unfortunately, just when we were beginning to build up our capital, my father's bicycle, not even a year old and being paid for on installment, was stolen by a Japanese soldier. Then, one evening, when I was on my way somewhere, another Japanese soldier stole mine. Whatever sympathy I once had for the Japanese began to wane and change to antipathy.

When the older and more experienced traders began to return to the market, what had been a reasonable source of income for us began to dry up, especially so after our stock decreased from lack of things to buy. By this point most of the people in the area had sold what goods they no longer had use for. This situation forced us to look for goods in other towns. My brother and I went by bicycle to Cepu but the only items we could find to purchase there were yarn, Bom cigarettes, and tobacco. After hearing that there was a surplus of cloves in Pati, we went there too.

Before coming home from the market, we would always try to buy snacks for the other kids and eggs, which I'd have one of the younger siblings cook specially for my mother. Mother had very little appetite and whenever I went into her room and saw how little of her meal she had eaten, I'd try to coax her to eat some more, but she would always fend me off with her own questions: "Have you eaten already? And what about your brothers and sisters?" All the children tried to make Mother happy but none of us knew how to make her well. In our area tuberculosis was rampant, affecting both neighbor and friend. At least every fifth household had a family member suffering from the disease. It was the curse of our small town and had sentenced not only my mother but also my newest sibling to untimely deaths. My mother wasn't able to nurse the baby so we found the money to buy cow's milk for the two of them. We did this cheerfully, out of devotion to her.

Because my father was so rarely at home we moved Mother into his room, which was far less drafty than her own room. But her health only got worse. In all practical terms I was now the family's eldest male, the household guardian, and every night I slept on two chairs directly outside my mother's room. Whenever she coughed I would wake and go into her room to check on her. Yet she would always be the first to speak, "Aren't you asleep? It's late. You should be in bed." If she saw me hesitating, she'd gently chase me away: "Go to sleep . . . You have to work tomorrow."

When leaving for the market or coming home with something in my arms, and even when keeping vigil over my mother at night, I was intensely aware of the pleasure that I derived from doing things for my parents, my seven brothers and sisters, my grandmother, and even for Nyi Kin, the old woman who worked as our household servant.

From the time I was a boy I felt indebted to my parents, and now that I was on the threshold of adulthood I vowed that, in as much as it was possible and to the best of my ability, I would try to repay that debt. But the gift of life my mother had given to me was not one that I could return, and her illness refused to go away. I was never envious of the kids my age who were carefree and had no responsibilities. Maybe I was just seventeen and my brother a bare fifteen, but we didn't ask for help from anyone.

One day, at around ten o'clock in the morning, my brother Koesalah, the third child, came to the market to find me. He reported, "Mother told me to tell you that she wants you to come home, that you don't have to sell today." Together we bundled my wares, rolled up the mats, and went home. There I found that Mother was in very serious condition. I immediately told one of my siblings to send telegrams to our grandparents' homes in Rembang and Ngadiluwih, and instructed the others to locate our father. I myself went to fetch the doctor, though I had no idea how I was going to pay him.

That same evening my mother's stepmother arrived from Rembang and, much to my irritation, immediately commandeered arrangements in the household. She ordered me to prepare a bed for my mother in my room. The doctor came, gave my mother and the baby shots of something, and then went home.

In my room I went to work on a bed for Mother. Hammer in hand, I started banging on wood, knowing full well the sound would disturb her. I wanted to refuse to carry out my stepgrandmother's command but didn't know how. She had come and with not even a how-do-you-do, had taken over my job of caring for Mother. I was crying as I worked. What could I do to show this woman I didn't want her here? Nothing! So I banged and pounded away, becoming all the more upset as I worked.

My stepgrandmother came into my room, looked over my work, and then said something to me in a loud and angry voice. I didn't want to hear what she said. My mind flashed back to a time in grade school when I had decorated the walls of my room with posters of American film stars and she had told me to tear them up, that God would not bestow His blessings on a household with such pictures on its walls. Another time—this was after I had finished grade school—she had suggested to me and my mother that I continue my studies at a Muslim boarding school. There wasn't a single person I knew who had gone to school at a *madrasah* whom I thought worthy of being a role model. Was that what she wanted for me? To be a person that people didn't look up to? And now here she was again, standing in my bedroom, all angry and bothered with me. Without saying a word to her, I threw down the hammer and left her standing alone in my room.

I stormed out of the house and tramped down the road to a machine shop where I found myself a bench and sat down, still seething with anger. For the next two hours I sat there, not saying a word. At around five o'clock, just when it was beginning to grow dark, one of my sisters came looking for me. "Mother wants you at home," she said. I jumped up and hurried on my way, letting my sister play catch-up behind me.

At home I went directly into Mother's dim room. From the fading light falling through the window slats, I could see that my mother was deathly still. Her arms had already been crossed and were resting on her chest. Her eyes were closed but a faint smile seemed to be on her lips.

"Mother," I whispered but she neither turned toward me nor opened her eyes.

I silently cursed my stepgrandmother and the doctor, too, who had given no indication at all that my mother was so close to death. My brothers and sisters were crying, and I could hear that the neighbors had already begun to arrive, but I stayed in the bedroom, wanting to be alone with my mother.

Victims of tuberculosis exude bacteria from their mouths and noses but I was sure my mother would not kill me with the same bacteria that had taken her life. I hugged her cool body and kissed her forehead but then was suddenly startled by a voice calling my name. I pulled my arms away from my mother's corpse and looked around to find that I was not alone in the room after all. In the room's dark corner there was the old and kindly-looking woman we called Mbok Slamet, who was always the first woman in the neighborhood to arrive at a person's home in time of calamity.

"Thank you, Mbok," I mumbled, knowing that she must have looked after my mother in her final moments. "Did she ask for anything?"

"No, she didn't."

My mother had died leaving no requests, willingly surrendering her children to their own lives. Mother, how very much you had to suffer. Mother, my dear mother. . . .

"You should go," Mbok Slamet advised. "You have things to do."

My father finally came home but as he appeared to have nothing to say to me, I had nothing to say to him. He looked nervous and at a loss at what to do. I knew he had no money, not a single cent. My brother Prawito and I would take care of doing the shopping: buying oil, rice, salt, spices, and cloth for Mother's burial shroud.

My real grandmother, my father's mother, had also appeared and was now cradling in her arms the newborn, who had been named Soesanti. "Dear God," she prayed, "You have taken this child's mother. Please return that life to this little one." But the baby, as if wishing to stay with my mother, died a few minutes later. In one part of my mind I viewed the death of both my mother and Soesanti as a release from their suffering. Maybe that kept me from the edge of despair. Even so, I regretted not having been with my mother during her final moments.

Our house that night was bright with lantern light. The furniture had been removed and mats placed on the floor. We had numerous visitors, many of whom stayed through the night, until the time of burial.

In the morning Mbok Slamet came to bathe my mother's corpse. She called me and the other children and told us to crawl under the bench on which my mother's body was to be washed. I refused and ordered my siblings to refuse as well. She then asked me, the oldest child of the family, to help her bathe my mother. As she rubbed the body clean, I was to pour dippers of water over the corpse. This I also refused to do. I simply couldn't make myself do it and, in the end, she did all the work herself.

After her job was finished, I asked Mbok Slamet to dispose of my mother's clothes, to burn them or throw them in the river. Now it was she who refused. "No, that wouldn't be right. I'll wash them in the river and, with water running over them, they'll be fine." I don't know how all the necessary preparations for the burial of my mother and sister were taken care of. I only knew how to pay for them.

And so, one morning in May of 1942, my mother was buried in the city's northern cemetery, in one grave with Soesanti. After everyone else had gone home, I kneeled beside the grave with my brother, my head bowed. I had never dreamed of this happening and that this place, this mound of earth, would be the final resting place for a woman I admired and loved. At the age of thirty-four, she was exactly twice my own age and had died leaving seven children behind. "Don't be disappointed if this is all we could manage to do for you in your final days," I implored.

My brother and I then left the cemetery, made our way to the main road, and returned home. There, Mbok Slamet immediately came to me with my mother's clothes. They had already been washed and aired to dry and were now neatly folded.

"You see how clean they are? There's nothing wrong with them."

"Please take them for yourself," I told the old woman who bowed her head and when turning to leave, held the bundle of clothing tightly to her chest.

Our kitchen was a large annex and was filled with women who were cooking yet another meal, the third one, for the *tahlil* prayer session that was to be held that evening. Old women, whom I recognized but probably hadn't spoken a word to in my entire life, were seated on the wooden sitting platform. I was grateful that they had come to share in our sorrow and I went into the house and to my mother's armoire, intending to divide up her clothes among them. I was incredibly shocked to discover that all my mother's prized *kain,* the batik wraparounds that she herself had made, were gone. Knowing that my mother hadn't sold them aroused my suspicion and I opened up the doors of the cupboard and the buffet. Many of our porcelain dishes were gone too. When I took the key to open the glass case in which were stored the silver-plated ware I heard someone whisper at my back, "You'll let me have those, won't you?"

I don't even recall who the woman was but when I said "Take them," she immediately took them all.

My mother left behind very little jewelry and what she did was of limited value though it was made of gold. Even so, I knew that she had not pawned them, because she had wanted to leave something for her daughters.

There were so many things to take care of that we didn't go anywhere for a week, not even to the market. When my brother and I did return, we found that another trader had taken our space. Counting our resources, we discovered that we didn't have enough money to buy new stock. We had only enough to pay the household's shopping expenses for one month. Fortunately for the family, schools had been reopened and Father began to teach again.

After Mother died I took to sleeping outside on a mat in front of the house. I'd stretch out in the open air and sleep until morning. When waking my body would be covered with a light coating of dew. For most of the ten days I slept outside, I was accompanied by two young men about my own age. Lying on my back, I'd stare at the moon floating across the rapidly moving clouds while Karmin Kenceng, one of the two, sang Javanese songs that he'd learned at *ketoprak* performances. I suppose that Karmin and the other boy, a friend of his, wanted to cheer me up or demonstrate their solidarity with me but there was an emptiness, a vacuum inside me that would not go away.

The moon floating through the sky and the Javanese songs evoked fond memories in me and also the regret that my mother would never see her children become self-sufficient adults in a position to show the devotion due her for her labors on our behalf.

One night, my two companions told me that they would be leaving the next morning for Sumatra. They were going to Palembang to look for work. They bid me a formal farewell but said they would stay with me one more night. The next day they would be departing for a destination they knew nothing about and where they had never been before. I didn't ask them where they had acquired the funds to make such a long trip. Maybe they hoped that I would give them a little extra money to help them on their way. But that is exactly what I couldn't do. All I had left was the shopping money for the house. The next day Karmin returned to say good-bye again. We shook hands and then he left. I never saw him again.

One by one, my former classmates also left town. There were few ways of earning a living in Blora. Arid soil made farming a bad bet, there was no industry to speak of, and handicrafts were being displaced by imported goods. For a long time, my hometown harbored a reputation as a source of prostitutes for the large cities. Was I to leave or to stay? If I stayed, would I share the same fate as those friends of mine who had not left town? Would I, like one of them, become a shiftless gambler who was now suffering from tuberculosis? Or a woodworker, as other friends had become?

The departure of Karmin and his friend made me feel lonely and ashamed. At seventeen, I was considered to be an adult. I should have been working, starting to build a life for myself, but I had no means to start a life and little opportunity for leaving the city. I worried about my two companions who, with no money in their pockets, had left the town, but envied them for their strong sense of purpose.

I couldn't be expected to earn enough to survive by teaching in Blora. There was a small radio repair shop in town and I spoke to its owner about the possibility of a job, but even I could see there was little or no work coming in. In all of Blora there couldn't have been more than half a dozen radio sets.

In the Dutch colonial era, poverty had held the town in its grip. Now, under Japanese authority, poverty wrestled with chaos. Though home industries had begun to appear, there were no buyers for their products and, one after another, they drowned in a sea of debt. The area's single constant source of revenue was the teak plantation and some people in the area, whose only skill was daring, had begun to earn money from the black market sale of wood.

What only a few months earlier had been the invincible Dutch East Indies government had collapsed beneath the winds of war in a matter of days, precisely at the time my own parent's income had reached its lowest point. This turnaround taught me just how temporal everything in the real world can really be. From history books at school my teachers had plucked lessons on how nations rose and fell. Even the *wayang* theater offered such lessons. "The king is dead. Long live the king!" Life, I had come to learn, is a river forever flowing to the sea, never returning to its source, one that human souls may ford but one time only.

Even one's good name will eventually disappear if one does not leave behind lasting values, because what is good, even what is very good, is not necessarily of lasting use. And what did my mother leave behind if not her stories and the moral value of her devotion as a mother and wife, and as an educator and guardian of her children?

My small hometown seemed to have nothing to offer me. When I looked at my siblings and at my father, I saw in them no reflection of myself. In the course of dealing with all the aggravations that arose at the time of my mother's death, family ties had for me lost much of their sacredness, especially when I saw none of my parents' foster children coming to the house to express their sympathy for me or my siblings.

My mother's death had taught me that while blood ties might be everlasting, friendships with people, even ones who had once been strangers, could be more binding. This knowledge made me regret that my friendship with Karmin Kenceng had been so brief. It also made me see my father more objectively. Though my estimation of his worth remained high, he had lost his frightening demeanor. I had found both his behavior and that of many of the people around me to be unsatisfactory.

I was left feeling alone. From recent experience I knew that no one was going to put out a hand to help me. At seventeen, I was already being forced by life to turn away from my family and search for a new life of my own.

The confluence of two events—the breaking of the Dutch lion's hold on Indonesia and the death of my mother—were the starting point for my diminished trust in man and his intentions.

My mother should not have had to spend so much time alone in her final days. People whom she had helped should have come by, if only to try to cheer her up. My feeling that she had been wronged fueled in me a desire for revenge, an emotion I managed to gain control over only after a long and difficult struggle. When I finally realized the havoc this desire can wreak I promised myself that I would never harbor it within me—I would not be like those people!—though I know now it was not completely possible for me to live up to my promise.

One evening in June, the family gathered at my mother's grave. One of the children read *Surat Yasin,* the prayer for the dead, and we all scattered flower petals that we had purchased at the market on my mother's grave. Two of my siblings began to cry. They were much too young to have lost their mother and the hope of ever seeing her again. Then I began to cry and, after that, the other children, too. Through my tears I promised myself that I would become a better, more useful person than all those people whom I considered to have acted unfairly and unjustly toward my mother.

Regardless of anything else, my mother was a symbol of devotion, sacrifice, and suffering for which she had never been properly recognized. My grandmother, my mother's biological mother, who was a village woman, didn't cry, but her eyes were red and she kept rubbing them with the back of her hand. I felt her tears possibly came not so much from losing her daughter, but from seeing her forlorn grandchildren, whom she could do nothing to help.

Before leaving the cemetery I silently asked my mother's leave. My brother and I were to go to Jakarta the following day and I would not be able to make this pilgrimage very often.

•

Before dawn, the next morning, my brother and I took leave from our father and made our way to the train station to board the local for Cepu. Our car was full of fish sellers from Rembang and vegetable sellers from Blora. Even with all their gaiety and laughter, I could not listen to them, though only a few months earlier I had been a seller, too, looking for trade in another town. I stared out the window northward and into the darkness.

About two miles away from where I sat was my mother's silent grave. There a small frangipani had begun to take root. I don't know who planted the tree—possibly my grandmother, to protect her daughter from the hot afternoon sun.

On my feet were my brown leather shoes, the first pair I had ever owned, the ones I had worn when leaving Blora to study in Surabaya. I remembered my mother, how she had given me the money to buy these shoes. And now I was wearing them to a place I didn't know, except from what I had discovered through my reading. I was happy to leave Blora, ready to discover the unknown and feel emotions I had never felt before. Was I ever to return? That I didn't know. I knew only that the hold of my birthplace had been broken. My brother and I weren't the first people to leave our town. People were always leaving and we were just two more names to add to the list. But we had to go, to find space in which to live.

People say that the sky and all that is beneath it is man's. I wondered then if this were true. My brother and I were alone with only the memories of our deceased mother as our helpmate and companion.

I recall a story once told me about a boy who, when leaving his village, is escorted by his family to the village limits. From there he makes his own way to the city to a teachers' college. What he doesn't know is that his departure is not just a separation from friends and family but a leave-taking from familiar ways of thinking, customs, institutions, and traditions. Leaving the village means entering the modern world, a country whose residents are not permitted ever to return to their place of origin.

Once, when I was boy and I was with my parents on a trip, we called in at my grandmother's house in Rembang. There I was teased for being a country bumpkin, a taunt that felt particularly harsh at the time. I wondered if the same taunt would be thrown at me upon my arrival in Jakarta. I had no way of knowing. When the local train finally arrived in Cepu, my bonds and ties with Blora began to loosen and fall away. I felt a stirring of freedom. At the station we were warned that our onward passage might be rough: a large number of bridges and sections of tracks were under repair. But I couldn't stop there. The call of adventure was much stronger and more inviting. I felt courageous, ready to face most anything as the express train moved out of the station and finally carried me away.

WORKING FOR
THE JAPANESE

(A Letter for Rina)

Picture a young man, seventeen years old, physically fit from regular exercise, and dressed in his best clothes—a white shirt and full-length white trousers. He enters a building on Jalan Pos Utara, the former office of the Aneta News Agency but now home of Domei, the Japanese news service. On the way into the building his eyes are fixed straight ahead; he doesn't notice the imposing roof or the tall transmission tower and barely takes note of the gilt *kanji* script on the pane of the glass window.

He is greeted by an office menial who shows him a place to sit and then goes off to report to his superior. The year is 1942 and the young man, a student at the Taman Siswa school, is none other than me.

The reception room is very small with adequate space for only a medium-sized lounge set. While waiting to be called, I try not to fidget as I mull over my uncertain future. A Japanese man no taller than myself and dressed in a white short-sleeve shirt and white trousers comes out to meet me. I stand up to greet him and, after we shake hands, he motions to me to take a seat. He speaks to me in English, a language I had just begun to study two weeks before. All I can say to him is yes and no. The man's name is Matano and he's head of the Domei News Java Service. He seems to be a polite, friendly, and educated man. He stands, then goes back inside. I can't see what's happening there because my vision is obstructed by a dividing wall. I listen to the clacking of typewriters and guess that the office has five of them at the very least.

Matano returns to the reception area and is followed by an office boy who places a typewriter on the small table in front of me. The Domei chief asks me to type a piece of Indonesian-language copy and then one in English. I had learned to touch-type only three weeks earlier, practicing my new skill day and night on a typewriter owned by my school for use in preparing telegrams. Typing at a speed of two hundred letters per minute, I pass the exam.

Matano nods and congratulates me. And suddenly I am employed as a typist for Domei. I am little more than a boy, but now, about to start my first real job, I am confident and feel that life has begun to open up for me.

On my first day of work, I was given my own desk, chair, and typewriter. My initial assignment was to type up short news articles on stencil paper. This I already knew how to do as I had been using stencil paper at my parents' house for years. No one had to teach me how to use the special correction fluid or how to insert the carbon paper.

I adapted to working at Domei quickly and, within a short time, the news became a part of my life. Through constant typing practice, within the space of two months I was able to type two hundred eighty letters per minute, making me the fastest typist in the office. Gradually I came to know the growing number of staff members and became familiar with some of the most well-known journalists of the time. These people were, as the title of the book goes, "My Universities." I listened to their conversations and chuckled at their jokes. Oddly enough, no one ever seemed to talk about the Pacific War, the very topic that filled the reams of pages I typed.

The entrance-level salary for underage staff members like myself was the grand sum of thirty rupiah, which I used to buy a new shirt and pair of shoes, pay my school fees, buy books, and treat my brother to a couple of meals.

•

I came to the job at Domei by way of my uncle Moedigdo, my father's youngest brother, who worked in the agency's summary section writing up English-language briefs of news items. A few months after my mother's death he had written from Jakarta asking my father to arrange passage for their mother to the capital. My father had other ideas, however, and sent me and my brother Prawito instead. I was seventeen, my brother fifteen.

The journey to Jakarta was a true adventure for me, the longest trip that I had ever made, and a strenuous one, too, because of its concurrence with the Japanese invasion of Java. When we finally arrived at the station we hired a horsecart and went directly to the dormitory where Uncle Moedigdo was supposed to be living. The dormitory had the grand name of "Soli Deo Honor" and was located on Jalan Kadiman right next to the Taman Siswa junior high school. There we found numerous young people—some sculpting, some playing violins and guitars, others painting and reading—but no Uncle Moedigdo. We were told that he had moved to the area of Kepu, which is where we then headed.

My uncle's house, conveniently located at a three-way intersection, appeared to be new. It was clean and nice-looking; its outer walls and verandah were unadorned. Even the interior walls were bare, giving it a modern, almost hygienic air. What furniture there was seemed new but the kitchen was empty—there was absolutely nothing there: no kettles, no cooking pans, just an empty open hearth. But Uncle Moedigdo was a bachelor and this was his first house. I was sure that I would be happy living there.

When he arrived home that day to find my brother and me at his house he addressed me in low-level *ngoko* Javanese, as would be his right in the Javanese feudal-linguistic tradition. Probably because I replied to him in *ngoko* and not in the high-level *kromo* a proper Javanese is supposed to use with his social superior, he immediately switched to Indonesian, which was the language we used together after that time.

My uncle was a hard worker and even at home he worked till late at night. It was he who taught us *kuntow*, a form of self-defense, and English.

For our part, my brother and I cooked, ironed, and in general, managed the upkeep of his home—this in addition to keeping up with our own studies after we had enrolled at Taman Siswa.

Among the belongings I had brought with me were a rectifier and other radio parts. Having been unable to find all the parts I needed to construct a radio in Blora, I had intended to look for the rest in Jakarta but because the Japanese declared radio spare parts to be contraband material, I was forced to destroy them and stop tinkering with radios. Having studied radio technology in school, I didn't know now what I was going to do.

In the evenings children marched past the house singing war songs. With their bodies covered in a camouflage of leaves and with wooden rifles in their hands, they'd scream in imitation of the Japanese.

In the early morning all sorts of peddlers passed by, hawking their wares in voices and words strange to my ears. I found it shocking to see women in short dresses and without their hair tied up in a *konde*, clattering down the asphalt road toward Nangka Market in their wooden sandals. Just as surprising was hearing men and women speak their minds, anywhere and everywhere they pleased, with an ease and candor I had never witnessed before. I concluded that the people of Jakarta were by nature an open, friendly, and cheerful lot, unlike the people of Central and East Java.

As my uncle didn't own a radio, I'd listen to our neighbor's through the open window for his was constantly on. What intrigued me at first was that he never changed the station but then I learned that after the arrival of the Japanese army (and until their departure) only one radio station was allowed to broadcast and all privately owned radio sets had been sealed, with their bands fixed on that one station only. For print media, the situation was worse. The Japanese had closed down almost all newspapers. They were not to reopen until after their departure.

My uncle had no library of his own so I spent much of my free time observing my surroundings: peddlers; shoppers on their way to market; the pedicabs going back and forth; the herd of goats that scrounged the neighborhood for any food they could find, even discarded shoes and sandals. (Two of the goats in the herd had only three legs and someone told me that the herd was owned by an Arab who would cut off a hind leg from one of his goats whenever he had a taste for goat satay. The person who told me that was joking, of course, but then one day when I saw that another three-legged goat had joined the herd, I began to wonder!)

The environment in which I now lived was unlike any that I had known before; everything was new and memorable for me. Without quite realizing it, I began to shed the influence of my Javanese upbringing, including my speech patterns, and within a week I had discarded my thick Javanese accent. I began to feel myself to be an Indonesian, a real Indonesian, a Javanese no longer, with an Indonesian sensibility.

I enrolled for courses and attended lectures that were held in the front hall of Soli Deo Honor. When the Japanese Military Command finally gave its imprimatur to Taman Siswa, this hall became the unofficial site of the school's junior-level classes and I became a second-level student.

Two of my teachers I liked very much. The first was my Indonesian-language teacher, an elderly man by the name of Mara Soetan. He was from a different generation, a different century in fact. He was a small, skinny little man whose spectacles appeared far too large and heavy for his nose to bear. He was missing some of his teeth and moved his body only with great hesitation. But he enjoyed talking about his life, his experiences as a teacher, and about what he called "sticky rice" polemics. He had a way of making historical characters come to life and an engaging way of recounting for us articles he'd found in newspapers and magazines. He piqued our interest in Plato and Aristotle, making us want to read the books that he recommended.

The other teacher I held in awe was Darmawidjaja, my history teacher who previously had been an editor for the newspaper *Asia Raya*. He was a tall, lean man with an ever-ready smile and a history lesson on his lips. His eyes shone brightly and his hands gesticulated wildly when he taught, as if the historical incidents he spoke of were events from his own life. Because of him the ancient kingdoms of Singasari, Dhaha, and Majapahit seemed to be neighboring towns, ones that my grandparents might have come from just yesterday. Historical events I had been ordered to memorize in primary school finally came to life and stimulated in me the urge to know more.

It was the influence of these two teachers that made me pick up my feet every Sunday morning and walk to the library of what is now the National Museum and peruse old books there. Though my knowledge of Dutch was rudimentary, it was the lever I used to push myself forward toward greater understanding.

Outside the walls of my home and school, as the Japanese Occupation moved forward, the country's state of decline became ever more evident. Food was harder to come by and more costly than ever before. Shops, street stalls, and the market were almost barren of goods.

As prices rose we were forced to move from the new and lovely house that we had been occupying to less costly accommodations. We sold most of the furniture and moved to a bamboo house in a *kampung,* one of the many inner-city "villages." The only source of illumination was one twenty-five watt bulb.

People grew thinner by the day, myself included, but in my newfound freedom and desire to get ahead, this was not a hindrance for me and it was around this time, and with this sense of spirit, that I began to work at Domei.

For me, my association with Domei and my work there were as exciting and pleasure-filled as a vacation in a new and exotic land. When I asked a person a question I was answered as an equal. As a result, I acquired a great deal of information that I never could have gotten from friends, teachers, or dictionaries.

As a student, I was granted shortened working hours and permitted to come in the evenings. I felt pampered, like a little prince. I began to try my hand at composition, writing feature stories on subjects I thought I knew something about but, invariably, they were rejected by the features editor and returned to me with nothing more than a smile. Not one to give up, I began to write articles for my school magazine, which I myself edited and even typed at the office on paper from the office's supply.

In my fourth month at Domei, just after pay day, I went to see Matano, the agency's director, to ask permission to buy some dictionaries. To buy any Dutch publication at that time one needed permission from a governmental agency and I had prepared a letter of request in Indonesian.

When I approached his desk he stopped working, put down his red pencil, and read my letter. He then looked at me.

"Do you have enough money to purchase them?"

"I think I have enough," I told him.

With that he signed the letter, affixed his seal, and jotted several Japanese words on the paper in gold-flecked red ink.

As it turned out my salary didn't cover the cost of the dictionaries and I had to add to that sum money I obtained from selling a ring my mother had given to me. But walking home that day with those beautiful dictionaries in my arms, I felt like the smartest, most important fellow in the world. The more I read the more I realized how very little I knew and how much more I needed to read. Unfortunately, reading materials were scarce. The only books available to me were ones I purchased at Balai Pustaka, the state publishing house, and Indonesia Sekarang, a second-hand bookstore, and the ones in the collection of the Museum library.

When going to the Balai Pustaka bookstore I had to pass by the Concordia Building—which later, for a time, became the Parliament Building—from whose bar-covered windows at sidewalk level came the giggles and shrieks of young women being fondled by Japanese soldiers. When reading in the Museum library I was forced to listen to the clanking of chains and the moans of prisoners being tortured by the military police at their headquarters adjacent to the museum on its right-hand side. Every time a cry of pain was heard, readers in the library would raise their heads, look around at one another, and wait to go back to their reading until the last "Dear God!" had faded.

Life was an arena full of attractions. One sideshow for me was the second-hand market where I'd spend hours gazing with longing at such things as motors, pliers, wrenches, soldering equipment, and other tools to which I had said good-bye only a few months earlier when forced to give up my dream of being a radio technician.

At the beginning of the new academic year, when I proudly came to take my place as a third-level student of Taman Siswa, the Japanese disbanded the school. I didn't know it then but the second level of junior high school would be the highest level of academic education that I would ever achieve.

During the Japanese Occupation, Indonesia—now that the Dutch East Indies had ceased to exist, the name was official—was divided in a way that made one think there had never been aspirations of forging a political unity. Java and Madura formed their own administrative unit beneath the Japanese Army. And just as if they were foreign countries, Sumatra, Bali, and other islands came beneath the authority of the Japanese Navy.

The Japanese soldiers turned out to be very much like the caricatures that had once appeared of them in the Dutch-language newspapers. They had huge teeth, some of them gold; they were shabbily dressed, and instead of talking they screamed, usually while thrusting their bayonets at the person they were speaking to. They also smelled so bad it was risky to breathe within sixteen feet of them. In time their appearance and smell improved, but that was to be expected: the first wave of soldiers to arrive in and to leave Java were front-line soldiers, responsible for securing the island, while the next wave was part of the Occupation Army, a more educated lot of men.

Unlike many of the Japanese employees of other agencies my boss, Matano, was a civilian, as was attested to by the badge with a cherry blossom that he wore on his hat or chest. Though he himself was a polite man, generally speaking, the Japanese newcomers—both soldiers and cherry blossoms—were greedy and corrupt, as well as rude. The air of authority that had attached itself to Europeans before the war was not evident in the Japanese. People didn't respect them. But they were afraid of them, a fear based on the frequent displays of torture by the soldiers.

The Japanese viewed Indonesians not as a lowly race so much as a herd of animals they owned and could do with as they pleased. They themselves were a higher race and in schools where Japanese history was taught, pupils learned that Emperor Hirohito was a descendant of the sun god Amaterasu.

As discipline among the Japanese improved, food supplies diminished. At first farmers were made to turn over to the military a certain percentage of their harvest but, later, demands came to be placed on their labor and their freedom of movement as well: many were turned into *romusha*, forced laborers, and were taken from their families to be sent off to build battlements for no recompense, and to die in strange lands with only the sky as their witness. After the war I learned that four million or more Javanese farmers had died as *romusha*, fodder for the sun god's militaristic descendants. Four million! The cities were filled with men who had fled the villages in their attempt to escape from death.

Batavia, such a neat and orderly city when I first arrived, was now a rubbish bin, piled high with inedible trash—"inedible" because anything that could be eaten, no matter its form or condition, had an empty stomach and ready mouth waiting for it.

In order to win their war the Japanese needed the assistance of the people they had colonized and they attempted to unite nationalists, religious leaders, and nobility under their power. (They also tried to exterminate all Communists, that being the very first thing they set out to do after setting foot in Java.) At the local level, through the neighborhood security unit known as *toonarigumi*, the Japanese kept an eye on all public activities. Women were made to join the Fujinkai. Young men were forced to register with Seinendan, the local division of the *keibodan* police. Nonetheless, all authority and all decision-making powers were held by the Japanese military.

At the office I spent my days typing reports about the activities that people engaged in, including their service in these surveillance organizations, for the purpose of winning the "Greater East Asia War."

Bold-faced headlines told of Japanese victories at land and sea. The silver screen ladled out depictions of Japanese victory and superiority across the board, from sports to war and even to comedy. The radio constantly blared Japanese and Indonesian military songs. But in Java, in the fields, along the road, and at intersections, were piles of the bodies of people dead from influenza and dysentery. For Indonesians, improved Japanese discipline and order meant hunger and destitution.

After I had grown accustomed to working at Domei, I began to explore the agency's large editorial office. There I found coveted dictionaries on the editors' desks and, against the wall behind the editors' desks, a large wooden cabinet behind whose wood-and-glass panel doors were several racks, on one of which sat a row of impressive-looking books: *Winkler Prins Encyclopedia*, the *Encyclopaedia Britannica*, an American *Who's Who*, three British-made atlases, and one set of green cloth-covered *Adat Recht*, Indonesian traditional law.

One day, when I asked a colleague a question that he wasn't able to answer, he pointed toward that imposing cabinet and suggested that I try to find the answer in the encyclopedia. Without asking permission, I opened the cabinet door. The creaking of the doors was so loud I was sure that everyone was looking at me. I glanced behind me but saw Matano still sitting calmly at his desk. I found the volume I was looking for and carried the book to my desk. There, for the first time—I had never used an encyclopedia before—I discovered what an encyclopedia is: a huge all-purpose dictionary. I was amazed to see how much Europeans knew and was distressed about my own scant knowledge. Henceforth I began to borrow volumes of the *Winkler Prins Encyclopedia* just to read. They became my teachers. I gave a silent prayer of thanks to my parents for having been educated in a school where Dutch was taught. Though I was far from fluent in the language, I was able to travel the road of discovery to places of which I had previously only dreamed. These books made me reassess my opinions of the Dutch. The emptiness of my life outside the office became less apparent than it had been. My world didn't feel so small anymore. Moreover, I saw that the world could be a pleasurable place. I dreamed of having my own set of encyclopedias. Such a dream! Such an impossibility! With my monthly wage I couldn't afford to buy even one volume.

•

A year went by, then another six months, and it was 1944 or 2604 Sumera on the Japanese calendar. One day I noticed an announcement posted on the wall: The agency was looking for two trainee-stenographers. One successful applicant was soon found among the staff: Hasnah Sutan. Diatas, a young Minangakabau woman who was a graduate of Middelbare Handelschool. After a week had gone by and the second slot still had not been filled, Matano called me to his office and offered me the position. I accepted it immediately.

The course was conducted in a small wing of the Volksraad, the People's Congress building, whose name had been changed to Chuoo Sangi-in. Our classroom was exceptionally beautiful and I would often find myself staring at the window's teak shutters, the teak-covered crossbeams that were so rich and deep in color, the room's fine molding, and the walls that were also covered in varnished teak. One wall of the room was stacked from floor to ceiling with racks of legal-size volumes I dared not touch. Heavy curtains of scarlet corduroy hung from the door and windows. The furniture was finely crafted. To my eyes even the refrigerator was beautiful.

On the first day of class Soekarno, the country's future president, addressed the students. First he spoke to us about the pressing need for courses such as the one we were now enrolled in as preparation for handling the governmental administration of Java and Madura. Then he proceeded to give us our first lesson on a topic I hadn't expected to hear mentioned at all: politics. Though that was the only time he visited our classroom, Mohamad Hatta, the future vice president, came to the school twice a week, from the beginning of the course until the end, to lecture on economics.

Our stenography teacher was a man by the name of Karundeng, a gifted teacher I'm likely never to forget. Already quite old at the time, he taught us the blind system of stenography. And in teaching he showed me the beauty of Indonesian. When he read a text for us to take down in stenogram, his lips opened and closed, protruded and puckered, pinched and swelled but none of us was distracted by either that or by his yellowed teeth. It was his voice we listened to. He spoke with absolute clarity, each word distinct yet joined so smoothly with the next word that together they might have formed a string of pearls. A short story by Usmar Ismail, which I had read three times before taking this course, suddenly became a work of exceptional beauty when he read it for us.

The course proceeded smoothly and in the seventh month we students began our on-the-job training. Our job site was familiar to us: the Chuoo Sangi-in plenary hall, which we often visited when the Council was in session. The room was split level and the lower level, where the representatives sat, appeared to be in a state of renovation, but that's where they had to sit, in tightly packed rows of carved teak chairs.

On the higher level, on one side of the room, was a large chair occupied by the Saikoo Sikikan, governor general of the Japanese Occupation Army. On the same level but on the other side of the room was another chair, this one occupied by Soekarno, chairman of the session.

For my first day of work I wore a pair of black pin-striped wool trousers. They were a second-hand pair, previously owned by a European I presume, which I had altered. My white shirt had once been a large tablecloth. My shoes were leather, goatskin that is, with raw rubber soles ever ready to abrogate their assigned duty. In my back trouser pocket were a few sheets of paper, six inches in width, while in my shirt pocket were six sharpened pencils standing upright.

Surprisingly, when going down to the lower level of the floor to take my place at the front of the room, I wasn't at all nervous. My heart wasn't pumping, my blood wasn't racing; I knew that everything would be all right. On both sides of the aisle I traversed were rows of chairs placed at three to six foot intervals. At the very front my fellow students and I came to a table along which were four sturdy-looking chairs of the same style on which the representatives sat. Before taking my seat I first turned toward my left, in the direction of Saikoo Sikikan, who was standing stiffly in front of his chair, and bowed to him in Japanese fashion. I then walked back along the table and toward the other side of the room where the session's chairman, Soekarno, was seated. I bowed again, then turned right and returned to my work station.

I performed this little ceremony as best I could, highly conscious that this was the start of my working career, a one-time event never to happen again. During the course of that first day, groups of four students worked for ten-minute stints on a rotational basis. After ten minutes of stenogram we would return to the classroom to transcribe the stenogram in Roman letters and then wait for the next stint to begin. Within two months we stenography students were, in effect, assistants to the Chuoo Sangi-in.

In the ninth month of our course, Hasnah Sutan Diatas and I were asked to do some extracurricular stenographic work for Muhamad Yamin, the poet, orator, and politician, who was scheduled to give a four-part lecture on Diponegoro, the Javanese rebel prince, at the Keimin Bunka Shidoosho Building. In total, the lecture was eight hours. Taking notes in stenogram for two hours proved to be nerve-racking work but by the time my course finished, *Diponegoro* was published as a book.

Though I was given a complimentary copy of the book, much more important to me was that at the age of nineteen I had actually contributed to the book's publication. I was also given an honorarium of thirty rupiah with which I bought myself two shirts, one white and one light blue.

I saw *Diponegoro* as my diploma: I was a full-fledged stenographer. I felt good inside, filled with hope and belief in myself. When final examinations were administered, both Hasnah and I were accorded a speed of one hundred eighty syllables per minute and graduated as second-class stenographers.

With our diplomas in hand we returned to Domei. Hasnah, being a Middelbare Handelschool graduate, was immediately given a desk in the editorial section, while I was sent back to being a typist with no increase in my salary at all.

With what seemed to be little chance for job promotion I began to feel frustrated working at Domei. In their defense, Domei's management was probably frustrated with me as well because of my relatively low educational level and my ignorance of foreign languages. Further disgruntlement was caused by an additional task assigned to me—that of teaching trainee stenographers for the agency. It's not that I was assigned too many students; it's that not a single one of them could write a proper Indonesian sentence.

Then I was given a new job: to prepare a detailed chronology of the Sino-Japanese War. But before I could finish the chronicle, my task was terminated. I was assigned to work in the clipping section but, soon thereafter, I was moved to archives where I began to spend my days perusing newspapers, separating their articles by classification, cutting them out and pasting them in the hundreds of folders that lined the archive's shelves. After I had achieved some degree of mastery in this work, the job began to bore me. Fortunately, I was then assigned to assist one of the senior journalists in his work, which turned out to be a learning experience that taught me interview techniques.

My longing for a better education led me to register as a noncredit student at the Islamic Institute, a newly-opened school on Jalan Gondangdia. I signed up for courses on philosophy and sociology, the fee for which was twenty-five rupiah per course. Part of the money I raised by selling the shirts I had purchased with my fee from making a stenogram of the Diponegoro lecture. The rest I obtained through making a stenogram of another lecture by Yamin, this one on the historical figure of Gajah Mada.

Because my sociology teacher never showed up for class, I enrolled for Arabic instead, but the only reason I mention my time at the school here is because of the change that took place in my thinking as a result of an experience there.

One day, the school's secretary came to me to ask for my assistance: "You're a stenographer, aren't you?" he asked.

"Yes," I told the man.

"Then take down for me the radio bulletin on housing affairs," he summarily ordered, as if I were his personal secretary.

It was not his words so much but the way he said them that caused me to leave the school with a lump of anger in my throat. "What had I become?" I asked myself. Whether inadvertently or not, the man had made me realize that a stenographer is a technician, little more than a skilled servant, which is something I never wanted to be. Yet with my vocational training and my status as a class-two stenographer I had, it seems, begun my working career as a slave.

For the first time I realized that I was not rebelling against the system that had placed me in a position I didn't want to be in. I suddenly remembered my longing to be free, to do the things I wanted to do, without having to concern myself with other people's wishes or having to swallow my disgust at being forced to kowtow to other people's demands.

A change was taking place in me. I was becoming an individualist. And though Jakarta might have been the right place for me, I was not (or at least not yet) the right person for Jakarta. All I could feel was frustration and unchanneled energy. If I were to clear my mind and formulate plans for my future life, I knew I would have to leave.

I submitted a letter of resignation to my supervisor, but found no response, then sent another to Matano, which went unanswered too. I knew that I had a moral debt to Domei to work for a full year following completion of my stenographic course but the agency was bridling my aspirations. It was a debt I was no longer willing to pay. I then sent another letter to my supervisor, but again got no reply.

During the Occupation, leaving the service of the Japanese without permission was equivalent to cutting off one's own head, literally as well as figuratively. That's what I imagined would happen to me if I didn't leave Jakarta and so, without an official letter of resignation from Domei, I left the city and traveled across Java to Blora.

From my hometown I then went to Kediri and on to Ngadiluwih where I walked southward to the isolated village of Tunjung. There I stayed at the home of my late aunt, my father's younger sister, and my uncle, the latter being the former village chief, who had also recently passed away. Like my mother before them, they had left behind a number of young children. At night I'd watch over my cousins as they slept, curled up next to one another on a large wooden sleeping platform with only gunny sacks as their blankets.

The poverty I saw there should not have come as a surprise to me. On my trip across Java I had seen people wearing clothes made from burlap and thin sheets of rubber. Even in Banyuwangi, where there was a surplus of rice production, people were wearing sarongs made of woven bamboo. Wherever they went they carried with them their roll of bamboo around their bodies. But what I was seeing in Tunjung was my cousins, my own family.

Behind the house was a coconut grove and a fish pond. At the back of the house were tools for making palm sugar. The region's slightly sandy soil was fertile from the eruptions of Mount Kelud. My cousins were living surrounded by an abundance of food. Why were they destitute? I could only blame the Japanese.

The village was a peaceful and tranquil place. No one there knew that I had run away from my work with the Japanese. Though I made the occasional visit to neighboring villages of Kandat and Paré, I spent most of my time in Tunjung thinking over the experience I had gained during the past three and a half years of Japanese Occupation.

I couldn't help but admire the Japanese for having broken the centuries-old colonial chains that had kept Southeast Asia bound to the French, the British, and the Dutch. As if Dai Nippon Teikoku, the kingdom of Greater Japan, were really a heavenly power, it had only to exhale a single breath to blow the past away. With my own eyes I had seen vanish in an instant the nobility, authority, and respect that had once been accorded to Western people in the land of my birth. As with many of my fellow Indonesians I had initially held great hope for the freedom from colonization that our "older brother" brought to us. But as with many others, my feelings had turned to disgust when I gained the awareness, knowledge, and understanding that Japan was just another colonizer, one that was even greedier and less civilized than previous ones. At the Chuoo Sangi-in I myself had taken down in my notes Japanese promises of freedom "at a later day," a day that was far too long in coming.

From the news I'd learned even before leaving Domei, it was difficult to conceal the fact that Japan was facing growing pressure despite the continued and thunderous cries of glorious Japanese victories. In the Pacific, Allied forces were advancing on the Solomon Islands and the Philippines. At home, the oil production centers of Kalimantan, Borneo, and Sumatra were now targets for American B-29 bombers. Several times they had flown over Jakarta but the Japanese anti-aircraft artillery was not powerful enough to reach them. In East Java the Allies had begun to upset the ground transportation system. Now, about the only cargo on many of the trains between Malang, Kediri, and Surabaya were bullet-riddled corpses.

Hunger ruled the people and uprisings by farmers in West Java and the Peta militia's rebellion in East Java were just two signs of growing unrest. Meanwhile, in West Papua, North Sulawesi, and Aceh, uprisings against the Japanese had resulted in rebel victory. In Java, however, the Japanese continued to track and hunt down anyone they considered to be their enemy.

Anyone with a discriminating intelligence could see that Japan was now in a defensive position, that all initiative was in the hands of the Allies. Japan's battlefront was too vast, with fighting units spread over an immense geographical distance. The Japanese military had overextended itself. The Japanese authorities called for Indonesia's young men to join Heiho and Peta, the civil defense and militia units they had established; but this, too, was evidence of the diminished pool of "home-grown" soldiers on which the Japanese army could depend for reinforcements. However, the death penalty doled out to those Peta soldiers who rebelled in Blitar made it equally clear that the Japanese were very averse to placing their trust in an Indonesian army. Everyone sensed that the downfall of Japanese military would come someday but few people, myself included, suspected that it would come as soon as it did.

The date was August 23, 1945, and in Tunjung news spread rapidly through the village that soldiers from the area were now returning, each of them with a bag of rice. Their weapons had been taken from them and they had been ordered not to return to their units.

I quickly made my way on foot to Ngadiluwih where I first heard the news that Indonesia was now free. In Kediri this news was manifested in the multitude of red-and-white national flags flying over the city. On seeing the Indonesian national flag I remembered again the promise that the Japanese had announced at the Chuoo Sangi-in. But then I learned Indonesian independence had not been a gift from Japan, that on August 17 Soekarno and Hatta had proclaimed independence of their own accord.

I went to Surabaya. On the train all the passengers said that since the proclamation of independence the Allied Forces had stopped attacking the trains. Surabaya was completely calm; there seemed to be almost no change at all, except for the national red-and-white flags flying everywhere. I continued my journey to Blora where, at the Piroekoenan pool hall, I watched a play about Japan's oppression of Indonesia, which had ended the day independence was proclaimed. Sitting there in that hall I felt myself to be out of touch. There were no newspapers to read and no radio stations to listen to. Nothing seemed to have changed in my hometown. I needed to experience this new state of independence. I gathered together my few pieces of clothing and at the very first opportunity made my way back to Jakarta and to a fate that was just as uncertain as the first day I walked into Domei.

FOR BETTER
OR FOR WORSE

(A Letter to Anggraini)

Today, July 13, 1975, I received your letter—or postcard, rather, since that's all the authorities will allow you to send—that you sent from Jakarta on March 19, 1975. Thank you for your birthday greetings and accept my prayers for a long life and lasting strength.

I'm sure you're wondering what I have to say about your first letter and your comments regarding the relationship between a child and her stepmother. Let me begin by saying that I believe it's almost instinctual for a stepmother to resent or dislike her stepchildren and for stepchildren to feel the same way about their stepmother. But I also believe that this instinct, if it is one, can be overcome through education. People can learn *not* to dislike—and not just your stepmother, for instance, but you as well.

Let me also say, right here and now, it's not true that your stepmother broke up my marriage with your mother. If that's what you think, you're wrong, and if you've accepted that or another explanation from someone else, you must rid yourself of that impression. The simple truth is your mama was never completely happy, never completely satisfied with me. The same thing can be said for me. At the time I moved out of our home on Kebon Jahé Kober I went to your grandfather and in all due humility officially returned your mother to him. I gave your grandfather a letter in which I outlined the reasons for my decision. The contents of that letter will not change, and neither will the words nor the meanings found therein. You may study the letter yourself if your mother thought it valuable enough to save.

You are twenty-two years old and therefore mature enough to comprehend the nature of our problem. But let me go back and start at the beginning . . .

After I stopped working for Domei, the Japanese news service, I left Jakarta and traveled around Java, spending much of my time in Kediri, East Java. After learning about the declaration of independence I immediately returned to Jakarta and enlisted in the People's Defense Force or Badan Keamanan Rakyat for which I served as a press officer. It was in that position that in 1946 I first saw your mother. I was stationed in Cikampek, outside of Jakarta, and she had come to the camp to sing for the men in service. Watching her as she sang in the open-air *pendopo* at the office of the district chief, the aspect that most attracted me to her was her physical well-being. She was a solid-looking woman with good posture, carrying herself in a confident and assured manner. I, on the other hand, just a lieutenant in the Indonesian Army, was pale and skinny as a rail. (At the time I'd been suffering from a stomach ailment for almost two months and hadn't been able to eat more than a couple spoons of rice each meal.) Furthermore, I was extremely timid, a nervous sort of person, which might help to explain why I was a chain-smoker too.

Not having yet recovered from the physically detrimental effects of the Japanese Occupation, I dreamed of having a wife who was strong, healthy, and brave. Your mother, who was tall and bold—so unlike my own mother, who was a small, thin, and wan-looking woman—met those requirements.

That first time I saw her I never did get up the nerve actually to introduce myself to her, but thereafter I often pictured her, she of the round face and large eyes. In the Dutch-language magazines of the time I'd often see pictures of American and European film stars, and their eyes were always so large, not at all like Indonesian eyes, not in the least like my mother's or father's eyes. Ever since I was a child, I'd thought large eyes to be more aesthetically pleasing; I wasn't attracted to the mongoloid features of my own race. And so it was your mother's eyes, with their hint of mixed blood, that enchanted me, though she herself, surrounded by narrow-eyed people as she was, often tried to hide them behind clear-glass spectacles.

A few months went by before I came to learn that your mother lived in a housing complex not far from my own lodgings and that sometimes she even came to bathe at a well outside my house. (Cikampek wasn't linked to the Jakarta municipal water system at the time and during the dry season water was scarce.) It was at that well I next ran into her again, but on that occasion, too, I didn't introduce myself.

On July 21, 1947, I was arrested by the Dutch military for possessing anti-Dutch political documents and was put in Bukitduri Prison in Jakarta. There, for the next year or so, I had very little contact with the outside world, but in late 1948 the Dutch authorities began to allow the prison's political prisoners to receive outside visitors—but only women; no males were allowed. And so it was that young women who sympathized with the Republican cause began to visit the political prisoners being held in the prisons of Dutch-occupied Jakarta. I was one of the fortunate recipients of their beneficence. Altogether eleven young women visited me, one of whom was your mama. You can imagine my delight the day she came to call on me. I didn't know her name—it was Arfah Iljas, as I then learned—but I certainly hadn't forgotten her face.

Each week thereafter she came to visit and, finally, I proposed to her, but on the condition that she "teach me to love her." My words angered her, but I didn't know what else to say. I didn't know the meaning of love between a man and a woman. I had never witnessed such a thing when I was growing up, neither at my parents' nor at my neighbors'. The love I knew was from books and, speaking honestly, I knew that it wasn't love I felt when I began to get to know your mother. Maybe it was my taciturnness that made her accept my proposal but, regardless of the reason, from that Sunday onward, whenever she came to the prison, she'd bring with her some kind of gift for me: food, cigarettes, writing paper. I wrote a great deal at Bukitduri. As you know it was there that I wrote my first published novel, *The Fugitive*.

Following the Renville negotiations between representatives of the Indonesian Republican forces and the Netherlands, one group of political prisoners after another began to be released; in Jakarta I was among the last nine people set free. This took place on December 12, 1949. Upon our release we were greeted by a representative of the Committee for Political Victims.

Because I had no place to go I was assigned lodgings at a warehouse under control of the Committee on Pegangsaan Timur. When I telephoned your mother that day she sounded so happy; she could hardly believe I was free. She immediately invited me to her house to meet her parents.

I wasn't just happy that day; I was ecstatic because there was now no doubt that the Dutch would recognize the sovereignty of the Republic of Indonesia. I also felt confident. I was a young nationalist, twenty-four years of age, whose works were beginning to circulate in the free world. For every short story I wrote, I received an honorarium of seventy-five guilders, enough money to buy five good shirts at the time. Even before I was freed your mother had begun to handle my writing fees, saving the money to buy the furniture that we would need after we got married.

I was a young man with a brilliant future ahead of me—at least that's what I thought. I saw myself as having boundless energy to write and also that, through my writing, I could relieve the pressure of my soul's upheavals, the personal suppression, and unspoken pain, as well as chart the dreams my lack of self-worth had not permitted me to explore.

There, I said it, I've told you my major weakness: my inferiority complex and a lack of self-worth stamped so deeply inside me that I thought I would never emerge from the abyss of repression. I was the proverbial snail who, when meeting something foreign or strange, immediately retracts into its shell. But at that point I had reason to believe my life had begun to change. People were reading my writings. And as my former cowardice vanished I began to feel like a new person, with my future in my own hands. Even so, I still hesitated when the driver from the Committee pulled up and stopped outside of Kebon Jahé Kober, the narrow street leading to your mother's home. I stepped out of the Committee's station wagon and stared down the lane for what seemed an interminable time. From the wide avenue on which the automobile was parked, the lane looked forbidding. At the end of the lane a boy of about twelve was hanging, bare-bottomed, from the edge of the drainage canal as he tried to relieve himself.

"Do you want me to wait?" the driver inquired.

"No, thank you very much."

As the station wagon moved away I stepped into the lane. The young boy I'd just seen served as a symbol for the entire lane and the drainage canal running between it and the wall of the European cemetery. I wasn't accustomed to such filth. What kind of lives did the people of this place lead that could keep them from seeing or prevent them from doing something about the sorry state of their surroundings? How did they see the world? I had no answers to my questions. I was completely new to this world.

Trying not to hold my hand over my nose, I walked to the end of the lane where it turned and, not far from the corner, located your mother's small home to which a *warung* was attached where neighbors could purchase their daily household needs. Next to that was a makeshift structure serving as a verandah for the house. I was shocked by the state of my surroundings—I had no idea that your mother lived in such an environment.

Your mother greeted me amiably and I returned the good cheer. After two and a half years of prison and forced labor, this was the first time that I was meeting your mother as a free man. She introduced me to your grandfather, a polite and reserved man, tall and healthy-looking as well, but already showing traces of silver in his hair. Then I met your grandmother, a large-boned woman with a round face just like your mother's. The atmosphere in the house was one of welcome and openness. Both the house and the furniture in it showed that the family was not well-off but, as I had never been taught to look down on poverty and was not afraid of being poor, I quickly put aside my thoughts of the drainage canal and miserable surroundings. It had not been that many hours since I left prison. Now I was in the free world among free people.

Three days later I was living in your mother's home. Your grandparents didn't object to my presence but did suggest that we marry quickly. Because in those first few days of freedom I had collected enough money for a wedding celebration and had already purchased a gold necklace as the bride price, I had no objection.

Thanks to the intercession of Dr. G. J. Resink, a "progressive" Dutchman who supported Indonesian independence and gave me the encouragement to write while I was in prison, manuscripts of the books I had written at Bukitduri were in the hands of several publishers.

Prior to our wedding I paid a visit to the offices of *Merdeka* where I met one of the paper's editors, a man who had been one of my teachers in junior high school. He immediately said to me, "Congratulations on receiving first prize!"

"First prize for what?" I didn't know what he was talking about. He then told me that my manuscript for *The Fugitive* had won first prize in a writing contest sponsored by Balai Pustaka, the government publishing house.

I didn't know what to say. I had once asked Professor Resink—or "Han" as his friends called him—about the fate of that particular manuscript but he told me that he had long ago turned it over to H. B. Jassin, Indonesia's foremost literary editor. But when I asked Jassin about the manuscript he confessed to knowing nothing about it. I assumed, therefore, that it had been lost.

"I've never liked contests and have never participated in one," I confessed to my former teacher.

"Nonetheless, you must stop by at Balai Pustaka," he told me.

A few days later I went to Balai Pustaka and there I met writers whose names I had known only from a distance, in prison. Face-to-face with them, I learned that they were not gods, and was surprised to find myself being able to speak freely with them. As if by some magic my sense of inferiority had disappeared; I had entered their circle and they greeted me as a friend, as if I were a peer.

I learned that I had indeed been awarded first prize in the Balai Pustaka novel-writing contest. H. B. Jassin had only pretended not to know what happened to the manuscript. In fact, he himself had submitted the manuscript on my behalf and had said nothing to me about it because he wanted to surprise me with the news.

In some ways the news made me feel small, as if it had diminished my self-respect—not because of my participation in a contest, but because the contest had been sponsored by Balai Pustaka the state-owned publishing house which, at that time, was still under Dutch control, and not under the control of the new government of the Republic of Indonesia.

The monetary prize was one thousand guilders, the largest amount of money I had ever received in my life.

On Friday, January 13, 1950, your mother and I were married.

When I met your mother she was working as a telephone operator at the Central Telephone Office in Gambir and was what we called a "cooperator," a person who worked for the colonial administration. Not long before our marriage she was transferred from the central office to the State Palace to work at the switchboard there. After we were married I asked her to leave the job. She assented on the condition that I find a job. I began to look for work and was offered numerous positions but their salaries were generally no larger than the honorarium paid for a single short story.

Though your mother and I had an inkling about our respective shortcomings prior to our marriage, it was only after we were husband and wife that our personal character faults became all too evident. I was a person unable to either give or take orders. Your mother was a person who liked to pout. Whenever we had something to discuss, instead of dealing with the problem she would seek a haven with her parents. Marriage is not just a matter of love or loving. It is a legal tie, a bond of obligation. And if the husband and wife are able to perform their duties to the best of their abilities, then everything will be all right. Marriage is a noble and respectable institution. And I had long ago promised myself that I would be—that I "must be"—a better husband than my father had been.

Another one of my faults was constantly comparing my wife to my mother, using my mother's qualities as the standard. Unfortunately, the simple fact is your mother didn't share the same qualities; in terms of education and personal capabilities, your mother's level was far below mine. Your mother hadn't graduated from high school. Even so, it wasn't right for me to compare her with my mother. I might not have known her well before we got married, but she was my wife, my helpmate whom I had chosen of my own volition.

From the job offers I received, I chose the one from Balai Pustaka and became the company's editor for modern Indonesian literature. This was such a grand-sounding and impressive title, but I myself had no idea what "modern literature" was supposed to be. I had read few world literary classics, much less studied them in any depth.

May 1, 1950 was my first day of work and upon my return home, even before I could tell of my experiences, I was handed a telegram: My father was on his deathbed. After borrowing money from Han, your mother and I immediately set off for Central Java.

In Blora I found myself in charge of making arrangements for the funeral. In that regard I believe I did everything I could do, to the best of my abilities, as a final offering for my father. The anger I had once felt toward him as a result of his treatment of and behavior toward my mother was forgotten.

My father's death came only five months after my release from prison. Everything was happening so fast. I was married and your mother and I were trying to start a life for ourselves. But now standing before me were my siblings, several of whom were still young and living in the family's ramshackle home. Another, my sister Koenmariatoen, was suffering from tuberculosis.

By the time we returned to Jakarta I was in a foul and bitter mood. The hope and pride I carried with me from prison had been deflated and I was once again my former self, a person lacking in self-confidence and easily given to depression.

The young nation's economy was in dire straits and with the value of money falling fast, life's difficulties started rising. Your mother and I argued frequently and I was often ill, taking to bed at least twice a month. My salary from Balai Pustaka was meaningless, and fees paid to me for the miscellaneous articles I published were less than a third of what they'd been when I was in prison. Many publishers treated my submissions as unsolicited contributions for which they need not pay. I seemed to be working day and night. A fellow writer warned me that this would be harmful for my career. But I didn't care. I was a madman with my work, a volcano spewing lava. Another writer said to me, "Pram, you're not writing anymore; you're shitting!" I didn't care. All I wanted was a reasonable life for myself and my family.

The numerous books I had purchased between 1945 and 1950 for the purpose of study—history, philosophy, economics, and literature from a wide variety of countries—remained untouched, lined up in neat rows in my bookcase.

I became irritable, easy to anger, and easy to fly off the handle. At work I began to acquire the reputation of being temperamental. I knew that my emotional ups and downs were affecting my judgment of the manuscripts I was assigned to read, but didn't know how to gain control of myself. I was floating, a piece of driftwood at sea.

One day I received an invitation requesting my presence at an international peace conference to be held in Zagreb. Why I had been shown such an honor, I was at a loss to understand. Although I wasn't able to attend the conference I did submit an address and when I received the conference bulletin I was flabbergasted to see my address printed alongside that of Eleanor Roosevelt, the world's most famous woman.

Before I could digest the meaning of this attention shown to me, my short story "Blora" was published simultaneously in English in

Indonesia and in Dutch in *Orientie*. Soon afterward, Spanish and German translations also appeared.

Because of the atmosphere of the time, because of the mood I was in, I didn't feel proud of these achievements. Instead, I felt suspicious. The publication of my works abroad was not, as I saw it, a barometer for the quality of my work but rather an indicator of the level of international curiosity toward the new country of Indonesia.

The more articles that appeared about me—and now I was being mentioned on the radio, too—the more suspicious I became. I thought my sudden rise to fame to be completely out of proportion to my talents. In my eyes Pramoedya Ananta Toer was a very young and very green writer only a few months into his literary career, unworthy of such fanfare.

Following the release of my novel *Guerrilla Family* in 1950, Professor A. Teeuw, the eminent Dutch literary scholar, published a very positive review of the book in the newspaper *Nieuwsgier*. Even that did not make me drop my guard and though I admit to clipping articles about myself and reviews of my books, I did this not to nurture fame but to try to see myself through the critical vision and assessment of others.

Despite the growing success of my literary career, most of my time was spent doing hack work. I was writing only to fill my plate with rice. Economic conditions forced me into that role. I worked nonstop—when watching films, doing woodwork, sitting alone, eating, bathing, even when in bed dreaming, it seemed. I knew this was detrimental to my health; in photographs from that time I look emaciated, as thin as I had been at the end of the Japanese Occupation.

My typewriter, the tool of my trade, was begging for forgiveness. I had purchased my portable six months earlier for the equivalent of my fee for three short articles. Now not even thirty articles would fetch me the same machine. Time and again, late at night, your mother would remind me to go to bed, but my typewriter was a siren whose call I couldn't ignore.

After the death of our father my three siblings from Blora, all of whom were in junior high school or senior high school, had moved to Jakarta. I had warned them, "All you'll get here is food and a roof over your heads. You yourselves will have to pay for your school fees, clothing, and other needs." Nonetheless, they were three more mouths to feed.

I also had to buy medicine for my sister Koenmariatoen, which was very expensive and hard to come by. Through connections of her husband, who was also suffering from tuberculosis, we did finally manage to find a place where she could be treated, at the Ngawen Sanatarium in Salatiga. But then he died and she, too, not long afterward.

Before my father died I had promised to finance the restoration of the family home but, due to rampant inflation, the estimated cost, including materials and wages, proved to be far off the mark, and the actual cost was ten times higher than had been anticipated.

On top of all this, Balai Pustaka was becoming a less and less tolerable place for me to work, even though it was a central meeting place for Indonesian and foreign writers and artists.

I write all of this not as an excuse for myself but to clarify the situation by putting my behavior in context. I contend that anyone who can function without an understanding of her surroundings must either be a god or an animal.

As I mentioned before, because of the situation we were in your mother and I fought often. While she tried to avoid resolution, I attempted to assuage her disgruntlement and dissatisfaction with me in the only way I knew how: by buying her gifts. This cycle repeated itself over and over again.

The root of almost every argument was my position and pursuant responsibilities as the oldest child in my family, but I didn't see that I had a choice in the matter. My siblings needed help. The family home had to be maintained. I saw its restoration as a symbolic offering on the part of a child to his parents. It was there my brothers and sisters had been born, and there, too, that my parents had taken their final breaths.

With all the pressures bearing down on me—the bureaucracy of Balai Pustaka, my personal difficulties at home, my sense of honor to my parents—within a period of only one and a half years my black head of hair turned to salt and pepper.

A respite from this stifling atmosphere came with the birth of our first child, your sister Ros. She was a healthy baby, resembling your mother in almost every feature. To help alleviate the pressure I was feeling, I left my job at Balai Pustaka and began to work out of home, which thereafter became a popular stopping place for writers, both young and old. At around that same time I and a number of fellow writers issued what became known as the "Gelanggang Testimonial" and established an organization by that same name. The purpose of both was to espouse and promote the ideal of universal humanism. Unfortunately, I was appointed secretary of the organization, thereby dooming it to failure as a result of my incompetence in running things.

At the national level, economic, political, and social conditions were on the decline. The country was rife with domestic unrest and civil disorder. Break-away movements threatened the country's unity; the various kinds of criminal acts associated with economic and social unrest threatened people's lives. There was rampant profiteering among government officials. Masses of veterans were now demanding that the government repay them for their service to the country. As best I could I stayed out of the fray. All I wanted to do—all I *could* do—was write. Not that I published everything I wrote; I believe I destroyed more writings than what made it into print.

In 1953 our second child, your sister Ety, was born. I was twenty-eight years old. That same year I received an invitation from Sticusa, the Foundation for Cultural Cooperation between the Netherlands, Indonesia, and Surinam, to spend a year in Holland. This was a great honor but it caused me tremendous anxiety. I could read Dutch but my spoken and written skills were virtually nonexistent. But then I recalled my mother's hope that I would someday study in Europe, and when I was told that I could bring along my wife and children, too, the offer was clinched. Even if I weren't going to Europe to study, I assumed some good would come out of it.

. The four of us—your mother and I, Ros and Ety—left for the Netherlands in June on the *Johan van Oldenbarneveldt*. Onboard that ship I felt like I was on holiday with nothing to trouble my mind. I had left my three siblings safely in the care of your kind and trustworthy grandparents, though I did promise that I would send some articles to help support them.

This was my first time on a sailing ship and I found it extremely pleasurable. I used my days onboard to reassess the past three years of my life. The invitation for me to visit Europe seemed almost like a command for me to begin to think more positively about myself.

When our ship entered the Ij Canal in Amsterdam, Dutch immigration authorities came onboard to check the passengers' papers. We took out our passports, my own as well as your mother's, which contained pictures of your two sisters as well, but when the officer checked them he discovered that your mother's passport did not have in it a stamped entry permit for the Netherlands. That caused a little bit of an uproar but we were finally allowed to disembark.

We were given a place to live on Oranje Nassau Laan in Amsterdam. When we arrived at our home-to-be we found sitting inside a number of gentlemen, members of Sticusa's board, including the director himself, who had come to welcome me. I was so stupid I didn't know who they were and was too embarrassed to ask. Why would bigwigs come to welcome Pramoedya Ananta Toer? It wasn't until after they'd gone that I found out who they were. I still blush to think of the incident.

Having arrived in the Netherlands in the summer it was somewhat easier for us to acclimate ourselves. During the day the temperature ranged between sixteen and eighteen degrees Celsius. We laughed about it, but even at those "high" temperatures we sometimes turned on the heater. We were yokels in the city, with little knowledge of European ways, especially everyday life. From the time of the Japanese Occupation I had lived in relatively deprived conditions. Now I was in a world where people didn't have to think about where the money was going to come from for the next meal, a difference I had felt immediately upon setting foot on ship. Of course this did nothing to change the fact that we ourselves were yokels.

Amsterdam turned out to be a clean and lovely city, not noise-filled and polluted like Jakarta. Being there made me especially pleased because your mother, with her parents being so far away, had only herself to depend on. I had to applaud her for it turned out she was not timid or hesitant in the least. I was pleased to see her able to take care of the children herself, and to do the cooking and shopping. I became convinced that our stay in the Netherlands would help to improve our married life. Ten thousand miles from Jakarta, there was no grandmother around to cook for or to bathe the children.

Then a problem, that same old problem, arose in me: my inferiority complex, which always chose to emerge when I was around people whose education was far better than my own. It also showed itself when I was with Dutch people, Indonesia's former masters and enemies. I didn't seem to know where to stand with them or how to treat them. I was prejudiced and constantly suspicious of them. When around them I was always tense, as if walking on eggshells. My suspicions of them deepened when it turned out the oral promises of assistance that Sticusa had given us in Jakarta did not jibe with reality. My grant was insufficient to meet our needs. We were forced to buy the heavier clothes that we needed on credit. We also had to pay from our own funds the rent of our house as well as the cost of utilities. We lost about one quarter of our monthly allowance as a result. This made things especially hard because, unaccustomed as we were to eating Dutch food, your mother prepared Indonesian meals, the cost of which was much higher.

Most of Sticusa's senior officers had formerly served their government in Indonesia—as district officers, estate managers, cabinet officials, and so on. To their credit, they were people who knew both Indonesia and its people but, on the negative side, they often seemed to act like teachers toward Indonesians. Perhaps they meant well, but it made me uncomfortable. Not everyone is willing to play the student's role or immediately agree to what his supposed teacher suggests.

I can't say that the other Indonesian grantees experienced the same difficulties; not even your mother did. I seemed to be the only one who was burdened by a sense of inferiority and felt unable to act happy and carefree. Not long after my arrival in the Netherlands, Sticusa held a symposium on modern Indonesian literature, the first one ever on the subject. I felt myself fortunate to attend but, still trapped in the cell of my inferiority complex, I didn't have the nerve to raise my voice; I could only listen.

This symposium was significant for me not because it was the first time that such a meeting of leading scholars had been held and not because it was the first time I was interviewed by the Dutch press, but because it was the first time I ever attended a cultural gathering in the true sense of the word. For the first time in my life I saw people debating differences without friction; I saw that differences in opinion need not cause an argument. So this was the way that healthy minds sought solutions! All these prominent people and they were able to discuss issues that perhaps had no direct relevance to themselves.

My friend Han was one of the symposium organizers and when he was to return to Indonesia, I escorted him to the airfield where he introduced me to the former foreign minister of the Netherlands. It was he, if I'm not mistaken, who gave the order for the so-called Second Police Action in 1948, which resulted in the deaths of so many fellow Indonesian soldiers. What I felt when shaking his hand that night might, I imagine, be likened to what Pierre Do Dinh felt upon first sight of the Arc de Triomphe in Paris: here he was, a child of the colony, staring at the victory monument of a people who had once colonized his country.

On that cool night at Schipol Airport I didn't know how to feel and on my way home I couldn't stop asking myself why the emotional burden of past history weighed so heavily on me. Weren't we both free people now? Was I emotionally unbalanced? Was I irrational? Were my feelings due to my sense of inferiority with its admixture of racial and historical shame? I didn't see other people bowing beneath the weight of these problems. They walked and talked freely, as if not carrying that burdensome load. Objectively, I knew that I was wrong but at times the inner self is so confused it fails to listen to rational thought. How was I to put new order into my life? That was the question to which I had no answer.

When I wanted to think about such things I'd go alone to Vondelpark, a large and beautifully maintained park that was not far from our place. One of my visits took place on a beautiful summer day. Scattered about the park were people—numerous couples but also people alone like myself—taking pleasure in the fresh outdoor air. I was relaxing on a park bench when a young woman sat down beside me and began to talk. She was friendly in both speech and manner and gave the impression of being well educated. By and by she began to speak to me about French literature, a subject I knew little about. The refreshing thing about her was that she didn't act toward me like a teacher; she engaged me in dialogue. But most importantly, that meeting left me with a strong and indelible impression: that I was not a colonial underling, that Asians and Europeans are equal.

Our acquaintance developed into a friendship and when she invited me to her place I accepted with alacrity. From our conversations together and my personal interaction with her I came to understand that if anyone should have a complex it was not I, the Asian, but the Europeans for their centuries-old sin of colonial domination. Why then was it that this woman, this new friend of mine, showed no signs of suffering from such a complex?

From our conversations I concluded that everyone has some kind of "complex," regardless of whether he or she is aware of it or not, and that the greatest source of strength one can draw on in the process of self-formation is human interaction, and the lessons that are to be learned from such alliances. Further, as human interaction is a matter of choice, one must always be willing to weigh and evaluate one's relationships; one's psychological and historical burdens can actually be turned around to become our sources of strength, not of weakness. Unfortunately, my newfound knowledge, so easy to accept in the abstract, was not so easily put into practice.

Your mother didn't know about this relationship of mine and I felt no need to tell her about it. I had a happy home life. I could listen to a wide selection of fine European music. With my adorable little Baby Olivetti I could work as if I didn't know the meaning of fatigue. And I had the children to play with, too. Ros had already begun to speak Dutch and had made lots of friends. Troops of them would often show up at our house to play. Ety wasn't old enough to mimic her older sister but she was her own source of enjoyment for me. Your mother and I often went to see films and concerts, and we frequently took walks with the two girls. I write this now to make it clear that when we were in the Netherlands there was no tension or threat of separation between your mother and myself.

I had begun to resolve the financial difficulties resulting from the high cost of Indonesian meals by compiling broadcast texts for Radio Hilversum, preparing written materials for Sticusa, and checking Indonesian translations of Dutch-language materials that were to be published in Indonesia. I also did editing work for the bilingual journal *De Evenaar-Chatullistiwa*.

The only real difficulty I faced was the ongoing struggle within myself. No one knew what I was experiencing inside, no one except myself. Even your mother was unaware. I viewed it as a personal problem that I would have to resolve alone. This is why my relationship with that woman was so fortunate; it helped to give me back my self-confidence. It also stirred in me the desire to study and improve myself.

You were already in your mother's womb at this time and, toward autumn, for practical reasons, your mother and sisters preceded me home. Other Indonesians who had been in the Netherlands during this same period also left. And though I had begun to adapt to life abroad, the time after their departure was a lonely one for me. To fill my time I sat in on lectures, attended theatrical performances, visited museums, and made trips to other cities. All in all I was pleased with the development in my outlook toward life but most pleasing of all for me was that I had begun to believe in myself.

Autumn in the Netherlands, with its smell of rotting leaves, its barren trees, brisk winds, and falling temperatures seemed to have a positive boost on my mental and physical health. I grew stronger and put on weight. I felt unencumbered, with freedom of movement in both my body and soul. I was able to work longer hours, sometimes up to twenty hours at a time, something that would have been impossible at home. But, in the end, I had to leave, and on January 1, 1954, I boarded a KLM plane to fly home. While on a strictly social level I viewed my stay in the Netherlands as a failure, in psychological terms I felt that the trip had done wonders for me.

•

Jakarta was just as it had been when I left six months previously. The city's poverty and, more particularly, the stench of the drainage canal near our house tortured my senses.

The state of my financial affairs seemed to be as murky and as difficult to clean up as the canal. Up until that time royalties from my books published by Balai Pustaka had been my major source of income, but a decree by the Minister of Education and Culture turned the company, a state-owned venture beneath that ministry's authority, from a literary publisher into little more than a printing company servicing only the Ministry's needs. No literary titles were being produced, no royalties were being paid. To make matters worse, other literary publishers that had previously subsidized their operations through government printing orders were now, because of Balai Pustaka's virtual monopoly on State printing concerns, being forced to shut their doors.

In no time at all my financial position was more precarious than it had been prior to my six-month "vacation" in Holland. But it felt even worse. The Netherlands had shown me the beauty of an organized society where a person's skills are valued and where everyone has not just the right but the opportunity to earn an honest living. In this respect at least, Indonesia had learned far too little from Holland during their three hundred and fifty years together. Either the Netherlands was not too good a teacher or Indonesia was a lousy student.

There was for me the occasional windfall of income from writing fees, but otherwise I was buried under debt. Your mother began to demand that I sell the family home in Blora. I tried to convince her that the situation would not last forever and that someday we would build our own home—by this time I had in fact managed to buy a very small piece of land—but she was not to be coddled by my words.

Possibly as a result of my stay in the Netherlands, I now found it impossible to do hack work. But even more impossible was trying to put meals on the table without a salary or wage.

When my sister Oemi Syafa'atoen in Blora got married, I, being the oldest male in the family, was obliged to act as her legal guardian and to take responsibility for all other matters connected to her wedding. This was yet another financial hardship but, in retrospect at least, balancing that burden for me was an invitation from the district information office of Blora to give a public lecture during my stay there.

It was the first time I had spoken to an unknown audience and I was delighted when finding myself unafraid or too nervous to speak. Certainly there were shortcomings in my talk but at least I wasn't afraid. Instead I felt empowered, with the strength to relieve myself of burdensome emotions. Regardless of what other people thought about my debut performance as an orator, I saw it as a victory over my inner self.

Then you were born. Ros resembled your mother and Ety looked like mine, but you had your own special look. Maybe in shape you resembled your mother but you were still very different. The important thing is you were healthy.

As you might glean from what I've already written, you were born at a time when I was experiencing serious social and economic constraints but psychological clarity as well. Though you brought the two of us happiness, my life with your mother was deteriorating as she grew more and more demanding. One of her greatest complaints was about my siblings, all three of whom were still in school. She wanted them out of the house and put her demand in writing, which she then forced me to read to my sister Koesaisah, the oldest of the three.

Telling my siblings that they would have to move was a heartbreaking thing for me to do and I felt completely wretched for having to do so. They were still so young and immature. They were orphans. What sort of brother did I turn out to be?

Your mother also needled me for not working hard enough. "All you do is sleep. My parents even have to feed you." And as her criticism changed to ridicule our house became a hell for me. I began to avoid coming home and would stay out till late at night at the homes of friends. If I had no other place to go, I'd sit in the park until I fell asleep as I waited for late night to come. That our relationship was approaching a critical juncture became very clear when one day your mother asked me for a divorce. That first time I didn't answer her; I was still thinking of the promise I had made to myself that I would be a better husband and father than my own had been. How could this have happened? My father was a failure in those respects, and now my own wife thought the same of me. Also in my mind was the thought that a marital crisis is never just one person's problem. At the very least it concerns two people, and more, if there are children born of the union.

Then your mother ordered me out of the house. Though I felt humiliated, I still didn't do anything. I kept asking myself, "Is this as far as I've progressed? Is this all that my experience has brought me to?" Was I to be thrown out like a piece of trash into the drainage canal outside the house?

When your mother ordered me out of the house a second time, I truly began to feel offended; both my pride and self-respect were hurt. I saw that her attitude toward me was not that of a wife toward her husband. Yet she was my wife. And she was your mother, your natural mother, but in my eyes she had lost all worth. In my heart she was no longer my wife. Even if our marriage were not officially dissolved, I was no longer the man she had married. I was someone else now, a person with a different attitude. I found myself unable to forgive her. Never in my life had I suffered such an insult.

Be that as it may I still tried to save our marriage. Aside from everything else, I felt that I owed a large moral debt to your grandparents. I asked your grandfather's brother to intercede for me. I hoped that he might be able to dampen your mother's temper. I warned him, however, that if your mother tried to throw me out again, I would leave for good. As you can see from what I've written thus far, the deterioration of our marriage did not take place in the span of a day. That is the reason I've compiled this chronology for you. Ignorance of the process might lead one to what appears to be a justifiable stance, but in fact is a mistaken conclusion.

It was at this time, in this very uncertain period of my life, that I received an invitation to attend the Gunung Agung Book Week being held in Deca Park. There were many stands at the fair, most of them being tended by young writers but two by a pair of sisters whose names I learned were Nuraini and Maimoenah Thamrin. Both women were easygoing, attractive, and friendly.

I'm not leading up to an excuse now. Everyone is free to judge my behavior, even my children. In this I feel a father must be willing to stand up before the bench over which his children preside as judges. He must be willing to give them the facts they need to render their verdict. And so, my daughter, here I am. This is your father standing before you.

Because my relationship with your mother—our married life—was beyond repair I didn't hesitate to seek the acquaintance of the Thamrin sisters, especially the older one, Maimoenah. I was not going to waste my life in the doldrums simply because of an unhappy married life. After all, didn't I, too, have the right to a life?

Maimoenah Thamrin delivered me from a life of uncertainty. My initial impression of her was that she was a very beautiful woman. Her eyes were bright and friendly. She didn't laugh at me with my baggy corduroy trousers which hung from my body like a blanket on a clothesline. She simply asked why I was so thin and pale. In speaking with her I noticed that she had a birthmark on her neck, but I still found her lovely, and throughout my travels in later days I would never come across a woman as enchanting as she.

I didn't try to hide my growing relationship with Maimoenah, neither from your mother nor her family. If you look at the articles about our unfolding relationship that were published in *Buku Kita* and *Kentjana* in early 1955, it should be clear that I was not running from public scrutiny.

Maybe what you've heard all this time are rumors—there certainly were lots of them making their rounds at the time—but now I'm the one who is talking. I feel no guilt for my actions because I knew that my relationship with your mother was causing me to become unbalanced. I knew that unless I did something I would very soon drown in the well of self-destruction.

I can't say whether your great-uncle Matsani attempted to intervene with your mother on my behalf, but the situation certainly didn't change. In fact, your mother ordered me out of the house for the third time. This time I knew I had to go.

I went to the director of Gunung Agung to ask for a loan which he gave me, no questions asked. With that money I rented a house in Kebayoran Baru. The house was simple but clean and well maintained. I then went to my father-in-law to ask his permission to leave—I wasn't about to wait around to be thrown out another time.

"Have you found a place?" your mother asked straightaway.

"Yes," I told her, "in Kebayoran Baru."

"Then that house is for me."

And so I turned over the contract for the house to your mother, and helped to move her there, too. I remember the day she and I made our way to Kebayoran, along with you children and all our furniture too. She may have insulted me; she may have hurt me; she may have lost all my respect; but she was your mother, the mother of my children. And for me she was now just a woman with whom I shared a house. She was no longer my wife. Therefore, I continued my relationship with Maimoenah Thamrin. Then, one morning, your mother asked me for the fourth time to leave. And so that same day I left, taking with me my clothes, books, tools, type-writer, and my old Sparta motorcycle.

I went to your grandfather to officially return your mother to him. Because for me he had always been such a wise, kind, humble, and helpful man, this was something I found difficult. It was hard for me to say to him, "Today I return your daughter to you. Forgive me for being unable to be your daughter's husband."

I also gave him a written list of my reasons for leaving as well as the customary pronouncement of divorce, thereby barring the possibility of reconciliation between your mother and I. Suddenly remembering all the kindness that he had shown me, I began to cry, but even through my tears I could see there to be no other way.

"And the children?" he asked me.

"Your daughter will not allow me to take them," I answered.

And with that our five years of married life was over. When leaving your grandfather's house, your mother screamed at me, "You'll never find another woman who can take care of you for five years!"

Was she right? Was her judgment true? Was I really such a bad husband? I don't think it's my right alone to judge. My children, too, must have their say, especially you.

A passing thought when leaving your mother that final time was that she would never again have the chance to scratch my face. I'm not lying to you in saying that your mother was always one to maintain and keep her fingernails sharp. You were so small when I left, the only one of my three children with your mother whom I had so little chance to rock in my arms and play with. Perhaps you'll think of Yudi, the eighth of my children and your youngest half-sibling, who was only two months old when I went away in 1965 and whom I have not seen since. I hope that you will acknowledge it was not I who wanted to leave you. As you know from customary and religious law, children are their mother's until they come of legal age.

Do you remember the time after our divorce I came to your grandparents' house? I came there that time not because I wanted to reconcile with your mother, which I knew would be futile, but to see you.

About your mother, I no longer have anything to say. You know her better than I. She raised you, after all. Just remember that a child must maintain a critical attitude toward her parents in order that she herself might be a better parent, one who is wiser than the generation preceding her.

I write this letter to you on my fiftieth birthday. You are a woman now, not the baby that I left behind twenty-one years ago. You now can see for yourself whether another woman could take care of me for five years. This year, Maimoenah Thamrin will have taken care of me for twenty years, and served me not just in the figurative sense but in the literal sense as well. She never chased me from my home, never scratched my face with her nails. She accompanied me from the incredible poverty that marked the early days of our life together and stood by me through both sorrow and happiness. After I was kidnapped and then imprisoned in 1960 and 1961 she took care of me. After my arrest in 1965, she queued outside the Military Prison to see me almost every visitation day of that year. And now, as I enter my tenth year of exile, she continues to care for our children and to do whatever she can to help me.

She has never asked for a divorce. During my first year of imprisonment I once suggested that we divorce and she marry again. She was still young and beautiful. But she chose to remain the wife of Pramoedya Ananta Toer.

I write this letter on my fiftieth birthday, my half-century mark, as written testimony for my children in hopes that they will better know their father. I write this answer to your letter to ensure that my words and their meaning do not change. I have no time for gossip or for the rumors that you might hear. Just as a rumor grows fat from being repeated, so, too, it will waste away and die when ignored.

You are an educated young woman with a higher level of schooling than your father. As such, you should be able to hold in high respect the value of wisdom.

My final words are not for you alone, but for everyone. Ten years ago I was forced to leave Maimoenah Thamrin. Since that time she has raised your five younger siblings and put them through school without ever once complaining. There are not many women in the world like her. I don't know what will happen in the years to come, but this is how it has been for the past ten years. Is this a woman who deserves to be hated? Anyone who truly knows her must respect her.

It would give me incredible pleasure to be able to speak these words to you, but that is not possible. I can only write them down for you, not knowing if ever you will be able to read them. But if you read them, you will know that I answered your letter and that at least for once in my life I gave a full accounting of my actions to you.

For you I wish eternal happiness, safety, and prosperity. With love, from your distant father . . .

A HOME TO LIVE IN

(A Letter for Astuti)

On Saturday, March 4, 1972, I was handed an envelope, inside of which was a letter from my daughter Astuti, my fourth child, whose pet name is Tieknong. The letter was typed—I myself had taught her to type, six years earlier, when she was in third grade—and, at two letter-size pages in length, was the longest letter I had yet to receive from her. In her letter she told me about her classes at Pharmaceutical School and her desire to get ahead. She also asked how I was doing, what I was eating, and whether I was taking care of myself. Most touching was when she told me that she continues to wait for me to come home and that everyday she says to herself, "When Daddy comes home, I'll hug him as hard as I can. Then I'll finally be free of all my longing."

A letter is such a personal thing, but here, on Buru, it's a public possession, to be read and perused by anyone curious about a fellow prisoner's family. Letters circulate from hand to hand, from one barracks to another, forever producing a flood of tears in their readers. In this I know I'm not mistaken for I am not the only one who's easily overcome by a letter.

For me a letter from a child is testimony of his or her love for their father. But how am I to answer my daughter's letter? How am I to reply? What can I do except to pray for her health and safety and hope that all her dreams will someday be realized.

Silently I write to her a letter that, like so many before, will never ever be sent:

You remember, Tieknong, don't you, the time when you and your sisters came to Salemba Prison and you were sitting on a mat in the grounds? What year was that—1968? You weren't even out of primary school. Do you remember how I sat you on my lap and whispered something in your ear, and then you nodded your head in reply?

And now you're in junior-level Pharmaceutical School. Congratulations! You did so well on your tests. When I was in school I never got a "9" or a "10," which means that you have achieved something I never did. And I see from your letter that you already know that good grades alone are not enough, that true achievement also requires *ausdauer*, resilience—not just to maintain what you've already achieved, but to go further and achieve those things you've not yet mastered.

You said you had forty minutes to complete your examination and yet you finished it in only fifteen minutes? Why hurry so? Is that necessary? When hurrying to finish something one sometimes isn't careful, and to be a scholar one must always be careful. Being able to do a job quickly is good, but only so long as you can still do it with care.

Thank you for being proud of having a father like me. Your pride makes me feel worthy of being your father though, frankly, I don't know if I can any longer be said to be a good father for my children.

You also said that you'd like to be famous. That's fine but keep in mind that "fame" itself should not be a goal. Fame is a form of compensation for a job well done. If you do something for someone and that person likes what you have done, you'll have a good name in his eyes. Fame is something that one must take care in developing and maintaining. What I'm getting at is that fame is the result of hard work, and not something one should seek.

It's good that you've been made assistant representative for your class. It will give you a chance to learn how to organize and to work within an organization. I myself never had such an opportunity until I was older. As a result I became a loner, caring little about social life. One might even say that I was asocial, unable to mix with others.

Your teacher said that you'll be a success, and with that I completely agree. In a free Indonesia, success is promised to each and every child who works and studies hard, who is able to learn from experience, who has ideals, and who is brave and honest.

I'm also happy that you want to further your education, not just for a degree of course, but for the knowledge and scholarship that comes with it, and because of the quality of the work itself. A degree itself is no guarantee of quality; scholarship and quality are synonymous. And for you to become a scholar doesn't necessarily mean that your mother must finance your education. You can do it yourself. In the end, if a person is going to get ahead, she must be willing and able to pay her own way and to make her own progress. Success toward one's goal will come from within oneself; it is not a gift that others can give.

To be smart one must also be healthy, and sports is good for that. Sports promotes good blood circulation, a prerequisite for physical health. But when you take part in sports you must try to achieve a proper balance in physical training. A person who works hard but uses only certain parts of the body will suffer from not using her other parts. Sports gives your body resiliency and flexibility; a body that's stiff is like a brittle twig that will break when bent. Remember, there's little benefit in being smart if poor physical health prevents one from being able to put one's wits to good ends.

There is a connection between sports and life. The course of a person's life is determined by both brain and brawn. Because sports gives one the opportunity to improve the condition of one's body and mind, active participation in sports also means maintaining and improving the state of one's physical and mental health. Sports is exercise for both the body and the mind.

In ancient India people thought that the state of one's health was determined by blood circulation. If certain parts of one's body were ailing it was because those parts were afflicted by poor blood circulation. They also maintained that proper breathing and balance were essential to good health; it was this view that gave birth to yoga.

The point of all this is that when a part of the body is not used it will diminish or weaken in strength.

The relationship between studying and sports is very important, not only for good health and clarity of thought, but also the balance between physical and mental work. An imbalance between the two can result in illness.

When I was a boy I'd often see old people so stooped over that when they walked they had to use a cane. Those people had obviously never exercised when they were young. And the senility in those days—there seemed to be many more people then who were senile, meaning that when they were young they hadn't been properly trained to use their memories. At that time senility seemed to affect numerous middle-aged people as well. Many of them, too, never seemed to find a proper balance.

There are some people who even make smiling a sport. Can you imagine having to train yourself to smile? I'm not talking about the unconscious act of smiling. That's no exercise or sport. But people can train themselves to smile when they are weary or when they want to sleep. This is a form of conscious training that can help to relax one's muscles and nerves. A person might be able to fall asleep when she's tense or nervous, but she's never going to get a proper rest. For that she must be free of tension, and a smile can help to achieve that. Smiling settles the soul, and releases pent-up tension. In turn sports can help to turn people into optimists and to free one's soul from pessimism.

I'm very sorry that you've never received answers to the letters that you've sent to me. Please believe that I answer your letters, at least the ones that I receive. And even if you yourself don't write to me, I still write to you. You just have to keep in mind that there are times in life when a person is not his own boss or the master of his own condition.

I was very surprised to learn that you had received a photograph of me. During all the time I've been here I have never, to my knowledge, been photographed. Someone must have taken the photograph without me knowing it. And how did you come to hear my voice? Was it a recording, or on the radio, or on television? I can't imagine where it could have been. Nonetheless, I'm pleased to know that you were able to recognize your father's voice.

If there are houses in the picture, the location would be Wanapura because there's a group of houses there on stilts. It would be a nice place for a person to study. The air is clean and there's almost no pollution, except when it's time for burning chaff or the dried brush in a jungle clearing. In those times the air is probably dirtier than Jakarta's.

As for places to study, I guess any place can be good, even the outhouse. I knew one man who always wrote difficult words on the wall of the outhouse, which he would memorize when he was in there. In some cities in Europe, announcements are plastered on the walls of public toilets. People are sure to read them. A person doesn't necessarily need books to study, or to read or to write. If books aren't available and you have nothing to write with, you can still study, can't you? Watching people, observing and memorizing their actions, listening to them speak is also studying. Of course, no amount of study can guarantee that a person will be smart. Studying means gathering knowledge but being smart means knowing how to put that knowledge to use. The intelligent person is one who can formulate conclusions on the basis of his knowledge and experience. A resolute person is one who is both capable of making decisions and able to implement what decisions he has made.

You need not cry over the loss of your father. Don't be sentimental. That you know your father loves you should be enough. That I know you love your father is more than enough for me. You study now without your father's help. The fact is, I'd probably be of little help to you anyway. You're studying subjects that I never studied in school. I don't know anything about your field of study.

Do you remember when you first told me that you wanted to study chemistry? I cherished such hopes for you because I, too, had once loved the subject, even though I lacked the requisite knowledge to do well in it. I was first introduced to the subject when I was in sixth grade. I'd been given a chemistry book to read and I became absorbed by the text. Unfortunately, as soon as they started talking about formulae, that's when I got lost.

I'm surprised to find you still think about the time when I was taken away. It wasn't possible for you to be with me at that time; it would have been too dangerous. You saw what happened to the house, didn't you, how it had been wrecked? River stones gathered by the crowd from the adjacent lot, where they had been piled in preparation for the construction of a neighbor's home became a rainstorm that fell on our home's walls. No single person could have thrown stones that size. A catapult was needed for that. Your mother was wise enough to remove you from the house before that happened.

One stone alone was enough to break the front door to pieces. Thank God you weren't there when that storm hit. So, please, don't get emotional thinking about me. When you think about me it should be enough for you to realize that I constantly pray for your success. At the same time you should be aware that success doesn't fall from the sky; success comes from hard work, diligence, and constant improvement of oneself.

I was surprised to read that you had an operation and am thankful to know that everything went well. I am also grateful to learn that your mother has recovered from her bout of tuberculosis. It was friends who told me about the time your mother fainted when coming to bring me food; she herself never said a word. But then she had to go into the hospital for treatment and she was forced to tell me. Before she went in she came to say good bye. We were given permission to meet face-to-face. She started to cry when I told her, "Nothing is going to happen. Be strong. It's only fear that you have to worry about."

And, oh, how I did worry about her health, and that of you and your sisters. I hold on to the belief that there are still in this world a great many kind people willing to help their fellow man. And because that is so, people must learn to show their thankfulness by performing good deeds.

You're right in that I have aged rapidly these past few years. A person's face is a picture of both his inner and outer self. I think it would be more accurate to say that I am thin, very thin. At present I weigh only one hundred seventeen pounds, twenty-two pounds less than my normal weight. Your concern about my food and clothing is a sign of the love that a child feels for her father. I just said that there are many kind people in this world willing to help others. I believe that the number of truly rotten people in this world is very few. Much more common are people who, for reasons of ignorance, do not concern themselves with humanitarianism.

Your mother looks young. That makes me very happy. A youthful woman is a bouquet of harmony. Remember that always. Yes, I think about your mother a great deal, especially with all the kids she has to care for, and many of them so young. When I was taken away I had nothing left to give her because everything had been destroyed—all that we had gathered, little by little, from the time I became an adult, even before you were born. I recall how very difficult it was to make a living good enough to raise you and your siblings. Yet I had to leave her and you behind with no home, no money, no nothing.

You said that the rest of the kids and your mother, too, are in good health. Wouldn't you say then that this is a reflection of all that your mother has done and that her way of approaching life is one worth emulating? I trust your mother now as much as I always have, I will always believe in her.

I'd like to tell you a story, one about the relationship between your mother and I, and our life together in the time before and shortly after you were born.

I first met your mother in October or November of 1954 at a book fair sponsored by Gunung Agung Publishers. She was working at one of the stands. She had got the job because one of the company's managers, a man by the name of Kopetsky, rented a house from her father, Haji Abdillah Thamrin, just two houses to the right of your grandfather's house.

At the time I met your mother I was in miserable straits, both socially and economically. My life had reached a crisis point. For some reason, from the time I was a teenager, I had it in my mind that I would never live to be older than thirty and the way I lived my life was based on that idea. The thought exercised such power over me that by the time I was twenty-nine, in 1954, I was literally feeling death's arms beckoning me and preparing myself to take them in my own.

Meeting your mother and getting to know her regenerated my spirit for life. I suddenly felt that with her beside me I could live.

Fortunately, I didn't know your mother's family. Given my condition at the time, if I had known her father owned several houses, I probably would not have approached her for fear of being accused of being a fortune hunter. You see, I had nothing at the time, no hope at all. Even my health was poor. But when I met your mother it was as if there were no other people in the world but us. There was no guile in our relationship, no conditions; it was a simple and beautiful thing with no pretense at all.

I found the fact that your mother could accept me as I was to be a miracle. She was just coming into bloom. A woman so beautiful and bright as she, with a gleam in her eye, had every right to demand a good life for herself, yet she accepted me. To this very day I've never asked her why she would accept for a mate this thin, pale, rag-tag of a man with absolutely nothing to his name.

Because of your mother I changed my mind about dying. I now believed that I would live and be happy. This was not just the sentimental thought of a young man in love. The world had begun to show me its other, more pleasant, aspects. Pessimism had stepped aside for optimism's reign.

Your mother and I never talked about "love" as it's shown in films, but it wasn't too long before I came to know that people had begun to gossip about my relationship with her. (As you know, I was still married to my first wife at the time.) One person confided, "Being the respected writer that you are, you have to think about more than just yourself. As part of the public domain you should not set a bad example." Another man, a Christian minister, advised me, "Your influence on Indonesian youth is substantial; you must be careful with that influence."

All the things that people were saying were in fact just a polite way of telling me not to cause a scandal. While I was grateful for their concern, I myself had never held much stock in the notions of love and influence that they described. Even today, I feel pretty much the same.

But I contacted your mother, and not for any scandalous reason, and she said that she would accept me—not just for the time being but for always. Doing this, she restored my belief in myself which, for a writer at least, is the same as being given a lease on a new life. Maybe a typist can live without self-belief, maybe people in other professions can, too, but for the unfettered spirit, self-belief is essential.

Your mother and I agreed to bind ourselves to each other and to go through life together, but before I asked her father for her hand, I first tested the waters with her mother who told me that before speaking to her husband I should first go to see his oldest sister, Hadidjah Thamrin.

Hadidjah Thamrin was a widow in her early fifties. The first time I visited her she was living in Batutulis Raya, an area I knew well because of my frequent visits there during the Japanese Occupation. One of my teachers, Mara Soetan, lived just down the lane and across the street from her house. At first all she had to say to my query was, "Why ask me? I have no objections. It's your affair." But, finally, after discussing the issues involved she agreed to talk about the matter with the other members of her family. It was an anxiety-filled few days before she gave me the green light. I could now talk to "Babé," the "old man."

Your grandfather received me at his home dressed as he always dressed: in a sarong, short-sleeved shirt, prayer cap, and clogs. He was tall and a fairly large man. In fact, when he was young, he might well have been considered a giant of a man. But when I first met him he was nearly seventy. In answer to my proposal he asked for a week to consider.

His answer, as it turned out, was no answer at all. "I hear that you're an agnostic," he said. "I also hear that you haven't divorced your first wife and that your father-in-law has worked hard to support you, even sending you to the Netherlands."

I replied to his statements. After all, he did have a right to an explanation.

I doubted, however, that he would grant my request. You can't imagine how happy I was when he finally agreed to give his daughter in marriage to me.

Because of my chronic lack of funds the days leading up to our marriage were a period of great tension. Part of the problem was that the Minister of Education and Culture had placed a freeze on all publishing activities with the exception of educational books. Almost all writers had lost their source of income.

Hearing that the writer Idrus, with whom I had previously worked at the State Publishing House, was now working at Timun Mas, I convinced him to introduce me to the company's director from whom I immediately requested and received a publication advance of 3,000 rupiah.

With that money in my hand I took off on a friend's used motorcycle to look for more money. I went to the Christian Publications Board on Kwitang but there found myself without the nerve to ask the director for more money and I took off again. At the intersection in front of Metropole Cinema a pedicab turned onto the street in front of me. A collision was unavoidable and I slammed into the pedicab, causing it to overturn with its passengers—a woman and her child—still inside. I, too, tipped over but landed on my feet on top of the cycle whose engine was still running.

At first dazed, I was finally brought back to the present by the sound of someone screaming at me, "Do something! Don't just stand there!" I immediately pushed my motorcycle to the curb and then proceeded to help the woman and her child, who had just come from Salemba Hospital, right up the road. The pedicab driver immediately insisted on compensation. "Sure," I told him, "but not until you take this woman back to the hospital."

The pedicab wasn't seriously damaged and could still be used to take the woman and her child to the hospital. I trailed behind. The check-up that followed showed no one to have suffered any broken bones but after giving the pedicab driver 2,000 rupiah in compensation and the rest of my money to the woman, I was without any funds once more.

•

Helping to make the situation a little brighter around the time of our wedding day was a promise of Nugroho Notosuanto to provide me with transport on the day of the wedding. I had come to know Nugroho when he, in his position as chairman of the Student Senate for the Faculty of Letters at the University of Indonesia, asked me to present a paper at a faculty-sponsored literary symposium.

I was living in temporary quarters at the time, sharing a hut with three of my younger siblings, Koesaisah, Koesalah, and Soesilo, which they had rented several months earlier after being forced out of their previous house. With its woven bamboo walls, the place was little more than a shack and was situated on the edge of a swamp, right next to a dike that encompassed a field of swamp cabbage.

At any rate, and I don't know how he had come by it, Nugroho owned a boat of a car, a big dark blue, nearly black, automobile, which on the morning of my wedding he somehow maneuvered to my shack. Think of the contrast between the two!

In the car with Nugroho was Ramadhan Kartahadimadja, an up-and-coming writer at the time, who was to be our witness. I, my three siblings, and my sister's fiancé piled into the car and took off for your mother's home. There we were, the entire groom's party, all riding in one automobile, and the groom didn't have a single cent in his pocket.

Arriving at your mother's home, we found your mother's father already waiting for us out at the end of the street. When catching sight of us he hurried back to the house and there waited for my party to march in.

The front verandah of the house had been cleared of its tables and chairs. Mats covered the floor, which is where we sat cross-legged and with our backs erect, beside the invited guests. Seated directly before me was the religious official who was to preside over the ceremony. Your mother was nowhere to be seen. As is customary, I first recited the profession of faith; it was then your mother made her presence known, a detached voice from inside the house. As nervous as I was, I was thankful that she wasn't seated in front of me, that it was only her voice I could hear. But with her clear answer to my prayer your mother became my wife.

Immediately after the ceremony was over the religious official opened his attaché and took out a book entitled *The Happiness of Marriage,* a volume of stock formulae for happiness. Book in hand, the official gave me a mini-lecture on happiness and then, not so subtly informed me of the price of the book. Of course I was expected to buy it. So there I sat, in full view of my new father-in-law and the wedding guests, groping my empty pocket as the blood rushed to my face. Everyone was staring and waiting. But just at the moment when my face was about ready to fall and I was to become the laughingstock of all, Ramadhan eased a bank note from his wallet and said to me, "Here, you dropped this at the house earlier."

With that, the price of the book was paid, and I now entered a new chapter in my life.

Following our marriage we were, like traditional newlyweds, confined to the house for two weeks. Because I had no money this was a particularly difficult time for me; it embarrassed me to no end to have to live off your grandfather's generosity. Fortunately, around this time, a poet and friend of mine, A. S. Dharta, stopped by the house with an English-language copy of Gorki's novel *Mother* to see if I would be interested in translating it into Indonesian. The 6,000 rupiah that he proceeded to count out convinced me I was up to the job.

I obtained from another friend the Dutch translation of the same book and, when comparing the English and Dutch language editions, discovered a number of differences. There were sections in the Dutch translation not found in the English version and vice versa but, having already taken the money, I felt I had no choice but to produce an Indonesian translation. Later, when my translation was published, it was strongly criticized in a review that appeared in *Indonesia Raya.* I must confess that I had to agree with the criticisms. Years later, on a visit to Russia, I had to put up with the barbed queries of students at the University of Leningrad.

Your mother took me to meet friends and family and I could see that she was happy to have me as her husband even though I owned nothing more than myself.

•

After our period of confinement I went house-hunting and found a place, nothing more than a shack, near the home of my siblings. The place measured only two hundred square feet and was situated on a sloping piece of land above a rice field. During the first hard rain after we moved in we discovered that the roof was a sieve. The water poured into the house and in no time at all had risen up to our calves. Your mother panicked and screamed for help, but what were we to do? The next time it rained, the same thing happened again. And the next time, too. About all you could do when the rain came in was to be more careful walking around the house in order not to cause waves.

I topped the floor several times with additional earth but every time it rained the soil seemed to be sucked into the ground. I then discovered that the plot of land on which the house was built had once been the site of an outhouse that had later been used to store lime. We were living on top of a filthy strainer.

We lived in that house for several months, and despite our poor living conditions my newly restored sense of confidence helped to improve my outlook on life and, gradually, led to a turn for the better in our economic situation.

I had been fairly apolitical up until that time. In fact, I had consciously avoided involving myself in any activity that could be described as political. But when I signed a letter protesting the detention of the journalist and writer Mochtar Lubis, my friend A. S. Dharta explained to me that my signing the letter was a political act, an instance of refusing to accept government authority.

"But I was just doing what I thought was right," I told him.

"Whether you thought it was right or not is irrelevant; yours was a political act," he said. "Nothing in this world is free of politics."

If that was a political act, how, I wondered, was I to reconcile my action with my opinion that all politics is dirty. To this, A. S. Dharta had to say, "Anything having to do with authority or the wielding of power is politics. There is good politics and there is dirty politics and just because there is dirty politics doesn't mean that everything political is that way."

Even so, I soon discovered that political views and, more particularly, public opinion of politics, are often based on popular perceptions, which may or may not have their basis in fact.

Our life was happy at that time. Oh, your mother and I had differences of opinion and disagreements, but we never fought. Your mother carried out her work as a housewife: she kept the floor and grounds of our little house well swept. She cleaned the furniture and made sure our bed was neat. She went shopping in her bare feet at the muddy and slippery market. When returning from the market she'd go straight to the well to scrub her feet with a palm-bristle brush. Thereafter she'd cook and serve our meal, wash the dishes, and only then, maybe, take a rest. She washed clothes twice a day. I began to eat regular daily meals though at times all we had to put on our rice was a little salt. But at least I was eating.

In the beginning our neighbors were skeptical of your mother, not quite willing to believe that she, who had been born into far better conditions, would stoop to do such menial work. But work she did and the neighbors, when seeing her do all the work by herself, began to stop by and volunteer to help cook or otherwise help out. Even my job of hauling water from the well eventually came to be taken over by a young lad from the neighborhood.

Your mother was always fit, ever ready to tackle the job at hand, and under her care I, too, began to regain my health. In your mother I found a wife who shared my own mother's values. Much like my mother, she was a woman who never asked anything from me or ordered me to do anything. She gave me complete freedom.

In our home I could work contentedly, though the ever-present rats and mice did their best to ruin our hard-won peace. To cope with that problem I first tore down the bamboo walls of the house and replaced them with boards and then, on top of the existing floor, I added another layer of soil and then, on top of that, a layer of plaster. I also installed a bathroom with a toilet. Prior to that time we had to relieve ourselves in the open drain that emptied into the field of swamp cabbage.

When we received an offer to move into an empty house located not too far from our first home we accepted it and moved into what was a fairly habitable place complete with electricity, cement, wooden walls, and a terrazzo floor. With the loan of a radio from a friend, our new home suddenly had style. Even so, your mother didn't change; she continued to perform all the tasks she considered to be her responsibility.

The improvement in our living situation was followed by improvement in our means of transport as well when I replaced my old Sparta motorcycle with an Ariel and then, later, with a BSA. Now, I had the freedom to come and go as I pleased.

And then your mother became pregnant with you. I was incredibly excited just waiting for you to be born. At first I hoped for a boy but your mother convinced me that it was useless to think about that.

It was the evening of July 7, 1956 when your mother felt the first contractions and asked me to take her to the maternity clinic on Sawah Besar. By coincidence, the clinic had once been one of the homes of M. H. Thamrin. Your mother had lived in that house when she was a girl.

Six hours after our arrival at the clinic you were born. Not a boy but a girl—my fourth child, my fourth daughter. I was happy and thankful.

Three days later, you and your mother were taken to your grandfather's home and five days after that you were brought home to our own house. Your arrival made life gleam and sparkle. Even when you cried your voice was for me a song from another world. Born to two people who loved each other and their life together, you yourself turned out to be a happy child, and there was nothing more that we could wish for.

In April 1958 we brought home a sister for you: Arina. Now the mother of two girls, your mother remained steadfast in carrying out her responsibilities as a housewife. As for me, I began to receive steady work from *Star Weekly*. For each article I produced for the journal, I earned an honorarium large enough to live for one month, albeit simply. At the national level, publishing activities had begun to recommence. Everything seemed to be going well. Life was getting better.

In July of 1956 I received a surprise visit from an official from the

Embassy of the People's Republic of China. He brought with him a letter seeking my acceptance of an invitation to attend the twenty-year commemoration of the death of Lu Hsun, the great Chinese writer. While I did know the writer's name I confess I knew little of his life history. I had heard him referred to as the Chinese Gorki, but knew little more than that. I had no more than a vague comprehension of the history of Chinese literature.

Though your mother didn't try to dissuade me from making the trip, my own lack of knowledge about China made me reluctant to accept the invitation. I weighed the offer a long time before finally paying a visit to the consular for Cultural Affairs at the Chinese embassy. The consular explained to me that the invitation had been prompted by a suggestion from Indonesia's own minister of Education and Culture, Dr. Prijono. The consular then presented me with an official invitation printed in Chinese with its English translation.

When calling on Dr. Prijono I learned from him that I was to act as an official representative of the Ministry at the commemorative events. The Ministry henceforth provided me with a letter with which to obtain a passport from the Passport Bureau of the Foreign Ministry.

About my trip to China there is little to say. Much more interesting is that upon my return to Indonesia, the *Star Weekly* refused to publish the article I had written about the trip. Other publications followed suit. It seems that because of my visit to China I was now considered a Communist. It was at this time, as I mentioned earlier, that I began to think not only about one's political views but how public perception is formed. Needless to say, I found the incident unsettling and not too long later, during a visit to a publisher, my surmise was confirmed when one of the staff members quipped, "So, you're studying to be a Communist."

Just because of public perception, the openness I had once found at that publishing house was suddenly gone. But life cannot stop because of public opinion, and to live one must work. Some doors might have been closed to me but other doors had opened and I began earning an income from editing manuscripts for publication.

•

In early 1958 we began to build the house in which you lived as a child, one not far from our old home. We had planned on building the house with wooden pillars and bamboo walls but when your grandfather visited the construction site, he advised against it. "In the long run it will cost you more. Better to put up solid walls!" And so, at his suggestion, we built the house with solid, freestanding walls.

Your mother and I both put our labor and our lives into building that house, and when it was finished we ourselves were surprised that we had managed to build such a large home for ourselves.

You were just a wee thing when we moved into the house but I remember you, crawling around on your little hands and knees, helping your mother to wash the floors. Your mother and I had no strength or money left but we now had our own home to live in. That is the home where your mother raised you. That is the home where you learned to read and write. That home was our pride. It was there that I hugged you for the last time, before the rainstorm of stones fell and I was taken away. We built that house for our use, not for anyone else's. I just wonder who's living there now.

III

LESSONS
FOR
MY
CHILDREN

Most of the material in this volume was written primarily as a dialogue with myself. This is true even of the letters I wrote for my children. I knew when composing these that I'd never be allowed to send them. Prisoners were only allowed to send postcards and even these had to be censored first. Always after writing a letter, I'd hide it somewhere. The only reason some of them still exist today is because I was able to smuggle them back home.

I have eight children. From my first marriage there are Pujarosmi, Indriarti, and Anggraini; and from my second marriage, Astuti, Arina, Setyaning Rakyat, Tatyana, and my only son, Yudistira.

I love all my children, and after my divorce from my first wife I visited my first three daughters as often as I could. I especially liked to be there to give them their allowances. I am deeply sorry that I had such a minor role to play in their education. The same can also be said of the children from my second marriage.

While undoubtedly one of the greatest losses I felt as a result of my imprisonment was the destruction of my library—I knew I would never be able to build up such a library again and would never be able to rewrite the manuscripts that were destroyed—another great loss, or perhaps "regret" might be the better word, was not being able to educate my children.

Knowing that my children were growing up under Indonesia's "New Order," a militaristic regime that was rife with intimidation and lies, I worried constantly about the kind of education they were receiving.

And though because of the distance of time and my diminished memory I could no longer imagine what my children even looked like, I tried, in my letters to them, to create a kind of dialogue. My letters might be seen as lessons but, even more than that, they represent a distillation of my hopes for them.

Constantly, throughout my years of imprisonment, I worried that I might never be able to see my children again. At the same time, however, I was always ready to die—I for one have never in my life underestimated the cruelty of the Indonesian army.

Despite the fact that my children were growing up under the influence of the New Order, I still didn't want them to move to Buru. I wanted them to live in a world of freedom.

When I was a child I swore to myself that I would be a better parent than my father had been to me. Unfortunately, I can't say that I have succeeded.

In that same vein I've also hoped that my children would be better than their father and would rise to greater heights. In fact I clearly remember a time, a visitation day at Salemba Prison before I was sent to Buru, during the Lebaran holidays, when my children came to visit me. I remember telling them that day to do their best to be better than me.

A person makes his own place in the world and, in my mind, children should not be obliged to their parents. My children have no obligation to me. They are free to determine their own course in life, just so long as they are able to take responsibility for the choices they make.

1998

SCIENCE,
RELIGION, AND
HEALTH CARE

❧

Dear Yudi,

There are many things in life that, once they are gone, will never come back—not just objects, but opinions, and times as well. For me, the Pandawa brothers, heroes of the *Mahabharata* and the *wayang* theater, will never come back, not even Yudhistira, the eldest of the five. That world is now gone and the only Yudhistira in my life is you, my youngest child, my one and only son.

You and all of your sisters were born into a free world. The colonial powers were gone. Unlike your father and mother, you were born the children of a free people.

When you and your sisters were born you all cried right away. Your eyes were open wide, as if shocked by the strangeness of the world. Your hands and legs twitched in the open air; blood reddened your cheeks. You suckled at your mother's breasts, finding nurture there for quite a few days.

Such was not the case with me. Obviously, I cannot claim to be a witness to my own birth but I was present at the birth of my siblings, the eight younger children who were born after me. And when they came into the world, both my sisters and brothers alike were unable to open their eyes. Their eyes remained closed, as long as a week after their births for some of them.

According to the *dukun* who acted as my mother's midwife, newborn babies should not be allowed to move. With their arms bound to their torsos and their legs trussed together they looked for all the world like cocoons. I was instructed to daub their lips with honey. As the oldest child, I was given the responsibility of burying their afterbirth. Each time, after another sibling was born, I would clean the placenta, seal it inside an earthen vessel, and bury it at the right side of the house. A child's after-birth was thought to be the child's older sibling. I'd also place flowers in the vessel, along with a letter that had been written in Javanese, Arabic, and Roman scripts. This, I was told, was to ensure that the child would be able to write those three scripts with a beautiful hand. The site where the older sibling was buried was surrounded by a miniature fence of woven bamboo and for forty days after its burial a candle marked the grave. The candle was placed there so that the older sibling could find its way to the younger sibling's bed.

Mornings and evenings would find the midwife at our house, tending to my mother's needs and bathing and retrussing the baby. Sometimes, before rebinding the baby, the midwife would massage the baby's chest until it began to bawl and scream. But still the baby's eyes remained closed. Two or three times a day the baby was force-fed a paste of pulverized banana. Occasionally, the baby would start to cough and choke. These things won't happen again. As a baby you had no such experiences, and I suspect that your own children won't have them either.

My childhood was a time of ignorance. My brothers and sisters weren't able to open their eyes for several days after birth because we knew next to nothing about matters of nutrition. Babies are weak when they're born and we, at that time, lived with a lack of animal, and even vegetable, protein. Even when I was an adolescent I'd still hear people say that eating meat gives people worms. Coconut was supposed to give people worms, too. A person was supposed to limit both his intake of food and his rest in order to achieve clarity of thought and to find guidance from above. A person was supposed to practice abstinence and fast regularly. As a consequence the Javanese grew thinner and thinner, progressively smaller, weaker, and less able with each succeeding generation.

When I was young I, too, practiced various forms of abstinence. For certain periods of time—one or two weeks—I'd eat no meat or maybe only green leafy matter. Doing so, I was told, would make me able to think more clearly and do better in school. There was no one around at the time to tell us this was nonsense, that such practices did not increase a child's intelligence and that, in fact, the reverse was true: a person's physical growth would be stunted from a lack of essential vitamins. Sometimes I'd fast on Mondays and Thursdays. But in my case it didn't seem to help. It appeared that is not how God made people smarter.

Later I came to know that all those clever Western people never went through such an ordeal to attain knowledge, that they were smart because of constant and systematic work, training, and study. I learned that a person could have fun, maybe go off on a picnic or play as a means of restoring one's vigor before starting to work or study again. And it's true—I found that no amount of knowledge can be had without doing the work oneself.

And the letters that were buried in the earthenware vessel along with the afterbirths of my siblings? They were of no value whatsoever, nothing but rubbish. How many placentas did I bury, and did any of my siblings ever learn to write in beautiful Javanese or Arabic script? As for their use of Roman script, most of them learned to use a typewriter.

I often laugh when remembering childhood experiences. But such were the rituals of the times. Even older people were fairly ignorant with little more than a child's knowledge. In order to be able to memorize the Koran, children were told to drink water that had been mixed with the ashes of a holy book. I never did that but, then, I was never very good at memorizing or reciting the Koran! And none of the people who were so free in giving their advice ever felt any sense of responsibility if the advice proved false or incorrect. They never apologized, probably never felt that they could be mistaken or wrong.

If the views my elders held when I was young were true, then obviously there would be no need for schools, prayer houses, textbooks, or printing presses. There would be no need for a postal service to send documents around the country. It would be enough for a person to meditate and fast; that would be the surest way to obtain expertise in the field a person wanted to excel in.

The smartest people at the time, or at least the people who were viewed as being the smartest, were *kiai, dukun,* and doctors. I won't say much about religious teachers or shamans but I would like to comment on my experience with doctors. You're probably asking if we even had doctors when I was young, and if there were, what did they teach people to make them as foolish as I make them out to be.

Before there were doctors, the *dukun* and the *kiai* held ultimate authority. It was they who controlled public opinion and, because they were thought to be closest to God, whatever they said was true and people didn't attempt to test the veracity of their words. What few doctors there were could not alter this backward view.

I remember when I was in the third grade at primary school and had to go to the hospital to have an ingrown toenail removed. I was so incredibly scared. There wasn't a single friend of mine—not a one—who didn't believe that the cream-colored salve I was supposed to use was made from people's brains. Of course my parents didn't believe such stuff, which is why they sent me to the hospital.

When the doctor was going to remove the infected toenail I wiggled and screamed so much that it took two adults to hold me down. Then someone sprayed an extremely cold liquid on my toe and when the nail was extracted I felt no pain at all. But that didn't stop me from crying. My toe was treated and bound and I was told to go home. And though I limped for a while I no longer suffered from fevers. The constant pain I had felt gradually disappeared. A few days later I was completely healed. My trust in doctors was born as a result of that experience.

When my mother was hospitalized for a period of several months, I visited her every evening and, during that time, my fear of doctors and the hospital gradually faded. But I still distrusted the white-robed workers and many of the patients; they gave me a strange feeling, as if they were aliens from another world. This I could possibly attribute to my rural upbringing and the fact that farmers always dressed in black or other dark-colored clothing.

At the hospital my mother had a double room with a window. You could see, not too far away, a large cemetery where cashew trees grew. Illness and the hospital were neighbors of death. My mother was never afraid of doctors, or at least never admitted to being so, and her attitude eased my fear of them as well. Even so, it took some time for me to rid myself of the creepy feeling that the hospital gave me.

I remember it being evening—the sun was going down and I had to leave my mother alone in her hospital room so close to the cemetery. Hearing the sound of people singing, I peeked through the door of the general practice room and found it full of men and women dressed in white. It was they who were singing. I didn't know it at the time but they were Christians conducting a religious ceremony. Onlookers such as myself were given a sheet of paper on which were printed God's commandments and their elucidation in Javanese. There were also pictures of angels and prophets. From then on, I always thought of the hospital—the doctors, nurses, staff, even the druggists in the hospital apothecary—as one and the same as Christianity.

Even though I never had a "proper" religious education my family was, at least nominally, Muslim. The community leaders, the *dukun* and the *kiai*, were also Muslim, but at the hospital, the nurses and the doctors were Christian. This difference in beliefs, this variance in point of view, was enough to make the general Muslim public unreceptive to doctors.

"Doctors" were but a tiny speck within the larger Islamic society. They had no significant influence; it was the *dukun* who still held sway. Nonetheless, knowledge and science, which depended not on mantra or intrigue, but on proven fact, could not be held back forever, and gradually came to be accepted by the public body.

Take my playmates, the kids my age, for example. Most all of them suffered from one illness or another because of lack of proper nutrition. When I say playmates, I don't mean classmates. I played with farm kids, almost all of whom suffered from yaws. At certain times of the year most all of them experienced eye problems, too, and whenever the planting season came around, they were felled by malaria. None of my family ever suffered from yaws, though I once did catch malaria. Most of the children my age suffered from parasitic worms, ascarisis, at the very least. These things combined took a definite toll on their health and growth.

I'm sure that you have never had to see the effects of yaws. In my village the infected parts of the body—generally the legs, mouth, nose—would be covered with verdigris; that's how it was treated. My playmates' bodies would be speckled with green, but even after they recovered, there were almost always permanent scars. At the market or night fair you'd see two or three people without noses who spoke with a nasal sound. Their noses had been eaten by yaws.

Once a year medical personnel from the public health service came to the village school to try to eradicate yaws. All the kids would be given a shot of *salvarsan,* a kind of penicillin. We were told that a few days before we had the shot we were to eat as much goat meat as possible. Believing in the shot's efficacy, my friends' parents would try their best to find the money to buy goat meat and serve it to their children with yaws. They did this for three days sometimes. As soon as the kids were given the shot of *salvarsan,* their sores, which they had lived with for months or maybe even years, would begin to dry and scab. After a few days, when the scab fell off, they would be scarred for the rest of their life.

Have any of your friends had yaws? The world you live in today is much better than the world of my youth.

Also because of lack of knowledge about nutrition, many people suffered from *bodok,* a Javanese word for one of the initial stages of leprosy. This illness usually spread through direct contact at the prayer house. In fact, the deeply religious *santri* people viewed contracting *bodok* as a sign of true faith. This illness, which might cause a person to suffer for months or years on end, would leave a person's body marked by thin-layered strips of darkened scars. But people didn't go to the hospital for this kind of illness; they simply ignored it. The same as yaws. Even when health workers couldn't come to the school, people still wouldn't go to the hospital. People went to the hospital only when told to do so by their superiors or because of an accident. And numerous accidents at the time can also be traced to ignorance. Many people were struck by lightning, especially during the harvest season. Or were injured in fights involving sharp weapons. It seemed like, when I was young, there was a fight almost every week. Most all of them took a human toll. That, too, you can blame on ignorance.

You live in a world of freedom. Yours is a happy life. When I was a boy parents instilled their children with all sorts of fears. We were taught to be afraid of the police, of the military, of anything that had to do with Europeans. Whenever an automobile passed by, we'd all run and hide. Older people told us that the car was coming to kidnap children. And when we heard the roar of a Harley-Davidson police motorcycle, the kind with a big sidecar, we'd also hide; we knew that the Dutchman who was driving the vehicle—and, in this regard, it didn't matter whether the "Dutchman" was the red-skinned variety from Europe or the black-skinned native variety—was coming to torture people, especially tradespeople who were selling their wares outside the market for lack of funds to rent a space inside. These people were coarse and ever ready to strike someone. Our parents' fear of them made us afraid of them as well.

When the civilian militia marched by the house with weapons in hand on their way to the firing range outside the city, pedestrians and vehicles moved as far off the road as possible, sometimes even into the drainage ditch! It was as if the men on parade weren't mortal, but creatures much more powerful than we. We were made to be afraid of them too. Whenever a child started crying, his parents would tell him to be quiet or a policeman or soldier would come to take him away.

These fears disturbed the children's mental growth. Even as adults they were still timid, some of them carrying their fear to their graves. For a wrong such as this you can place the blame squarely on the ignorance of their parents.

People also frightened us with superstition and evil spirits. There were all sorts of spirits they could name. If you read *The Tale of Abdullah*, which was written more than a century ago by the Malay writer Abdullah bin Abdul-kadir Munsyi, you'll find the Malay names for these spirits. Each name represents another bit of nonsense, something to fill the gap in people's knowledge of science. Many people, too many people, even educated people continued to believe in them as adults, especially when they were at death's door. My feeling is that people who believe in such things will always live in a corral of fear; their spirits will never be free. The problem is that people who believe in bad spirits always try to make other people as frightened as themselves. Superstition is like an infectious disease. Unlike in science, where findings must always be backed by proof, in life no one seems to feel the need to provide proof for the existence of spirits. Acceptance of their existence is proof enough.

Because of superstition we were afraid of the dark, the domain of those spirits whose names our parents would mention to frighten us. In the field or at home, people were afraid of being alone for that's when spirits would appear. Any unexpected sound or occurrence was sure to raise goose bumps. At the prayer house, when learning to recite the Koran, we were made frightened by the horrors and torture of hell. Everything was scary, and everything seemed to be aimed at teaching us to believe that human beings are powerless. All this pressure, from intangible and unknown forces, filled our souls with fear. To make things even worse, a vendor from the big city once came to my town to sell pictures of *borak*, Mohammed's winged steed, and the various tortures of hell. These were later pasted on the walls of the prayer house for all of us to see.

I hope that during your childhood you never have to experience such things. I don't want for you to have to cringe the way I found myself cringing when I was small. The soul, like the body, must grow and develop; fear is a burden that can only paralyze its development.

The lessons that parents taught their children when I was young shackled their souls and bound them forever to darkness. In other countries children are able to live in brightness and cheer, infused with courage and the spirit of freedom, the very capital necessary for becoming useful adults at a later day.

You must not experience what I went through. No, you mustn't. My childhood was one of enslavement by fear, ignorance, and illness. You are the child of a free people. You are a cheerful child. In your freedom and liberty, you must take care never to be small-minded or fearful.

Fortunately, I did not have to go on receiving such awful instruction forever—and, remember, it wasn't my own parents who educated me that way. After entering the fifth form of primary school, more and more of my instruction came from school and the books that I read. I began to ignore what my religious teachers said. I no longer trusted them. One day at school my teacher told us about bacilli and bacteria. That evening the *kiai* told us about a devil by the name of Basil who lived in people's stomachs. He said that a prayer or a mantra would cause this devil to flee but that he would return if we forgot to say our prayers. I never went back to that teacher for further instruction. Much as with the other *kiai* who taught me to recite the Koran, he, too, was given to talking about obscene things, subjects that were never raised in school.

I remember when I was in the second grade one of my teachers, a man by the name of Haji Sodik, told us students about hell and all its tortures. Even as an adult, his tales stick in my mind. I fault him for knowing nothing about children's needs and for poisoning our minds with tales of torture and sadism detrimental to healthy mental growth.

My school library had books with stories about evil spirits that were just as bad as the ones that the older people told us about. These days, I'm afraid, there are even more books about such things, and many more stories of violence and sadism. Such books can only have been written by people who are as ignorant as the old people of my youth. Remember that you don't have to read them. I'm afraid that their effect will be unnecessary stress caused by unnecessary fears.

When I was young, old people had odd views about everything. People thought that God could be frightened and bribed, or cajoled to grant a person's wishes. (I'm afraid to say that these days, though it is more commonly understood that such a thing is impossible, there are still people who attempt to use His power to frighten, to bribe, and to negotiate with others.) In days past God's powers were depicted in various guises. Among some peoples, He is seen in numerous gods. It was with growth in monotheism that these gods began to fall and people began to look more to the "One God" and His authority.

There are those who hold that a person's position can be ascribed to destiny and, because of the desire for unlimited power, many will stop at nothing to obtain that power. Among some peoples this view led to the development of mystical knowledge and astrology. When I was young, old people had astrological calculations for days and weeks, even for the letters in one's name, and with almost computer-like skill were able to determine one's destined fate for such and such a day, for one's marriage, travel plans, and so on. I'm sure there are still Javanese who believe such things but, trust me, these people are nothing more than puppets made of flesh and bone. They allow their lives to be controlled by calculations whose veracity can never be proved. They are not free and will never be able to free themselves from their mystical shackles.

This so-called mystical power both deprives people of the initiative to undertake something that astrological calculations supposedly forbid and gives people excessive confidence in embarking on ventures that are sanctioned. The damage this causes to one's personality is permanent; such a person will never be able to think independently. He will forever be stunted because creativity springs only from the unbound soul. He will never make a meaningful contribution to life or to humanity.

People who understand that superstition can be traced to the lack of knowledge are able to use other people's ignorance to both obtain and maintain power and wealth. In a paper presented by Setiadi Harsono in 1964 at a conference on Javanese literature in Yogyakarta, the author superbly illustrated how Javanese kings used superstition to maintain power. In his paper the author talked about the role of Nyai Roro Kidul, Queen of the Southern Sea, in the Mataram kingdom. In *The Chronicle of Java* (*Babad Tanah Jawi*), the first king of Mataram is said to have married the Queen of the Southern Sea. Once this belief gained public acceptance, the king was able to frighten his subjects into doing whatever he ordered them to do; forever watching over the people and their activities were the children of Nyai Roro Kidul, her very own thought police.

There were a number of rich people who used similar tales to enrich themselves. I remember one story of how a man had used a certain supernatural being to obtain his wealth and that if someone stole from him, the thief would find his plunder changed into maggots. Coinci-dentally, the wealthy man happened to be a meat salesman.

People of simple mind, those who are ignorant of science and knowledge and hold to superstitious beliefs, fall prey to the power of the *dukun*. The *dukun* is a person who is supposed to know how to make use of God's power and these simpletons will, at the *dukun*'s behest, work themselves to the bone just to avoid doing something they don't want to do or to obtain something they long for.

I'm sure that such deception still takes place today and just as certain that the victims are always people who are ignorant, people who can't control their desires, or people who have abandoned science and knowledge for fear of not wanting something to happen. But you are the child of free people. You have a free soul and need not fall into the *dukun*'s clutches, either for reasons of fear, desire, and ignorance, or for lack of knowledge.

I recall that a common piece of advice was to restrain oneself from excessive knowledge. Knowledge leads to unhappiness and makes people permanently dissatisfied. I eventually came to realize that the origin of such a poisonous belief was some people's desire to have others fall into their power.

People with royal titles were thought to be of noble pedigree and were honored as such. Meanwhile, a person who graduated from school, no matter how great his academic achievements, was thought to be of little consequence for lack of a royal title. The older people praised the titled person, not caring whether he had the brains of a goat or a buffalo.

For you the situation today is different. Whomsoever is lacking in knowledge will himself be isolated, only able to nod or shake his head, and having no mastery over the issue at hand, unable to engage in coherent discourse. No honor will be shown to him.

Americans hold the view that a person worthy of respect is one who has found success in life, regardless of what field that person is in, whether it be trade, science, industry, military, or politics. The Japanese are of the opinion that a person worthy of respect is one who has many friends. The Javanese once thought that the person worthy of respect is one who holds power over others and is able to control their life and death. What is the Indonesian concept of respect? I can't say I know. But I do believe that those who contribute to the betterment of humanity—whether they are American, Japanese, or Indonesian—will forever be persons worthy of respect. Maybe such people won't find success, maybe they won't have many friends, maybe they won't have any power, but the family of man will respect their deeds. That is the principle to which I adhere.

A person cannot contribute to humanity without knowledge, and a person who has the soul of a slave and is bound by superstition cannot contribute at all. Only a person with a free soul, a person who has no use for fear, can contribute to this world's betterment. I pray that is how it will be for you, my youngest child.

THE CASTE SYSTEM AND THE REVOLUTION

(*Fragments of Two Letters*)

Dear Et,

If no one has ever taken the time to tell you about the Indonesian rev-olution, then let me tell you a story. To understand it you must first understand the Hindu caste system. In India the highest caste is the *brah-min* caste, whose male members are traditionally assigned to the priesthood or to leadership positions. Beneath that caste there is the *satria*, or warrior caste, whose male members traditionally served in the military; the *vaisya*, whose members are generally traders and business people; the *sudra*, com-prising farmers and other common people; and, at the very bottom of the social order, the *harijan* or pariah. In Indonesia, the system is somewhat dif-ferent because, following the emasculation of indigenous business class through feudalization and colonization, the *vaisya* caste was effectively dis-carded.

Indonesia's first president, Soekarno, and the ideologues he associated with were members of the *brahmin* caste as became most evident when he first read out the Proclamation of Independence. He spoke with hesita-tion in his voice, an indication that his ties with the common people, members of the *sudra* caste, were loose at best and that he was uncertain of or unable to gauge their political strength and aspirations. Then, too, his voice might have trembled because, with the pending arrival of the Allied Forces, victors of World War II, he could not be certain of what the Japanese military occupation force might do, just where they might throw the weight of their munitions.

Following the Proclamation, a fairy-tale reality took hold. No one knew what was to happen. Few suspected that Indonesia would explode into a revolution that would spread to both land and sea. What the people did know was that something had to change. They had reached a critical point in their lives, the very apex of social, economic, and political life. It was a time of crisis.

When the British Army, as representatives of the Allied Forces, landed in Indonesia they released Europeans from the internment camps that the Japanese had established in the Jakarta area. Some they armed, and these men took to forming vigilante squads, hunting down both Indonesian nationalists and Japanese soldiers. This was the spark that transformed the "crisis" I just mentioned into an actual revolution. Whereas before, young people around Jakarta had armed themselves for the purpose of safeguarding their own neighborhoods, now the city's pariahs, people from the Senen area of town, began to take the offensive and leave their home base to stage attacks.

"Senen," as you know, refers to the area surrounding Senen Market, which encompasses a radius of approximately a half mile. It was here that crops from the interior were stored, distributed, and sold. Everything was for sale at Senen, from rubber clothing and tires, to second-hand clothes, second-hand books, and all other kinds of used goods. At Senen the medicine men rolled out their mats to compete for customers' attention. Senen was the center of street theater and also home for Jakarta's pariahs: the city's unemployed, prostitutes, and pickpockets. The things that made Senen special were its filth, its odors, and its masses of vendors. It was Senen where the disempowered went, where escapees from Japanese forced-labor squads concealed themselves and tried to find rest for their bodies and souls while recovering from hunger and dysentery.

Some people might blush when told that the Indonesian revolution was begun by pariahs—the lowest order of the caste system—but that's the truth, at least as I witnessed it. Those who are embarrassed might recall the story of Ken Arok who in the eleventh century initiated the major historical shift in Java from a Hindu to an indigenous Javanese outlook. His particular success came from raising his status from that of pariah to the son of the Hindu gods, Brahma, Siva, and Vishnu. The difference in twentieth-century Indonesia was that the pariahs from Senen were unable to put themselves into leadership positions, which were then being held by the country's ideologues and *brahmins*.

Unfortunately, the *brahmins* were not nearly as revolutionary as their ideas and during this time of crisis they came to be left far behind the *satria*, the military caste that had occupied positions of power in both the country's colonial and precolonial eras.

Members of the *satria* caste are raised to defend the interests of whomever is in authority, and when they found a niche for themselves in the country's power structure, they began to use their position to reap personal gain. And with that Indonesia's "revolution" sadly and prematurely came to an end, long before its goals had been achieved.

As the *satria* were gaining strength, Indonesia's *brahmins*, who had guided the nationalist movement during the colonial period but were now hopelessly out of touch with grass-roots developments, were busy trying to negotiate a settlement to the burgeoning conflict. As they were doing this the *sudra* were arming themselves and forming fighting cadres. They rejected the *brahmins'* decision to negotiate and sometimes showed their position through the muzzles of their guns. Nonetheless, the *brahmins* continued their negotiations and, as part of the eventual settlement, began to strip the *sudra* troops of their weapons. Weapons, they insisted, were to remain in the hands of the *satria*. This effort to strip the people of their weapons and the rebellion and the killings that ensued were among the main reasons that I chose to say good-bye to the military.

It is not because I disapprove of militarism that I write this now. Personally, I feel that without Indonesia's military experience, the

Indonesian people would have had to face many more obstacles in their establishment of a free and independent country. Indonesia's military experience gave people the opportunity to learn how to think and to act in an organized manner as well as to be able to make decisions in whatever conditions that might arise. Blame for the failure of Indonesia's *brahmins* I place squarely on their lack of military experience. This is not to suggest that they should have changed castes, but that in an emergency situation, in a time of danger and social crisis, it is very easy to run out of ideas when trying to find one's way out of an unknown battlefield alone.

Don't think that I don't hold in high regard our country's history of armed opposition to colonialism or that I don't honor the endeavors of the *brahmins* and ideologues to secure our independence. To both I award the highest level of respect, but not without taking into account their shortcomings. Similarly, I offer the highest esteem for the *sudra*, who made possible the struggle for independence by providing and paying for the foundation on which this struggle could proceed. The regrettable thing is that in confronting the colonial powers, Indonesia's three castes proved incapable of joining together to deliver a unified blow.

In the end, it was not the Indonesian military that pushed the Dutch out of Indonesia. It was because of American financial interests that the Netherlands was finally forced to leave. And sadly, when Indonesia's sovereignty was finally restored on December 29, 1949, the event was followed not by social unification but by social caste-ification instead. National freedom had been achieved but not so the aspirations behind independence.

One must never ignore the fact that the Indonesian revolution was made possible by a break in the link between the imperialistic powers who controlled the world at that time. Simply put, a vacuum of power permitted the revolution to happen. One cannot say the same thing about the end of Soekarno's reign. By 1965, when he was toppled, a strongly competitive force emerged—multinational capital—which saw in Indonesia a source of raw materials, cheap labor, and a large market. This is the lever that prized Soekarno from his position. The great *brahmin*, who had dreamed of an Indonesia with political sovereignty, economic independence, and cultural integrity was unable to hold back the forces of multinational capital.

Perhaps history will one day remind us that "capital" is not just a stack of money: Capital is the energy that has, over the last four centuries, altered the face of the world and driven away to reservations, jungles, and the outback those peoples who would not compromise. Capital has joined together the peoples of all nations and races through war, trade, destruction, and financial assistance. It has brought people out of their cocoons to fly as economic butterflies.

Don't think me to be anticapitalist. I'm not that at all. I'm simply cognizant of the fact that capital has the power to effect change, something that has been almost continually demonstrated ever since the sixteenth century. No, it's not capital I dislike. It's the arbitrary use of capital power that I abhor.

In *Hawaii*, Michener wrote that when the gods are replaced, kings will fall. In Indonesia, when the gods were replaced, it was the *brahmins* who fell and the *satria* who rose to power. They were tired of working with the *brahmins* and took back the determinant position they had occupied in the days before independence.

They were now an established force; they were the new kids on the block, without need of dreams or ideology. Anything could be had with power except freedom from opposition, perhaps, which is why I and hundreds of thousands of other people were rounded up and imprisoned. Which is why hundreds of thousands more were killed.

After my internment, new political prisoners informed me that the number of people killed by the military in just a few months already surpassed the entire number of people who had died in the Vietnam War. And these were not men killed on the battlefield, but defenseless people without arms and even the intent to resist. They were killed like rats in a gutter. It was once remarked that Indonesians are "the most gentle people on earth." The world must therefore have been amazed when these very same people embarked on a rampage of murder of a scale with very few comparisons in the history of man.

Traditionally, when praying to or trying to appease the "local" gods, people sacrifice buffaloes, chickens, or goats or leave them offerings of flowers. It seems that for the new multinational gods, Indonesia's *satria* had prepared an almost unsurpassable human sacrifice.

As I write here, all I can ask is when will this vicious and blood-filled circle end? When can we fly to the unknown? I'm afraid that it's not me or you who will provide the answers. These are to be found by the generation not yet born.

Ever since you were a baby you've been quiet and sickly. Do you remember the last time we saw each other, in 1968 when we were separated from each other by a wire fence? You didn't look very well that day, but do you know what I thought of when I looked into your face? The distant past of my own childhood. You had my mother's face. The only difference was in your eyes. Your grandmother's eyes were fairly small, one might even say narrow, but your eyes are large, almost like your mama's.

My mother, your grandmother, was an archetype of womanly perfection, the standard by which I have always judged women. She wasn't a beautiful woman and she was often ill but reflected from within her was the wisdom, the intelligence, and the courage to face both life and death.

Because I loved my mother, my assessment of her virtues cannot be entirely objective, and as I age I see even fewer shortcomings in her. Perhaps other people who knew her as adults might say that she was a magnet for failure and defeat. But think whatever they may, I—as her son and, more particularly, her firstborn—will hold to my own point of view. She was my teacher, the person who shaped and guided me, the person who laid the foundation on which I have conducted my life up to this very day.

Though only a graduate of Hollandsch Inlandsche School, the Dutch medium primary school for Indonesians, my mother's many inner strengths would have helped her become successful in a great many fields—if only she had been male. But she was born in a different era, a woman bound by nine children and the obligations of her family and husband, a woman burdened by frailty and poor health, which together undermined her strength and contributed to her abbreviated life span.

My mother was a person of inestimable value, the flame that burns so bright it leaves no ash. For me, she was a revolution on an individual scale, a woman who not only gave birth to her children, but who set down the ethical guidelines that her children would follow in life. Do not be surprised, therefore, that when I look back at the past I see the Indonesian revolution embodied in the form of a woman—my mother, Pradnya Paramita, Hindu Goddess of the Most High Wisdom.

The Indonesian revolution represents not just a link in the process of human and social evolution; not just a restructuring of the old and worn; not just a new momentum or a turning around; and not just the erection of a new set of conditions atop the rubble of the old. The Revolution of 1945 was more. Most especially it represents emancipation: the opening of a new room in the house of humanity, expansion of a new building block in humanitarian development.

I use the term "emancipation" because the fundamental reason behind the revolution was freedom for the Indonesian people from the tyranny of enslavement and oppression that had once held them down. Because there is value and goodness in humankind and because man has inalienable rights that must be respected, in this house of humanity there is not and never shall be room for antihumanitarianism.

The world in which you live is very different from the world in which I grew up, but I do feel that it is those who have been most oppressed who can best understand the meaning of humanitarianism. Those who have had their rights usurped know best the meaning of self-respect. Those who have been endangered by illness most easily recognize the value of good health. And whomever cannot understand the meaning of humanitarianism or is unable to show respect for others—no matter the reasons!—is a person who has never really thought about anyone but himself.

The revolution that gave birth to the Indonesian people and the nation that is Indonesia erased the centuries-long slate of colonialism and restored self-respect and honor to millions of this world's inhabitants. It changed the map of power and affected, to some degree, the thinking of people around the world. It changed the world itself.

The Indonesian Revolution may be called the first revolution of this century or, at the very least, the first one after World War II. One could argue that the Vietnamese Revolution began a few days earlier, but it was the Indonesian Revolution that first had an impact on the international world. Without the Indonesian Revolution, it might have been much longer before India, Burma, and the Philippines found their freedom. The Indonesian Revolution also sparked the call for revolution in Africa, a call that ultimately awakened all of the world's colonized peoples and signaled the end to European hegemony and domination of world history.

Perhaps, in a sense, it could be no other way. After all, wasn't the world colonized by Europe because of Indonesia's spice islands? One could say that it was Indonesia's destiny to be in the vanguard of the decolonization process.

Over the years I've heard lots of criticism about the results of the Indonesian Revolution and it may very well be criticized because, in certain regards, the results have fallen far short of original aspirations. But one should realize that the revolution could not possibly fill all the hopes of every Indonesian. While the needs and dreams of men are unending, the capability of humankind is limited.

No, there is no revolution that can fulfill the hopes of everyone, yet sometimes people forget that "results" are nothing more than the product of thought and the realization of that thought through action; all the rest depends on the situation, the conditions, and, possibly, Mahakala, the god of time. If indeed the results of something are lacking then one must put on trial the thoughts and actions that preceded them. The trial will reveal where the error lies and, in this instance, the highest court is history, because history takes no sides. Some say history takes sides, but I say it does not. Bias might be found in the politics of history, but not in history itself.

There are times in this exile of mine when I feel so lonely that I begin to fantasize about having been born a European and having equal rights with my fellow citizens under law and not having to serve a sentence for which I have never been tried. These thoughts always lead me back to the past, to the revolution, and to the question of how we—how I—could have let this happen. "Weren't you there to stop it?" I ask myself. Does this current atavism reflect the mental state of a people who are not free? Did the fires of revolution fail to spark the flame of freedom? Is that why we can't respect the rights of others—simply because they are different from us?

In centuries past our ancestors tried to bribe the gods to grant them their wishes. Their bribes, or "offerings" if you will, were usually called sacrifices. If, however, the offering was given without thought of recompense, the term used was not "sacrifice" but "gift." A sacrifice might be in the form of flowers, a cow, a buffalo, a chicken, a human, or even a deed that the supplicant thought would be pleasing to the gods. So what about me? What about my own situation? Now that eleven years have passed, what am I—a sacrifice or a gift? Who will answer that?

There is no such thing as a blank human being; man is shaped by conditions, situations, and obligations, yet he also occupies a more primary, more noble position than those same factors. It is man who determines values; without man, conditions, situations, and obligations do not exist. All that exists is, as Buddhists say, *sunyata* or emptiness.

If I close my eyes and view the world through the eye of my soul, what I see emanating from the soul of the Indonesian people is a flame that has spread across the world, over seas and continents, and has sparked the risings of the many unfortunate peoples who were colonized in the last four centuries. The Indonesian Revolution is a beautiful thing, the mother of everything. I once thought that when this goddess appeared, she would provide the foundation on which to build everything of which we had ever dreamed. But in the end the revolution faltered, lasting only a few months, a number of days easy to count, and was followed by a war of independence.

So, my dearest daughter, in writing to you about the Indonesian Revolution, I hope that you will want to give it some of your attention and set aside some of your time to study it. Once you learn of its strengths and weaknesses, its successes and failures, you will also come to know that its success is the success of its actors, the people participating in it, and that its failure is the failure of our ancestors. This might make you want to know your ancestors better: their dreams, desires, intellect, passions, pretenses, and achievements.

And when you have taken it all in and are able to comprehend it all, you will then understand that past events shape the present. And those events could not have happened without our mother, the Indonesian Revolution.

GEOGRAPHY

Dear Yudi,

How are you doing in geography now? Have you made any progress? You must have, I'm sure. Do you have a world map at home? If not, you must acquire one, but not a primary-school atlas. You need a large, comprehensive one. Without one, how will you ever get ahead in class?

Now take your atlas, open it up to "Asia," and listen to what your father has to say . . .

In 1958, before you, Rita, and Yana were born, I made a trip around Asia. I left Jakarta on a Qantas flight for Singapore, a transit stop, where I caught a Cathay Pacific flight to Bangkok. After a night in Bangkok, I left the following morning on an Air India plane for New Delhi.

Now look at the map, Yudi, and tell me what countries, rivers, mountains, and cities did the planes that I was on fly over before I arrived at my destination?

I arrived in New Delhi in the afternoon. The bus that took me from the airport to my hotel passed by narrow and dirty streets. Twice it had to stop because of a cow crossing the road. Indians show great respect toward cattle because they help the Indian farmer till the earth and provide milk for India's children. In India cows are treated with the deference commonly shown to one's mother. Another three times the bus stopped because the driver got into arguments with the drivers of other vehicles.

Most of the buildings along the road were four or five stories in height. All of them seemed to be painted gray, which made for a very depressing scene, almost like England. If it weren't for the large numbers of people and the incredible amount of filth on the streets, I might have sworn that I was in an English town.

The hotel I stayed in was quiet with very few guests. After arranging my things in my room I left the hotel and went out for a walk along the river. On the riverbank I stopped to watch a man who was fishing. When the man noticed me, he immediately came up the bank and began speaking to me in rapid Indian-English, all the while shaking his head back and forth. The man ordered me to take hold of his fishing pole and then proceeded to give me a fishing lesson.

At dusk I saw a young and well-dressed man come down to the river. He took off his clothes, folded them neatly, then proceeded to bathe. After his bath he put on a pair of ragged underclothes, picked up his bundle of neatly folded apparel, and then went to find a place to lie down on the sidewalk. When he found a spot he stretched out with no mat or anything else between his body and the pavement!

At night I went for another walk, this time heading toward the city's gloomy center, its walkways dark from lack of lights. In front of the buildings I passed, rows of people, as close together as fish drying in the sun, were sleeping on mats on the sidewalk. Here and there cattle lowed and chewed on their cud.

I also saw grand-looking cars drive up and park outside a night club. From these coaches, Indian goddesses emerged. As they walked among the poor who were lying on the sidewalk they raised the ends of their saris to make sure they didn't become dirty. The difference between the haves and the have-nots was both obvious and extreme. In that respect, at least, Indonesia was far better off than India was at the time.

The first time I heard of India was in primary school. My mother often told me about Gandhi, India's national hero, and about his teachings and the struggle he waged for independence. His teachings, including that of *swadesi*, limiting one's material consumption to home-produced goods, had a strong influence on Indonesia's nationalists, including my own family. In the 1930s my family's home in Blora was one of the centers of the nationalist movement, and it was there that I first heard of the valor shown by the Indian people in facing British colonialism. The Indonesian struggle against the Dutch was very much influenced as a result.

When I was in junior high school I was taught that India was the mother culture of Asia, the home of Hinduism and Buddhism, both religions with comprehensive philosophical bases and all-encompassing worldviews. In junior high school, I learned of the Indian scholar, Professor Bose, a botanist who theorized that plants have emotions and are particularly sensitive to pain.

After the Japanese military occupation of Indonesia, I learned the name of another Indian: Subhash Chandra Bose, a man who came to be equated with Wang Ching-wei from China and Soekarno and Hatta from Indonesia for having cooperated with the Japanese during the occupation. Following the defeat of the Japanese, Subhash Chandra Bose and Wang Ching-wei were not heard of again. Soekarno and Hatta, on the other hand, were raised by the force of the Indonesian Revolution to become important world figures.

If you are asking why that was, Yudi, it was because in Indonesia's revolution, in its struggle to break free from colonialism, the colonized countries of Asia and Africa found a model for their own aspirations. National independence for Burma, India, the Philippines, Malaya, and Singapore would not have been achieved so readily without Indonesia first freeing itself through armed struggle. In short, Yudi, with Japan's defeat, India was no longer Indonesia's teacher. The opposite was true: Indonesia was now the teacher for other colonized countries and peoples.

During the revolution I learned of another side of India: its poverty, caste oppression, and its periods of mass starvation and death. This side of India surprised me. How could this country, the source of two of the world's great religions and reputedly the mother culture of Southeast

Asia, be so incapable of taking care of itself? Even in the midst of the revolution Indonesia managed to send to India rice, shirting, and calico cloth.

Because I was very interested in India I scraped together the money to
buy a four-volume set of books on Buddhism. To my disappointment
these books did not provide me with the key to understanding twentieth-
century India.

In a book by Rene Füllop-Miller about Gandhi, the author quotes
Gandhi as saying something like, "It's a sin to bring a child into the world,
even through legal marriage, because, in doing so, one gives to that child
the burden of hunger and suffering." Füllop-Miller also wrote that
Gandhi viewed technology as the source of India's hunger. I thought
Gandhi's opinion to be naive but, in historical terms, both in modern and
ancient times, India has had a significant influence on Indonesia, especially
in literature and language, but also in sculpture, dance, and philosophy.

In the late 1930s another wave of Indian influence appeared, a wave of
theosophy that caused even your father to study the speeches of
Krishnamurti. Sometimes, when thinking about that, I find myself having
to smile, but at that time a large number of semi-educated Indonesians
were influenced by this new Indian-based theosophy.

During the revolution I came to learn first-hand about several Indian
ethnic groups, particularly the Gurkhas and the Sikhs, who were serving in
the Rajputana Division of the British army. I met Indian Muslims, too—
keep in mind that India was still under British hegemony and hadn't yet
been split into two countries, India and Pakistan. At that time the entire
subcontinent was called India. The Gurkha soldiers were especially effective in serving the interests of the English and Dutch in their attempt to
reinstate colonialism in Indonesia, but many of the Muslim Indian soldiers went AWOL, fleeing their divisions and surrendering or joining the
Indonesian side. Their flight to our side helped diminish Great Britain's
power in its attempt to hold back the Indonesian Revolution.

All of this is to say, Yudi, that a great deal of Indonesia's experience is
linked to India. You might already know that the word "Indonesia" itself
means "Islands of India."

There's yet another influence from India that came to Indonesia in the 1930s. This was the influence radiated by Rabindranath Tagore, the renowned writer, educator, and philosopher. Even in junior high school I had already read many of his works through their translation into Indonesian.

Tagore was very respected in Indonesia, not only for his being awarded the Nobel Prize for literature but also for his success in developing an educational system completely distinct from the educational model given to India by its British colonizers.

There are still many other things I should tell you about India. As I mentioned earlier, when I was in New Delhi in 1958, Indonesia was in a much better situation than India. People were not dying of hunger in Indonesia and caste oppression was nonexistent. Indonesia had gained its freedom through revolution and not as a gift from its former colonizer. Walking on Indian soil, I felt like a tourist, not a student. New Delhi contained quite an array of multistory buildings; in Indonesia at that time there were almost none. But I wasn't particularly impressed, because buildings are not, for me at least, a standard for judging human worth. Buildings can even oppress people, as could be seen from the row after row of people sleeping on sidewalks in front of those buildings.

The following morning I went to the airport to start the next leg of my journey. The Aeroflot airplane I was to board was there and waiting. It was a huge craft, an Ilyusin jet plane that was at least two or three times larger than any plane I had ever been on. The plane was divided into three large cabins and could carry more than a hundred passengers. It was to be my first flight on a jet.

It's time now, Yudi, to take out the map again and draw a straight line, northward from New Delhi to Tashkent. Tell me, what hills and mountains do you pass?

The morning was clear and beautiful; from my view in the plane the barren ground below looked completely white, until the plane had crossed a high mountainous wall whose peaks and rims were covered with snow. On the other side of the mountain new sights came into view: large

concrete viaducts to contain and channel melted snow from the mountain peaks to the barren ground below and on to massive tracts of rich
green agricultural land.

My plane was late in landing in Tashkent and by the time I arrived at
the hotel at midday the conference I was there to attend, the Asian and
African Writers' Conference, had already begun.

At the end of the conference I received an invitation to go to
Turkmenistan so, instead of heading home, I boarded a small Ilyusin—
another Aeroflot-owned plane but not a jet this time—and flew north-
west to Ashkhabad, the capital, whose name means "City of Love."

Look at the map again, Yudi. Have you located Ashkhabad?

Turkemenistan is an arid country about the size of Java, but Ashkhabad
is located in an oasis whose soil is far richer than the dry and sandy plains
that surround the city. The city's population was around forty thousand,
about the same size as Blora. The difference with Blora is that it did not have
an airfield, though Blora does have a train station, which Ashkhabad did not
have. Ashkhabad also had very wide roads but almost no cars.

As soon as I and the other invited guests landed, cameras began to
flash. In addition to the Indonesian delegation, Indian and North
Vietnamese delegations were there as well. We were taken directly to a
guest house. Our official host was Turkmenistan's Minister of Culture.

A very memorable event for me in Turkmenistan was a visit to a village located outside of Ashkhabad, several hundred yards off the main
road and reachable only by foot. When we arrived, all the men of the village came out to welcome us, but not the women—their customs, it
seems, were like the Arabs, the ancient Arabs that is. We saw one or two
women, but only from a distance; their eyes were the only visible part of
their body.

All the children of the village gathered around the meeting place to
watch us. It seems that children are the same everywhere, always happy to
stare at the foreign visitors. And if you had been a child from that village,
I am sure that you would have been in the crowd, watching me, too.

None of us in the group knew the reason we had been brought to this village and, not knowing the schedule of events, we had all taken care to eat before going. It turned out the reason we had been brought to that village was for a traditional goat feast. Unfortunately, none of the delegates had much of an appetite, and I'm afraid that the hosts were very disappointed in us. I wish I had known that we were going to eat.

In both Uzbekistan and Turkmenistan goat is the main source of meat, and one of the favorite dishes is *sashlik*, which is very similar to Indonesian satay: grilled skewers of goat meat. The only real difference is that in Indonesia the meat is cut into small pieces, whereas in this part of the world, large chunks of meat are used, and the meat is served with huge portions of purple onion, one plate per person! The people love onions for its purported efficacy in building strength and agility as well as preventing cramps.

I'll never forget the huge earthenware cooking pot that was set down before us containing a kind of goat stew with pieces of meat the size of giant fists. I had no idea how the dish was supposed to be eaten—we weren't given any utensils—and the dish went untouched. Maybe we were supposed to eat it with our hands.

The villagers were pleased to meet fellow Muslims from different countries. When speaking to them, even through an interpreter, they were able to hear Arabic loan words and, as such, felt themselves to be part of a larger and shared culture. But because of the confusion over the food I felt very embarrassed with them.

That trip was followed by a visit to Firuzi, a village on the Iranian border. We made the journey by car, traveling on a beautiful highway that cut through the desert in an absolutely straight line for a distance of about forty miles. On the side of the road, every third of a mile or so, were stone statues. If I'm correct in my guess, then there were one hundred twenty statues along the road from Ashkhabad to Firuzi. Because the statues were positioned somewhat distant from the roadway I wasn't able to get a clear look at them. But, given their location, it was apparent that the Ashkhabad-Firuzi Highway was the country's major tourist route.

Firuzi itself was, by Javanese standards, too spread out to be called a village. There was a large rest house made of stone, but no real residential area. Its main attraction is a giant tree, which people stare at in awe. For the desert, I suppose, it is worthy of interest.

When looking at that tree I was reminded of a trip to the Netherlands where a Dutch friend of mine had tried to convince me to visit a local tourist site, a large rock. As I had seen plenty of large rocks in my time, I declined my friend's offer.

I've also seen lots of giant trees. There are quite a few here in Buru. I came across one when I was working on the road gang. I don't know the name of the tree, and it wasn't that old, at least not in the thousands of years. I guessed it to be, at most, four hundred years old. Do you know how to estimate a tree's age? If you don't, you must ask your botany teacher.

The next day I continued my journey by plane to other foreign lands. The first place we stopped was Cen-tu in southern China. Look at the map in front of you, Yudi, and find southern China. I wasn't feeling well when I was there but did manage to view the area's cultural artifacts, in particular the ancient Buddhist monuments. Leaving Cen-tu on a China Airways flight, I flew south and passed over a high mountain range. The plane began its flight over Burmese territory and our first stop was to be Mandalay. Look at your map and say the word: "Man-da-lay." It looked to me like Bangkok, and from the plane, I could see a countless number of beautiful pagodas.

The Burmese people dress very simply with a locally made sarong, a collarless cotton shirt, and head-cloth. Because they don't use belts they are constantly having to make adjustments to the sarong at their waist. Their head-cloth is simple in style and, like their shirts, also made from white cotton.

The Mandalay air terminal was very basic, as was the restaurant located there. Only two people got off the plane and as there were no new passengers getting on, our plane left soon thereafter.

In preparation for my trip I hadn't really bothered to check my ticket and, given the amount of Chinese written on it, there wouldn't have been much use anyway. Besides, I trusted the airline's agents to do their jobs but a mistake had been made and I had to pay a dear price for it: When the plane landed in Rangoon, the capital of Burma and the final stop on our flight, there was no one to arrange my onward flight. I looked at my ticket and found that China Airways did not take responsibility for passengers after they had disembarked in Rangoon.

My trip to attend the Tashkent Conference had come about as a follow-up to the Asia Africa Conference in Bandung, meaning that it was, in effect, government business that I was on. Even so, the government did not pay our costs. All we got from the government was its blessing, an exit permit, an official government passport, and a suit. Having used up all my own funds, I was in a difficult position. On top of everything else, I was not feeling well. It was early evening; night was coming on.

A bus driver finally came to my aid and took me, his sole passenger, out of the airport and into Rangoon. He must have assumed that I had very little money because he began to search for the simplest accommodation possible. But I didn't have even a single cent in my pocket and I asked him to take me to the Indonesian embassy.

At the embassy the guard, an Indian man, wouldn't allow me inside because, as he told me, the office was already closed. Meanwhile, the bus driver was still waiting, apparently not wanting to see a stranger stranded in his land.

As I was wondering what to do, an embassy staff person came out of the building carrying a tennis racket. I immediately begged his assistance. I asked him for a place to sleep—no food was necessary; nothing more than a platform and a mat where I could rest until the next flight out of Rangoon. The staffer told me that the ambassador was away and that he had to leave immediately. To that, I said that if the Indonesian embassy wasn't able to help an Indonesian citizen who had been stranded in a foreign country, particularly one such as myself who was acting as an official representative of the country, I would have no other choice but to take this problem to the Burmese press.

In my experience and that of other Indonesians I know, who have relayed to me their experiences in traveling abroad, it appears that most staff members in Indonesian embassies are of the opinion that Indonesians who come to an embassy are nothing but a nuisance, beggars one and all. That is why, in dealing with this embassy staff member, I acted the way I did.

Upon hearing from me that I intended to talk to the Burmese press, the embassy staffer repeated that the ambassador was away but that the first secretary was in. He then escorted me to the first secretary's home which, like the homes of rich Burmese, was surrounded by a high steel fence.

After learning that I was ill and wanted a mat to sleep on and a roof to cover my head, the man revealed his true character: "It's only when you people are stranded that you come to us," he told me. "Go find a hotel. There's no place here."

If I hadn't felt so ill I might have been tempted to strike the man, just to make a scene. I looked at the gate barring the entrance to the residence and thought that it was intended to keep me out too. I also thought about all the rice that Burma was importing at that time and started to imagine how lovely the inner garden of the residence must be.

Staring at the face of the first secretary, the image that then came to my mind was of a character from a Dostoyevsky novel. In my life I had met so many people like that. As a young boy my parents had shown me that colonial government officials were loyal only to their superiors and that they would do nothing to help their subordinates; their only goal in life was to maintain their own plum positions. That is also the way they treated wives, children, neighbors, anyone.

I repeated my threat to this man, saying that I would take my case to the Burmese press and, if necessary, the Burmese Immigration Service.

Finally the man was compelled to do something, and he had me taken to the Railway Hotel, which was located above the Rangoon Train Station, a place of constant din and noise. Now that I had found a room, I couldn't leave, so ill was I. No one came to see me, and for that I was thankful, but I didn't have money to call a doctor. It was a struggle even to bathe. During my trip the hotels I had stayed in had all been reasonable, but at the Railway Hotel the water I ran into the tub was muddy and yellow in color. I wasn't able to bathe the whole time I was there.

Rangoon, Burma's capital, is not a large city, and the houses were similar in style to houses in Indonesia at the time. I saw no multistory residences. The place had a relaxed air, with bald and crimson-robed nonworking Buddhist monks wandering the streets among the hard-working Burmese women. I could tell from the huge flocks of crows that gathered at the sides of the roads motorized vehicles were few and far between. There were so many crows there.

I'm ashamed to say that I had never read any Burmese literature and that I was ignorant of Burmese history as well. Further, because I wasn't able to go anywhere, this single visit of mine to that country was for naught. The only thing I got from that visit was ill treatment at the hands of Indonesian government officials who, no different from their colleagues at home, seemed unaware that I was giving twenty percent of every cent I earned to the state. This thought made me bitter, as if my trip had no meaning or mission whatsoever.

On Thursday, my third day in Rangoon, my health began to improve, and early that morning the staffer from the Indonesian embassy came to tell me that he had got me a seat on a flight. I was to leave that day on KLM, the Dutch airlines, for Bangkok. In Bangkok I was to change to a Garuda flight and fly to Jakarta by way of Palembang.

Aboard the KLM plane, I thought again of my loss at not knowing Burma: the face of its people, its history, and the conditions of the country at the time. I knew almost nothing about Burma, only that Suyono, a foster brother of mine, had died there when serving as a nonregular soldier in the Japanese army. The facial features of the Burmese, their physical features in general, were similar to the Javanese, even the color of their skin. The one difference that I could see was that because of their different historical backgrounds the Burmese were able to live simple lives while the Javanese, and Indonesians in general, were easily tempted by material wealth. I wondered if one reason might be that most Burmese are Buddhists while most Indonesians are Muslim.

Also, as a final note to my ordeal in Rangoon, after my return to Indonesia I received a letter from the Indonesian embassy in Rangoon, which included an invoice for the cost of my hotel room and instructions to pay the money to the Foreign Ministry. The figure was shockingly high, equivalent to approximately ten days in a five-star hotel. I sent Rangoon a letter by return mail with a carbon copy directed to the Minister of Foreign Affairs Subandrio. I heard no more from Rangoon after that.

In December 1958, two months after my return, I was given an audience with President Soekarno at which I gave him a copy of the set of resolutions that had been passed at the first Asian and African Writers Conference in Tashkent. At that meeting, the president was accompanied by several adjutants and cabinet ministers. When speaking to me, the president addressed me as "Mas" Pram. His use of the Javanese term of address and the familiar short form of my name struck me as somewhat odd, but I did not object.

I suggested to the president that with Indonesia having already established close relations with many "newly emerging forces" countries, it might be useful, whenever Indonesia sent a formal invitation to another country for a state visit, also to include an invitation for a writer of that country. "The writer," I told him, "is much more likely to be able to present a broader picture of Indonesia to his fellow countrymen."

"Take that down and see to it that it is carried out," the president immediately said to a governmental minister. "And you, *Mas* Pram, will act as host to the writers who come here," he then said to me.

I began to fumble for excuses but he cut me off: "Guided democracy means guided in every aspect," he intoned.

"But division of labor is important too," I added.

I don't believe President Soekarno liked me very much. He thought I was arrogant.

•

So there, Yudi, now you have gone with me on my trip to India, Uzbekistan, Turkmenistan, and Burma. Isn't that a geography lesson?

Now about other things: I know you like to fish, and fishing is fine as long as it doesn't cut into your study time. But for you to go fishing in the open sea would make me very worried. Can you swim? If you can't, then I forbid you to go. You can't count on friends coming to your rescue if you're in danger. They might not be able to. You have to be able to help yourself. And if you can't do that, then don't take unnecessary risks.

And how is that chicken of yours, the one with the gimp leg? Is it better now? What kind is it—a free-range chicken or the domesticated kind? If you're smart enough to raise one chicken, then why not raise a whole coop, forty layers, for example? With that you should be able to make a good and steady source of income.

It's harvest time here and in the afternoon the white clouds of smoke from the burning chaff fill the sky, erasing the forests and mountain behind its screen. *Dali* and *sriti* birds dart here and there in pursuit of fleeing insects. Once-green fields are now a medley of shades: piles of straw, my mates who are thrashing the rice, grazing cattle, and black stumps are all that remain of the former jungle.

The heat is incredible. It has rained a few times, but still not enough, and the level of the Wai Apo River is far below normal.

I wrote this letter over a period of a few days, Yudi, when I was down with dysentery. But I'm on the mend now; at least the bleeding has stopped, and my mates have been feeding me Manadonese porridge every day, with four eggs. Have you ever had Manadonese porridge? It's a rice porridge that is cooked with different kinds of vegetables, and some salt and meat. But my porridge had no meat, just vegetables and rice. My mates have also been giving me medicine to take: a diuretic, an antibiotic, and rehydration packs.

I close this letter longing to receive your next loving letter to me. Hugs and kisses for my distant son.

MUSIC, SPORTS, SELF-DEFENSE, AND A STORY

My sweet daughter Yana,

I am very pleased to learn that you like music—but I hope not the sappy kind, of questionable worth. I once read somewhere that a woman must love music and that one who doesn't will find life to be unbearable in times when she is confronted by sorrow. Whether this is true I'm not sure, but I am very pleased that you like music—good music, that is.

In order to appreciate good music, you must listen to it regularly. For a start I suggest that you listen to instrumentals. One cassette I think you would like is "The Soul of Spain." It's not heavy music and contains more than a dozen Spanish songs. Listen to it carefully. Once you're accustomed to hearing the songs you'll be able to remember both the individual pieces and their titles. Then I'll send you other suggestions.

Quite a few of the men here have made their own musical instruments: violins, guitars, cellos, and even drums. At my new unit, in Indrapura, many of them have been studying classical violin, fortunately not the kind of rah-rah music that seems to be so popular now, which might be good for making money but is not likely to be of lasting value.

The more kinds of music you know, the less foreign you'll feel as you begin to explore the world.

It's too bad that you haven't begun to study self-defense. If you can master the art of self-defense, you won't have to be so timid. It will give you greater confidence in yourself.

Congratulations on your good report card! And your penmanship is so neat that it's a joy to read. Even so, I was surprised to read that you get out of school at 12:40 but don't arrive home until "01:30"! You mean "13:30" don't you? You're too young to be staying out until 1:30 in the morning. In fact, even when you're home and studying, you shouldn't stay up past 10 o'clock at night. If you do have to study past that time, take two vitamin-B complex tablets before going to bed.

You say that all Yudi does is play. You have to remember, that's the way boys are, all over the world. Boys seem to need more exercise than girls; they need to use their muscles more so that they can grow up to be men. If Yudi comes home bloodied or bruised, that wouldn't surprise me either, but do tell Mama that Yudi must have his own household responsibilities. He has certain obligations to fill, first of all to be loyal to his home, his parents, his family, and his roots. He's not to play or go out of the house until he has finished his duties, and finished them well.

In your next letter, let me know what chores Yudi has been assigned and whether or not he's doing them cheerfully and well. I worry about his circle of friends. Are they good kids that he's playing with? I wouldn't want him to grow up to be a juvenile delinquent. Tell Mama to watch his behavior and speech. I don't want him making trouble for other people. And make sure that his hair is cut short and combed neatly. I don't want him looking uncivilized.

After you visited Mbok and Mul and saw what a sad state they're living in, what did you do? There's no use in feeling pity for someone if you're not going to do something to help. If a person really does feel something, then he or she must do something about it—whether it be through thought or action. I hope you'll keep this in mind: Though one doesn't have to feel pity for another, one is still obliged to help. If you see someone who has suffered misfortune, don't just say, "Oh, that's too bad." You must do something. Europeans, who seem to have a more highly developed sense of self-respect, would feel humiliated if pitied by others. In Europe, Yana, a laborer whose job is loading freight doesn't want help; that's his job, and through that job he makes a living. He'd feel insulted if someone felt pity for him. You see, even a coolie's work is noble when it causes no harm for others and gives him benefit. He does his job, no matter how hard it might be, with full awareness of what he's doing. Do you understand what I'm trying to say?

I'd like to tell you a story about a friend of mine. The story starts in 1960, before I was sent away, when I was on a trip to Russia to see a development project that was being undertaken completely by young men and women.

It was late October 1960, if I'm not mistaken, and I was on a jet plane flying from Moscow to Irkutsk. Below me, the whole world was white, completely shrouded in snow. Only here and there, in forests, where tips of trees poked through, were specks of green.

When the plane landed that day the temperature outside was 35 degrees below zero Celsius. Though only four o'clock in the evening, it was already growing dark. Accompanied by my translator, a muscular and good-looking young Russian man who had graduated from the Academy for Foreign Cultures, I made my way into the city, past silent wooden houses and over lonely and frightening stone roads.

After arriving at my hotel I didn't leave until the next day when my translator picked me up at nine o'clock to take me to the Irkutsk air terminal from where we were to fly to Bratsk, site of the youth project I had been invited to see.

Our plane that day was a jet that resembled a Dakota. We flew north and after a four- or five-hour flight finally landed in Bratsk sometime around four o'clock. It was already dark and the temperature outside was 45 degrees below zero Celsius.

A car took me and my translator to our hotel whose manager, a bear of an older woman, greeted me with an all-encompassing hug. "Oh, my son from warmer climates," she says to me. "You must be so cold!" As embarrassed as I felt, I had to admit that I found some comfort in the heat of her arms.

The voluble but very kind manager then pattered away, but in a moment had returned with several bottles of vodka. "Drink this," she tells me. "Drink lots of it so that you are warm." She then proceeds to pour me several shot glasses, one directly after another, which I immediately consumed.

In Moscow a few days earlier I had been served vodka but didn't like it. It tasted and smelled like kerosene. But this vodka was different, invigorating. I drank sixteen shots and wasn't sick at all.

Dinner that night included servings of black and brown caviar whose smell alone was enough to make me want to throw up.

I was glad that I had come to Bratsk in October, for I was told that in the first part of the year the temperature can drop to 75 degrees Celsius below zero, causing birds to fall dead from the sky. Even people, newcomers especially but sometimes local inhabitants as well, sometimes faint on the street or in their homes. At night the radiators of cars not in use are removed from the vehicles because sudden freezing can cause them to explode.

In the morning I began my tour of the Bratsk youth project. The primary facility under construction was a dam that, when finished, was to be the largest dam in the world. The lake created behind the dam blocking the Amudaryanya River was to be the largest manmade lake in the world, with an area greater in size than West Java. At the time of my visit, work had already been going on for eleven years. The runway on which we landed the evening before was at the base of the dam. Eventually the city of Bratsk would be submerged. Some of the young people working at the project were still in school. A few dozen had already become engineers during their time of employment there.

The sides of the dam were mountain ridges while the dam itself was made of poured concrete. On top of the dam were two roads, with the uppermost one, which was six lanes wide, reserved for motor vehicles, and the lower one for a railway. Everything was covered with snow and was white as chalk. It was incredibly cold. I was wearing only a light Dacron suit and a heavy overcoat. Walking on top of the dam was like walking on a large field, not like a dam at all. The snow formed a thick white blanket. Every two hundred yards or so we'd come to a wooden shack. Inside were electric heaters glowing bright red, and people were constantly running in and out to stay warm.

That evening I was given the opportunity to interview the project's chief engineer, a young Mongol who looked too tired to carry on a respectable conversation. In our brief discussion of the project, he said that everything was done by machines and that the only things the machines didn't do was to wipe one's bottom. That's when our conversation ended.

For entertainment that night I watched a play put on by project workers. In my opinion, the play wasn't very good, especially when compared with the dramatic performances I had seen in the larger cities of Europe. My opinion wasn't well received. "You are too critical," I was told. What can I say? When it comes to art I demand a great deal from others and even more from myself.

The next day I left Bratsk and its astonishing dam to return to Irkutsk. It was still light when I returned, so I left my stone hotel and spent some time walking around. I visited the city museum, another stone building, which contained a display of geological artifacts.

When I returned to the hotel, I found a letter waiting for me from a person named Kaiga who requested to meet me the next morning, prior to my departure. The letter gave me no hint as to what it was the woman wanted to see me about. The next morning a young woman of about twenty-four appeared at the hotel. This was Kaiga. With her black hair, narrow eyes, rounded cheeks and face, she looked like your sister Rina. She was hefty for her size, a mix of Mongol and Russian blood.

She spoke to me in fluent English: "I heard that you are to leave Irkutsk today, so I had to come to see you. I'm hoping you might be able to help me." Her voice was plaintive, as if she were, indeed, in need of help. "Who knows . . . anything at all . . . the smallest thing would make me happy," she added.

I looked at my watch because it was almost time for me to leave. Her request took the form of a tale: "Some time ago a delegation of young Indonesians passed through Irkutsk on the way to attend the Youth Festival in Vienna. The delegation had boarded the train in Canton and went to Peking where the members then got on the Trans-Siberian Rail for Europe. But here, in Irkutsk, one of the delegates had to be removed from the train because he was ill and was taken to the hospital.

"I was his nurse," she said, "and after he had recovered he left Irkutsk to return to Indonesia. He promised that he would write, but I still haven't heard from him."

She seemed so sad, her eyes so sorrowful.

"What is his name?" I asked.

She pronounced his name slowly: "Kaihatu . . . Do you know him?"

"No, I don't," I told her, while thinking that she must not know Indonesia was a country of almost fourteen thousand islands.

"That's too bad," she said, "but even so, I hope you will help me make contact with him. I've written this letter for him." She lifted a bundle from where it had been resting on her lap and placed it on the table. "It's up to you, of course, but I hope that you will give this package to him. It's just two books, not enough to overload you on your flight. If you wish, you can read them on the plane."

She then said good-bye and rushed off to work. I immediately left for the airport.

As Kaiga suggested, I read the two books in the plane. One was a children's story, written in English, about an old hag of a horse. I could see that it wasn't the story that was important, but the words Kaiga had used to fill the book's blank pages. Together they formed a mournful call for her lover from the snow-covered plains of Siberia.

After my return home, I stored the package in the armoire, intending to give the packet to Kaihatu if I ever found him. But I didn't know the person, didn't even know what he looked like. At the same time, I can't say that I went out of my way to find him either. It's for that reason I feel that I wronged Kaiga and the reason I'm telling you this story. It's my apology to her.

Now let's jump to 1969: You weren't even in school but, by that time, I had already been locked up in Salemba Prison for four years. Can you still remember the prison with its large field inside bordered all the way around by cell blocks?

In June of that year the prisoners were moved around and I found myself in Cellblock R. I lost some of my old cellmates but got a number of new ones as well, one of whom was a man by the name of Kaihatu.

When first meeting him I didn't know why his name sparked a dim memory for me. Something inside my mind kept forcing me to try to recall where I had heard his name and, finally, a few days later, I remembered Kaiga and her request. But I hesitated. Maybe this man wasn't the one Kaiga had meant. There might be many Kaihatus; it was a family name, after all.

I began to observe him. He was tall and thin, skinny in fact, with dark skin, wavy hair, a straight nose, and protruding lips. He looked to be a mixture of Moluccan and Northern European blood. He wasn't a handsome man, not very interesting-looking at all, especially in his present state. Like the rest of the prisoners, he, too, was suffering from hunger. His stomach was so thin that it affected his posture, making him unable to stand straight. He also suffered from low blood pressure and spent much of his time sleeping. When he was awake, he would play the guitar. At times, as his fingers picked the strings, he'd also sing.

Because the guitar and his music seemed to be his only friends, I found it reasonable to assume that he might be the Kaihatu who had once gone to Vienna to attend the Youth Festival. One evening, after engineering a meeting alone with him, I put the question to him: "Your name is Kaihatu, isn't it? Have you ever been abroad?"

"No," he answered coldly.

"But you like music, don't you?"

"Yes."

I asked him whether he had once gone to the Vienna Festival as a member of Indonesia's youth delegation. Again he said no, and this made me wonder whether he was Kaiga's friend or not.

I told him about my visit to Ikurtsk. He listened to me talk, but didn't reply. Finally I asked him, "Do you know the name Kaiga?"

He coughed and shook his head, then bowed and picked up his guitar. "It's him," I said to myself.

In July of 1969, five hundred prisoners were removed from the Salemba Prison, myself included, and transferred to Nusa Kambangan Island where we were put in Karang Tengah Prison. A few days later, I and thirty other prisoners were moved to Limusbuntu Prison, our final stepping-stone for our departure to Buru on August 16, 1969.

The group I was in was the first group of political prisoners to land on Buru and we were placed in Unit 3, the island's most isolated camp, which later came to take the name Wanayasa. One Sunday morning, three months after our arrival, Kaihatu appeared at the camp. He looked healthier and smiled and laughed more readily than before. I didn't raise the subject of Irkutsk or Kaiga.

He was living in Unit 2 (later known as Wanareja), which seemed to be a holding tank for prisoners the authorities particularly disliked.

On November 14, 1973, I was transferred to Unit 1, now known as Wanapura, which is located further up the Wai Apo. As it turned out, Kaihatu had been transferred there, too. But now he was extremely thin. His stoop appeared to be permanent and his skin much darker in color. The trousers he wore were much too short, having shrunk from age, water, and mud. The hollows of his eyes were very deep, making his eyes look much larger. Ever since I'd known him he had been a man of few words but now, though he did try hard, it was virtually impossible for him to express himself. Every three or four words would be followed by a low and deep cough. I thought he might be suffering from tuberculosis. He was constantly clearing his throat or coughing. He spoke slowly, and his breath came in gasps.

I learned that he was often tortured by the soldiers, many of whom were also Moluccan. An official from the Ministry of Information, another Moluccan who was stationed at my camp, was said to find special pleasure in having the Moluccan soldiers torture Kaihatu. By this point Kaihatu had almost no flesh on his bones.

Many of the prisoners didn't particularly care for Kaihatu either, but that was because he was obstinate and stubborn. Kaihatu was one man who preferred death to doing something that went against his conscience. As frail as he was, he never cried out under torture. He was taller than me but weighed no more than one hundred pounds—more likely, ninety-five.

At the end of the workday I'd often find him fishing in the ditch beside the road for minnows. They were no larger than a thumb or index finger but they helped him to stave off his hunger. I, too, was hungry; it was a time of famine. The rice harvest had been eaten by insects and we were surviving on sago balls, which, if you waited too long to eat, became rubbery and hard. Prisoners took to calling them *dandem celeng* or "pig stones," which were rocks for throwing at wild boar.

As thin as he was and coughing constantly, he managed to visit me a few times. He also invited me to visit his place, which wasn't all that far away, only about forty yards from where I lived. He shared his hut with two other men.

Once when I was there, sitting with him, he suddenly started to laugh and he pulled out a grilled *mujair* fish, a very large one.

"Eat up," he told me. "It was a good day."

After uttering that long sentence, he could hardly breathe.

From our late-night conversations, I pieced together the story that in October 1965, at the time of the upheaval, he had been an employee of the Office for Culture in Kebayoran. In 1966, shortly after the change of currency, he had used his connections with several prominent Moluccans to secure for himself a substantial loan of tens of millions of rupiah, which he used to purchase a camphor factory, the one and only one in Indonesia at the time. Suddenly, from being a person with nothing, he became a rich man.

Unfortunately, he was also naive and had little knowledge about the rapaciousness of evil men. Branded as a Communist, he was removed from his position, and thrown into this state of indeterminable detention, but I surmised that the real motive behind his downfall had been others' greed.

Kaihatu's parents and family were Dutch citizens and lived in the Netherlands and, once he was in prison, he found himself a man almost completely alone. Once he received a letter from Europe in which it was mentioned that a care package had been sent to him, but he never received the package. He received other letters from the Moluccas telling him the same thing, but those packages didn't arrive either. Be that as it may, he never asked for help from anyone.

Packages I received always contained Iso-Nicotinezuur Hydraside, which I'd give to him. He drank the medicine happily.

Even when times began to get better and we experienced a good harvest and an increase in our protein intake, he was still thin. His cough had become almost nonstop, and when he was out walking he looked as if he could not focus on the world around him. He seemed to be a man living in his own dreams.

In early 1974, I asked him again if he had ever been to Siberia. He coughed and scratched his head, then looked at me and nodded, "Yes, I have."

I suddenly wanted to blow up. "Then you know of Kaiga, the woman in Irkutsk?"

"Yes, I do."

"So for fourteen years I've been looking for a man by the name of Kaihatu and it turns out to be you!"

"I know . . . I'm sorry," he apologized, "but I was still young."

"What? Do you think you're the only one who has ever been young?" I looked at his graying hair, then told him about the package that Kaiga had sent him and the story of the broken-down horse.

"Supposing that what happened hadn't happened," I told him. "That package would now have been in my armoire for fourteen years."

I then told him about the night of October 13, 1965, when a group of vandals had destroyed my home and belongings. "The package for you was also destroyed," I added apologetically. "I'm sorry."

Sitting there, so stooped, he resembled the nag that Kaiga had described. "It's through you that I'm also apologizing to Kaiga." He said nothing to this. "You knew her, didn't you?"

"Yes," he finally whispered.

Nothing more was said about Siberia, Irkutsk, or Kaiga. His cough was growing worse.

I didn't know him on the outside, when he was still a free man. He might have been a good-looking man at one point. He was taller than I. With his height and some weight and, added to that, some money, he might have been very attractive indeed.

In exile here he composed a tune, which he titled "Karang Tumaritis"; the lyrics were by someone else.

So it is, Yana, that each and every person has experiences. They may be great or small, deep or high, boring or exciting. But for me the amazing thing always is "experience" itself. Their value is subjective, and they depend very much on the person who's judging them. What I'm trying to tell you is that experience when not assessed, either by the person experiencing it or by someone else, will be as a sheet of paper torn from the book of life, absent of meaning. Experiences are none other than the building stones of life. Therefore, learn to evaluate your own experiences.

LANGUAGES, SOCIAL SCIENCE, AND NUTRITION

My daughter Rita,

I received your letter of July 1977. It's really too bad that you weren't able to go to Surabaya. I lived there once, for quite some time, but the last time I visited the city was in 1964 when I was on a tour of Java. I can't say I like Surabaya very much. For me, it's a bit like Medan—I just don't feel comfortable there.

You said that you're not interested in seeing Borobudur and Prambanan? Why not? A visit to those two ancient temples would provide a good lesson for you on what your ancestors were able to do. There's nothing to see in Surabaya, it's just hurly-burly, but at Borobudur you can study reliefs that depict the lives of your ancestors in the eighth century: their houses, ships, clothing, tools, and customs. The temple presents a display of their wealth of knowledge, including at least one foreign language: Sanskrit. You'd be amazed that your ancestors of twelve centuries ago could build such magnificent structures. Each stone is laid with precise reckoning, just so, according to plan.

If you get red marks in your report card, that's normal. You shouldn't worry too much. There are times when a person just can't seem to get excited about something, a school subject for instance, but at other times—when she discovers how useful the subject might be to her life—she gets all fired up.

When I was in primary school, I hated to study and it wasn't until my mother, your grandmother, died, that I came to the realization that I had an obligation to fulfill my mother's wishes; I wouldn't fail in achieving the dreams she had for me. So, I began to study and began to like doing so. I studied any and every subject, most of them without a teacher, the English language included. Because at that time there weren't many lesson books in Indonesian, like it or not I had to study foreign languages in order to increase my knowledge.

Three languages were taught when I was in primary school: Javanese, Dutch, and Malay. At my school we studied formal Javanese for half a year, in the fourth grade, and Malay for half a year, in the fifth grade. The language of instruction from grades one to three was Javanese, while from grades four to seven it was Dutch. The students had to know those three languages, both written and spoken.

By the time I was in seventh grade, I had a fair knowledge of Dutch and this greatly helped me in my studies. My father had his own library, including an extensive selection of Dutch books, and publishers both in Java and in the Netherlands would send him complimentary copies of their publications.

For an Indonesian speaker, Dutch is a far more difficult language to learn than English. Except for its use of adverbs English seems to share more grammatical similarities with Indonesian than Dutch. Even if you use Indonesian grammar in stringing together an English sentence you can usually be understood. The most difficult thing about English is its idioms and pronunciation. I, too, experienced many difficulties, but mainly because I had to study on my own. Maybe your teacher isn't very good at his job.

Remember that if you don't understand something, or even think that you don't understand something, ask your teacher. Don't be shy or embarrassed about asking questions. In studying a language you can't be shy or embarrassed about writing or speaking. Even if you make a mistake, someone will correct you. Make it a habit of using English with your sisters and, again, don't be embarrassed about making mistakes. There's nothing wrong with making a mistake; it's not your own language, after all. On the other hand, if you're using Indonesian, you should be much more accurate and make far fewer mistakes.

Don't look on studying foreign languages as a burden, Rita. Think of it as a game. By playing with a foreign language you'll gradually come to enjoy it. In time you'll become an addict and want to study other foreign languages, too. I once studied Italian at the Dante Alighieri course in Jakarta, Spanish in the Netherlands, and French in Bukitduri Prison. Maybe I didn't master them, but that's because I didn't get a chance to put them to use.

More recently, at Salemba Prison, I studied Old Javanese, German, and French. Because of the lack of books and teachers, my comprehension of Old Javanese and French is very limited, but I now have a fair knowledge of German, at least enough to read.

My father once tried teaching me Arabic, but I failed to master it. That I regret because its knowledge would have been helpful for my work. After leaving home I tried studying Arabic again, this time at the Islamic College in Jakarta, but then the revolution came along and, with the school's closing, my studies effectively came to an end. Yes, indeed, I do regret not knowing Old Javanese and Arabic. My work would be much easier if I knew them.

As for social science, I'm surprised you find that subject difficult, especially since it deals with the relationship between man and the world and his environment. It is the study of people, the study of oneself. Maybe your teacher isn't explaining things clearly or maybe there are other things you'd rather think about than study.

Look on a knowledge of social science as capital for advancement in life. With mastery of the subject you'll not be easily confused by the mistakes people make in speaking or writing. You'll better understand the society in which you live, and be better prepared to play a leadership role.

Make it a habit to read newspapers and magazines for this will give you a boost in your studies. Ask Uncle Han what magazines and newspapers would be best for you. Once you get in the habit of reading, you'll be sure to discover the enjoyment that comes from a knowledge of social science; intellectual pleasure is one that cannot be purchased with money.

You asked about me trapping animals. I've never been one for that. The one time I went along on a deer hunt, a huge wild boar caught sight of us, forcing me to scramble up a tree. Matyani, a friend of mine from Cengkareng, hunts crocodiles. He takes a dagger, jumps into the river or swamp, and then overpowers them. He contends that crocodiles are near-powerless in water and argues that they're very dangerous on land where they can attack with both their snout and their tails.

Monkeys? There are no monkeys here. Monkeys aren't native to the Moluccan Islands. And the number of deer here is dwindling. I suspect they're not native to the region either, that they were brought in by settlers along with cattle and buffalo.

Why would you want a gift of maleleuca oil? Isn't it easy to come by in Jakarta? Visitors to Buru usually take back birds as gifts. Every day the swamp and the forest are filled with a choir of birds' voices, a virtual canon of song. There are numerous kinds of cockatoos: red ones, green ones, and red-and-green ones. There are both large ones and small ones as well. A friend of mine has a pet bulbul, which is about the ugliest bird you can imagine but it can speak. My friend feeds his bulbul palm sap, and now the thing is huge, a giant among its race. Even though it's not kept in a cage, it always comes home to drink. Of course, the only place it's going to get palm sap is from its master's hand.

I wouldn't suggest that you try eating civet cat, not if there's something better to eat. But here we don't always have a choice of what to eat. When food was really scarce some of the men ate raw baby mice. One man I know eats live *cicak* lizards and another one live *walang sangit*, that smelly kind of locust.

Have you ever heard of *oret*? Oret are a kind of worm that lives in the bark of *kapok* trees. They're fat, cream-colored worms about the size of a thumb. When there's no other source of protein around, we dine on them too. But you throw away the head first so that only the fatty part of the body remains.

When pounding sago in the marsh you find an especially large amount of worms in the rotting wood. Don't stop pounding! Just pulverize them along with the sago and cook them up, too. But some of the men like to eat them raw.

A man I know who was suffering from tuberculosis got better by eating fetal mice every day. There are an abundance or mice and rats here, in all shapes and sizes. The fields of elephant grass are a haven for them and what with our fields located nearby, they've become very fat. But now that we have chickens, ducks, and geese to eat, we're not eating them anymore. We've cut down on dogs and cats too.

I recall another time when food was hard to come by. A group of men were out in the forest sawing wood. When taking a break near the river, they saw what looked to be a piece of meat floating downstream. They caught it, roasted it, and when they thought it was done, began to eat it, but still there was blood inside. Surprised, they took a better look at the thing and do you know what they discovered they were eating? A baby's placenta! One of the locals must have thrown it in the river. All of the men threw up immediately, right then and there, and started to curse and swear. But that's how it is, Rita, when you're trying to stay alive and healthy.

There's almost no fruit to be found in the jungle here, and what there is, is almost inedible. There are candlenuts but the variety here have very thick shells. But did you know that you can break a shell open with the midrib of a banana leaf? It's strange but true: you place the candlenut on the top of a banana leaf cone, strike it with the midrib, and—lo and behold!—the shell breaks right open.

Once we found a *keluak* tree but didn't know at the time that you can't simply cook the raw fruit. It wasn't until later that we learned you first have to boil it and bury it in mud or soil for about three weeks. Sometimes we'll come across wild nutmeg. The trees are very tall with roots that rise about one yard from the ground, making the tree look like a person who's tiptoeing through the mud and not wanting to get spattered.

All in all, conditions are better now than they used to be, but the men are getting older and starting to lose their strength. There's no reduction of the work load, though!

So, you say you're having problems in social science. With a better grasp on the subject, I'm very sure that you'll be better able to understand—not just feel—what I'm telling you now. Why is it that people force themselves to eat live *cicak*? Or a baby's placenta? Or fetal mice? Social science can provide the answers. It's up to you, however, to find the reasons.

On a different subject, Rita, yesterday I was looking at an old photograph of you, the one in which you're standing with Yudi and Yana beneath a coconut tree. Directly in back of the tree is a bamboo fence. Yana has on white shoes and Yudi, black. See if you can find that picture in the family album.

As I recall, that tree is not the boundary to our property; a person would never use a coconut tree to mark a boundary. Take a look at the title for our land and check the measurements against reality. Make accurate measurements of the length and width of the property and then tell me if there's a discrepancy. If there is one, try to find out the reason. I wouldn't want someone else's land, but then I wouldn't want someone else taking our land either, not without our permission. And tell Mama to make a few photocopies of the title and to store the copies in different places so that we'll always be sure to have at least one. It's important that we have some kind of legal guarantee if any action is required.

Thank you for reminding me to be careful when taking a bath in the river. Once, one of my friends fell in and disappeared for a long time before coming up and finding a handhold on the edge of the raft. It was five in the morning. I grabbed his hand and pulled him up. The water was up over the riverbank at the time, and was a thick yellow color. Right now, the Wai Apo is very far down, so low that in some places you can even wade across. Stumps of trees and clumps of bamboo that were torn from the banks by flood waters are now visible. When the water is this low, you can't take a boat very far up river, especially not a fifteen-ton boat. All the boats have to dock much farther down river.

The soil here is new and loose and the topsoil so thin that it's not at all stable. Even a drainage channel of less than one yard deep and one yard wide can cause extensive landslides and erosion.

Four years ago, about one hundred yards from where I'm working now, we dug a canal six feet wide and six feet deep. That canal is now a river bed thirty feet wide and almost thirty feet deep.

In 1971 a crew of us excavated a canal measuring six feet wide, two feet deep, and two miles long. In the process we had to remove a hill, the layers of soil in which were different kinds of colors—gray, blue, yellow, red, and pink. That is why we christened the canal "Bantalawarna," which means "colored layers." We discovered that the soil, when mixed with a little starch, could be used as paint and, in the end, our barracks came to be all sorts of different colors. But anyway, that canal is now a river, a real river. The soil's instability makes irrigation a very expensive and never-ending task.

I remember when we dug that canal and what hard work it was. Because the work site was so far away we had set off from camp by five-thirty in the morning and often worked until eight o'clock at night. The canal cut through jungles, fields of the local settlers, bamboo groves, and forests. In the fields of elephant grass we were scorched by the sun. In the jungle we wrestled with trees, prying them up by their roots. But worst by far were clumps of rattan: thorns is all they are—long, thin, razor-sharp thorns that pierce your skin and break off inside. If you find yourself standing under a rattan vine, before you know it, your skin starts to itch and become red and inflamed. Just brushing up against one makes your skin start to swell. And the mosquitoes! Don't even ask! In the jungle, Rita, they are incredible.

That canal I just told you about is no longer usable because it, too, has turned into a river.

We once had to "dig" the craziest ditch imaginable, one that traversed a stretch of low land and marsh. For that one we didn't have to dig so much as to build mounds for the canal on both its sides. As you can imagine, working in the swamp made it very difficult for us to find enough earth to build those mounds. In the end, we were forced to ferry it in by raft from quite far away. We used poles to pull and drive the rafts forward. That idiotic canal turned out to be more than one mile in length and then, when we let water through it, it couldn't be used anyway. The water proved to be more powerful than our ability to cope with it using our primitive tools, working methods, and knowledge about the primitive area in which we were living.

It's between seasons right now and the sky is a constant gray. Out at sea, the easterly winds churn up tall waves and make it impossible for small boats to call into Namlea. That's why I have no onionskin paper on which to write.

For the past three months there hasn't been any lightning but when it does come, it comes down hard. Several men have been killed by lightning. One man was in the storehouse when lightning struck the building. He was knocked to the ground, unconscious, with blood coming out of his ears. He didn't die but he did lose his hearing.

In Jakarta now it must be hotter than ever. It's hot here, too, and with the water level falling the swamps have begun to recede, distinguishing themselves from the rivers and ponds. With the water in the swamps so low, the *mujair* fish that live there are beginning to suffer from both lack of food and room in which to move around. This makes it very easy for us to catch them with hook, net, or trap. *Mujair* tastes best when eaten with *colo-colo*, a kind of chili sauce made with chilies and citron. All you have to do is to grill them, though I think they taste best when you wrap them first in mud or in the sheath of a banana trunk, and then cover them with hot coals. You don't get nearly so bored eating them that way as you do when frying or salting them.

It will be time for the tuna season soon. The kind of tuna found in the Java Sea is small but here, in the Moluccas, the tuna are very large. An odd thing about tuna is that when you cook the fish, the outer layer of flesh is darker than the layer inside. That's because the dark part is where the fish's veins are found, which is why tuna are always at risk of freezing to death when swimming in cold water. To keep from dying the fish must continue moving at all times, at a speed of about twenty miles per hour. Any slower and the blood will freeze, which is why it's impossible to catch live tuna. As soon as it hits a net and stops moving, its blood freezes and it dies.

That's enough for now, Rita. In your next letter tell me a story about something interesting that you've experienced, or maybe about a dream that you've had, or about your lessons, or your teachers. Write clearly. You don't have a boyfriend, do you? You're too young for that but remember, when you do start going out, you must ask permission from your mother or father first. We don't want you sneaking around. Be open with us always.

Hugs and kisses for my Rita.

PHYSICAL AND SPIRITUAL WELL-BEING, CAREER CHOICES

Dear Tieknong,

I received your letter and the photographs that you sent on August 12, 1977. As your birthday was in July I'm afraid that this letter, my birthday gift for you, is going to arrive awfully late. I hope that's all right.

On June 30, I traveled from headquarters to Savanajaya on bicycle to attend the wedding of a friend, a distance of twelve miles. This was my second time in Savanajaya. The first was in 1973 when I traveled there on foot from Wanayasa, a distance of fifteen miles. I left at one o'clock in the afternoon and didn't arrive until ten o'clock at night.

During the past twelve years I've always gotten around on foot—the last time I had ridden a bicycle was in 1963—so I can't tell you how wonderful it was to be on a bicycle again, effortlessly traversing the hills and dales. I felt like I was being jet-propelled when speeding down the hills.

I have many memories of bicycles and during the ride to Savanajaya I thought fondly of my first bicycle, which my mother gave to me when I was in seventh grade. Two years later, when I moved to Surabaya to continue my studies, I took that bicycle with me but later Mother bought me a new one, along with a wristwatch and two gold rings. In 1942, during the early days of the Japanese Occupation, a Japanese soldier took my new bicycle from me on the road beside the Blora cemetery and I was without a bicycle until 1943, when I was in Jakarta and bought my own, a Hercules. I'm not sure what happened to that bicycle but I think I might have given it to Uncle Prawit. In 1950, a few months after my release from Bukitduri Prison, where I had been imprisoned by the Dutch, I bought myself a new bicycle. That one I think I gave to Uncle Tjus.

When I was still in school, during vacations I'd travel for hundreds of miles on bicycle; once I even cycled around Madura Island. In 1955, when I was much younger and stronger than I am now, I rode a bicycle from Central Jakarta to Kebayoran Lama and back without stopping, a distance of around twenty miles.

But as I'm sure you're not interested in reading about bicycles, let's get back to the wedding: the marriage ceremony for my friend and his bride was held in Namlea, a proa-ride away across Kayeli Bay. They were married in a civil ceremony because the priest was still on vacation in Java. They left at five o'clock in the morning and returned to Savanajaya at two o'clock in the afternoon almost faint from motion sickness.

Their ceremony was marred by something quite disgusting: Before he married them the presiding officer made the couple promise that they would remain on Buru. What this means, in effect, is that when and if my friend is released he'll still be a prisoner. All I could think about when that was happening was, What kind of civilization is this here in Indonesia when the government can so blatantly interfere in one's personal affairs? Is this the Indonesia that I had dreamed of when I was young? How very different reality is from dreams! Supposing I had been that young man, I would have refused.

The bridegroom was from Unit 3–Wanayasa and I was elected to stand as the unit's representative and to serve as the official host at the reception. The day before the wedding, one of the men in Wanayasa had been gored by a bull, a large one about the size of a buffalo. Fortunately, he was not seriously injured, but the bull was slaughtered anyway and the meat donated to Savanajaya where the reception was being held. Other units sent cartloads of vegetables and fruit. In addition to the prisoners and their families who lived in Savanajaya, there were also present guests from all the other units. There must have been about three hundred people in all. Eggs, rice, and other food flowed in from all directions.

The wedding reception that evening, which was held at the unit's arts building, was made festive by the music of a live band and a very fine comedy performance. What with a soccer match that was also held that night, Savanajaya was in a truly celebratory mood. Plates of meat—duck, chicken, goose, and beef—lined the tables, ready to fill hungry stomachs. Unfortunately, there was no goat, my favorite food and the most expensive kind of meat here, which I haven't had since my arrival. The sight of the plates of beef reminded me of another prisoner from my unit, a man by the name of Yadi, who was also gored by a bull. He wasn't as lucky as the other man and died after the bull stuck its horn into his chest. I say this just as a reminder, Tieknong, that when cattle, bulls especially, are worked too hard they are likely to turn on their masters. Buffalo are different; they're forever placid, like half-wit children.

The reception broke up at two o'clock in the morning. Even though Savanajaya is located on the coast, the weather there is extremely cold. The southerly winds that sweep down from the mountains cause people's teeth to chatter. That night the temperature there dropped to thirteen degrees Celsius! I was reminded of the first time I visited the Netherlands in 1953. In the summer, when I arrived, it was only sixteen degrees and in December, when snow started to fall, the temperature inside the house fell as low as ten degrees.

Because I had no place of my own to sleep that night, I went to the unit storeroom and borrowed a pallet, a mosquito net, and a mat. I slept on only half of the mat and used the other half to cover myself. I must have looked like a human eggroll but because of the cold, my eyes wouldn't close the whole night through.

At ten o'clock in the morning, I left Savanajaya but on my way back to headquarters stopped in at Unit 15–Indrapura to catch up on a little sleep. Maybe I haven't told you, but Unit 15 is to be my new unit; I'm to be transferred there soon. The unit is located in the hills where the air is fresh and cool. There the prisoners don't bathe in the river; bath water comes from a mountain spring, which is funneled into the camp through a one hundred fifty-yard bamboo pipe. The water is clean and fresh and also used to fill the terraced carp ponds that the men have built. The ponds were seeded with Priangan carp from West Java and some are now as big around as a human thigh. The fish are a frequent object of theft, but it's not the men in the unit who are stealing them.

The men at Indrapura planted papaya trees along the road that runs through the unit and any hungry passerby is welcome to stop and eat until he's full. He may even take some home if he wants. Even with this benef-icence there are too many papayas to eat and many fall, overripe, to the ground.

As fresh as the water is there, it's also difficult to control because the riverbed has a silicate base and during the dry season, in some spots along the course, the water suddenly disappears, dropping beneath this stone base not to reappear until a few hundred yards further down the bed. A section of the road that took me back to headquarters runs alongside the edge of a gorge; the soil there is a kind of hard red clay, made even harder with the presence of small black stones that shine much like iron ore when split apart. Imagine the difficulty we had in carving out this road with only shovels and pickaxes as tools.

During the rainy season, the bridges that we build are often washed away by heavy rain. You have no idea how much it floods here. In times of heavy rain a torrent pours down the mountain like water from a pitcher; no matter how good the swimmer, he could never survive the flood waters here. I know of a local man who was tossed by the current against a tree and killed instantly. His body was never found. At least ten men so far have died because of the dangerous waters.

Then when the dry season comes, the temperature rises as high as 36 degrees Celsius. Steam rises from the plains of elephant grass which, as with the arid stands of maleleuca trees, sometimes bursts into flame. Did I ever tell you about the time during the 1971 dry season when all the streams dried up and thousands of birds circled the air to plunder dying fish? At that time I saw with my own eyes a one-mile stretch of riverbed whose dry base was covered with dead fish. When the water level in the marshes falls, you can catch huge eels, some of them up to seven feet in length. In those times there's an absolute overabundance of fish and more have to be buried than eaten.

But in the rainy season the water is so high that platter-size snappers and sharks with razor-sharp teeth are able to swim up river from Kayeli Bay. A snapper that swims nine miles upstream is certain to die of exhaustion, but a few days ago a man who had set up a hook and line caught himself a small shark about one and a half feet in size. The man transferred the shark to the drainage canal but of course it died; it's used to living in salt water, after all. And it didn't taste good either; its flesh wasn't firm at all.

But now on to other things . . . I hope that once you're out of school you will trace our family tree. For the present you can work on your mother's family tree, that of the Thamrin family. I once started to do it myself but only got as far as Thamrin Muhammad Tabri, your mother's grandfather.

As for the manuscript that I am working on, I'm almost finished, but I've had to stop until I can obtain supplementary material. Once I've gotten that I'll go back and rework the manuscript from the beginning.

Hearing your tale about looking for work was humorous. I know that many ship's passengers, who pass through Namlea on the way to Irian, say that it's hard to find work in Java. For some reason I'm reminded of my mother, your grandmother Saidah, whose father, your great-grandfather, was a religious leader and man of some standing in Rembang. She was insistent that I not become a bureaucrat or work with the government civil service. She wanted me to be independent and free, able to do whatever I wanted to do, with the qualification, of course, that I not impinge on another person's freedom.

To be independent, she said, requires that a person believes in himself, and it is a goal that requires daily, near-constant practice. But as a result of her instruction, I became an independent person, one who is able to take care of himself. And that's why my mother was always making me work, giving me preparation for taking on any kind of job at all. She told me to be prepared to do any kind of work that was offered to me and that no job is less honorable than another unless it causes detriment to others.

I strove to fulfill my mother's hopes and for the most part believe that I succeeded. Because of her training, I never had a problem finding employment, though to be truthful I've only ever held two real jobs in my life. The first was at Domei News Agency from 1942 to 1945 where I started out at the age of seventeen as a typist but later rose to become a stenographer, then a junior archivist and, finally, an editor. The second was at the Balai Pustaka Publishing House, where I worked from 1950 to 1951 as an editor of modern Indonesian literature. During the time between these two jobs, from 1945 and 1947, I was serving in the nationalist armed forces, but this I viewed as a duty, not a job.

There was another time, between 1963 and 1965, when I taught a course on literature at one of the universities in Jakarta but I don't think of that as a real job either since I was doing it only because I myself wanted to learn about academic life. Moreover, my own education had never prepared me for a teaching job at even the most elementary of levels.

In telling you all this I'm not trying to convince you to follow in my footsteps. Your career must be your own choice. And because I've not had the opportunity to watch over you and supervise your growth, I can't say that I know you in the way that a father should know his daughter. My only advice is that you be whatever you want to be as long as in doing so you don't bring harm to yourself, your family, or other people. From your letters I believe you have a gift for writing but that you yourself don't realize it and have never consciously tried to develop your writing skills.

In the photographs you sent, you look pale and out of sorts, not your normal self. You said that you were having stomach problems. Be careful. Once you get sick with one thing, other illnesses are likely to follow. I'd like to tell you something about this: My father once put down in writing his hopes for me and my siblings. For me, he hoped that I would become a person of intellect. He warned me, however, that I must watch my health. In particular, he said, I must look after my stomach. The odd thing is, I've always suffered from stomach ailments, from the time I was a boy up until my time of exile on Buru. Until my late teens I was always coming down with something. I was sick so often that I seem to have lived my life in an illness-induced blur.

For a time I never thought that I would live past the age of thirty. I guess I was wrong about that, as I'm well past thirty now. When I was thirty-five and on one of my trips abroad, I vowed that I would try to improve my health. I was in Bucharest, capital of Romania at the time, so the first thing I did was make an appointment for a physical examination at the clinic of a Dr. Anna Arslan. She herself was in the United States but her assistant examined me. When the results of the tests came in, I was more surprised than anyone else to learn that I was suffering from hardening of the arteries, especially in areas around my joints. I was given a series of injections as a remedy but they left me almost paralyzed. Can you remember back to the time when in the evenings your mama used to massage my arms?

From Romania I went to Germany where I made an appointment at the Berlin municipal hospital. During my examination there, the doctors were stone silent as they checked first the left side of my face and then the right, which had swollen abnormally. They couldn't find a solution. In Prague someone suggested that my blood was too thick and I needed a complete transfusion of new blood. In Budapest it was another story altogether. The sum of it is that in Europe I wasn't able to find a cure for my malady. After some time back in Indonesia I went for a checkup at the Central Army Hospital. The three doctors who examined me concurred that I was experiencing calcification of my joints and suggested bonereplacement therapy.

After returning home from the hospital that day I came across in the backyard a length of flatcar railing, which I fashioned into a dumbbell. I said to myself that if I was going to get healthy, I would get healthy, and if I was going to die, then I'd die. In addition to lifting weights I worked out on a set of exercise bars that I constructed and, whenever possible, went jogging in the morning. Gradually, the physical deterioration that I had experienced began to reverse itself, though my body never did return to prime condition.

Can you guess the meaning of this experience for me? From it I learned that one must fight to overcome one's own weaknesses. And that is what you, too, must do—whatever weakness in whatever field. I learned that sometimes you must fight your own self in order to attain the condition you hope to achieve.

As for that stomach ailment of yours, I told you already that I, too, suffered from intestinal disorders. During my time in the nationalist forces the bouts were very frequent and, whenever they came on, I'd lose my appetite. For a period of a couple months I wasn't able to eat more than a few spoonfuls of rice per meal. If I came down with diarrhea or dysentery, it was sure to last at least three weeks. There was no medicine for such things at the time; the only remedy I had was to eat turmeric.

When I was imprisoned by the Dutch in Bukitduri Prison, I fell ill again. At first I thought it was just the normal stomach upset, but this time it proved to be something else. For four days I couldn't relieve myself. I couldn't pass gas either, and neither the Indonesian nor the Dutch doctors knew what to do. The cramps were so bad that even to get up was painful. On the fourth day of my illness—it was a Sunday, as I recall—my cell-mate received a package of food from his family. In it was a bottle of sliced and pickled shallots in a red chili pepper brine. I asked him for some of the pickles, but he didn't want to give them to me, saying that the doctor had told me I was not to eat anything except porridge and other soft food. I kept at him until he finally gave in and, lo and behold, after drinking two large spoonfuls of the pickles' spicy brine, do you know what happened? The cramps suddenly ceased. The pain disappeared and I was immediately able to relieve myself.

Once, there was a neighbor of mine in Tanah Abang who was suffering from a similar problem and who got better after following my suggestion of drinking two tablespoons of vinegar. This might just be a coincidence but I don't think it was.

Here on Buru there have been six men I treated the same way and they all got better, even after the doctor hadn't been able to find a way to help them. As long as you're not suffering from an intestinal infection, you might want to try this remedy too. On Buru this vinegar solution is now known as "Pram's medicine."

A stomach illness can be the source of emotional and nervous disorders. It can upset you, make you unstable, anxious, and frightened. In the end these negative feelings begin to affect the other parts of your body as well and you find yourself unable to function normally.

Gas and constipation used to affect me, too, but not here in Buru. My explanation for this is that every night we set outside the water we're to use as drinking water the following day. The dew that falls is supposed to purify it. According to Hindu teachings, dew or naturally distilled water is the basis of life. I don't know if I put much weight in that theory given the number of nuclear bombs that have been tested in the atmosphere. But the fact is, I'm healthy now and no longer given to stomach upsets or colds. I began doing this in 1971, and my first experience in drinking the dew-cleansed water was discombobulating; I could feel the cold water twisting its way through me, like a snake slithering through my intestines. But I kept up with the practice, drinking the water every morning right after waking, and after about a month all my stomach problems disappeared. I've not been affected since. Maybe this is something you should try, too. The only problem with it is the frequency one has to urinate, because you have to drink almost a quart at a time.

One thing I've not been able to fend off is the diminishment of my eyesight. I know that every two days or so I should spend some time staring closely at green leaves in order to obtain a dose of chlorophyll, but I never seem to be able to find the time. Maybe I should put some leaves in my room to have them there when I'm working. As is, all I see is white paper.

Still, in regard to health, there's something strange that I've learned about sties. People used to say that if a sty appeared on your left eye, then you were to tie a cotton string around the ring finger of your right hand. Such foolishness, I thought. But earlier this year when I got a sty in my right eye I remembered that old wives' tale, and though I had already been given some salve, I also massaged the base of my left ring finger. And it went away! I tried this remedy on a friend and it worked for him too.

Another way I've learned to treat sties is the Chinese method. A sty is a kind of festering and when, for example, a sty appears in your right eye a boil is just as likely to appear on the upper right part of your back. The same is true for the left. You must lance the boil and extract from it the white thread inside. Once that has been removed, the sty will disappear forever.

If you're feeling dizzy or have a headache, try pinching the muscle between your thumb and index finger. After a few minutes of this, the pain you're feeling will be gone. It's strange, but true. In Buru the arts of reflexology and acupuncture are very popular and have done wonders for many of my friends.

But now onto other, more important things. You said that you feel ashamed of yourself for all the things your parents have done for you. You mustn't feel that way. Be proud of having parents who are willing to work hard for you and, at the same time, equip yourself to be able to do the same for your children in the time to come. The love of parents for their children is made manifest in the things they do for them. Your mother and I are proud to have children like you. I'm not ashamed of any of my children. For that, I think the credit goes to the fact that all of you were born and raised in an environment full of love and affection.

Your feelings are an indication of an inferiority complex. You must rid yourself of them. Lift your head up and face the world, for life is a constant struggle against travail. Even plants, when blocked from the sun, will move toward the light. That's what life is: a search for the sun. Each person is unique; there is not, nor has there ever been, nor will there ever be another person like that person in the world. You are your own person. Each person has her own specialty, skills, ideals, and dreams. All I can say is that whoever lacks the courage to fly or is afraid of the sun is a worm. Similarities between people are biological, but even one's basic needs can differ from another's.

Your mother and I know very well that you want to make us happy and to please us, but you should not think about that. You must build your own life for yourself and your future children. Don't permit your journey forward to be hindered by your parents' past. They have had their own time in this world and that time is not yours. Your time is the future, one that you yourself must build. Your parents cannot build it for you.

I don't like seeing you always frowning in photographs. Always remember that failure is the best teacher. Accept this as a fact of life and learn from it. And don't be unrealistic, even in your dreams. A person who spends her entire life trying to achieve the impossible must be prepared to shoulder the burden of disappointment.

With everything I've told you, Tieknong, I hope that I have shown you a way to cure you of your physical and spiritual travails. But supposing your problem is due to an emotional or neurological disorder—which is something that can happen to anyone—I'll now explain a remedy my mother once showed to me and which I still practice to this day: Whenever you lie down to sleep, whether it be in the afternoon or at night, adjust your body until you have found its most relaxed position. Don't use too high a pillow or a bolster either. Regulate your breathing and then listen to the sound of your breath going in and out, in and out. Let your thoughts go and try to think of nothing at all. Try not to feel anything at all. If you can do this, you'll feel much better the next day and be able to work harder.

Before sleeping, offer up sincere thanks for your well-being and the measure of good fortune you found that day. Smile when you do this and then free your mind so that your muscles can relax and rest. Thinking causes muscles to tense. Thus if, for example, you start thinking about that mean teacher of yours, the one who frightens you so much, without your even being aware of it, your heart will start to beat faster and your body will adopt a defensive position. Maybe you will fall asleep but unless you have first relieved yourself of tensions they will stay with you during your sleeping hours, and when you awake in the morning you'll still feel tense, tired, and out of sorts.

What my mother taught me was a form of *samadhi* or meditation. There are many levels of meditation, but mastery of the initial level is sufficient for one to survive—culturally, emotionally, intellectually, spiritually, and physically. The road to good health is to trust in a better future. Adhere to that hope and you will end each day with a feeling of contentment.

As for your future, you are an adult and are free to choose for yourself your husband, though I would voice the hope that when making your choice, you choose not only a man that you love but one who is civilized, educated, and loyal. No one is perfect; every person has his shortcomings. Nonetheless, exercise caution in your choice and make sure that your prospective husband suffers from no mental, physical, or genetic illness. No matter how strongly you love a man, if he suffers from a genetic illness then you had best let him go. If because of your love you are unwilling to let him go, then you must be prepared not to have children. No good can come from producing children who will forever burden their parents or society.

I would never suggest that "wealth" be a factor in your choice of a husband. Material wealth has never tempted me and no amount of goods could ever sway my heart, my mind, or my soul. Principles are far more valuable than fancy feathers. To the cause of national freedom, your grandfather gave away most of his wealth, and in so doing he bankrupted himself. Maybe he has never been officially recognized for his contribution to national independence, but in my eyes he is still very much a hero. To be sure, he had his weaknesses and made mistakes, yet he left behind something far more valuable than monetary wealth: the knowledge in me that the strength to adhere to one's principles comes from having to struggle with adversity, and that the more difficulties one faces, the stronger one must be in order to remain true to one's goals, not only for personal gain but for the greater good of society.

No doubt you will find that, with growth in the population and an inverse decrease in living space and opportunities for advancement, your life will be one of ever greater challenges. Technology, with its promise of progress for the future, is today's Messiah, but beware of false promises. Destruction of the environment and the spread of disease continue to threaten human life and, regardless of our efforts to halt the cycle of decline, to institute reforms, to correct false attitudes, and to create a healthier worldview, wherever you look the signs of decline in the quality of human life are evident. At times, the hope of progress seems unrealistic and all we can do is to check a further decline.

I'm sure you understand what I'm saying—namely that, because your future children's generation will have to face challenges more serious than my generation or your generation ever had to face, the issue of "heritage" must forever be one of preeminent consideration; you must prepare yourself to give your children the kind of education they will need to find solutions to those challenges. A mother must be understanding, dynamic, and flexible. She must be strong, much stronger than a man. I myself believe that the future will be determined by women. The power of women has been seen before. Witness in the Christian faith four centuries before Mohammad a growth in the cult of Mary; in the Buddhist faith, the emergence of the goddesses Locana, Pandarawasini, Mamki, and Tara; and, long before that, in ancient Greece, the goddesses Demeter, Hera, and Athena. But their times were times of slavery and women did not provide answers to the challenges that were presented to them. Life then was controlled by brute force. Now, in this day and age, through education and social change, women have gained power and strength and are no longer the chattel of men, not simply one accessory for a successful male, as we were taught by our Javanese ancestors.

Male hegemony over the ways of the world is now being challenged. Of all the wars that have taken place—all of which were started by men—none have made life any better for the human race. Women being the fount of love within the human race must therefore take life-determining power as their own. The world's age-old values are now fossils, in both shape and form, and it is up to women to use their hands and hearts to give them new content and spirit.

I am very concerned about the challenges that future generations will face. What will happen when force is a thing of the past? Call me a Malthusian or a neo-Malthusian if you will, but the principles of Malthusian thought are absolutely true. It's up to us to figure out how to apply them.

In 1948, when I first studied Malthusian thought, my life, my world-view, everything was completely bound up in the nationalist struggle. Now I can see that I was wrong. The problems that we faced then were not those of a particular cross section of humanity but of all humankind. In 1948, I nodded my head in agreement when told that expansion of capital was the reason that United States first fired on Yokohama and opened the doors to Japan. Capital-rich United States was out to make the world its home. It wasn't until later I learned that what one calls "the United States" or "the American people" was nothing more than a handful of men who controlled the American economy and, with it, life in the United States itself.

Such is the case when talking of other peoples as well. Certainly, capital can be used to expand living space, but for a limited number of people only. Put forth as a possible solution to this problem at the time was the nationalization and socialization of the sources of production on which the majority of people depend. But, in the end, this idea capitulated to the power of capital. It also gave rise to the fantasy that it would be possible to cooperate with foreign capital. As a solution to this Malthusian problem there are those who advocate the formation of a new social organization and system and feel that this can only take place through radical change in the old system and organization.

So it is, Tieknong, that our century, the twentieth century, has been marked by a search for a solution to the problem of ever-diminishing living-space. Existentialism, a philosophy that was born or, more accurately, became popular after World War II, promoted the view that man must not be an intellectual blank. He must work toward the common good of all mankind and not reside within the cocoon of his own personal problems. Man must use not only his brain to think—he must use his heart, his hands, his feet, and his mouth. The challenge for your generation and your children's generation, therefore, is to obtain more knowledge than the preceding generations. This century is the age for finding solutions to the problem of "man as man," and not "man as animal."

When I was in my twenties, I thought that being a good person meant being a pacifist, that that was enough. It turns out that I was wrong: I came to see that man finds meaning in his existence only through the active demonstration of his human self, a cosmos comprising the entire constellation of life's factors: culture, civilization, tradition, history, ideals, facts, physical conditions, one's mental state, the ecology, and so on. In other words, while I once thought that man was a barren and soulless, completely self-confined entity, today I see him as a gigantic force, with every square inch of his skin forming its own macrocosm.

But maybe I'm boring you, so let me tell you a little story about Japan and one of its noble deeds: In 1943, when I was eighteen years old, an announcement appeared in the newspaper about opportunities provided by the Japanese military government for junior high school students to continue their studies in Japan. Because I was working at the Domei News Agency at the time, I had ready access to official news, but I never heard how this program was administered. It was only later that I began to hear rumors that the candidates accepted for admission to this program were all young and attractive female students. Rumor also had it that these young women, most of whom were the daughters of respected and educated families, were sent not to Japan but to Japanese military installations scattered around Indonesia. There they were given not an opportunity for further education but were forced to service the sexual needs of Japanese soldiers.

The Japanese authorities insisted that the rumors were "the poisonous whispers of enemy spies," and no in-depth discussion or investigation of these rumors ever took place. The families of these young women never received any letters from their daughters, and when the revolution broke out these girls, most of whom were no more than fifteen or sixteen, were considered lost.

But do you know what happened to them? The rumors were true.

And now, at a time when Japanese goods are flooding Indonesian mar-
kets—as if Indonesia itself were the rubbish heap of Japanese industrial
production—some of those women who as girls were deceived by the
Japanese are still to be found here on Buru Island. They are old now and
live in a state of misery. The ones I learned of are chattel, just one more
item in a native clan's belongings, communal possessions with absolutely
no rights of their own.

As to how these Javanese women came to reside in this backward area
varies but the one I find most believable was told to me by a prisoner who
met one of the women: One day in 1974 the man was out by himself working in a field. Toward evening, when looking up from his work, he spotted a middle-aged woman sitting quietly beneath a bush. In her arms she
held a baby about nine months of age, but the child did not appear to be
her own. She just sat there, saying nothing, doing nothing. Her skin was
dirty and her clothing ragged. She wore no shoes and her hair was
unkempt. My friend went up to her and was given a real shock when she
began to speak to him in High Javanese, explaining that she was the wife
of the village chief and would like to request some cassava. She was fam-
ished.

In the conversation that ensued the woman related that she was the
daughter of a deputy village chief from Wonogiri. In 1943, when she was
fourteen years old, the Japanese promised to send her to a school for mid-
wives and to find employment for her at a hospital in Ambon. Her parents gave her their permission and she and forty other young women of
various ages were taken first to a dormitory in Semarang and then by ship
to Ambon where they were placed in a dormitory guarded by Japanese soldiers and *heiho*, Indonesian soldiers serving for the Japanese. At first they
were not given any work to do; they ate, slept, and generally whiled the
time away. Then the young women were divided into smaller groups
based on age; she and her group were taken by ship to Ceram where they
were placed in another dormitory. It was there that their real duties began:
They were the Japanese officers' sexual toys. When new girls were brought
in, most of them from Java but some from other parts of the country as

well, she was transported to Manipah, a small island off the north coast of Buru. Again she was placed in a dormitory, this one surrounded by a high fence and guarded by *heiho*.

When the Japanese were defeated, the women were left to fend for themselves. She herself was taken by a Burunese man to Buru Island but not long after her arrival on the island, the man died and she was taken by his beneficiary further into Buru's interior. After my friend gave the woman some cassava to eat she rose and adjusted the sling that held the baby to her chest. "I'd like to return to Java when you go home," she said, "but all of you seem to be happy living here. You've made roads, rice fields, bridges, houses, and dams . . ." And then the woman disappeared into the bamboo grove, not to return again.

My dearest Tieknong, who has been raised by your mother in an environment of peace and love—can you possibly imagine how that woman must have suffered as a girl of fourteen when her dream of becoming a midwife was shattered by the cruelty of the Japanese? Can you imagine being separated from everyone you love and all the people who love you, not to mention having to experience the decline in everything you recognize as civilization and culture?

This brief tale of this one nameless woman is but a grain of sand in an insurmountable dune of tales, representing no more than a hint of the condition in which your countrymen are forced to live. Odd, isn't it, that there should exist such tales of hardship in the land of your birth. But knowing them, as you do, I hope they will give you the forbearance to deal with your own situation. You must not be weak. To bear life's challenges you must be strong. Gather your strength to make yourself strong and you will be strong.

The slippers you sent me I wear continually, except in the bath and when I'm in bed. They were the perfect gift. I just don't know how many months they'll last. My gifts to you are the things I've told you here in this letter. In closing, let me tell you a little about my own life here: Since November 14, 1973, I've not had to work in the fields, which means, for all practical purposes, that I've not been working for my own food. I survive by the sweat of my friends. It is they who provide me with food and drink. The only thing I have to do for myself is to get my own bath water. My food ration is three plates of rice a day plus some greens, but my mates don't leave it at that. They always try to make sure I get something extra, and even help to keep me supplied with cigarettes, clothing, sugar, and soap. Each month they give me two reams of onionskin paper, a typing ribbon, and carbon paper, and when my rickety old typewriter finally broke, they rushed to fix it for me. When I'm sick they take care of me. They love me, Tieknong, and I love them. I shall never forget their kindness.

Many of the prisoners travel a good distance to see me, some from as far away as five miles, with gifts of bananas, papayas, or fish for me. I know that I can't repay their kindness individually but I swear that someday I'll find a way to make it up to them, even if they themselves have given no thought to recompense at all. In the twelve years that I've been here I've met so many, so very many good-hearted people. They help me to remember the things I have forgotten. They air their complaints to me, and ask me for advice on dealing with family problems. I feel now that their families are my family, too.

As the days pass, more and more of them die, out of sight of the people they love and the people who love them. And here they now are, by themselves, alone and silent in untended graves on the mountainside and the arid plain. A wooden post, a makeshift gravestone, with their dates of birth and death, is all that marks their graves.

Most of those who have died are younger than your father. And sometimes, after they're dead, a long-awaited letter arrives from home— two, four, even five years late. Such things as this make me cry. Two months ago one of the men, a man by the name of Mulyoso, was killed by a fellow prisoner. The man who killed him, who was only twenty-seven years of age, had been sixteen when he was brought here! A few days after Mulyoso's burial a package from his mother and family in Semarang arrived, a sign of affection the deceased had been waiting for twelve years to receive.

These past twelve years have been a period of intense hardship for me. So many of my friends are now dead. Life is to be devoted to the continued safety and prosperity of humankind. And suffering, as Buddha taught, is always the result of stupidity and ignorance.

There, my precious Tieknong, for your twenty-first birthday I have written you this letter. I'm enclosing with it a photograph that was taken four months ago. I hope you like it. It was taken in my room. The copy I sent previously must not have arrived. It's a wonder, isn't it, that two millennia ago Rome and Byzantium were able to maintain reliable postal systems. With all the technological marvels of this day and age, you would think poor postal service would no longer be a problem.

I don't want you or the family to worry about me. I live among very cultured and civilized men. When I ask for their help, they give it freely, as long as it is in their power to do so. These men are the shining lights of Indonesia's intelligentsia. They have no tolerance for pretence and use none of the lofty phrases or elegant deceptions that seem to have pervaded the outside world. I have many famous friends, names of people you would recognize, but I also count among my friends numerous young people who in the world outside never found the chance to demonstrate the true extent of their capabilities.

The first time I was imprisoned was in July 1947 at the age of twenty-two. I was a member of the nation's younger generation. Now, at fifty-two, I am one of the older generation and I'm still in prison! But I know that you for one are not ashamed to have a father who is a prisoner.

This is the best greeting that I can give you for your birthday. I wish you happiness and safety, now and forever. Strengthen your body and soul. Nothing ever comes by itself. Each and every thing is the result of human labor.

Kisses and hugs for you, your mother, and the other kids.

IV

❧

DELIVERANCE

When I arrived on Buru, the island, or at least the central eastern section where the penal colony was established, had no roads to speak of except those within the coastal villages located there. Being among the first group of prisoners sent to the island, we were placed in the deepest interior, on the low plain beside the Wai Apo River, reachable only by motorized river craft.

The only supplies promised us were rice, salt, sugar, and some other basic foodstuffs to last us six months, after which we were expected to be on our own. In fact we didn't receive even half the amount of food promised us and were never allotted any sugar. In no time at all, not only the volume but also the quality of our rations diminished and all that we were left with was discards.

As I said before, the barracks in which we had to live were extremely basic. Each unit had a clinic, with a stethoscope, some operating tools, and a bit of disinfectant, but that was about it for medical supplies. The clinic doctors were themselves political prisoners as were the paramedics.

Knowing that we had to depend on ourselves to live forced me to stay alert and, in that regard, I didn't change throughout my years on

Buru. Even as the time for release came—I never called it "freedom"—my attitude remained the same: I was ready to die. Nonetheless, I did want to remain alive long enough to witness the fall of the New Order regime.

That I was prepared to die is not to say that I was willing my death. This was not suicide I was choosing but rather, the route of the Javanese mystic who surrenders his soul to life's force. "Take my life if I am of no use. Kill me if there is no reason for me to go on." I was willing for that to happen, which is what, I believe, kept my mental health stable.

In 1973 after I received permission to write, my fellow prisoners built a room for me within the barracks in which I would have some privacy. Unfortunately, I had almost no reading material save for the occasional religious tract and used copies of *The Catholic Digest* that the priest from Namlea brought for us. Given the circumstances, I was forced to rely on memory for historical detail.

During my time on Buru I wasn't able to write nearly the number of works I had hoped to during that period of my life but I did produce the following:

- *This Earth of Mankind*, comprising a tetralogy of novels (*This Earth of Mankind, Child of All Nations, Footsteps, House of Glass*) intended to help correct the accepted colonial version of the history of the rise of Indonesian nationalism;
- *A Changing Tide (Arus Balik)*, a historical novel that I hoped would stimulate the awareness that Indonesia is a maritime not a land-based country;
- *Arok and Dedes (Arok dan Dedes)*, a novel about that period of Javanese history in the eleventh century when Hinduism was being subsumed by Javanese indigenous beliefs;
- *Mangir*, a drama about the establishment of the Mataram dynasty in the late sixteenth century;
- *Whirlpool (Mata Pusaran)*, a novel about the fall of Majapahit as a result of the decadence and moral erosion of its rulers.

I also worked on, but didn't succeed in finishing, an encyclopedia that was intended to be an updated Indonesian version of the classic *Netherlands East*

Indies Encyclopedia. This manuscript, too, was confiscated and destroyed prior to my release.

And then, of course, were all the notes, letters, and essays that were collected after my release to form a two-volume Indonesian edition, *Nyanyai Tunggal Seorang Bisu,* and also from which the present volume emerged.

The time I found for writing was a gift from my fellow prisoners who took over my fieldwork for me. While at an individual level the authorities granted me no significant preferential treatment, I do realize that the authorities were forced to act more carefully toward me because the eyes of the international press were on me.

Regardless of my special status, if that is how it can be described, imprisonment is a terrible thing for it means the severance of communication with the outside world. We prisoners were unable to convey our feelings and opinions about the treatment meted out to us. It goes without saying that the trauma of the mass killings that took place in 1965 and the years following effectively silenced the voices of many who might have otherwise protested. And in this regard, I am probably an exception, one among the very few prisoners who was not about to give up the right to air his view to whomever, whenever, or wherever.

As hard as my life has been I have no desire for revenge. If I wish for anything it is for all the things that have been stolen from my life to be returned to me.

Before my release, before my return to Java, I never once tried to imagine what my life would be like afterward. Realist that I am, I have always based my assumptions on existing realities. Thus, before my deliverance from Buru became a reality, there could be no release for me, not even in my imagination.

Did I gain anything, did I learn anything, was there any benefit for me, from my time of imprisonment?

I came to know well the mind, the heart, and even the hypocritical face of the New Order regime. I learned ways of maintaining my health at almost no cost; that life is actually very simple but has been made complex by a small group of authoritarian people for a glittering lifestyle; that the slaughter Indonesia experienced is a demonstration of cannibalism, of an animal devouring its foe just to make itself feel stronger. Then, too, I also learned that a smile, even a false smile, is an antidote for stress and feelings of hopelessness, that even as it relaxes one's muscles, it serves to soothe one's nerves.

1998

THE FIRST RELEASE

When the Hindus discovered and gave meaning to the word "release," humanity found the key to open a door behind which there were no ghosts of fear, worry, sorrow, pain, or death. The Buddha Siddhartha later gave the word "release" another meaning—deliverance from everything worldly, from all things of the flesh. In doing so he proffered the key to another door, behind which was a world not of the flesh.

Now as I write "The First Release" at the top of this sheet of paper I look outside my window and see that the sky is windless and gray. Dark clouds cover the entire expanse and the Batabual mountains, which form the walls of my prison, and the stands of *meranti* trees, my prison's bars, are completely enveloped within it. Such is the climate at the time of this first release! But just as days may be gray, people, too, may be gray—regardless of whether they find release.

Release, release! Ever since the word was first discovered, its meaning has been the same: freedom from unwelcome realities, deliverance unto a better world. So it is with Hinduism and Buddhism, too.

Release! Throughout the ages, humankind has longed for release— in the days of slavery, in feudal times, in the age of expansion, in the

modern era, in my own time. And release, a synonym for which is freedom, occupies a special corner in my heart and in the hearts of all the
prisoners here. For a man who has been without freedom for twelve
years and who has had his rights and his possessions taken from him,
"release" seems to be an intangible dream. Tempered by severe hardship, the word is hard, harder than steel. Polished and honed by travail,
it gleams and glows. Release is a dream and that dream is a diamond in
my heart.

In the last months of 1965 I was moved from one prison in Jakarta to
another. Each move was ushered by the rumor that this move was in
preparation for my release. But in early 1966, I was put back in my original holding pen. Release? What were you thinking of? You're a public
figure, after all!

In July 1969, I was sent to Nusa Kambangan, the island prison off
the southern coast of Central Java, which no one has been allowed to
write about ever since colonial times. And then, on the evening of
August 16, 1969—as a gift to commemorate the twenty-fourth anniver-
sary of Indonesian independence—I was put on a ship bound for Buru
Island, to be sent on to "a new life," we prisoners were told. *"Selamat
jalan,* good-bye," the military official intoned over the ship's loudspeaker.

After our arrival in Buru there was no more talk about "release."
The term we now heard was "socialization," which was usually followed by "through transmigration."

"Socialization through transmigration"? What did this phrase
mean? Within the context of our exile, no one had a clue what "socialization" meant. But from use of the word "transmigration" the infer-
ence was clear: We prisoners were never to leave Buru Island; we were
to remain in exile until our deaths. So, with this answer in their minds,
the prisoners began to prepare themselves for life on this desolate isle
and, like the *meranti* trees in Buru's forests, put roots down in the
island's arid soil.

"If the natives can live here, surely you can, too," one official told us. "After all, you are much more civilized." More civilized? What did that have to do with it? "Where grass can grow, man can sink even deeper roots . . ." On and on the man went in his far too imitable style.

"Transmigration," defined as a system for resettling inhabitants of overpopulated islands to less populated regions, was a familiar term to me. When I was a boy, the family who lived in the house right behind my parents' home transmigrated to Lampung. People didn't call it transmigration, though; they called it *"boyongan,"* which means "resettlement" or "emigration" in Javanese. As a student in primary school I knew that the Dutch word for it was *"kolonisatie"* or "colonization," but that term, as I later came to learn, was a euphemism too. Following independence the terms "colonization" and "emigration" were replaced by a new English-based word: *"transmigrasi"* or "transmigration."

Regardless of the term used, Indonesia's transmigration program, which was originally established by Governor General Van Heutsz in 1904, has as its goal turning Java into an Eden. From the first part of the century up until the present time, that goal has remained unaltered. But its realization demands the scooping-up of all undesirable inhabitants and the dumping of them elsewhere.

We here on Buru might not have any civil rights and might not always be able to comprehend everything said to us, but we don't lack feeling. So no matter how glossy the phrase "socialization through transmigration" might be, we knew from the time that it was first spoken, that any thought of freedom was to be buried together with our other memories of the calamitous events of 1965.

Release . . . Such was the promise made two years ago to a newly arrived group of prisoners from Nusa Kambangan. When the ship came to pick them up, it carried them not to the freedom that had been promised them, but onward to an even more distant place of exile, to Buru Island.

Release . . . Was that release?

•

During the first few months of this year, 1977, a number of officials often mentioned the possibility of our release. One of them, speaking with good intentions no doubt, compared our situation to the sinking of a well and said that there were only two inches left to go. For us, though, even if only one inch were left, we knew that the final layer to be removed was of steel that no ax or hoe could pry apart. As a result, official announcements on this matter were consistently met with tightened lips and other signs of wary disbelief.

If twelve years of imprisonment had taught the men anything it was disbelief. At times a glimmer of hope might arise but, instead of vanquishing disbelief, it inevitably was squashed by disbelief's feet, much like the skulls on which Siva the Destroyer God stands. Disbelief is a bitter thing; it is the bile of unfulfillment, the bastard child of a culture that does not keep its promises.

With all that said, a change in climate did indeed begin to take place, one that was stirred by data-collection activities within the units. Lists were made of the chronically ill, those who were mentally or physically handicapped, the names of prisoners above sixty years of age, prisoners about the age of fifty-five, above the age of fifty, and so on.

The cycle of the prisoner's world on Buru was upset. Where the voices first emanated from, we do not know, but their sound grew louder and more insistent: release was imminent. Even I was to be released. And then in November, over the television at camp headquarters, came the announcement: One thousand five hundred of the political prisoners on Buru were to be released on December 15 of that year.

Release! Release! But then other voices, like the rumble of thunder that comes with clouds, cast doubt on this forecast. "Who says that being released means freedom?" "Being released might not mean being set free." But with the chuckles and laughter that accompanied such comments, the position of the God of Disbelief began to be shaken. Why not, after all? Hadn't the modern age taught us that man is born to be free and that only man—other people that is—can reduce or take that freedom away. Animals cannot. Idols cannot. Even God cannot.

We began to count the days until December 15, but even among the prison officials there were those who were skeptical and unable to believe the day of release was nigh. "How can they be released?" one of them asked. "Even their shit helps to turn a profit here!"

The older prisoners—and more than eighty percent of the men were fifty years or older—began to prepare their possessions. "Take everything. Everything. Even your rotten clothes," one of the officers sagely suggested, "after all, you might just be moved to another place."

Twelve years had taught the prisoners to always seek alternative meanings to words. I for one had learned that lesson the first day of my detention when, on October 13, 1965, a military commander made his way through the crowd that was destroying my home and said to me, "Follow me, sir. I'll take you to safety." And I had followed that man through the crowd outside my home and to the open-back truck that was waiting for me with my hands tied behind my back, the rope linked with a noose around my neck. A hangman's noose, we had called it during the revolution. Once I was in the truck and the vehicle started moving, one of the guards smashed my face with the metal and wooden butt of his gun. Fortunately I had time to turn away and, in so doing, saved my left eye from injury, but my cheekbone was cracked. At any rate, that is how I came to know the meaning of "being taken to safety" and when I came to distrust the obvious meaning of words. Times change, I guess, and so do the meanings of words. The words themselves are not misnomers. Not at all. Blame the old dictionaries for the source of misunderstanding and always be prepared to look for the hidden meanings of words, ones not likely to be found in any standard dictionary.

It seemed to me that the entire penal colony, the more than eleven thousand prisoners in all of the island's units, "knew" that I was to be included in the first batch of prisoners released. I had no idea how everyone was so sure about this since I had no information myself and, for my part, certainly wasn't counting on being released until it actually happened. While I knew well the feeling of longing for freedom, for my own freedom, my entire experience had taught me that some matters were out of one's hands.

Word spread that an advance team of journalists was coming but, in the end, only one appeared at my door, a reporter from *De Telegraaf* of Amsterdam. The evening that he visited me he confirmed the news that one thousand five hundred political prisoners from Buru were to be released. He told me the prisoners were to leave on two passenger ships that would depart Namlea on December 20. Disembarkation would take place in Surabaya.

When I asked him if he believed the information, he merely shrugged his shoulders, which gave me as much reassurance as the local inhabitants who for years had been saying, "You won't be here long," and "Soon you'll be taken back to your home in Java on a white ship flying a red flag." But, in fact, there was an incredible amount of activity going on. The units were ordered to prepare and store nine cubic yards of firewood. Prisoners who had previously requested permission to marry—either local women or the daughters of other prisoners whose families had moved to the island—were informed that a mass wedding ceremony would be held for them on December 19. This announcement caused many to shake their head; there was no time to prepare. "Shit," one prisoner muttered, "getting married here is no different from corvée labor; you simply got no choice!"

The change of climate, the nature of things to come, could not be predicted. Prepare! Make plans! The days were filled with tension; the nights even more. Would the dream finally come true? Had we been wrong in doubting? Might we now dare to believe?

Talk among the local inhabitants of our imminent departure increased. Many, no doubt, were concerned about the future. In Namlea, at the administrative office for the penal colony, was a map of Buru with a large red circle on it. The circle encompassed a nucleus of 350 thousand acres, an area much larger than either Monaco or Liechtenstein. That was the penal colony or, as the authorities had begun to call it, the Buru Island "Humanitarian Project."

Public worry mounted. Over the years the people of Namlea had begun to switch from sago as their staple food to rice, which the prisoners produced. During our time on Buru, rice had flowed from the penal colony to Namlea and Ambon with the prisoners receiving the smallest portion of the selling price. Growth in regional trade, which had multiplied a thousand times over since our arrival, was also a direct result of the expansion of agricultural and forestry production on the penal colony.

New buildings dotted the city of Namlea. Each stopping place between the penal colony and harbor, and the factory and the colony benefited from the prisoners' presence, for some measure of profit was left behind there as well. Further, in terms of our purchases, we always had to pay the highest price going. There was no such thing as a free market; the products of our sweat and work were channeled through a military-controlled marketing agency from which we had to purchase our needs as well. A swell life was to be had by many islanders but few among them were prisoners. No, once the prisoners left Buru, the island's quality of life would suffer greatly.

It was impossible for me to conceal my discomfort and embarrassment from those fellow prisoners who came to say good-bye to me, most of whom expressed the hope that my manuscripts would soon be published. I couldn't blame them for believing the rumor. The local inhabitants and military officials had also heard it on Radio Ambon.

The first day only a half dozen men came, but after that the number grew daily, each one of them just as sure as the last that I was to be released. There were those who came from distant units, six to twelve miles away, traveling on foot through the jungle, beneath the heat, and over muddy paths without proper protection against the rain.

For years these men had supported me, helped me to fulfill my needs, from tobacco to matches, and from soap to medicine. I had listened to their words, to their worries about their families and their future, and to their suggestions on what I should write. Now I found myself without the courage to look at them; I myself wasn't convinced that I was to be released.

Some of the men just sat around, close to me, without even saying a word. Some asked me to leave behind something for them: a bit of writing or something else to remember me by. Others said they were glad I was to leave, "For when you go, you'll take with you a part of me."

As the days went by, more and more prisoners came to convey questions, advice, or requests:

"Can you really believe this is happening?"

"Be careful, they might be making ready to take you to the killing grounds."

"Won't your wife and children be happy!"

"Do you think you'll stay in Indonesia?"

"You should leave the country at the first possible opportunity!"

"Once you're gone, I'll take your room . . . I can have your room, can't I? . . . I'll put in a request so that I can stay in your room."

"Write about us so that the most vital part of our lives, which has been stolen from us, will not be forgotten as it has already been for our predecessors who were banished by the Dutch."

A gangly young man came to my room and gave me a package wrapped in plastic containing thirty-two feet of plastic rope, a pair of nylon socks, soap, toothpaste, and a can of milk. He then left without saying a word.

Another prisoner, who had been off doing corvée in another unit for a week, also came by and silently placed six duck eggs in my room.

A friend, a tailor by trade, gave me a sporty-looking wool hat that he had made along with the written message, "When you get back to Jakarta, you can stop wearing your grass hat!"

What with all the requests and bits of advice, in the end I was forced to yield to my sense of discomfort and shame. Thereafter I listened to my fellow prisoners' words but with a growing feeling of emptiness.

•

In order to wake up early, between 4:30 and 5:00 A.M., so that I would have time to exercise and carry out my daily tasks, I kept a strict schedule, always trying to make sure that I was in bed by 10:00 P.M. at the latest. Only something extraordinary could affect my schedule. And so it was on that night, the night of December 14, after I was already asleep, when very late someone came knocking on my door. The urgency of my unknown visitor's voice caused me to light my lamp and open the door for him. Outside, I found one of the prison office workers.

"Your name is on the release list!" he announced straightaway. "You should be ready in case you have to leave tomorrow."

He then went on to tell me that TVRI, the State-owned television station, had just announced the release of fifteen hundred political prisoners from Buru. Just as the Dutch reporter had said, the prisoners were to be picked up by two ships on December 20 and would arrive in Surabaya on December 25.

"After the television was turned off," he continued, "we were told that we had to stay and do office work. That's how I learned the prisoners' numbers. Lists have already been sent to some of the units. They'll be announced tomorrow. You should get your papers together."

I was in a sweat that night, going through my papers, selecting the ones I wanted to keep. For three hours, beneath the light of two candles—all the available electrical power was being used for overtime work at the office—I was busy making choices, my heart still trembling from disbelief.

In the morning, my drowsiness made me neglect doing my exercises. Instead, after boiling my drinking water, I walked for a half hour.

The sun wasn't up; fog still reigned.

At six o'clock prisoners from other units, those whose names had been called at morning roll, began to arrive at headquarters. So, it was true; after more than twelve years, there was finally going to be a release.

The arrival of prisoners carrying with them what few possessions they owned stirred a welter of emotions. Shoeless men with bone-thin legs dressed in rags; patched plastic buckets hanging from their shoulders; bundles wrapped in plastic outer bags for fertilizer carried under their arms. What could possibly be in them? Nowhere on their faces was happiness or delight—only worry. They stared forward, looking neither left nor right, as if it were with their hearts that they were trying to see what was out there, beckoning to them.

Was this really a freedom parade, this assortment of souls who had somehow managed to pass successfully through countless portals of death for so many years? A parade of life's remains, they had the good parts of their lives sucked out of them during their twelve years here. These were men with bad hearts or crippled limbs resulting from accidents or from the carrying out sadistic orders with no recourse to medical services; men who were dependent on their mates for nursing care and medicine; men with ruined kidneys from lack of sugar, lack of rest, nonstop work.

My exercise that morning was giving encouragement to these men and extending nervous and hurried farewells. Almost all the men were older than I. One old man, who hobbled into camp after walking for six miles, stopped beside me and clutched my hand. He stroked his white beard and mustache, then yawned from the weariness of his journey. "Where are they moving us now?" he asked plaintively.

"I don't know, but I pray that you'll be safe," was all that I could tell him. It would not have been right to add my doubts to his burden of twelve years. He then hobbled away, supporting his weight on a cane far too short for his height. The old and brittle stick had probably broken on the way.

A tall thin man, stooped beneath the gunny-cloth pack on his back, walked slowly into camp and stopped to greet me. He was a man I had known before, in the free world. He hugged and kissed me, then whispered, "Good-bye, my friend, good-bye." He didn't seem to want to let go.

"Good-bye! Good luck!" I said, while attempting to free myself from his embrace.

Twelve years ago, he had been a strong man, a person out to conquer the world. Now he was stooped and suffering from acute psychosis. "Crazy," the men said of him but, even in the best of times, how narrow is the line between sanity and insanity? In this case we were talking about a period of severe mental stress lasting more than twelve long years. Twelve years of constant anger and recurrent shouts. How many minds would not eventually break beneath such weight?

December 15, 1977. What a day for emotions! Prisoners whose faces I had never seen because they had been unable to leave their units due to poor health or lack of strength, shuffled as best they could down the path to the four waiting sloops that would carry them to Namlea Harbor at 7:00 A.M. Men who lacked even the strength to drag themselves across the thresholds of their barracks were carried on chairs or litters. I saw in my mind a time 1,970 years earlier when Israelites had left their homes in search of Jesus Christ. I saw wave after wave of men streaming in to witness the coming of Christ.

From among the moans of helplessness came a whimper from one of the stretchers: "Why move me now? I'd rather die here in the care of my friends." I bowed my head. Yes, this was life's remains; once the sap had been sucked out, all that was left was a hull, nothing more than fiber. The sarong that covered the man on the stretcher slid off with the bobbing of his transport to reveal a pasty, chalk-colored face. One of the man's cheeks was missing, eaten away by cancer. He might very well find his final resting place at the bottom of the Banda Sea was the thought that came to my mind—if the ships do come, that is, and actually leave for Java.

All the men in my unit spent the day arranging for the departure of fellow prisoners: preparing supplies, cooking, checking lists, transporting belongings to the sloops. As busy as they were, none could dismiss the questions hanging above them like daggers over their hearts: Where are my friends being taken? When will I be dragged away?

In the afternoon some of the men who had been trying to learn whether or not I was to leave came to my room to inform me, "Your name is not on the list." In an instant the visitors who had filled my room were gone. But later, others came in to say farewell. Several requested that I pray for them to find the strength to continue to bear their burden.

At eight o'clock that night I finally closed and locked my door. Completely sapped of my strength, I immediately lay down and fell asleep. I couldn't have been asleep too long—two or three hours at most—when I was startled awake by a rap on my door. "Now who?" I lit my lamp and opened the door. Standing just outside were two men. One was a younger man with long hair and light-colored skin. I didn't recognize him but stuck out my hand in greeting.

"I'm sorry to disturb you," the visitor apologized straightaway.

The other man, who was fairly stout, then took my hand and shook it heartily. "Hello, Pram!" he barked in a voice like that of a prison officer.

Immediately my instincts told me to be careful. Twelve years without freedom had forced me to think about each step I took, about each word I spoke. The walls of my prison were not just the mountains in the distance but the awareness that I, a political prisoner, might not show the proper attitude toward authority. Years of living like this had made me feel as if I were constantly walking a tightrope.

"Don't you remember me?" the man asked. "It's me—Trisno."

"Trisno Juwono?"

"Yes."

"Come in," I told him.

The long-haired youth followed with a look of surprise, as if he were seeing an exotic caged animal. "I'm a reporter now," Trisno then said. "I couldn't survive as an author so I'm working as a reporter for *Pikiran Rakyat* in Bandung." Slapping his protruding paunch, he then informed me that he had a car, two wives, and lots of girlfriends. "Disgusting!" was all I could think. "Twelve years, and he still hasn't changed," I said silently to myself as he chirped on about his frequent travels abroad.

After Trisno had finished his recitation of achievements, the long-haired youth began to talk: he too was a reporter, and before coming to Buru, had visited my family in Jakarta a couple of times. He'd even brought with him a note from one of my children—"Are you really coming home, Papa? Is it true what the newspapers and magazines are saying?"—and also a message from my wife: "Twelve years have passed and I hope that I and the children won't be disappointed again. After I heard there was to be a release, two more weeks of waiting seems so long. I don't know what I'm supposed to do. I'm so confused. But the children are beaming and happy and are making their own plans. All sorts of things. They're all so sure that your name is on the list. All I do is pray, day and night, that this time my prayers will be answered."

I asked the young man his name.

"I'm Sindhunata, from *Kompas*."

"How old are you?" I inquired.

"Twenty-six . . ."

Almost the same age as my oldest daughter; only one year younger. He could be my son. Immediately I felt a fatherly feeling toward him.

Trisno excused himself and left. After that Sindhunata and I were able to speak more freely. I first asked him about life at my home.

"It's good," he told me, "very good in fact. Your wife is working hard selling ice snacks. The children are doing well. Your daughter Titiek plans on going on to school at the university."

"But do you think my wife and children really want me to come home?"

His voice broke: "Of course, of course they do. They love you."

"Really? They always say so in their letters, but I don't know if it's really true."

"They do love you and hope to be back together with you soon."

"Someone told me that my wife had remarried."

"That's a lie, just a lie."

"It would be all right if she did. She has the right."

"But it's not true," he insisted. He now looked tongue-tied.

"My wife, is she still beautiful?"

"She is, just a little older-looking is all."

"Who looks older—me or her?"

"You, a little . . ."

For a moment it was late 1954 and I was introducing myself to my future wife at a book fair in Deca Park. I thought of our marriage, how peaceful our life had been until December 1960 when I was kidnapped and held, incommunicado, with my wife not knowing where I was, for a period of two months. When I was finally freed a year later we had a respite until I was again forcibly taken away in October 1965 . . . I returned to the present.

"The first time I saw her at Salemba Prison after my arrest I suggested that she find herself a new husband. She was still young and beautiful."

"But, no," the young man interrupted. "She's still waiting for you."

For four days, one day after the other, the political prisoners whose names had been called flowed into Command Headquarters from the outlying units. Many stopped to say good-bye: among them, the old, the physically handicapped, the mentally defective, and the "children." Yes, some of the prisoners were between twenty-three and twenty-seven years of age, virtual children in this prison of old men. Lower their ages by between eight to twelve years and you'll have the age that they were taken in "for safety reasons."

Most of these youngsters were here for reasons of love: when their fathers had disappeared they had searched the jails and prisons and, when finally locating them, had not wanted to be separated from them. So, instead of being returned to their homes by the authorities, they were sent into exile as *"tapol-kecil"* or "little political prisoners" as we called them before they became full-fledged political prisoners.

To each of my visitors I gave a small slap on the cheek as a means of lightening the burden they felt from parting. When hugging one of the men who had come to say good-bye, he began to cry, which caused me to follow suit. After that I avoided embraces. Because of the years we had spent together we were now family, more close-knit than maybe even our own, and the pain of one family member was the pain of all.

Not all the prisoners who wanted to say good-bye were able to do so, because my room became filled with journalists. There must have been close to a score of representatives from the print and electronic media. I welcomed them, one and all. Being able to talk to people who were free from the bonds of this place made me feel as if I, too, were free. It had a calming effect. I felt like a human being again; not a pharaoh's slave, not a prostrate idolater, but a human being.

A good part of that day and the days that followed were spent answering journalists' questions. There were times when I was literally gasping for breath from speaking so much. My time with the journalists represented an initial release for me. The pressure on me was suddenly, if only momentarily, lifted. How long had it been? Twelve long years! And now the tadpoles that had hatched and grown inside me wanted to croak loudly their right to be free.

Of all the questions and answers from those sessions I note here but a fraction of them:

"In Jakarta we heard that you were to be released. Now that we're here, you're saying that might not be true. Don't you want to be free?"

"Freedom is my right. I didn't obtain either my freedom or my citizenship at no cost. As with others, I, too, got them through work, struggle, and war."

"What will you do after you're free?"

"I'll clean up my manuscripts. I have no reference books to do that here."

"But didn't you write a novel? Do you need reference books for that?"

"I feel that I do."

"Is there freedom for you in writing?"

"If I find freedom in writing, it is also because of work."

"Do you think that the books you've written here are better than your earlier works?"

"Of course I do. I'm twice as old now as when I first started writing and my years in this world have given me more options to choose from. Even this twelve-year period of no freedom or civil rights represents a period of aggregation."

"What do you intend to do after your release?"

This particular question gave me pause. I wasn't sure of the appropriate answer. As a writer, I would have to repeat what I always said—that I would write. But as a father, I wanted nothing more than to lift up my son, my youngest child, and throw him into the air. I had done that with his sisters when they were children but not with him for he was too young, only two months old, when I was taken away. Now he's twelve, going on thirteen. I might not have the strength to do it, but I wanted to try. Then, too, if I were speaking as a husband, my answer would have to be something else altogether. There would be numerous family matters for me to settle along with debts both of a spiritual and material nature. I saw no use in talking about these things.

"Didn't you once oppose the demand by Amnesty International for the release of Mochtar Lubis?"

"Where was that printed?" (I didn't recall ever having done such a thing.)

"In *Bintang Timur*."

"I wasn't the only person writing for *Bintang Timur*. What I do remember is that in 1956 I was among the first people to protest his detention."

"But that was in the 1950s; the 1960s were different."

I was uncertain of both my memory and the course of this particular examination. What did this person think, I asked myself. That I was one of those people who never did wrong? I wanted to shout that I have always been prepared, at any moment, to ask forgiveness for the mistakes that I have made.

"Did you ever hear of the activities undertaken by Amnesty International for the release of the political prisoners, on behalf of the prisoners and you personally?"

"No, but I am thankful to the organization for its work."

"Do you still believe that literature cannot be separated from politics?"

"Just as politics cannot be separated from life, life cannot be separated from politics. People who consider themselves to be nonpolitical are no different; they've already been assimilated with the current political views—they just don't feel it anymore. This is normal. Throughout history, almost all literary works have been political. People must broaden their understanding and accept the fact that politics, not political parties, is tied in with anything and everything that is related to power. As long as man is a social animal, he will participate in political activity. Showing respect for the flag, singing the national anthem, and paying taxes are political statements. Look at the Javanese literary classics; don't they support the power structure of their time? What I'm saying is that a political work can also be a literary work."

"But isn't politics dirty?"

"There is dirty politics and there is clean."

"What do you have to say about your ten years of detention?"

"It's not been ten years; it's going on thirteen. I view this period of almost thirteen years as one consequence of the nation-building process."

"And your own feelings? Your personal feelings?"

"They're not important. As an individual I am not important in this process."

"What about if Indonesian society doesn't want to accept you back? What would you think about that?"

"Easy—I've always been willing to leave. As Amir Pasaribu once said, 'It is better to be a foreigner in a foreign land than a stranger in one's own land.' "

"What is your religion?"

"Officially, Islam."

"Do you pray."

"I meditate."

"You appear to be in good health. People were saying, at the time of the attorney general's visit in 1969, that you were looking quite old."

"I've had the fortune to be aided by family and friends."

"Do you have to work in the fields?"

"I used to, but now I'm permitted to write, though sometimes I help with the hoeing and I prepare firewood for the kitchen every day."

"How long has that been?"

"Ever since General Sumitro's visit in 1973. At the very least I'm able to channel myself into my work, though I can't say any one of them is actually finished."

"What all have you had to do here?"

"What everyone else has had to do: clearing jungle, building roads, opening up fields; clearing savanna; plotting and tilling rice fields; sawing wood for lumber; ironmongery, and so on. The only jobs I haven't done are working as a raftsman and beating sago."

"How do you ease your longing for your family?"

"That's easy; I pray for their safety, prosperity, and happiness."

"What are your thoughts about your children after being separated from them for so long?"

"I'm very sad that the opportunity to help educate them was taken from me. They have grown, like grass, without me watering them. Even so, I trust in their mother's judgment."

"You have a typewriter. Who gave that to you?"

"It's an old one that had been discarded; friends helped me fix it so that it could be used again."

"I read in a newspaper that the president once sent you a typewriter."

"If so, I never received it."

"When do you write?"

"Whenever . . . Writing is the only kind of work I feel capable of doing."

"During the day or at night?"

"Mostly during the day."

"How many hours a day?"

"As many as I am able."

"What's your work schedule like?"

"I wake up at four-thirty or five o'clock and start right in, doing exercises in place, push-ups included. After getting out of bed, I boil water for the group—the carving, painting, and mapping group. After taking care of my toilet, I walk for a quarter of an hour and then do some more exercise: pull-ups, dumbbells, tai-chi, after which I run for one or two miles. Or jog, I should say, as I don't run very fast. Finally, I get the wood ready for the kitchen, and then I begin to write."

"What has the president sent you?"

"Just a letter."

"Would you mind talking about your membership in Lekra?"

"My membership in the Institute of People's Culture and in all other organizations has always been honorary. I'm not an organization man."

"Do you still hold that art is for the people?"

"Who else if not for the people? At the very least my work is not for myself, though it is of myself."

"Were the works produced by Lekra writers of the standard you had hoped?"

"No."

"What is your opinion of Marxism?"

"I've never studied the subject."

"But there are certain groups of artists who oppose you."

"I have no objection to that. In seeking the truth many roads are open; what's important is that one's focus remain on the truth, not on disagreement. Siti Sundari, an essayist from the first part of the century, once wrote, 'Beras menjadi putih bukan hanya karena tertumbuk alu, tetapi teru-tama karena pergeseran dengan sesama beras karena tumbukan alu . . . The color of rice changes to white not only with the beating of the pestle, but because of the rubbing of one kernel against the other kernels of rice that are being beaten . . .' "

"And that's the reason that you raised the banner of art for the people?"

"My words, my writing, my actions—these have never been for myself alone, either directly or indirectly. There is no such thing as an artist who creates art only for himself. That is masturbation. There's a social aspect to it, and the greater the development of the social aspect, the better it is. No one wants to eat just to eat. I can assume, can't I, that the notion of man as a political animal has not been banned?"

For four days the penal colony's human dregs made their way from upriver to Namlea harbor: gray-haired men with pulmonary disorders and cancer, their chests filled with feelings of uncertainty, their backs bowed from the weight of nothing more than their final hopes.

Journalists discovered an invalid in Unit 2. That was Mulyana who was imprisoned at the age of fourteen and had fallen from a palm tree on Buru when he was tapping for sugar. Then there was the prisoner whose legs were now useless, the bones in them having been pulverized by soldiers' bullets when he couldn't run as fast as they had ordered. And what about the two prisoners from Savanajaya, the unit where political prisoners with families lived, who were first told they would be leaving but then, after arriving at headquarters, were told that they would not be going after all. One of the two fell over in a dead faint; he'd already sold all of his possessions, including all his rice.

Another prisoner, a skeletal, middle-aged man with gray hair, told me that he didn't want to leave, that his calling was here on Buru. "I am the Messiah," he said, "the sole and only perpetual pupil of God." Of course, ten years earlier, at Salemba Prison in Jakarta he had said to me, "I am Jesus Christ and can live from my own saliva."

The night found me exhausted and I had little energy when Sindhunata, the *Kompas* reporter, again came to my room to talk. After his arrival, the assistant intelligence officer knocked on my door and was followed into my room by Warwick Beutler, a reporter from ABC, who gave me a copy of *Heap of Ashes*, translations of a number of older short stories of mine by Harry Aveling.

After the officer left, I thanked my guest for taking the time and effort to bring me this gift. Most surprising about the book for me was its cover, a picture of my wife and children that had been taken four years previously.

Sindhunata tried to persuade me to record a message for my family on tape. He said that he would play it for my children. I told him that I had once tried doing that, but when I later listened to a playback of the tape, my voice sounded so authoritarian to my ear I decided not to send it. I worried my children would be afraid when hearing it.

"You mustn't worry about that," he told me, and so I gave him the older recording. The tape contained a story about a dog—it was meant for my son, my youngest child. A story about a dog! But I was thinking at the time that people who can't show concern for other people might at least be able to sympathize with a dog.

Finally, the young and sympathetic reporter from *Kompas* said good-bye but the ABC reporter stayed behind a while longer to talk to me and record my views on Indonesian culture. Unable to organize my thoughts in a logical, systematic fashion, I'd be embarrassed now to hear repeated what I said. By the time he left I was already prone on my sleeping platform, the copy of *Heap of Ashes* close beside me.

The date was December 19, 1977, and still my name had not been called. Knowing the limited value of freedom for Indonesians, a citizenry yet to benefit from *habeas corpus,* I shouldn't have been surprised. Human rights might be respected in Europe and the United States, but not so in Indonesia, where the status of political prisoners remains unchanged. The Universal Declaration of Human Rights is a wonderful document but means nothing for those who put greater value on weapons than they do on the rights of mankind.

At 5:30 in the morning, David Jenkins from the *Far Eastern Economic Review* came to see me. He wanted to use this last opportunity to talk to me in relative calm. He measured the size of my room—8¼ by 9 feet of floor space, 8¼ feet in height—and then asked me about my belongings, what manuscripts and few items of clothing I owned. After he had finished his task, he took his leave. He and the rest of the reporters were to leave that day.

My meeting with free people—the foreign and domestic journalists—had given me something wonderful to think about: that the larger
world still recognized our existence, our life. And that as long as there
was life, that life would have meaning. My—our—existence was still
recognized. We had life and our life had meaning.

The last sloop to go was finally filled with prisoners. They weren't
required to wear their unit ID tags. When I was a boy, dogs had to have
tags that could be purchased at the local colonial-government office. If
a dog had a tag it wouldn't be shot.

One thousand five hundred and one political prisoners, my mates,
were departing for Java, leaving behind the remnants of their life in this
place as well as those friends who would never return but would forever
lie in graves on the hills and in the valleys of the Wai Apo plain.

Tens of men had drowned in Buru's rivers. Many more had died
from their own generosity, expending too much of their energy on their
fellow prisoners, working continuously in the hope of being able to
raise their quality of life to a level higher than that of the island's wild
pigs. For the sake of their friends they gave their sweat; in the end, their
bodies, too, enriched Buru's soil.

How many lives were cut short? By hepatitis, ascites, and cancer, or
from being crushed by falling trees. Or from suicide caused by their
incomprehension of the world they inhabited, one their parents had
never sung about in lullabies.

When entering Kayeli Bay, the prisoners ventured into waters that
had swallowed their mates, those many men who had felled *meranti* in
the jungle, hauled the trunks to the Wai Apo, bound them together in a
raft, and steered them down the river to this bay, only to disappear
beneath the waves. Meaning that in the end their hard work and the
dangers it entailed had not been for their fellow prisoners or even for
themselves; it had merely served as proof of their status as political prisoners. There will be no legal accounting for their deaths. Not even an
official announcement for their families.

To you now leaving I wish good luck on your journey to a free world. Good-bye forever to the twelve years spent here and to the euphemisms and foul phrases dressed up in fancy costume.

After the men had departed, a young man who prior to his imprisonment had been a mathematics and physics student came to my room. "We'd all hoped that you'd be released," he told me, "but that you weren't is kind of nice too. At least we still have someone who's a father to us here."

His words reminded me of a carpenter from Surabaya whom I had met six years ago in Wanayasa. He had told me, "We're all hoping that you'll be freed. It doesn't matter if we have to stay, as long as you are freed."

I almost couldn't bear to listen to the young man. His clear-eyed innocence and his willingness to give me anything I wanted from him raised before me the picture of a stern-faced judge who was pounding his gavel and pointing at me. What had I done for this man and others like him, he wanted to know, that they should want to help me? What had I done to deserve such kindness? And at that very moment I finally understood the reason why I had frequently fallen afoul of the authorities and been punished for offenses unknown to me during my term of imprisonment. Twice at the Salemba Prison I had been transferred to the criminal wing and here on Buru for two years I had been placed in isolation in Wanayasa. In the eyes of the judge, the willingness of my friends to help me was a crime. Any kind of spiritual link between prisoners was punishable.

With the twentieth century nearing its end, I wonder if there is any other place in the world where the attitudes of former times—the Stone Age, the age of slavery, the feudal era, and the colonial age—continue to thrive as they do in Indonesia.

As the hours went by more and more of the prisoners, these "reporters" without positions, came to see me. They laughed loudly and made all sorts of comments on why my release had been delayed.

"Until you are home with your family without any conditions on your release, you'll never really believe you're free. An unconditional release! Of course, all you guys were sentenced for twelve years and there were no conditions on that either!"

Everyone was smiling. The visit to the unit by the journalists had been the first time in a dozen years we met visitors who didn't carry a bag of prejudice, duties, insults, or advice with them. For the first time in this period we had the chance to reveal ourselves—our lungs, gall bladders, hearts, livers, kidneys, nerves, and skin. Yes, even skin, for there's not one man among us whose skin isn't marked by curious disfigurements and mysterious scars, which together form a map, a secret guide, to our life here on Buru Island.

The journalists had seemed more familiar with us than even our own relatives. Mercy, I know now, is one aspect of democracy and the journalists had removed from us at least a ton's worth of burden. Now that they were gone, we would begin to take on a new burden, one ounce atop another ounce, until another ton had formed. But, for the time being, so what? At least for once real people had been given a chance to visit this grand "Humanitarian Project."

The prisoners who had been assigned to work at Namlea harbor, arranging for the food and provisions of the prisoners who were being sent home, now began to return to camp. From them we heard another piece of news: that the prisoners who were to be released had to sign two statements. The first statement included promises not to spread or propagate Marxist-Leninist communism; not to upset the security, order, and political stability; not to ever again betray the Indonesian people and the state; not to initiate litigation proceedings against or demand redress from the Indonesian government, and so on. It ended with the following statement: "And I, having had no force put upon me, do therefore willingly take this oath before the representative of the government of the Republic of Indonesia, and willingly accept responsibility for any and whatever consequences may occur as a result of the violation of this oath."

The second statement, which the prisoners had to write and sign in their own hand, was a written testimony that they had never been tortured and never had to undertake forced labor.

This is what the prisoners had to sign before they were released. Before they could have their freedom they had to be first sworn in as slaves! About this time, the ship of free slaves should be leaving Kayeli Bay and entering the Banda Sea . . .

I enjoyed reading *Heap of Ashes* and attempted to read the stories in the collection as the creations of someone else—a person of a different culture, nation, and language—but found myself unable and could not stop the tears from welling in my eyes. As a result, I finally had to stop and I just kept turning the pages until I reached the final story, "The Silent Center of Life's Day," a section from my diary that I had written in late 1954. There I paused, too, as I recalled that at that time there almost seemed to be no way out for me from the social, spiritual, and familial problems I was facing.

I leafed through that final section of the book with my heart trembling. My stomach felt like I was riding in an empty truck on a bumpy road. My cheeks grew wet with my tears as I thought of that time twenty years ago. How quickly time had passed! I saw myself as a young man in his twenties, wandering without direction, roaring and bellowing in my loneliness— "bearing my own wounds," as the poet Chairil Anwar once wrote. How well I knew that other animals, even animals from the same herd, could not understand the pain another animal was feeling.

Look at me now. The markings of my past, ever more evident by the day, are the lines and crow's-feet on my face. I've begun to lose my teeth; my eyes now need the added appendage of spectacles. My hearing, too, has begun to play games with me. My hair is receding and losing its pigment; bald spots show on my scalp. The muscles that hold my head erect appear to have lost their strength and I nod more frequently now, both as a sign of understanding and not understanding. Only twenty years! I, who was once the soloist, singing in pain alone and without witness, have been led by age to decrepitude. I'm an old man now, only good for looking after grandchildren. My lips at a different time had moved with mantra and trembled with prayers to the One and Everything for strength and endurance; they had hissed at things not to my liking and praised the things I viewed with pleasure. Now they curl with the understanding smiles of age. My heart is more peaceful than it once was, not upset by the ripples and waves of youth, as I silently attempt to comprehend the things within my grasp.

Age has its own agenda and passes its own verdict. I once thought that I would not live to be past thirty. That age is now long past. Gone, too, is the time when I craved my body's destruction. I recall someone saying at that time, "Let him holler; he'll soon wear himself out." Now what I hear is, "Let him be. It won't be long before he dies anyway." I have lost my voice. Were I able to sing, would anyone hear this mute's soliloquy?

The time in prison and exile, now going on thirteen years, has not been an easy one. And still I wait for my release.

In the end, the First Release turned out to be a reality. The return of the prisoners to their families was announced on national television and radio. But more significantly, in the images that were aired—in the warmth of the welcome given to the prisoners upon their return—it was apparent that the Indonesian people were willing to accept the former prisoners back within their fold.

On Buru the days crawl by more slowly, as if time is averse to continue its cycle. One after another the men have succumbed to daydreams or illness. The tension of their wait has been heightened by a clearer recognition of the low value that is placed in Indonesia on individual freedom. Of how cheap the tears and prayers are of the families they left behind, twelve years before. They have a newfound respect for countries where people can demand justice from their courts even in the face of negative public opinion, where people can state their opinion to anyone they wish, where people may marry without the testimony of a third party; where people may utilize their bodies as they wish, for themselves and for whatever purpose; and where people may do a thousand other things with no thought of having to ask permission.

There was a time when the people of Indonesia wanted, demanded, and fought for national freedom. Now that it's been won, personal freedom is trammeled. I've often heard people say, "Your country is beautiful, a virtual paradise." When will the people of Indonesia be as beautiful as their land, with a civilization and culture that contributes to the greater beauty of humankind and no longer smothers and strangles the mind?

Now, as I think of setting down my pen, the sky has a dirty cast. Surely, though, the clouds are not eternal. Twilight is fading to darkness and it's time for roll call—just as happens every day, to be counted off, only one in a number. Such a pity it is that the deer and wild boar of this island will never be able to understand these notes of mine, even if they could be freed from their illiteracy.

THE DEAD AND THE
MISSING

It was the same event that brought us together between the years of 1965 and 1970 when we were arrested, with no official writ of detention, by the authorities of the New Order government. In legal terms, one could say, we were kidnapped. Our families were not told where we were held; our whereabouts were concealed from them. When we were transferred from one place of concealment to another, they were again not informed. Even when we were taken to Buru Island, where we were made to carry out a sentence of hard labor without even the benefit of a mock trial, they were left in the dark.

After our strength had been siphoned from us, after we had been force-fed lectures and sermons on the merits of being upstanding citizens and of devoting one's life to God and the creation of a society based on *Pancasila*, the New Order government's unwavering ideology, the authorities remained close-mouthed, not deigning to send word to those families whose loved ones had been murdered or had died as a result of overexhaustion or work-related accidents. This was the reason I asked representatives from each of the units to supply me with data on the prisoners who had died.

However much information is contained in the table below, the sum total is still incomplete as the data-gathering process was terminated in 1978—that being prior to the release of all the prisoners in 1979—when prisoners who were working in the service of our jailers made it known that they knew who was collecting data and that those men would suffer certain consequences if the data collection were to continue. Their threats were effective and the data collection ended.

The primary intent of this "Table of the Dead and Missing" is as a resource, an index of information for the families of those political prisoners who died in exile. Its existence stands as a monument for Buru Island and the history of mankind.

Before the last shipload of prisoners left Buru Island for Java, the prisoners attempted to ensure that the graves of those they left behind would not be lost to time or nefarious minds; they carved the names and addresses of those who had died on cement blocks and buried the blocks alongside the prisoners' graves, their hope being that, someday, when a dead prisoner's loved ones visited the island, even if they could not find their loved one's bones, they might at least find a cement block with his name carved on it. Alas, even this work remained unfinished. Once again, the authorities threatened official action against persons involved in such a "hero-making" exercise. To the families of those prisoners who died on Buru but whose names are not mentioned herein, I must therefore offer my heartfelt apologies.

TRANSLATOR'S NOTE:

"The Table of the Dead and Missing" is arranged in alphabetical order based on the prisoners' first name. Many Indonesians (though not all) do not use surnames or "last names." Thus, in a name such as "Usup Tiono bin Hartorejo," "Hartorejo," is most likely *not* the person's surname but rather the man's father's "first" name and he himself would be referred to as "Mr. Usup" while his children might (but not necessarily) use "Usup" as their final name.

Among the dead and missing are a number of women and children. This apparent anomaly is due to the fact that in 1975, the government, in an attempt to persuade the prisoners to stay on Buru and not return to their respective homes, established a new administrative unit known as Unit 4 or "Savanajaya Village," a "family village," and urged prisoners to convince their families to move to Buru. Conditions in Savanajaya were little better than in the other units and illness was common. Lack of medical care also meant that, for women, pregnancy was a life-threatening process, one that frequently ended in the death of either or both the mother and her child.

In looking at the educational level of prisoners, be aware that the original list (as it appeared in the Indonesian-language edition of this book) included almost thirty kinds of educational degrees, many of which have no exact Western equivalent. Any given prisoner's education level is, thus, "approximate." Also keep in mind that an educational degree obtained by a person who was born in the 1920s (when opportunities for education by Indonesians under the Dutch rule were very limited) represents, in relative terms, a much higher level of education than for someone born, for example, in the 1940s.

Given the fact that most of the prisoners listed in the table had been accused of being God-rejecting Communists, one must also view the column entitled "Religion" with a certain degree of irony.

On a final note, the number of "dependents" includes only a prisoner's direct dependents—his spouse and children—and not extended-family members who may have lived with the prisoner or his family prior to his incarceration. Adding up the total number of dependents for the prisoners gives one an inkling of just how many people were directly affected by the prisoners' forced exile and their subsequent deaths.

—Willem Samuels

A number of abbreviations are used in the following table. These are as follows:

Unit Number or Code and Unit Name	Other Abbreviations
1 = Wanapura	B = Buddhist
2 = Wanareja	BI = Bank Indonesia Training School
3 = Wanayasa	C = Catholic
4 = Savanajaya	Dependents = No. of direct family dependents
5 = Wanakarta	HS = High School
6 = Wanawangi	I = Islam
7 = Wanasurya	IS = Islamic School
8 = Wanakencana	JHS = Junior High School
9 = Wanamulya	Jkt. = Jakarta
10 = Wanadharma	n.a. = Information not available
11 = Wanasari	P = Protestant
12 = Bhirawa Wanajaya	PS = Primary School
13 = Giripura	Rel. = Religion
14 = Bantalarejo	STT = Secondary (Level) Teachers Training
15 = Indrapura	VS = Vocational School
16 = Indrakarya	TLA = Tertiary Level Academy
17 = Argabhakti	U = University
18 = Adhipura	VSS = Vocational Secondary School
JK = Jiku Kecil Isolation Camp	
R = Ronggolawe	
S = Siwunggaling	
T = Trunojoyo	

THE DEAD AND MISSING

No.	Name	Unit Code	Photo ID No.	Former Address	Yr. of birth	Age/date of death	Dependents	Educ.	Rel.	Cause of Death (or "Disappearance")
1.	Abd Kohar Acep bin Zainudin	2	0464	Balimester, Jatinegara, Jkt.	1947	34	0	JHS	P	typhoid
2.	Abdulgani bin Arif	JK/2	292	Jati Pulo, Tanah Abang, Jkt.	1944	31	0	PS	I	shot dead
3.	Abdulmanan bin Badu	15	1280	Kayumanis 5A, Jatinegara, Jkt.	1913	64	0	n.a.	n.a.	tuberculosis
4.	Abuhadi bin Tondoyitno	2	0899	Sosrowijayan GT/199, Yogyakarta	194-	11/12/74	0	HS	P	shot dead
5.	Ada Suhada bin Saroji	16	0351	Wanareja, Garut	1927	47	4	n.a.	n.a.	tuberculosis
6.	Agus Suroto bin Sukar Harjowtiirto	2	0089	Jetisharjo D. 6/304, Cipari, Yogyakarta	1946	28	0	VSS	P	shot dead
7.	Agus Syafei	11	129/82	Pranti, Penganti, Surabaya	1944	33	0	n.a.	n.a.	hepatitis
8.	Ahmad Ngaspan	6	4167	Gabus, Pati	1935	38	3	PS	I	cirrhosis of the liver
9.	Akhlan bin Mashar	2	0536	Mulyoharjo, Pemalang	1937	37	0	PS	P	heart attack
10.	Akhmad bin Sarpan	2	99/83	Kutabedah, Kedungkandang, Malang	1935	39	2	None	I	shot dead
11.	Akhmad Suhaimi	10	1803	Jl. Tikukur III/3, Bukitduri, Jkt.	1925	46	8	PS	I	abdominal tumor
12.	Akhmad Sumanta	10	0893	Ngantai Girang, Cianjur	1931	44	5	VSS	I	ascites
13.	Alex Temu	JK/1	1275	Jl. Mataram, Kulitan, Semarang	1937	36	2	JHS	C	murdered
14.	Alhadi a.l. Mingun bin Kromodimejo	1	1464	Bayeman Gg. Buto 365, Magelang	1930	41	4	n.a.	n.a.	fell ill and died in Namlea
15.	Amir Nasution	16	3256	Bondangan, Batutulis, Bogor	1917	58	11	n.a.	n.a.	hepatitis
16.	Amir Simangunsong	S	252/REH	Jl. Panglima Sudirman 46, Kediri	1934	42	5	n.a.	n.a.	n.a.
17.	Antenius Mardiman	3	0-091	1) Jl. Brigjen Sudiarto 554, Solo 2) Macanan DN II/5/73, Yogyakarta	1945	32	0	U	P	decompensation, TB, hepatitis & nephritis
18.	Antonius Suhaimi bin Irosemono	4	2028	1) Jl. Gunung Sahari 77, Jkt. 2) Pedurenan Masjid, Jkt.	1930	43	2	VS	C	suicide by hanging

No. Name	Unit Code	Photo ID No.	Former Address	Yr. of birth	Age/date of death	Dependents	Educ.	Rel.	Cause of Death (or "Disappearance")
19. Aris Pranowo bin Prawiro	12	1243	Pisangan Lama, Jkt.	1925	46	4	n.a.	n.a.	tuberculosis
20. Arsal bin Dasmin	7	2153	Sengon, Subah, Batang	1934	40	2	PS	I	hepatitis
21. Arsat Rahmana	4	-	C 1, Savanajaya, Buru	(?)	12 mos.	n.a.	n.a.	I	broncho pneumonia & otitis externa
22. Awang Rasawan	JK/2	0219	Desa Susukan, Ciawi Gebang, Kuningan	1937	36	3	STT	I	shot dead
23. Bakran Cokrohartono	2	2368	Pasar Kliwon Surakarta	1930	45	1	PS	I	cancer of the scapula
24. Basri	8	2183	Wonokerto, Simbangtulis, Batang	1936	37	1	n.a.	n.a.	hepatitis
25. Basron bin Hadri	16	01731	Cikadu, Sukamarah, Cianjur	1929	44	5	n.a.	n.a.	hepatitis
26. Bejo Harejosiswoyo	13	4130	Cangkringan, Banyudono, Boyolali	1937	40	3	JHS	I	chronic glomerulonephritis
27. Bernadus Hadi Susanto	S	3656	Wanadri III/957, Semarang	1924	53	3	n.a.	n.a.	n.a.
28. Budiono bin Gonowisastro	14	2900	1) Pasar Made Petak Rw.5/12, Kebayoran Lama Jkt. 2) Cilandak, Jkt.	1916	57	7	VS	I	tuberculosis & malaria
29. Bunawar	R	7979	Tangerang, Peninggaran, Pekalongan	1940	37	0	n.a.	P	exudative pleurisy
30. Busro	1	0086	Ngrembes, Bringin, Salatiga	1929	44	2	n.a.	n.a.	hepatitis
31. Cahya Kartika	4	-	A 32, Savanajaya, Buru	(?)	8 mos.	n.a.	n.a.	C	ileus
32. Cecek bin Karta	R	02776	Cikoromena, Antapani, Cicadas, Bandung	1926	51	6	n.a.	I	irreversible dehydration
33. Ciptono Surakhman	S	101	Kedung Tarukan VI/33, Surabaya	1931	44	n.a.	n.a.	n.a.	drowned in the Wai Apo
34. Dakri bin Carmi	2	1651	Kampung Pesayangan Talang, Tegal	1933	43	1	PS	P	?
35. Dakun al. Laskun	11	462/62	Prunggahan Kulon, Tuban	1943	33	0	PS	I	tuberculosis
36. Darmani bin Baidin	2	459/62	Senari, Tuban	1926	50	4	PS	P	cirrhosis & hepatitis
37. Darmosuwito al. Wahkhid	6	3404	Pendem, Jenalas, Gemolong, Sragen	1937	34	1	PS	I	crushed by a falling tree
38. Darmoyo Wagiran	3	A-306	Sokar Ngantang, Batu, Malang	1931	46	2	PS	P	liver cancer
39. Darsim al. Dwijopranoto	5	2230	Kediri, Karangluwes, Purwokerto	1941	31	2	STT	I	shot dead

No. Name	Unit Code	Photo ID No.	Former Address	Yr. of birth	Age / date of death	Dependents	Educ.	Rel.	Cause of Death (or "Disappearance")
40. Darsun Toha bin Matwirejo	2	0041	Kalimanah, Purbalingga	1948	26	0	PS	C	shot dead
41. Dasran bin Paiman	17	200/REH	Tanjung Pandan, Surabaya	1935	37	1	HS	I	broncho pneumonia
42. Dasuro	1	0720	Kasepuhan, Batang, Pekalongan	1925	49	4	n.a.	n.a.	disgestive disorder
43. Daud bin Citro	10	2358	Simbang, Batang (Pekalongan)	1939	37	2	PS	C	high blood pressure
44. Domo	10	51/REH	Krisik, Randisari, Blitar	1938	39		PS	C	tuberculosis
45. Eddy Kusnadi bin H. Karnaen	14	3028	Kampung Duri Pulo Rt.11/12, Kebayoran Lama, Jkt.	1920	54	5	PS	I	decompensation
46. Endang Supadi Gadion bin Abdulgani	2	0893	Wirogunan 1172, Yogyakarta	1933	41	0	B-I	P	shot dead
47. Entong Madrais bin Usman	12	1687	Kampung Condet, Balaikambang, Pasar Minggu, Jkt.	1937	37	6	n.a.	n.a.	tuberculosis
48. Ewon Sarwan bin Aswapi	12	0425	1) Banaraga, Ciamis 2) Babakan Baru, Tasikmalaya	1928	48	2	n.a.	n.a.	mental syndrome
49. Frans Pardi bin Parwilaijah	7	1916	Gunung Wungkal, Pati	1946	23	0	None	P	drowned
50. Gadrah Sumini bin Kartorejo	4	-	A 46, Savanajaya, Buru	1970s.	8	n.a.	n.a.	I	ascariasis & ileus
51. Gatot Widodo bin Abuwijaya	JK/2	0872	Joyonegaran II/36, Yogyakarta	1949	24	0	HS	C	shot dead
52. Glenter	1	1143	Muncang, Comal, Pemalang	1939	37	1	n.a.	n.a.	died suddenly in his sleep
53. Harjito	3	A-676	Kademangan, Blitar	1934	43		HS	I	ileus perforation
54. Harjo	10	0505	Mangun Jaya, Ciamis	1930	47	n.a.	PS	P	murdered by local resident
55. Harjosumarto bin Tukimin	1	1134	Jangka, Karanganyar, Solo	1937	38	0	n.a.	n.a.	peritonitis
56. Harry Adhi Saputra	15	01799	Jl. Rangkas Betung 7, Bandung	1931	41	5	n.a.	n.a.	pharyngitis
57. Haryanto bin Somosentono	2	0099	Komplek Gaya Motor, Cilincing, Jkt.	194-	11/12/74	0	VSS	P	shot dead
58. Hermawan Brotohadi Tenoyo	10	1763	Kramat Kwitang 3/2/03, Jkt.	1927	46	3	HS	P	acute colitis
59. Idi NM Hulaemi	T	001940	Sawahlempai, Cinideung, Tasikmalaya	1919	56	1	n.a.	I	died walking from

No. Name	Unit Code	Photo ID No.	Former Address	Yr. of birth	Age/date of death	Dependents	Educ.	Rel.	Cause of Death (or "Disappearance")
60. Ignatius Mokh. Tohir	3	A-461	Tembok Dukuh Gang Gang Sanggan, Surabaya	1928	58	6	PS	C	malaria
61. Iranto al. Joyokamto	3	A-602	Gubeng Trowongan Kertojoyo, Surabaya	1929	42	4	n.a.	P	kidney stones
62. Irwansyah Saad bin Karel Hendrin	17	1175/REH	Bakang Hilir, Sampit, Kalimantan Tengah	1928	45	0	TLA	C	suicide by drowning
63. Ismulyadi	1	1072	Samodra Gumelar, Ajibarang, Purwokerto	1936	39	5	n.a.	n.a.	suicide by poison
64. Isnarto bin Atmomiharjo	4	0530	Pasar Minggu Rt.8 Rk.1, Jkt.	1943	30	0	HS	I	cirrhosis & hepatitis
65. Jacobus Banawi	1	0103	Pekalipan Selatan, Cirebon	1926	49	5	n.a.	n.a.	suicide by hanging
66. Jajang	10	0970	Cimenteng, Cianjur	1935	30	S	PS	I	tumor
67. Jamal	8	361/02	Sawahan II/62, Lamongan	1930	41	6	n.a.	n.a.	meningoencephalitis
68. Jambari	1	0679	Warungasem, Batang, Pekalongan	1925	50	3	n.a.	n.a.	malaria
69. Jantje Nelwan	14	2795	1) Astama Polri, Kebayoran Lama, Jkt. 2) Rawabadak Blok II Kebayoran, Jkt.	1940	33	0	JHS	P	cirrhosis & hepatitis
70. Jawadi	5	1475	Singosaren, Bantul	1943	29	2	PS	I	shot dead
71. Jayadi bin Joyosuwito	17	689/82	Sidomulyo, Tuban	1938	37	2	STT	I	cirrhosis & hepatitis
72. Jembrang Suwardi Martosuwarno	2	0420	Sidareja, Cilacap	1932	42	5	PS	P	shot dead
73. Joyokamto al. Imam Sukardi	3	A-615	Kampung Sawo, Babat, Lamongan	1938	33	5	PS	I	heart failure
74. Jumadidan bin Toprojo	8	2013	Cangkring, Cekulo, Kudus	1940	32	0	n.a.	n.a.	tuberculosis
75. Jumain bin Sumosuwardi	5	3438	Guwo Tlogowungu, Pati	1950	24	0	PS	P	acute hepatitis
76. Jumea bin Ebet	14	1027	Kramat Sawah Gang 13, Jkt.	1918	56	3	n.a.	I	cirrhosis & hepatitis
77. Kadiyat bin Sukoutomo	2	0104	1) Muja-muju UH I/36, Yogyakarta 2) Kalimanah, Purbalingga	1948	26	0	JHS	P	shot dead
78. Kadri bin Roto	8	1779	Tajur, Kandang Serang, Pekalongan	1943	31	0	n.a.	n.a.	hepatitis
79. Kamlun bin Incing	2	0191	Kampung Baru, Legon, Tanggerang	1931	41	4	PS	I	tuberculosis

No. Name	Unit Code	Photo ID No.	Former Address	Yr. of birth	Age/ date of death	Dependents	Educ.	Rel.	Cause of Death (or "Disappearance")
80. Kapsah (Mrs. Kasnap)	4	-	A 23, Sawanajaya, Buru	1935	40	n.a.	n.a.	I	died in childbirth
81. Kardi bin Armawijaya	12	1706	Bukitduri Tanjakan Rt.4/V, Jkt.	1934	40	n.a.	PS	I	drowned while rafting
82. Kardi bin Sumopaing	11	3008	Bektiharjo, Tuban	1947	30	0	PS	P	hepatitis
83. Kardono	R	02309	Desa Pesindangan, Cirebon	1939	39	n.a.	n.a.	C	kidney failure
84. Kariyun	7	2152	Sumbung, Tulis, Batang	1937	35	4	PS	I	decompensation
85. Karso H.P. bin Kartiwijoyo	2	1979	Ds. Kajar, Dawe, Kudus.	1933	44	4	STT	C	fell from a tree
86. Kartosugi al. Sugimo bin Karyodijoyo	6	3899	Bulurejo (Krejo), Karanganyar	1931	46	2	BH	I	bone cancer
87. Kasimin bin Karsodimejo	2	0169	Gang Pabrik Es No.121, Cawang, Jkt.	1944	30	0	PS	P	shot dead
88. Kasiyadi	11	735/82	Tanjung, Lamongan	1930	41	5	PS	P	malaria
89. Kasmodan Wijaya	T	5578	Ny. Mariem, Serongan, Solo	1919	57	3	PS	P	cerebrovascular accident
90. Kasno Kartodimejo bin Harjokasim	6	3825	Katerban, Kutoarjo, Purworejo	1930	41	3	PS	I	apoplexy Cercori
91. Kasri bin Kasturi	17	1220/84	Jl. Setro V/53, Surabaya	1935	41	1	JHS	I	cirrhosis & hepatitis
92. Kasurun	S	1059	Tembokdukuh, Surabaya	1924	51	n.a.	n.a.	n.a.	drowned in the Wai Apo
93. Kaswan bin Tapyan	2	0564	Gandu, Comal, Pemalang	1942	32	0	VSS	P	shot dead
94. Katam Siswohartono	2	0452	Karangpucung, Cilacap	1938	36	1	STT	P	shot dead
95. Kayun bin Tohir Dulkhaji	3	00-94	1) Karanganyar, Kebumen 2) Sosrowijayan I/206, Yogyakarta	1942	30	0	U	P	suicide by poison
96. Kholil Yohannes	1	0455	Wanareja, Majenang, Cilacap	1931	41	5	n.a.	n.a.	tuberculosis
97. Kiban al. Mowijoyo	8	452/82	Siding, Bulu, Tuban	1930	43	0	n.a.	n.a.	liver ailment
98. Krisogonus Sadimin	1	0331	Magersari, Rembang	1932	41	3	n.a.	n.a.	tuberculosis
99. Kusiman bin Prawirodiharjo	2	1019	Gaduhbajen Pantalan Jetis Bantul	1940	31	0	U	I	drowned
100. Latip bin Matkalim	16	910/84	Jl. Rajawali Sidomulyo 37, Surabaya	1925	52	6	n.a.	n.a.	uremia

No. Name	Unit Code	Photo ID No.	Former Address	Yr. of birth	Age/date of death	Dependents	Educ.	Rel.	Cause of Death (or "Disappearance")
101. Legimin bin Surobarjan	11	614/82	Kebonagung, Jombang	1947	28	0	PS	P	tuberculosis
102. Liliek Setyati	4	-	C 22, Savanajaya, Buru	1973	3 mos.	n.a.	n.a.	I	enteritis ileus
103. Lucas Rubiyanto	8	1774	Blimbing, Tawangsari, Sukoharjo	1948	27	0	n.a.	n.a.	tuberculosis
104. Luther Marsono	3	A-415	Demakjaya Gang 10/45, Surabaya	1933	39	5	n.a.	P	lung and rectal cancer
105. M. Mudakir	6	4284	Kaligondang, Sumbermulyo, Bantul	1936	42	n.a.	PS	P	cancer & hepatitis
106. M. Sentot	6	3841	Kentangsari, Kedungjati, Purwodadi	1939	34	n.a.	STT	I	acute pharyngitis
107. M. Toha	6	3395	1) Tegal Suruh, Sragi, Pekalongan 2) Sukareja, Kasesi, Pekalongan	1942	31	1	IS	I	brain trauma following torture
108. Magi Hadimartono	13	4087	Kuripan, Purwodadi	1941	35	1	STT	C	pleurisy/tuberculosis
109. Manari bin Kertosentono	11	098/82	Mulyoagung, Bojonegoro	1948	23	1	PS	I	tuberculosis
110. Mansyur	T	02026	1) Ny. Ayum Rumesah, Cikoneng, Ciamis 2) Babakan, Gianyar, Garut	1917	59	3	PS	I	tetanus
111. Mardi bin Sarmijan	1	0319	Srihombo, Borang, Lasem, Rembang	1940	30	2	n.a.	n.a.	drowned in the Wai Apo
112. Mardi Sudarto bin Kanadi	4	-	A 45, Savanajaya, Buru	1963	14	n.a.	n.a.	P	broncho pneumonia
113. Mardono bin Sutikno	11	738/82	Brondong, Lamongan	1948	28	0	JHS	C	tuberculosis
114. Margono	5	3395	Tawangharjo, Pati	1940	32	3	PS	P	shot dead
115. Markus Kastran bin Sardi	6	3887	1) Mlangsen, Blora 2) Tamansari, Purwodadi	1930	47	3	PS	P	hepatoma
116. Marlena bin Suparno	4	-	A 32, Savanajaya, Buru	1973	13 days	n.a.	n.a.	C	premature birth & diabetes
117. Marsaid bin Marsain	2	0272	1) Kampung Kolong Balareja Tanggerang 2) Unie Kampung Tanjung Priuk, Jkt.	1933	36	3	PS	I	fell from a tree
118. Marsum bin Dullah Iksan	14	2358	Kampung Bali, Matraman, Jkt.	1938	37	0	PS	I	shot dead
119. Martodiharjo	5	3863	Karangkemiri Kemangkon, Purbalingga	1929	43	0	PS	I	shot dead

No. Name	Unit Code	Photo ID No.	Former Address	Yr. of birth	Age/date of death	Dependents	Educ.	Rel.	Cause of Death (or "Disappearance")
120. Martosudirojo al. Suwiji	S	6740	Prawito, Nusukan, Solo	1925	51	0	n.a.	n.a.	high blood pressure
121. Marwat Budiono bin Sartiman	2	0601	Blimbing, Pemalang	193-	11/12/74	2	JHS	P	shot dead
122. Marykul bin Kamso	2	0633	1) Siman, Ponorogo, Madiun 2) Tanjung Priuk, Jkt.	1940	34	0	VSS	C	shot dead
123. Maskito bin Mashud	13	2684	Sunggingan Kidul 28, Kudus	1934	38	3	n.a.	I	hepatitis/ascites
124. Masno Manen bin Jaya	15	0115	Harya Mukti, Cirebon	1940	37	3	n.a.	I	n.a.
125. Mastur	S	5278	Sarirejo, Guntur, Demak	1930	45	n.a.	n.a.	n.a.	drowned in the Wai Apo
126. Matosin	3	A-407	Tembok Lor III/12, Surabaya	-	12/16/69	n.a.	PS	I	escaped/disappeared
127. Mayadi bin Tawil	12	0569	Bangodua, Kalangenan, Cirebon	1927	49	7	PS	n.a.	tuberculosis
128. Miad	3	0-072	Kampung Sidoger, Sukajaya, Cigudeg, Bogor	1932	44	3	STT	I	gastric ulcer
129. Misbah bin Ali	14	1274	Solitude RK.IV, Jatinegara, Jkt.	1929	44	3	PS	I	cirrhosis & hepatitis
130. Misnan bin Amat	16	3523	Pintu Air III/010/002 Pasar Baru, Jkt.	1918	54	3	n.a.	n.a.	tuberculosis
131. Mitro Sutarno al. Sudiro Petrus	12	2146	Simpruk Atas Rt.02/05, Grogol Udik, Kebayoran Lama, Jkt.	1935	38	4	n.a.	n.a.	hepatitis
132. Mokh. Rubadi al. Prayit Subagyo bin Munasr	11	1988	Melati Lor, Kudus	1938	40	n.a.	PS	P	swelling of the spleen
133. Momon Ranapriyatna	16	01641	Cisondari, Pasirjambu, Bandung	1924	49	7	n.a.	n.a.	n.a.
134. Mudakir bin Sarjo	2	0663	1) Cahro, Blado, Batang 2) Gumawang Wiradesa, Pekalongan	1940	30	2	STT	I	drowned
135. Muhadi bin Sahudi	7	2955	Jl. Stasiun 10, Banjarnegara	1947	24	0	PS	C	drowned
136. Mujiyana	4	0928	1) D 24, Savanajaya, Buru 2) Klinter Lor III/61 Yogyakarta	1931	45	3	n.a.	P	acute tuberculosis
137. Mukhroni	1	1235	Jl. Manggis 5/12B, Semarang	1929	44	2	n.a.	n.a.	heart decompensation

No. Name	Unit Code	Photo ID No.	Former Address	Yr. of birth	Age/date of death	Dependents	Educ.	Rel.	Cause of Death (or "Disappearance")
138. Mukhtar Kasbulah	3	0-739	Salatiga	1926	45	4	n.a.	I	cancer of the prostate
139. Mukidi bin Markasan	JK/2	27430	Jl. Taman Siswa, Slawi, Tegal	1930	46	3	n.a.	n.a.	suicide
140. Mukirin bin Amatjalal	1	0199	Bedowo, Jambu, Ambarawa	1933	45	0	n.a.	n.a.	suicide by hanging
141. Mulani bin Kasmo	11	719/82	Batokan, Banjeng, Surabaya	1940	37	0	PS	I	hepatitis
142. Mulyadi Sastrodiwiryo	14	0984	Kampung Dukuh Sawah R.t.9 Rk.II, Kebayoran Lama, Jkt.	1940	33	0	JHS	P	tropical malaria
143. Mulyono	11	3006	Majakan, Pendowoharjo, Sleman	1947	30	0	TLA	I	uremia
144. Mulyoso	16	2414	Utankayu, Gang Duren 11, Jkt.	1934	43	0	n.a.	n.a.	murdered (by fellow prisoner)
145. Mumun bin H. Abdullah	16	01511	Cibendawa, Cijeruk, Bogor	1926	46	7	n.a.	n.a.	cancer & typhoid
146. Munajid bin Asmorejo	15	01794	Jl. Elang 18, Bandung	1947	28	0	n.a.	n.a.	murder by drowning
147. Munawi al. Munaji	4	69/REH	1) A 62. Savanajaya, Buru 2) Sawah Pulo Tengah I/24, Surabaya	1925	51	0	n.a.	I	tuberculosis
148. Mustaji	JK/17	68/REH	Jl. Banjaran II/26, Kediri	1937	35	3	U	I	suicide by hanging
149. Mustar bin Sali	15	1933	Petojo Binatu 11/29, Jkt.	1929	43	5	n.a.	n.a.	malaria
150. Nair Effendi bin Mangkupawiro	15	2619	Cikini Kecil, Jkt.	1937	40	5	n.a.	n.a.	typhoid
151. Nawijan	1	0773	Gondolayu, Yogyakarta	1934	41	2	n.a.	n.a.	Calebral Costa
152. Ngadiman al. Palil	7	3147	Kebon Arum, Klaten	1945	28	0	JHS	C	tuberculosis
153. Ngasiman	5	4195	Wonorejo, Guntur, Demak	1935	37	4	PS	C	shot dead
154. Ngatmin bin Mangundikromo	5	4466	Ngernak, Bendo, Pedan, Klaten	1950	25	0	JHS	P	shot dead
155. Ngatmin Sudaryanto	1	0764	Caleban UH X/56, Yogyakarta	1939	36	1	n.a.	n.a.	suicide by poison
156. NM Rasidi bin Wiryotasman	6	4238	Sikucing, Weleri, Kendal	1920	55	3	JHS	P	cirrhosis & hepatitis
157. Nono Sudiyono bin Prawirodiharjo	JK/2	0028	Jl. Ledok, Gondomanan 10, Yogyakarta	1945	28	1	JHS	C	murdered

No. Name	Unit Code	Photo ID No.	Former Address	Yr. of birth	Age/date of death	Dependents	Educ.	Rel.	Cause of Death (or "Disappearance")
158. Nuri Suhadi bin Subakir	2	0075	Kramat Raya 81, Jkt.	1944	30	0	PS	I	shot dead
159. Oei Beng Kie	1	6017	Bawang, Batang, Pekalongan	1935	38	3	n.a.	n.a.	hepatitis
160. Oei Kim Liok bin Oei Oen Sen	2	0072	Jurumudi, Panjang, Batuceper, Tanggerang	1945	29	0	PS	B	shot dead
161. Opa Mustafa	15	01706	Pandak, Cianjur	1944	31	0	n.a.	n.a.	n.a.
162. P. Harnopawiro	6	4284	Dalemen, Gatak, Sukoharjo	1935	43	n.a.	BH	C	hepatoma
163. Paimin al. Hadisumarto	7	3511	Somopura, Jogonalan, Klaten	1935	43	n.a.	PS	C	abdominal disorder
164. Paimin bin Surotiko	5	3865	Menurejo, Wonogiri	1928	45	2	PS	P	liver cancer
165. Pangi bin Rapal	13	3430	Kramas, Ungaran	1936	36	0	n.a.	I	hepatitis/ascites
166. Parjiman Pawirosumarto	5	2800	Tegalrejo, Rt.2/28, Yogyakarta	1935	39	4	PS	P	gored by a bull
167. Parno al. Partokromo	17	6279	1) Mencolo, Juwono, Pati 2) Karangrejo, Juwono, Pati	1935	37	3	PS	P	nephritis
168. Petrus Ngatiman	5	3807	Caturharjo, Bantul	1944	38	n.a.	PS	P	shot dead
169. Praptodihardjo al. Tumino	1	1104	Krian, Sukoharjo	1931	42	6	n.a.	n.a.	tuberculosis
170. Prastiwi Andayani	4	-	C 13, Savanajaya, Buru	1973	19 mos.	n.a.	n.a.	I	pneumonia
171. Prawoto bin Mertodimejo	JK/8	3379	Jangkot, Baturetno, Wonogiri	1933	39	3	STT	P	died under interrogation
172. Raharjo	3	0-738	1) Jl. Kepolisian 4, Solo 2) Jl. Dr. Suprapman 14, Rembang	1932	44	0	STT	P	kidney failure
173. Ramaun bin Madya	2	0102	Pegambiran Lemahwungkuk, Cirebon	1931	43	2	PS	I	abcessed liver
174. Rangun bin Ramin	3	A-594	1) Jl. Jarak 30, Surabaya 2) Putat Jaya 628, Surabaya	1927	47	7	None	P	cirrhosis & hepatitis
175. Rasmadi	1	5825	Caruk, Tirto, Pekalongan	1930	46	0	n.a.	n.a.	died suddenly in his sleep
176. Rebo Poniman	1	1294	Jarak Pusor, Banjararum, Kl. Progo, Yogyakarta	1944	27	0	n.a.	n.a.	suicide by poison

No. Name	Unit Code	Photo ID No.	Former Address	Yr. of birth	Age/date of death	Dependents	Educ.	Rel.	Cause of Death (or "Disappearance")
177. Rimin Sunaryoko Mangunsudarmo	3	A-404	Tambaksari, Surabaya	1916	56	7	PS	P	hepatitis & tuberculosis
178. Ronggo	11								bronchio asthma
179. Ronggowijoyo. K.	4	125/81	Jl. Taman Pahlawan 7, Kediri	1928	58	5	n.a.	n.a.	tuberculosis
180. S. Resosalinem bin Karsiprayitno	6	3086	Bejalen, Ambarawa	1930	42	3	PS	P	killed by a wild boar
181. Sa'iban bin Sa'an	14	864	Jembatan Merah Rt.17/12, Jkt.	1921	56		I	I	tuberculosis
182. Sadino	5	3340	Tawangharjo, Pati	1947	25	n.a.	PS	C	shot dead after escape
183. Sadirin bin Sodikromo	2	108/83	Klayatan I/17, Malang	1928	49	5	PS	I	tuberculosis, chronic lung problems
184. Sahad Utomo bin Mansarip	17	1257/84	Jl. Penjara 8, Surabaya	1931	46	2	JHS	C	leprosy
185. Sakhrun bin Ramad	1	5833	Pasirsari, Tirto, Pekalongan	1928	46	4	n.a.	n.a.	crushed by falling tree
186. Sampan Pujohandoyo	15	3207	Menteng Rawapanjang, Jkt.	1939	38	1	n.a.	n.a.	tuberculosis
187. Samsuri	10	0925	Pasirbalang, Sukaraja, Sukabumi	1943	34	0	PS	I	septic shock
188. Samtiar bin Syafei	3	083	1) Lubuktinggi, Payakumbuh 2) Kramat VII/13, Salemba, Jkt.	1930	52	0	JHS	I	anemia & tuberculosis
189. Samyono	5	3302	Krapak, Pati	1941	31	n.a.	VSS	I	escaped, then caught and taken away
190. Sanari bin Wahar	18	5947	Pecabean, Pangkah, Tegal	1941	37	0	n.a.	n.a.	typhoid
191. Sanrusdi al Kadri bin Martorejo	1	043	Jambusari, Jeruklegi, Cilacap	1927	46	1	n.a.	n.a.	suicide by poison
192. Sapari	5	3333	Ketanggan, Pati	1943	29	n.a.	STT	C	shot dead after escape
193. Sapari al Imam bin Tirtorejo	16	996/84	Dinoyo Lor II/14, Surabaya	1929	47	0	n.a.	n.a.	n.a.
194. Sardi Mokh. Sambudi bin Imam Rejo	2	0625	Pademangan III Gang 32, Rt.10/2, Jkt.	1923	51	4	STT	P	shot dead
195. Saridar bin Nawitana	13	2279	Karangpetir, Kalimanah, Purbalingga	1943	33	0	STT	P	struck by lightning
196. Sarimin	7	3722	Kotagede, Bantul, Yogyakarta	1940	34	0	STT	P	decompensation
197. Sarna	10	0586	Ds. Glimus, Penawangan, Ciamis	1933	39	4	PS	C	speared by a local resident

No. Name	Unit Code	Photo ID No.	Former Address	Yr. of birth	Age/ date of death	Depen- dents	Educ.	Rel.	Cause of Death (or "Disappearance")
198. Sarpin	3	A-476	Besawo, Jatirogo, Tuban	1913	58	4	STT	I	lung cancer
199. Sastrodimejo al. Suparman	8	3233	Kagokan, Gatak, Sukoharjo	1928	44	4	n.a.	n.a.	tuberculosis
200. Simon Prawito al. Sukarnen	S	6241	Loh Gawe, Kudus	1935	40	n.a.	n.a.	n.a.	drowned in the Wai Apo
201. Siswosarjono	1	0862	Donoharjo, Ngnaglik, Sleman	1934	41	3	n.a.	n.a.	tuberculosis
202. Siti Aminah	4	-			10/30/75	n.a.	n.a.	I	stillborn
203. Siti Rahayu (Mrs. Sugeng Haryono)	4	-	Kampung Bogis Rt.9 Rw.12, Jkt.	1939	34	n.a.	n.a.	I	bacillary dysentry
204. Slamet bin Kromodirjo	13	2614	Duwet, Baki, Sukoharjo	1945	26	0	JHS	P	drowned
205. Slamet bin Wirjo	8	1813	Kwasen, Kesesi, Pekalongan	1937	41	4	n.a.	n.a.	typhoid
206. Slamet Hardiyanto bin Dursalam Stefanus	18	5595	Dipowinatan MP V/200, Yogyakarta	1933	42	0	VSS	C	struck by lightning
207. Slamet Prasojo	3	A-704	1) Karangwaru, Tuban 2) Bayu Urip, Tuban	1938	39	1	STT	I	cerebrovascular accident
208. Sobar Matius bin Miat	2	0457	Cipawi, Sidareja, Cilacap	1941	33	0	PS	P	shot dead
209. Soma bin Misra	16	0884	Comblong, Bandung	1927	47	0	n.a.	n.a.	tuberculosis
210. Somopawiro al. Sagi	8	2048	Butuk, Ngrampal, Sragen	1934	39	2	n.a.	n.a.	struck by lightning
211. Somotenoyo	8	1552	Rejosari, Purwosari, Purworejo	1937	37	3	n.a.	n.a.	liver ailment
212. Sri Sunarto Barnadus	16	3353	Kayumanis III, Jatinegara, Jkt.	1926	48	1	n.a.	n.a.	hepatitis
213. St. Sardi	R	489/032	Pandean Gang I, Malang	1929	47	n.a.	n.a.	C	entritis, acidosis & dehydration
214. Stefanus Dwijosumarto	5	4550	Troketen Pedan, Klaten	1944	28	2	PS	C	shot dead
215. Subandi	S	147	Karang Gayam II/11, Surabaya	1933	42	n.a.	n.a.	n.a.	drowned in the Wai Apo
216. Subarto bin Mangkupawiro	15	1488	Ketandan Wetan, Yogyakarta	1929	46	5	n.a.	n.a.	malaria
217. Subeno	3	A-503	1) Jl. Pancana I/69, Surabaya 2) Petemuan Gang II, Jl. Pucang Sewu	1933	43	2		I	hepatitis & ascites

No. Name	Unit Code	Photo ID No.	Former Address	Yr. of birth	Age/ date of death	Dependents	Educ.	Rel.	Cause of Death (or "Disappearance")
218. Sucipto Ciptoharjono	2	1637	Karangjambu Balapulang, Tegal	1924	53	6	VS	C	hematemis
219. Sudarno	5	4200	Jl. Pemuda 75, Demak	1935	37	3	STT	P	shot dead
220. Sudirman	S	5072	Banjararjo, Karanganyar	1938	37	n.a.	n.a.	n.a.	drowned in the Wai Apo
221. Sugiarto Purwoatmojo	8	3529	Gledeg, Karanganom, Klaten	1940	31	2	n.a.	n.a.	tuberculosis
222. Sugiman Philipus bin Martodimejo	2	0120	Nusupan, Priyonggo, Gamping, Sleman	194-	11/12/74	0	HS	C	shot dead
223. Sugiono bin Sukanto	2	0552	Mulyoharjo, Pemalang	1931	41	4	JHS	I	suicide by poison
224. Sugito bin Kartosentono	1	1373	Janturan UH-II/36, Yogyakarta	1937	47	2	n.a.	n.a.	drowned in the Wai Apo
225. Suhadi bin Rusman	13	2447	Sale, Rembang	1941	31	0	n.a.	P	appendicitis
226. Suhardi al. Prawirosumarto	5	3768	Jl. Remujung, Yogyakarta	1933	42	3	PS	P	tuberculosis & pneumonia
227. Suhardi bin Amat Bakri	2	0770	1) Panggungharjo Sewon Bantul 2) Ngleran Wetan 100, Kudus	1928	41	2	JHS	C	asthma
228. Suharjo Kartosudarmo	2	0748	Umbulharjo 4/31, Yogyakarta	1944	30	0	STT	P	shot dead
229. Suharjono	JK/1	0112	Gondolayu, Jetis, Yogyakarta	1949	24	0	HS	P	tortured to death
230. Suharman	10	0483	Ds. Sudimaka, Penawangan, Ciamis	1927	45	0	None	C	speared by a local resident
231. Suharto bin Salimin	4	2780	Jomblang Perbalan 747, Semarang	1933	43	3	HS	C	cardiac asthma
232. Sujadi Hadisuwarno bin Atmodisasro	17	997/84	Jl. Gundi Gang 2/64, Surabaya	1928	50	n.a.	PS	I	cirrhosis & hepatitis
233. Sukardi	5	3559	Kutoharjo, Pati	1936	36	2	VSS	P	shot dead
234. Sukardi Wiryosudarmo	2	0410	Bugangan II/257, Semarang	1930	45	3	PS	P	heart decompensation
235. Sukarmin bin Sanmustar	2	0427	Menteng Rawapanjang, Rt.20 Rw.3, Melayu Besar, Jkt.	1944	30	0	PS	C	shot dead
236. Sukarni	1	0394	Sluko, Rembang	1942	36	0	n.a.	n.a.	hepatitis
237. Sukarno bin Kartorejo	2	0969	Tanahtinggi, Gedongbaru, Petojo, Jkt.	193-	11/12/74	0	PS	P	shot dead

No. Name	Unit Code	Photo ID No.	Former Address	Yr. of birth	Age/ date of death	Depen- dents	Educ.	Rel.	Cause of Death (or "Disappearance")
238. Sukawi bin Astropoyo	8	2067	Karangwono, Tambakwono, Pati	1934	44	1	n.a.	n.a.	drowned
239. Sukoco Haryono	15	01455	Kaum Kidul Dawuan, Cikampek	1926	49	3	n.a.	n.a.	liver ailment
240. Sdigi bin Kasrun	13	2390	Karangwono, Tambakwono, Pati	1939	33	0	JHS	P	tuberculosis
241. Sumadi Atmomadjono	8	3214	Sumberejo, Tawangsari, Sukoharjo	1935	40	5	n.a.	n.a.	tumor
242. Sumandi	10	2200	Jl. Lodan 29a, Jkt.	1930	47	2	JHS	P	kidney failure & high blood pressure
243. Sumardi bin Wagimin Wignyo	2	0125	Brotokusman MGIV/123A, Yogyakarta	1945	29	0	HS	C	shot dead
244. Sumidi bin Wiryodikromo	1	0871	Bumijo Lor III/340, Yogyakarta	1949	22	0	n.a.	n.a.	crushed by a falling tree
245. Sunar bin Samadi	17	6297	Dukuh Alit, Juwana, Pati	1942	33	0	PS	P	drowned
246. Sunarno Kartowardoyo	14	3028	Warakas Gang. B No.2 Tanjung Priuk, Jkt.	1926	51	7	PS	I	cirrhosis & hepatitis
247. Suparno Junaedi	10	1663	Pejaten, Pasar Minggu, Jkt.	1935	42	n.a.	PS	B	abdominal disorder
248. Supandi bin Akhmad	10	0897	Sukabumi (?), Batang (?)	1941	34	2	PS	I	crushed by falling lumber
249. Supardi B	3	A-616	Gilang K.A., Babat, Lamongan	1918	58	2	PS	I	cancer of the prostate
250. Supardi bin Rasijan	1	0690	Setono, Batang, Pekalongan	1934	40	1	n.a.	n.a.	tuberculosis
251. Supardi Nitisudarmo	T	303/82	Sekapu Ujung, Ujung Langkah, Gresik	1920	56	2	PS	I	cirrosis of the liver/ hepatitis
252. Suparjan	1	0237	Pedalangan, Semarang	1929	49	4	n.a.	n.a.	kidney ailment
253. Suparman al. Hoping bin Suparto	12	15O	Tanah Abang III/2a, Jkt.	1943	31	n.a.	PS	I	drowned while rafting
254. Suparman bin Sanhuri	15	02234	Panawangan, Ciamis	1927	46	2	n.a.	n.a.	tuberculosis
255. Suparno Paulus Pranotoraharjo bin Tarunowiwo	2	2449	Cililitan Besar Rt.005/09, Jkt.	1935	43	0	U	P	hepatoma
256. Suparso Wiryosudarto	14	2756	Tanah Tinggi Gebang Baru Rt.16/13, Jkt.	1942	35	0	VSS	I	uricacidemia & nephritis
257. Supiyan	11	576/82	Wonoayu, Sidoarjo	1930	41	4	PS	I	crushed by falling tree
258. Supriyadi Harjoyo Saputro	4	3296	Jl. Gumur 22 C, Solo	1940	33	0	HS	P	gastroenteritis

No. Name	Unit Code	Photo ID No.	Former Address	Yr. of birth	Age/date of death	Dependents	Educ.	Rel.	Cause of Death (or "Disappearance")
259. Suproyo	3	0-880	Bumijo Lor DI 3/40, Yogyakarta	1928	58	3	U	C	hepatitis
260. Suradi	10	0715	Bangas, Majalengka	1927	44	3	PS	I	hepatitis
261. Suradi b Kartowirejo	13	2297	Jati, Gatak, Sukoharjo	1946	26	0	JHS	P	struck by lightning
262. Suradi Purwanto	17	1222/84	Semboro, Tanggal, Jember	1940	35	1	PS	I	cirrhosis & hepatitis
263. Suratin al. Hadisuwito bin Sastroprayitno	7	1858	Semangat, Cepu	1930	58	n.a.	PS	C	hepatoma
264. Suratin bin Ronosastro	2	360/82	Kandangrejo Kedungpring Lamongan	1934	41	1	PS	I	tuberculosis
265. Suratman al. Simon bin Marso Mangun	18	6119	Brengkelan, Purworejo	1939	34	0	PS	P	hepatitis
266. Suripno	8	3528	Karanganom, Klaten	1948	26	0	n.a.	n.a.	n.a.
267. Suripto bin Sastrodadi	8	2887	Pondokan Kayu, Pati	1945	27	0	n.a.	n.a.	suicide
268. Suroto Noyolelono	14	3034	Kemayoran Gempol Rt.13/10, Jkt.	1945	32	0	JHS	P	drowned in Kayeli Bay
269. Susanto bin Sudomo	2	0563	Krayo, Randudongkal, Pemalang	1949	25	0	STT	P	shot dead
270. Sutadi Wiradinata	13	2130	Paseban Timur IV/D76, Jkt.	1927	50	6	HS	I	pleurisy/tuberculosis
271. Sutamat	11	326/82	Kradenanrejo, Lamongan	1926	56	3	PS	I	Kekara poisoning
272. Sutar bin Sastrosudarmo	16	3479	Rawasari, Rawakerbo, Jkt.	1920	52	6	n.a.	n.a.	pharyngitis
273. Sutarji al. Miskun	5	3968	Kalimanah, Purbalingga	1944	28	1	PS	I	shot dead
274. Sutarno Sastrodiharjo	R	8455	Tegalsari, Weru, Sukoharjo	1926	51	4	n.a.	P	hepatitis
275. Sutoyo bin Hadiwikarto	2	0331	Kampung Bugis Kemayoran, Rt.30/15, Jkt.	1943	21	0	PS	P	shot dead
276. Sutrisno	17	116/83	1) Suronatan VII/1, Mojokerto 2) Mawartunggal 3, Jember	1929	47	6	JHS	I	throat cancer
277. Sutrisno bin Kromodimejo	13	2322	Kranjan, Gatak, Sukoharjo	1939	33	0	HS	P	peritonitis/perforated intestine

No. Name	Unit Code	Photo ID No.	Former Address	Yr. of birth	Age/date of death	Dependents	Educ.	Rel.	Cause of Death (or "Disappearance")
278. Suttino bin Sonorejo	14	3005	Kampung Tomang, Tanah-Tinggi Rt.16/13, Jkt.	1934	39	0	PS	P	skull fracture (struck by falling beam)
279. Suwarno bin Hadiprayitno	8	1588	Pandak Sumpyuh, Banyumas	1930	41	4	n.a.	n.a.	n.a.
280. Suwarno Ciptosupono	JK/1	0861	Juwiring, Pedan, Klaten	1933	40	0	STT	I	shot dead
281. Suwarno Pribadi	3	A-441	Blauran III/14, Surabaya	-	12/16/69	n.a.	PS	I	escaped/disappeared
282. Suwendra bin Nursaman	2	0231	Gadingan, Sliyeg, Indramayu	1934	40	5	PS	I	shot dead
283. Suwondo al. Darto	13	20/81	Sidotopo Kidul, Surabaya	1935	40	2	PS	P	chronic glomerulonephritis
284. Suwoto	5	3447	Pohgading, Pan	1941	31	3	PS	I	shot dead
285. Suyadi	3	A-506	Wringin Anom, Surabaya	1937	36	2	STT	I	gored by a bull
286. Suyoto	17	935/84	Demakjaya V/8, Surabaya	1937	40	7	VSS	I	cirrhosis & hepatitis
287. Syamsuddin	3	0 - 592	Prumpung, Kebon Jeruk, Jatinegara.	1940	36	0	PS	I	drowned in the Wai Apo
288. T. Mulud Siswomiharjo	12	013/81	Jl. Cenderawasih Gang Gereja, Madiun	1939	32	2	n.a.	n.a.	hepatitis
289. Tasiil bin Karso	5	4231	Karanganyar, Pekalongan	1932	41	3	PS	I	cirrhosis of the liver
290. Taslim Subroto	16	01738	Merak, Serang	1929	44	5	n.a.	n.a.	tuberculosis
291. Taswadi bin Waryat	2	1688	Margodoyo Sumurpanggang, Tegal	1935	41	1	PS	I	cirrhosis & hepatitis
292. Teguh Sudarnadi Sumantri	4	779/84	Jl. Ubi II/I, Surabaya	1938	34	3	U	I	suicide by hanging
293. Tien Wahyuningsih	4	-	C 9, Savanajaya, Buru	1976	5 mos.	n.a.	n.a.	C	fever & ileus
294. Tika bin Dina	14	3461	Kramat Pulo Gundul, Jkt.	1920	51	5	n.a.	I	ileus
295. Titis Kamalasari bin Susilanto	4	-	A 5, Savanajaya, Buru	1976	12 mos.	n.a.	n.a.	C	run over by a cart
296. Todan	1	0592	Muncang, Comal, Pemalang	1935	41	0	n.a.	n.a.	died suddenly in his sleep
297. Usmawanto bin Kasman	4	-	D 9, Savanajaya, Buru	1964	12	n.a.	n.a.	C	decompensation, hepatitis & edema
298. Usup Tiono bin Hartorejo	1	0165	Tegalrejo, Salatiga	1945	31	0	n.a.	n.a.	tuberculosis

No. Name	Unit Code	Photo ID No.	Former Address	Yr. of birth	Age/ date of death	Depen- dents	Educ.	Rel.	Cause of Death (or "Disappearance")
299. Wahyono	R	5095	Sragi, Pekalongan	1931	47	7	n.a.	P	hemmorrhage
300. Wahyudin bin Samin	10	1662	Jl. Baturaja VI/5, Jkt.	1932	39	5	PS	I	speared by a local resident
301. Walujo Sudradjat	S	02111	Ciniru, Kuningan	1928	48	8	n.a.	n.a.	tuberculosis
302. Waluyo Slamet bin Astrodikromo	2	0426	Menteng Rawapanjang, Rt.19 Rk.3 Melayubesar, Jkt.	1935	42	0	JHS	P	hepatic coma
303. Warimin bin Jasmo	13	118/83	Mangunrejo, Kepanjen, Malang	1939	35	0	JHS	P	suicide by hanging
304. Warsum bin Towikromo	10	2418	Tahunan, Sale, Rembang	1941	33	n.a.	PS	P	obstruction of the duodenum
305. Warta Sacadipura	JK/2	038	Tanah Merdeka, Tegalan, Jatinegara, Jkt.	1933	39	0	HS	I	asthma/heart problems
306. Wartam bin Sanrais	12	1858	Rawabadak II/41,Tanjung Priuk, Jkt.	1931	43	n.a.	PS	I	drowned while rafting
307. Wartono al. Sastroyuwono bin Munadi	13	2539	Doro, Pekalongan	1941	31	2	HS	P	dental problems
308. Widoyo bin Sanggan	2	0554	Mojo, Pemalang	1944	30	0	PS	P	shot dead
309. Wiryono bin Prawirosumarto	14	3539	Rawakerbo Rt.1/9 Cempaka Putih, Jkt.	1925	48	2	PS	P	cirrhosis & hepatitis
310. Wolo Arjo Sujalal	17	1233/84	Krembangan Makam 5, Surabaya	1926	50	4	PS	I	cirrhosis & hepatitis.
311. Yosodimejo al. Y asir	T	6408	Ny. Maryatun, Jatiprobo, Polokarto, Sukoharjo, Solo	1921	56	6	PS	I	uremia
312. Yosoharjono	1	1212	Cawas, Pedan, Klaten	1937	40	2	n.a.	n.a.	hepatitis
313. Yusman bin Karsiprayitno	6	3089	Candirejo, Tuntang, Salatiga	1935	37	1	VS	I	cirrhosis of the liver
314. Yusuf bin Jaji	2	0161	Jl. Kartini Rt.29 Rw.13, Jkt.	1942	32	0	PS	I	shot dead
315. Yusup Lambertus Nakadismus bin Atma	2	0161	Sindangheula Kotawetan, Garut	1946	31	n.a.	PS	P	hepatic coma

THOSE WHO WERE TRANSFERRED

No. Name	Orig. Unit	Photo ID No.	Former Address	Age	Educ.	Rel.	Date of Transfer	Destination
316. Azhar Munandar	-		Kebayoran Baru, Jkt.	-	U	I	8/14/72	Jakarta
317. Bahsan	16	2393	Palmerah Barat 58, Jkt.	-	JHS	I	-	Namlea
318. Daddy al. Syan *	1	727	Cipari. Ciawi, Bogor	36	HS	I	9/8/75	Namlea
319. Gunung Suwardi	12	2150	Karet Belakang 24/X. Jkt.	-		C	-	Namlea
320. Rakhmat Kusumobroto	14	3556	Batu, Malang	52	HS	I	8/14/72	Namlea
321. Sadimun bin Astrawirya	3	660	Gandaria Ilir 7/V Kebayoran Baru, Jkt.	-	PS	P	-	Namlea
322. Samiyono	5	3382	Kropak, Pati	31	VSS	I	3/73	(See Unit 5 No. 3)
323. Sudrio	R	4365	Kampung Jawa, Rawasari Rt. 11/03	-	PS	I	-	Jakarta
324. Sukadi *	1	729	Abdul Rakhman Saleh, Jkt.	30	HS	I	9/8/75	Jakarta
325. Tarfi Af. Nasution *	3	728	Gang Api No. 1, Bogor	29	HS	I	9/8/75	Jakarta

* Prisoner Nos. 318, 324, and 325 were not in fact political prisoners. From the time of their arrival in Buru at the end of 1969 until the time of their departure in September of 1975, they were given no duties and were not forced to do any of the work the political prisoners had to do, even though they were sharing quarters with them.

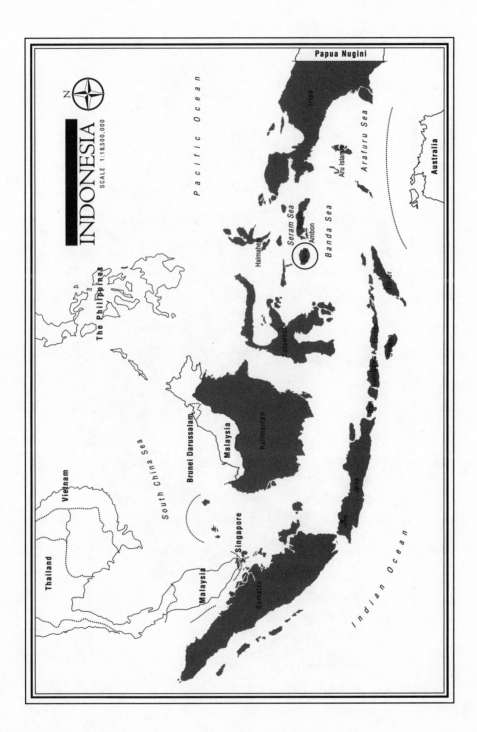

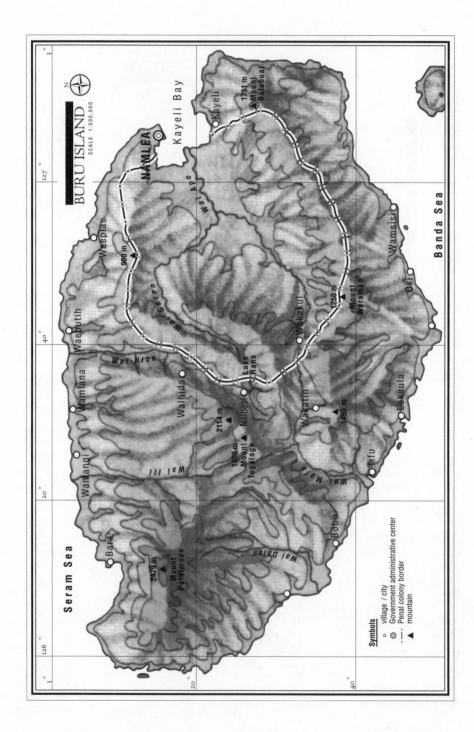

BURU ISLAND
SCALE 1:500.000

Symbols
○ village / city
◎ Government administrative center
–·–·– Penal colony border
▲ mountain

Seram Sea

Banda Sea

Kayeli Bay

NAMLEA

Waeplau

Waeputih

Wamlana

Wamangi

Bara

Mount Palamada 2429 m

Mount Tegalago 1400 m

Nalbessi 2114 m

Walhida

Lake Rana

Wakatin 1450 m

Wakakul

Mount Waraman 1250 m

Kayeli

Mount Batabual 1731 m

Wamsisi

Oki

Leksula

Tifu

Bobo

900 m

Wai Apo

Geren

Wai Nibe

Wai Ili

Wai Dalan

Wai Mala

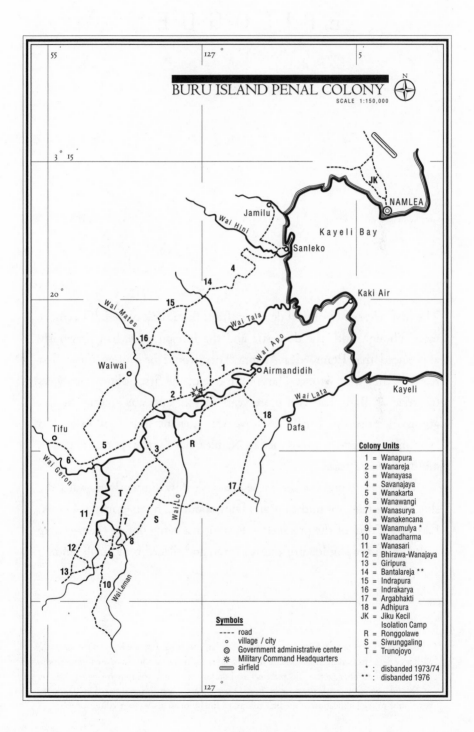

BURU ISLAND PENAL COLONY
SCALE 1:150,000

N

Kayeli Bay

Jamilu

Sanleko

Kaki Air

Waiwai

Airmandidih

Kayeli

Tifu

Dafa

Colony Units

1 = Wanapura
2 = Wanareja
3 = Wanayasa
4 = Savanajaya
5 = Wanakarta
6 = Wanawangi
7 = Wanasurya
8 = Wanakencana
9 = Wanamulya *
10 = Wanadharma
11 = Wanasari
12 = Bhirawa-Wanajaya
13 = Giripura
14 = Bantalareja **
15 = Indrapura
16 = Indrakarya
17 = Argabhakti
18 = Adhipura
JK = Jiku Kecil
       Isolation Camp
R = Ronggolawe
S = Siwunggaling
T = Trunojoyo

 * : disbanded 1973/74
** : disbanded 1976

Symbols

---- road
o village / city
◎ Government administrative center
✳ Military Command Headquarters
▭ airfield

E P I L O G U E *

The first release of political detainees from Buru took place in December 1977. Though both the domestic and the foreign press had previously announced that Pramoedya Ananta Toer would be among those first released, they were wrong. The author, one of the first political prisoners to arrive on Buru, had two more years to wait and was among the last group of prisoners finally to leave that distant island of exile. On November 12, 1979, they were led to Namlea, Buru's main port, and placed on the *Tanjung Pandan*.

On the third night of the *Tanjung Pandan*'s slow journey homeward, the ship weighed anchor midsea near a buoy about six hours north of Gresik, East Java. Forty of the prisoners—Pramoedya being one of them—were culled from the shipload of human cargo and placed on a small landing

---

* This epilogue was prepared by Joesoef Isak, who has served as Pramoedya's editor since the author's release from Buru Island, and is the person primarily responsible for the continued publication of the author's work. This piece is based on his epilogue to the Dutch-language edition of *The Mute's Soliloquy*, entitled *Lied van een Stomme (Song of a Mute)*, which was released in 1988, seven years prior to the publication of the first volume of the Indonesian-language edition in 1995.

craft that carried them to the port of Tanjung Perak in Surabaya. These prisoners had been classified by the Indonesian authorities as "diehards." They were "stubborn and noncooperative troublemakers" who persisted in adhering to the "old ideology."

Upon their arrival in Surabaya the prisoners were immediately loaded onto a bus that took them on the circuitous southern land route through the cities of Solo and Yogyakarta to the town of Magelang, Central Java, site of one of Indonesian military's largest military bases. At the prison on this base, the men from the *Tanjung Pandan* found themselves banded together with other "political diehards" recently released from prisons and detention centers in Java.

On December 18, 1979, after having been detained in Magelang for almost a month, the prisoners were transported to a military camp in Banyumanik, a small city about four and a half miles south of Semarang, Central Java's administrative center located on the north coast. On December 20, after two nights there, they were then taken to Semarang where, on that same day, a ceremony was held for their release.

After their official release, Pramoedya and other "former" prisoners from Jakarta were placed on special busses bound for Jakarta. Upon their arrival in the middle of the night, they were taken to Salemba Prison, the site where many of them had first been incarcerated fourteen years before.

On the following day, authority for the prisoners' custody was transferred to the Military District Command Offices of the respective areas in which they lived. Custody for Pramoedya, whose family home was located in the Utan Kayu area, came under the authority of the East Jakarta Military District Command. At the release ceremony that was later held at this office, Pramoedya and other prisoners whose homes were in East Jakarta were informed of their "compulsory duty" to report to the office once a week.

That day, December 21, 1977, marked the end of Pramoedya's fourteen years of physical imprisonment, a period of time during which no charges had ever been brought against him. For fourteen years he had been imprisoned with no legal redress whatsoever.

After their release from prison, how much freedom was in fact granted to Pramoedya and the hundreds of thousands of other political prisoners? In fact, very little at all. Not only were they barred by the government from employment in any government agency or in any company considered by the government to be "vital" to national interests, they were also barred from working for any branch of the mass media. Further, if they wished to travel outside the city or area in which they resided, they first had to obtain a special travel permit from the civil and military agencies responsible for their custody. To move residences they also had to obtain special permission, even if it be from one street to another street close by. In addition, they were obliged to carry on their person at all times a special identity card stamped with the code "ET" for "ex-*tapol*" or "former political detainee."

Another restriction placed on the political prisoners' "freedom" was in the field of publishing. Newspapers were banned from publishing any articles written by them; publishers were forbidden to publish their books.

Despite these restrictions, Pramoedya has, since his release, published five novels, a two-volume set of memoirs (on which this volume is based), and two biographical works. He also edited a collection of "prenationalist" literature and is now preparing for publication a play. All his published works have been banned by the Indonesian government, this on top of the blanket ban which remains on his earlier works.

Ever fearful of abduction, Pramoedya today spends most of his time at home, looking after his grandchildren, tending his garden, keeping his clipping file up to date, and writing the occasional article.

The Soeharto regime, which wholeheartedly sanctioned, if not directly undertook, the murder of hundreds of thousands of Indonesian citizens at the time of its birth and tortured and imprisoned hundreds of thousands more, came to an end in 1998. Since that time, numerous officials, both civil and military, have made promises of basic reform. One wonders, however, if anyone will actually take the initiative to establish new policies regarding former political prisoners. So ingrained is the view that the political prisoners must have somehow deserved their fate, the possibility of true restoration of their freedom and civil rights is slight.

Pramoedya himself is of the opinion that basic human rights, and, for that matter, his personal civil rights, are not a gift that the government or any other power can bestow on its citizens. The very fact that one is born a human being as an Indonesian citizen makes those rights one's own. It is on the basis of this principle that the author works: he writes and will continue to write, for that is his profession and his personal choice of occupation. It is not easy for Pramoedya to be a writer in his own country. For that reason the Latin phrase, *"Verba amini proferre et vitam imedere vero . . ."* might be applied to him: "He who expresses himself freely risks his soul for truth."

—Joesoef Isak

A NOTE ON THE TRANSLATION

The publication of this translation is a story in itself, albeit one far less interesting than the autobiographical tale found within. The fact that the materials from which this translation was produced survived the author's incarceration on Buru Island is a minor miracle.

The author notes in his foreword that the material found herein was written "under adverse conditions." This very much understates the case since the author himself can name prisoners who were beaten to death for the simple crime of possessing paper.

The author also states that "there is no grand plan" to his notes. This is true, at least in the sense that the author did not prepare or was not consciously working with an outline when putting down on paper the various pieces of text on which this memoir is based. More than a decade ago, when his editor, Joesoef Isak, presented me with a copy of the original typescript and conveyed to me the author's request that I not only translate the eight hundred or so pages of "raw text" that he carried with him, but that I also edit and shape the material in such a way as to make it more easily understandable for and accessible to the English-language reader, I first hesitated; I didn't know for sure if I wanted to accept the burden of editorial freedom that was being given to me. Having worked as a translator for more than a

dozen years by that time, I was well aware that it is a far easier task to produce a polished translation from a "finished" manuscript than from one of
lesser coherence. Further, as Pramoedya himself is as gifted an editor as he
is a writer, I worried that I would not be able to live up to his trust in me.
I can only pray that I have not disappointed him.

The task I accepted that day proved far more difficult and far more
time-consuming than I had ever imagined, one reason being that even
before the editing process could begin I felt it necessary to produce a near-
finished translation of all the material that had been given to me. I might
have chosen first to edit the Indonesian and omit from the translation
stage those sections which I felt might not "work" in English—doing so
would have saved me a great deal of time—but my experience as a translator had also taught me that sometimes there is no way of telling if a text
is going to work in English until it has been translated. Time and again,
texts that I deemed of interest in Indonesian have proven to be less so in
English, just as other texts, which originally I might have considered dis-
cardable, have proved to be true gems in their English translation.

The above comment serves to throw light not just on the difficulty I
had to face as a translator but also on my far more precarious position as
editor. To produce an English-language volume that was comprehensible
to the English-language reader and of manageable length, it was necessary
for me to excise from the original text a great deal of information—several
hundred pages worth, in fact—that the scholar of Indonesia might have
preferred I retain. In the end, however, because this volume is aimed at the
general reader, one who does not read Indonesian and has no detailed
knowledge of Indonesian history, this is what determined my editorial pol-
icy, particularly in regard to what material to delete and what to keep.

The true scholar of Indonesia who is conducting research into
Pramoedya may refer to the two-volume Indonesian-language edition of
the author's writings from Buru Island. Though this book is not based
on that edition but, rather, on the original unedited typescript, almost all
of the material found in English translation herein can also be found in
the Indonesian edition. Unfortunately, for access to the Indonesian orig-

inal of that small percentage of material available only in this volume, the scholar will have to wait until Pramoedya's papers have been deposited in a public collection.

The author did not not originally intend the written materials that appear herein to stand alone, within a single volume, much less as his first official memoir. For that reason I would like to remind the reader that there is, as he said, "no grand plan here," and that the original typescript contained numerous instances of repetition that both the author and I thought would be better to delete in this volume.

I would like to extend my thanks to the Department of Lanuages and Cultures of Southeast Asia and Oceania of Leiden University for a scholar-in-residence grant which was provided to me in 1997. Without this assistance, the translation might still be unfinished to this day. During my stay in Leiden, Henk Maier, professor of Indonesian Studies at the department and a fellow translator of Pramoedya's work, was kind enough to provide a home for me and to discuss with me many finer points of Pramoedya's work during six weeks of damp and chilly Leiden nights. Wim Stokhof, director of the International Institute for Asian Studies in Leiden, deserves special thanks for supporting my request for assistance and also for providing me with an office in the institute's hallowed halls. The helpfulness of the institute's administrative staff was incomparable as was Dick van der Meij, also of the institute, who frequently served as my Dutch-language informant.

A publishing advance from Hyperion East in 1998 allowed me once again to take enough time off my job to finalize work on this volume. To William Schwalbe and his colleagues at Hyperion, I raise a toast for their generosity and understanding.

Final thanks must go to the author himself and to Joesoef Isak for their active participation in the translation and publication of this volume. Both gentlemen were there for me at almost any hour of the day or night to answer yet another query. I am exceedingly grateful to Pramoedya for conducting a line-by-line read-through of the edited manuscript—the first time he had read what he had written, albeit in English translation, since Buru Island—and providing numerous suggestions and the many corrections that I incorporated into the final draft.

The author and I spent many hours talking of his childhood, his marriages and his children, his role as a writer, and his life as a political prisoner. His readiness to supervise my work gave me the necessary willpower to try to transform his Indonesian words of hope and despair into English-language siblings. His active participation in the publication process helped allay my fears. I will forever be grateful for the privilege of watching him take this "child," born on the arid island of Buru more than two decades ago, and shape it into the being it is today.

—Willem Samuels